THE STRUGGLE FOR SIGNIFICANCE

Second Edition

John H. Brennecke

Robert G. Amick

Mt. San Antonio College

GLENCOE PRESS
A division of Benziger Bruce & Glencoe, Inc.
Beverly Hills

διά Ζωῆ καί ᾽Αγαπῆ

For Life and Love

Glencoe Press
A division of Benziger Bruce and Glencoe, Inc.
8701 Wilshire Boulevard
Beverly Hills, California 90211
Collier-Macmillan Canada, Ltd.

Library of Congress Catalog Card Number: 74-6609

First printing, 1975

Contents

Preface to the Second Edition

Since the first publication of *The Struggle for Significance*, the world and its people have gone far and grown much older. We wish we could add *wiser*. Movement doesn't always mean progress; nor does maturation always mean growth. Yet, the past four years have taught us a million new things. We hope we have the skill to assimilate them into our beings so that we can, eventually, be wiser, more mature, more whole.

What changes? In 1971, this book was one of the first textbooks dedicated to a humanistic approach to the study of human behavior. Now there are dozens. We are glad for the company! In 1971, astronauts had just become acquainted with the surface of the moon. Now our rockets have left that dead sphere and are hurtling out beyond Jupiter, circling the earth in Skylabs, preparing for our first touchdown on Mars. We've seen science grow by leaps and bounds.

But what about humanity? We've had setbacks: Watergate, the resignation of a vice-president and president under pressure, a recurrence of the Mideast wars, continued tensions in Southeast Asia in spite of massive pullouts of American troops, an energy crisis of devastating proportions, and an increase in crime and violence. It's about time, many are saying, to give up on the so-called human race.

To deny that these matters have been tense and disturbing would be to become an ostrich. But what about the humanity resident in individual human beings? As teachers and therapists, we find ourselves encouraged as we encounter growing numbers of people who are tired of being shackled by the past memories and even the present's ugly reminders of our inhumanity to each other. They want to grow and to go beyond, to push out the frontiers of human existence to find something higher, nobler, better, fuller, richer in the process of being human. They have sought out thousands of ways of going about it: a resurgence of fundamental Christianity (the "Jesus People"); renewed interest in transactional analysis and in Far Eastern thought, biofeedback mechanisms, meditation, diet, yoga, newer and more radical forms of psychotherapy, and body awareness techniques; groups meeting to share their searches (often replacing the encounter and sensitivity groups of the late 1960s); and exploration of many other methods and techniques.

People are changing and are evincing an interest in changing even more, in developing toward Wholeness, toward uncovering more of the latent dimensions and potentials within themselves. So, too, we have found ourselves changing. While the problems of sexism, racism, elitism, injustice, and irrelevance are still with us, we find on the campuses less unrest, less violence, less vocal and physical protest, and a new interest in "getting down" on the realities of existence.

The rhetoric of revolution is being replaced by the quieter, more serious dialogue among concerned and searching students with instructors who are more interested in joining the dialogue and the search than in posturing as authority figures. Fewer students appear on the campus, but those that do seem dedicated to finding themselves and their place in the scheme of things.

There is confusion and disquiet still. It's often masked by gimmickry and sensationalism that distract us. We still find ourselves caught up in trips back into nostalgia ("Captain Marvel lives again!" "Long live Fred Astaire pants and high-heeled pumps") and games that fill empty hours. But there is also a newer quiet, and the slower freeway speeds are only symbolic of it all.

So, what to do with a book that spoke to its times in 1971, when in so many ways those times are changed? Obviously, it's necessary to change those parts of the book that no longer relate to the present. Obviously it's necessary to bring the book up to date. There are vast portions of the book that still speak to the ongoing need of people to discover their personal significance, but it's also necessary now to point out that our individual significance is bound up more than ever with a universal, global, even cosmic, significance and identity. R. Buckminster Fuller, Paul Ehrlich, and others in the ecological movement remind us that we are all passengers on "Spaceship Earth," and we are rushing headlong into a future and must prepare to absorb the "future shock" of the future that is already with us: the eternal now.

So, in preparing this revised edition, we've tried to put outworn and no longer pertinent ideas and terms into the attic and elaborate on those portions that are still vital and viable, infusing it all with the longer perspective of global consciousness. Perhaps the existential movement is slowing down, but our existential concerns have not.

It's a painful thing to try to do, to stand outside of our own experience and comment on it. We've never pretended to be totally successful at that kind of objectivity. Living is still a subjective experience and this book is similarly subjective. But we hope through this revised edition we can share our newer insights and add them to your own.

Life still goes on.

Jack H. Brennecke
Robert G. Amick

January, 1975

Preface

As a caring person approaches his beloved, so the preface of a book conceived in love should woo its reader toward involvement in the book itself. In these few pages we want to hint at our enthusiasms and tell enough so that the reader will feel he's missing something important and unique if he doesn't continue reading.

In our research, our teaching, our professional consulting work in community health clinics and in private practice, we have learned much that is too good to keep secret. We've learned that few people fit the Grand Designs of the theorists. We've found even fewer who could be fully described solely as a mechanism composed of stimulus-response bonds, or reduced to nothing more than an *id* fighting it out with a *superego* under the umpireship of a data-processing *ego*.

The need we have long felt and which we are trying to meet here is for a statement, comment, or a personalistic description of just what it means to be alive, to face the fact of death, to discover our own selfhood and identity, to struggle to live significantly in a world such as ours.

The situation is often gloomy. We try not to be, not because we don't see what is going on, but because there is a tremendous challenge in being alive today. We try to paint the background of existence with a broad brush, using whatever colors we find in nature. The foreground and details are painted with a finer brush, often dipped in the lifeblood of existence. We deal with hopelessness, not by catering to it, but by confronting it with what we continue to find all about us: hope springing significantly—if not eternally—from countless human breasts. In spite of the welter of confusing cries and curses, there is hope in the fact that the words come from *human* voices, not TV speakers alone, nor alone from computerized feedback units, nor just from the printed page. In all the hatred and violence we find hope, because real human beings are refusing to cop out on a plea of *instinctive aggression* or economic determinism. They are still willing to wrestle with the facts of learning and feeling and working problems through.

In spite of the emptiness of countless lives and jobs and textbooks and eyes and churches and bedrooms, hope is to be found in the few people who are willing to struggle to keep meaning and significance alive and well in their lives. These are the people who cry out that though they may die with a whimper, they're determined not to live with one. These are the people, the human people, the meaningfully existing selves-in-becoming, who inspire these authors and this book. These are the people who are doing their human "thing" in their own way, who come into our lives, classrooms, social scenes, and consulting rooms and who give us the spark by which to see the hope.

This book has a few goals. One is to give the individual student and casual reader some idea of the importance of life and of living it fully, experimentally, excitingly. We say to the reader: You have only this one short life. Turn on to *it*. Drugs, gurus, flowers, Zen riddles, and fast cars don't make it; living fully, openly, as a full-fledged, full-functioning human being does!

Another goal is to help the reader realize that there are still caring people around. It does make a difference in living this difficult thing called life if you can know that there are people who also laugh, hurt, love, give birth, seek, find, lose, share, and die.

Another of our goals is to acknowledge to the thousands of students, clients in *therapy* and *sensitivity groups,* friends, and loved ones that they have added to our lives and insights. This sounds like the "I wish to acknowledge . . ." part of a typical preface. It isn't quite. Here we want to point out in a personalistic way that we each grow from contact with one another. One of the few obligations we have in life is to share that growth with others. Amazing though it may seem, in a world of nearly four billion people we can still be cold and lonely, unless we know of and acknowledge the love and caring of others.

Theme of the book? With gritted teeth—for the task is one of oversimplifying a complex duty—we'd say that the theme is "the agony and the ecstasy of being fully and wonderfully alive." We hope you find here some of the following: To be a person is to be unique and at the same time to know of your kinship with every other living thing. To be a person is to be independent and dependent and interdependent. To be a person is to know that you have needs and motives, that you learn, value, love, work, play, adapt, maladapt, feel good, feel bad, feel right, feel wrong, . . . In short, to be a person is to know that you must live.

Though we are aiming at students enrolled in personality and adjustment psychology courses, we feel there are many general principles in the book. The traditional emphases are often shunned or ignored, partly because they are no longer meaningful to our point of view and partly because they *are* just traditional. Each of us needs to live experimentally. This means taking the customary, the traditional, the usual, and subjecting it to the experimentation of living experience. We are all very much alike in the sense of being living, breathing, loving, bleeding, climbing, slipping, human animals whose selfhoods are always in the frustrating process of becoming. We are all unique in that we will have to live our lives in our own way, on our own terms.

Life goes on and may we all catch a good ride!

Jack H. Brennecke
Robert G. Amick

January, 1971

1

Significant Selfhood:

An introduction to a way of living

"Oh, this business we've got now—it's been going on for a long time now, not just since the last war. Maybe the actual jobs weren't being taken from the people, but the sense of participation, the sense of importance was. . . . Even then there was a lot of talk about know-how winning the war of production—know-how, not people, not the mediocre *people running most of the machines. . . . They were participating in the economy all right, but not in a way that was very satisfying to the ego. . . . Things, gentlemen, are ripe for a phony Messiah, . . ."*

"Messiah?"

"Sooner or later someone's going to catch the imagination of these people with some new magic. At the bottom of it will be a promise of regaining the feeling of participation, the feeling of being needed on earth ——hell, dignity!"

KURT VONNEGUT, JR.
Player Piano[1]

1. Kurt Vonnegut, Jr.,
Player Piano (New
York: Avon Books,
1967), pp. 92–94.

This is a great and yet frightening time to be alive. If you can open your eyes wide enough and for long enough to look around, you might be impressed with the awesome wonder of life. You're also likely to be impressed by a great number of confusing experiences. It's confusing to try to understand interplanetary technology, the electronic wonders of TV and biofeedback,[2] problems among nations, DNA structures, political scandal, drugs, acne, Alice Cooper, the various movements for human liberation, and what you might make of your own life. And each of these is tied in with the larger confusion which we call *life*—not the Life that is the concern of theory-builders and philosophers, but *life* as each human being knows it most intimately and best: a personal living existence.

Among the urgent issues to which contemporary psychology is addressing itself is the crisis of significance. As we survey the world in which we live and move and work and play, we often come up short and are filled with the question: what part do I play in all this? Everything is so big, so complex, so technical, or organized, and so impersonal. Does my life even matter in this whole thing? When a person asks himself this question, he is experiencing the crisis we have come to call *insignificance*.

The excerpt from Kurt Vonnegut's fascinating novel *Player Piano* picks up this theme. *Player Piano* was first printed in 1952. Even then, when technology had only begun to impress itself upon the masses of people, a few sensitive people were concerned about the loss of man's sense of participation, of involvement, of importance. One of the things we feel each human being must do in the process called adjustment is to look at his life, his sense of selfhood, his identity, and evaluate them. Somewhere in this process—which the thinking man will realize may take an entire lifetime—may come the realization that life is a precious experience that occurs but once for each individual. The sense of *Self,* the conscious appreciation of the fullness of personhood, is also a precious experience. Too many of us live semi-lives, live only partially, deluding and hiding ourselves, hiding from ourselves, leaving parts of our selfhood out of the experiencing of life. In the eleven chapters that follow, we would like to look carefully at the process of living significantly, an experience that is possible for every living human being. We want to begin at the beginning.

The beginning is not at birth—we'll get there eventually. The real beginning is at death. A full understanding and appreciation of life must begin with a realization that it will end. Each of us will die someday. Think about this: the only certain thing a man can expect

---

2. At the end of this book, beginning on page 365, you'll find a Glossary defining several hundred of the terms used in these pages (*biofeedback* is one). Whenever you're uncertain of the meaning of some term that appears here, check its definition in the Glossary.

in his life is death. Death is not usually considered a friend, even to one writhing in the throes of a terminal disease. Some consider it a finality to selfhood; some look upon it as a necessary step into the "unknown" (and they fear that unknown); others are angry, thinking "too soon," or "unfair." Nevertheless, a mature, fully involved-in-life interest in life must include the fact of death. We are born, and we die. In between we live. Both life and death are realities.

The Existential Question

What do people do with the fact of human finitude, which existentialists call *the* existential fact? Many people shrug and say: "Everybody's got to die." That's copping out; they are trying to take comfort in a group fact. *Each* of us, individually and very personally, will die.

To live fully and vitally, meaningfully and significantly, we must know and acknowledge the fact that sometime or other we will *not* be living in the physical sense which we now experience. This knowledge must be more than intellectual. It must be a knowing down deep in the marrow of our bones, in every sinew, every nerve ending, indeed in every single cell.

In America and most of the Western world the common view is that first we exist and then we do not exist. Life and death are in separate boxes. Death, the opposite of living, is a tragic and terrible thing to most people, despite the teachings of Christian theology to the contrary. Being bombarded on all sides with this dichotomous way of viewing life—in movies, books, TV, funeral homes—adds to the firmness with which we hold onto it. Religions, especially Christian groups, add to the dichotomy by speaking of the "other" world, of heaven or hell, and contrasting it to our present world. Plato had much to do with this kind of dualistic thinking, but Christian theologians have perfected it to the point that any other way of thinking seems unnatural.

Living and dying are both part of life. Biologists tell us that thousands of body cells die each day in each individual. But since they also admit that dead cells are replaced with new ones, the death of cells doesn't really seem convincing evidence that total self-death is inevitable. Yet cell deterioration and replacement *is* an important clue to the fact that death is a natural part of the life of the smallest microorganism and the largest redwood tree. And of human beings.

Apart from the biological arguments we might use the facts of history. Even the greatest men in history have died. The wish for immortality or prolonged life may be a universal wish, but no scientific evidence has ever produced a person who has lived forever, and only a few who exceed ordinary life-spans by a couple of decades. Existential anxiety—the fear and dread of death—may be one of the most basic fears in man. Indeed we are finding evidence that it underlies many other kinds of anxiety.

People have all sorts of ways of cushioning or even avoiding a realistic acceptance of the fact of death. Many people put it out of their thoughts by alluding to their youth: "Death? Oh, yeah, when you're old . . . older. Me? I'm 18 (or 25 or 60), and my life's just beginning. I'm gonna live a thousand years!"

Some people use religious faith: "Sure, I'll die; it's God's will. But there is a God and there's a heaven, and since I'm saved, I've got a nice cushy place waiting for me up there. What's the big deal?"

Others block death out: "I'm gonna live so fast and furious, death's gonna have to have a 747 jet to catch me!"

Some people are so frightened by death that they absolutely refuse to let the thought of it enter their consciousness: "Why must you dwell on it? Don't speak about it; it's bad luck. Me, I never think about it."

Others numb themselves with liquor or drugs: "Grow old along with me; the best is yet to be. Drink up; trip out! With what we got in us, we can take on death and anybody he brings along to help 'im!" Those are rough games and the competition isn't very equalized.

Some escape into some form of "mental illness" and thereby beat death to the punch by assuming a living-death type of existence: "That old Grim Reaper won't find me out here on the funny farm." Trouble is, "he's" been there quite often.

We don't know anything about death, really. Few people are convinced by those who have claimed communication with "the other side." So, death is the Great Mystery for most of us. Dying, on the other hand, is a bit easier to understand, because the living are able to observe that. No, the firsthand experience of dying still belongs to those who have died, but we know enough from their reports and close observations to realize that dying still represents a painfully real and traumatic experience.

The increase in human life-spans, the halting of formerly terminal diseases, newer medications: all of these have brought with them problems undreamed of by pioneering scientists. When does life begin? When does it cease to be meaningful? When does it leave the body? Have we the right to end life? Have we the right to create it or program it?

Suicide is a major problem in our country, as it is in many other nations of the world. But if the fear of death is as universal as it often appears to be, why do so many people try to die? We don't know much about the real reasons behind suicide among those who succeed, but from studying those who fail in their suicidal attempts, we learn that the reasons are as many as there are attempts. Dr. Thomas Szasz, a psychiatrist with controversial views about many matters in human behavior, believes we will get much further in our efforts to understand the human experience if we stop viewing suicides as "psychotic." This compassionate and hardworking man (often called the Ralph Nader of mental health) says the person who kills himself is not at all similar in motives to the one who tries but fails, and further that people in these two categories differ from those who are psychiatrically diagnosed as "suicidal" in intent.

Szasz feels that those who kill themselves really wanted to die, but the person who threatens or attempts "unsuccessfully" to commit suicide really intends to improve his life.

> Put differently, successful suicide is generally an expression of an individual's desire for greater autonomy—in particular, for self-control over his own death; whereas unsuccessful suicide is generally an expression of an individual's desire for more control over others—in particular, for compelling persons close to him to comply with his wishes.[3]

Whatever the full range of motives for suicide, the frequency of suicide attempts (whether successful in bringing death or not) is on an upswing. How can this be? Most of us recoil at the thought of death. We don't like to talk about it, think about it, be reminded of it. Yet, a significant number of our fellow humans seem to seek death out, invite it in, or at least taunt it and flirt with it.

We think this puzzling situation merits far more research than it's getting, but for our purposes let's say that the fact of suicide—and the statistical increase in the numbers of suicides—may indicate that death is a powerful factor in human life, much more powerful and influential than we've really thought.

Death and ideas about death have, of course, been present since the beginning of life. It isn't too farfetched to conclude that most of our past and present religious, philosophical, and even scientific theories and researches have been motivated by the need to understand very important events in human existence; and the one so far unanswered question about human experience has to do with what we do about death: the end of physical human experience.

Existentialism is a movement in philosophy that has been around quite awhile, but most vividly promoted by Europeans like Sören Kierkegaard, Karl Jaspers, Jean-Paul Sartre, and Albert Camus, and by Americans Paul Tillich and Rollo May. *The main tenet of existential thinking is that each of us is going to die; the only choice we have in that matter is when; if we choose to live until we die naturally, then we tacitly acknowledge that we have only so much time and that we don't even know just how much.*

Since life is not open-ended and since we don't know how long it will last, hadn't we better do some living? Find ways of making the most of the time we do have? Discover the meaning in every single event in our lives, so we can do some choosing and attempt to develop the most significant aspects of our existence? Should we waste a precious moment? Can we not squeeze a whole lot more pleasure and significance out of this life that is, as the existentialists say, all we have?

3. Thomas S. Szasz, "The Ethics of Suicide," *The Antioch Review*, Vol. XXXI, No. 1, Spring 1971.

The Marriage of Existentialism and Psychology

The existential thinkers have made their way into other areas of human experience. Their message is a vital one that should be heeded. People interested in human behavior need to consider the ways in which a person's attitudes toward death influence the way he lives his life. Viktor Frankl, Jean-Paul Sartre, Aaron Ungersma, Binswanger, Buytendijk, May, Allport, Rogers: these are the names of the pioneers in the application of existential insights to the construction of personality theory and the treatment of emotional problems. All of them have noted in their research and clinical work that the people around them have been impressed by the facts spelled out by existentialism, without even knowing it was existentialism. Like the man who discovered he had "been speaking prose all the time," the patients and clients stressed their fears and anxieties about living, wondering whether any life that would end in nothingness could be worth living. The theme of "meaning" entered the work of these clinicians and gradually a new branch of psychology emerged. It is called by different names, but taking their common elements and combining them, we use the general term *existential psychology.*

Existential psychology has many followers. Its findings and procedures are beginning to be adapted by many practitioners and teachers in America. Most textbooks written in the past few years mention the new school of thought. And existential psychology has laid the foundation for an even newer school, *humanistic psychology*, the theoretical and practical applications of many facets of psychological study, including existential psychology, to the problems of man. Humanistic psychologists work with not only those who are emotionally disturbed, but also with people who have more ordinary problems in living.

The express purpose of this brief bit of history is to show that our present concern is living fully and fully living. We take as our premise that man's life is finite, that it will end someday. We are going to try to demonstrate some of the ways in which a human being can actualize (bring into actuality) his hidden potentials for selfhood. We feel this can only be done experimentally, by continually challenging ourselves and our environment, by taking risks, by experiencing the unknowns, and by showing some of what Paul Tillich calls "the Courage to Be." If we choose to live, we choose not only joy and love, peace and fulfillment; we must also accept the other ingredients in the package: pain, anxiety, conflict, hurt, anger, fear, frustration, and eventually death.

Humanistic psychology is indebted not only to experimental and *clinical* approaches in psychology, but also to existentialism as a way of grasping reality. Many of the insights of the humanistic psychologists have also been found in writings of Zen Buddhists and Taoists.

Purpose in Living

In Eastern philosophies, the question about the purpose of life or living is hardly ever raised. In America and other parts of the West, people are more pragmatic. They have been raised on a diet of goals, purposes, functions, and success versus failure. They look for the point or purpose or use in every action, word, book, film, play, and experience.

Our culture has conditioned us—and very well, too!—to seek the practical "reason why" in virtually every important sphere of our lives. Most of us design our work so that we can always demonstrate that there is a purpose to be found, a task (always noble) to be done, an end result to show for our efforts. Similarly, our schools get caught up in the need to educate students to answer previously determined questions on an exam so that grades can be given and diplomas or degrees awarded and transcripts forwarded: all to show that the educational process "works" and has "purpose" and is thereby justified as significant.

The lives of religious people are filled with similar concerns: sermons must have key points and final summary (a justification for the sermon?); our rituals must demonstrate their effectiveness; offerings must go somewhere; churches are still judged successful if their programs "work" well enough to bring in larger numbers of members.

In economic, governmental, and other social institutions, there has to be a working structure with specific functions demonstrably serving general functions. Accounts must be kept, and results or reports must be made periodically to let someone know that everything is working well.

Purposive Pragmatism, the eternal seeking for the reason-why or the goal-in-justifiable-terms, while not totally bad or unhealthy, is what ties so many people up. It keeps them from experiencing life and its fascinations, from undertaking any project—be it a course in anthropology or creative writing, a hobby or sport, a civic service, or recreation—unless they can find a socially "valid" answer to the question "What for?" The person who expresses a desire to take up golf invariably finds it necessary to add, "The exercise would be good for my health," not "Because I've always wanted to."

All of us to some extent need to find a purpose or goal in existence. *Everybody* has to know where he's going, we say. Every great person in history has set up guidelines and goals for his life. Agreed. There is certainly nothing wrong with goals. We all need them. But many people overstructure their lives for careers and achievement and end up feeling intensely guilty if they can't build the structure according to plan. Or they feel envious and even resentful of others who "make it." Possibly the worst problem of all is that they feel that their lives, once structured, have a purpose and that thus, as individuals, they are justified in using up earthspace and breathing earthair. We maintain that this attitude is unfortunate. None of us asked to be here or had anything to do with getting here. We have as much right to be here as anyone, and we do not have to "contribute" anything or "produce" anything or even "be" anything special in order to show good cause for our continued existence.

Many older people, born or raised in the economic slumps of the 1930s, have found it difficult—if not impossible—to understand life in any terms other than those identifying this "purposive pragmatism." They looked with scorn on the Beatniks of the 1950s, the Hippies of the 1960s, and find scant comfort in the nostalgic returns to the past in the early 1970s. Common questions heard from hardworking, established, fairly comfortable middle-class adults are "What do they do to earn the right to raise hell or riot or protest?" "Who pays the taxes to support these bums?" "Who minds the store while these kooks are 'finding themselves' through all their extravagant and irresponsible orgies and 'trips'?" "When are these unwashed, unshaven parasites going to settle down, join the human race [read: *"be like me"*], and pick up their fair share of the load of responsibility for building and continuing our way of life?"

We have no simple rebuttal to these arguments. But we do have a basic commitment to the intrinsic worth of each human being, including those labeled "kooks," "creeps," "weirdos," and "troublemakers." None of us has to do anything for another person *as a way of paying back the debt of being here.*

But, once each individual is guaranteed the simple right to be here and is enabled by those who care about him to survive and grow and become what he potentially is, he *will* become, we believe, productive and contributing and caring and compassionate. He *will* feel the self-worth of each other person because he feels his *own* self-worth.

Our only purpose in life, if "purpose" is needed, is to be what we are, fully, vitally, in a context of other people having the same right. The realization of the needs of others ought to produce, in sensitive people, the necessary checks and balances to make sure we "do our thing" without infringing on the important rights and needs of other thingdoers. In fact, in order to guarantee the satisfaction of our deepest needs, we must be concerned about the need-satisfaction of others.

In short, we can state realistically but not pessimistically that our only real goal is Death, and thus our big challenge is to live significantly, fully, meaningfully.

A full life depends on a total realization of just how short and limited that life might be. With life's ending in sight, the time still available becomes more valuable for meeting the challenge. The more

time each of us spends searching for *purpose* in living, the less time we have for *living* itself.

Life is given! It is not earned, not entrusted, not lent or rented, just given. And we don't have to get bogged down in philosophical or theological arguments about who gave it. But when someone out of a relationship of love gives you a gift, you don't need to say "thank you," or return it, or give a gift in return. The idea is to take it, unwrap it, appreciate it, use it, and enjoy it.

Existence and Being are gifts, with all the rights and privileges attached. Filling them with meaning and significance is up to the individual who receives them.

Selfhood

Let's regroup. By way of introduction we've tried to set forth the facts with which each individual has to grapple. We are conceived, we grow, we grow into *something*, we die. Death is a part of the life cycle and must be included in the full picture of human life.

But what is the "something" we grow into? We are born as units: individual cases of *Homo sapiens*, solitary examples of "people." We develop into something that has its potential in our human nature: human beings. We become "persons." There are many ways of describing this. Some speak of *soul*, while others talk about *spirit*. Some speak of *personality*, and others use the term *ego*. We call it *Selfhood*. As human beings unfold, like flowers blossoming from nib to bud into full-blown flowerhood, they become conscious of who and what they are.

The *Self* is the term for our awareness of our Being, potential and actual, latent and manifest. Reaching this awareness is a complicated process, but each of us, with or without the help of others, can come to a fuller, higher, finer, more satisfying understanding of just who and what he or she is. Actually, we'll find that we must do business with two concepts of selfhood: the self, which is like the *ego* of Sigmund Freud, the conscious, personally developed sense of one's own uniqueness; and the Self, the Suprapersonal identity, which binds us together with all living things. This is confusing, but throughout human history it has been a source of importance and inspiration to people concerned about developing human lives.

Our individual searches for significant personal selfhood and our collective searches for significant universal (or cosmic) Selfhood take many differing forms. We utilize others as models, heroes and heroines, ideals, and patterns, but there is also a uniqueness and individuation possible for each of us that goes beyond any copying process.

In the chapters which follow we'll outline the general patterns used in the processes of finding Selfhood. We'll try to show, in general terms, how each of us can make actual the hidden parts of the Self. Our definition of adjustment is *the process of attempting to bring into actuality all the latent potential aspects of Selfhood, trying to face and experience those aspects of reality that make this Self-actualization difficult, and trying to adapt to and have some* effect *on that reality.* In short, life is a series of successes and failures, hellos and good-byes, highs and lows, peaks and valleys, births and deaths; the fully actualizing Self experiences them all and deals with them effectively. It is more than "coping" or "battling" life. Self-actualization often means knowing when to "ride with" and fully experience those many life encounters that are difficult and painful. We do this with the joys and pleasures; why not also with the rest of life?

In a sense, the self is like a tool kit that contains the necessary tools (and often weapons) to work effectively with life. In another sense, the self is like a makeup kit in which we carry the materials for wearing the many faces or aspects of our being. Herb Gardner said it very well in his hit play and film *A Thousand Clowns.* Self-actualizing Murray Burns tells an uptight young girl that her sorrow over losing a man and a job may be a blessing:

SANDRA: What am I going to do? This is an awful day.
MURRAY: *(He sits on the swivel chair next to the bed)* Miss Markowitz, this
    is a beautiful day and I'll tell you why. My dear, you are really a jolly

old girl and you are well rid of Albert. You have been given a rare opportunity to return the unused portion and have your money refunded.

SANDRA: But . . . my work . . . what am I going to . . .

MURRAY: You are a lover, Dr. Markowitz, you are a lover of things and people so you took up work where you could get at as many of them as possible; and it just turned out that there were too many of them and too much that moves you. Damn it, please be glad that it turned out you are not reasonable and sensible. Have all the gratitude you can, that you are capable of embarrassment and joy and are a marathon crier.

SANDRA: *(Looking directly at him)* There is a kind of relief that it's gone . . . the job, and even Albert. But I know what it is, it's just irresponsible . . . I don't have the vaguest idea who I am. . . .

MURRAY: *(He takes her hand)* It's just there's all these Sandras running around who you never met before, and it's confusing at first, fantastic, like a Chinese fire drill. But god *damn,* isn't it great to find out how many Sandras there are? Like those little cars in the circus, this tiny red car comes out and putters around, suddenly its doors open and out come a thousand clowns, whooping and hollering and raising hell.[4]

In the course of living, even within the same hour of any day, we exhibit many aspects of ourselves.

The Struggle for Significance

Rather than spend good time, paper, and energy discussing what might be considered a *good* life, a *well-adjusted* life, or a *full* life, we'd like to introduce you to a rather new concept labeled "Significance." We are indebted, and make full acknowledgment of our debt, to Dr. Rollo May for his work in introducing it and in developing it meaningfully for us. In his fascinating and vital little book *Psychology and the Human Dilemma,* Dr. May asks a question that has time-, tradition-, and mind-blowing implications.

> . . . Is not one of the central problems of modern Western man that he experiences himself as without significance as an individual? Let us focus on that aspect of his image of himself which is his doubt whether he can act and his half-aware conviction that even if he did act it would do no good.[5]

4. Herb Gardner, *A Thousand Clowns* (New York: Random House, 1961), pp. 45–46.
5. Rollo May, *Psychology and the Human Dilemma* (Princeton: D. Van Nostrand Co., 1967), p. 25.

We feel that "Wow!" forming in our minds each time we read this and consider what it could and does mean for each human being in the here and now, and especially in the near future. A human being, with all the potential and actualized abilities he has, who still can feel that he doesn't matter! Man, the master of the world, able to doubt that what he is and does is significant.

> . . . Self-doubt which reflects the tremendous technological power that surges up every moment about him to dwarf overwhelmingly his own puny efforts.[6]

Man, seeing himself, for all his created and expressed potency, as *impotent* is more than a Frankenstein's monster turning on and destroying his creator. In that act, the monster was admitting Frankenstein's power and demonstrating that the only way to go round that power was to kill the man having it. The act of self-doubting is more pernicious. The monster creations and programs of man have become so powerful that, mindless as they are, they can afford to sweep him aside as being too unimportant to waste energy on killing him.

That is the stimulus, the challenge, the threat to the very existence of man as man that leads us to explore the "dilemma" that Dr. May describes. We propose, with the help of thoughtful and insightful people from many different times and backgrounds, to present the problem and explore its dimensions. We hope to show that Man's Ultimate Concern is more than what in the past has been listed as seeking happiness, enlightenment, wisdom, control, power, salvation, adjustment, or even identity. The concern of each of us is to find some way of getting alive, staying alive, fulfilling that aliveness, and making it (and ourselves) *count* in the scheme of things.

The Romans had a sign in their shops that read *Caveat Emptor.* "Let the buyer beware" is a very old cryptic phrase demonstrating an ancient concern that people should only purchase if they are aware of the possible consequences. Some of the difficulties to be encountered in absorbing this set of ideas are set out here for you to peruse, carefully, thoughtfully. You may, for instance, find that in looking into this dilemma it will defeat you, or at least knock you down emotionally. It's very difficult to confront the problems of life.

If you are interested in finding your Self, becoming who you actually are, in discovering not only your identity, but what worth that identity has, you may be in for hard work. So, buyer beware! You may be in for frustration, self-pity, self-hatred, and defeat. But you may also attain a rich and rewarding life and come to value the person that you find you really are.

6. Ibid., p. 26.

Adjustment

Each author who writes on the subject of Personal and Social Adjustment defines "adjustment" differently: "ability to balance demands of the *ego* with *id* and *superego* demands"; "being effective in reason, emotion, and interpersonal relations"; a definition having to do with reaching some sort of external, socially established goal; and so forth. The difficulty we have found with most of these approaches is in seeing "adjustment" in terms of something outside of, and apart from, the life of any human being. The definitions are, or have been, society's definitions. The goals too are usually those of the society. Attempts are even made to write a universal definition of "adjustment" so that each person, whatever his nation or culture, can reach some set of standards, hopefully agreed on by all nations and cultures.

Abraham Maslow has taught us a better lesson. He and others in the existential and humanistic branches of psychology have brought to our attention the fact that every human being carries within his own life the only real and possible "goals" or "standards" by which to measure adjustment—the actualization of Selfhood. This may mean, for some, that personal adjustment may take place at the expense of social adjustment. People who attain Self-Actualization are neither sociopaths nor anarchists. They know that we live in social worlds and benefit greatly from social experiences. Therefore, the attempt they make is to "actualize" their Selfhood as fully as possible while keeping a realistic understanding of the social demands made upon them. This often calls for compromise in behavior, though not always for compromise in thought and attitude.

The requirements for Self-Actualization include a full appreciation of the social relations and needs of each person. Every Self-Actualizing individual, then, is as fully and meaningfully himself as he can be without infringing upon or limiting the Selfhood of any other human being. As Schweitzer understood, "I am Life Affirming Itself in the midst of other Lives Affirming Themselves."

The search for significance has to be a very personal, even solitary experience: each person must figure out his own identity and live out his own life. Though it may be, it need not be a *lonely* search. There are currently on earth at this moment 3.5 billion other human beings who may also be interested in what it means to Be Alive.

The struggle to be alive, stay alive, to find meaning and significance in life is perhaps the only real purpose man has. The experience of discovering that you are a Being-in-the-process-of-becoming is a wonderful and fearsome one. But it can be so much more rewarding and thrilling than the mere ongoing, business-as-usual type of life lived

by so many people that we find it difficult to believe that you won't be stimulated and goaded and challenged by this idea. At the very least, we feel, you will have to do something with the ideas we are discussing. You may be able to forget or repress them, but they will remain part of your experience. Dealing with the "facts of life" in a realistic fashion is a part of the struggle.

Living life fully is not a straight-line path toward some external other-directed goal of adjusting or "mental health" or "perfection." It's trying to reach the end of your own life by experiencing it all deeply, richly, dangerously, riskily, and humanly. Life is "blood, sweat, and tears" *and* joy and glory. The challenge of living fully is well illustrated by a poem from the fertile mind of the contemporary American poet Dwayne Tipton Canon:

THOU

Lord, light my fire with purpose beyond the thought
    that life, happy or unhappy, successful or unsuccessful, is
        extraordinarily interesting.

Mighty warriors, celebrated and honored, allow me the pleasure
    of loving the multitudes of mankind, of escaping intolerance, a
        unique adventure.

Beautiful stars, is it so wrong to embrace the sun, to enjoy spring air, and
    to love, to think, and
        act courageously?

Powerful faith, do not betray me in my hour of need and despair, a
    superior man is marked by rising the fallen hawks and doves, an
        ultimate triumph.

Mountain peaks, do not reject me while my direction wavers, for
    all things must change to something new, to something strange, for
        flowers grow.

Ocean winds, might you offer more than fresh silence to my solitude, and
    allow me the conviction that only little minds are subdued by misfortune,
        and sadly mistaken?

Dark granite, forget your cold rewards, your solidarity is needed, a
    virtuous deed should never be delayed, the impulse is too strong, and
        hesitation unnecessary.

Bold rose, do not weary of life, your thorny stems lead inward to secret doors,
    and are doors outwards, out of self, out of smallness, out of wrong,
        to eternal peace.

—Canon, 1971

Summary

We have looked at the many crises each of us faces. The one with which we want to deal is that of *insignificance:* the feeling that our personal existence is not only meaningless but doesn't matter, isn't relevant or even related to anything or anybody at all. To begin the discussion, we must confront the most important fact of life: our own mortality. Man's significance is directly related to how he lives his life in accord with a full appreciation of the fact that he will someday die. This is dealing with the existential anxiety that all of us must confront one time or another in our lives. Existentialism and psychology have come closer together in the past few years, vitalizing scientific psychology and relating existential philosophy more directly to man's behavior. Humanistic psychology picks up on the very real dilemmas of human existence and attempts to guarantee that all our study and research can be applied to make human life more fulfilling, richer, and more significant.

Selfhood is described as one's consciousness of who he is. Significant personal selfhood is the goal and aim of this book. We are attempting to show people how they can actualize their own selves for more significant, meaningful, and, above all, joyful living.

Suggested Readings:

At the end of each chapter appears a list of books, articles, and other materials that may aid you in understanding the material in the chapter. Also, if any aspect of a particular point stimulates your further interest, the following materials will help. Some of these are found in our book of readings designed to accompany this work: *Significance: The Struggle We Share.*

Bugental, James F. T., ed. *Challenges of Humanistic Psychology.* New York: McGraw-Hill Book Co., Inc., 1967.

Buhler, Charlotte. "Loneliness in Maturity." *Journal of Humanistic Psychology* 9 (1969): 167–181.

Frankl, Viktor. *Man's Search for Meaning.* New York: Washington Square Press, 1963.

Fromm, Erich. *The Sane Society.* New York: Holt, Rinehart & Winston, Inc., 1955.

Gale, Raymond F. *Developmental Behavior: A Humanistic Approach.* New York: Macmillan, 1969.

Giorgi, A. *Psychology as a Human Science.* New York: Harper and Row, 1971.

Goble, Frank. *The Third Force: The Psychology of Abraham Maslow.* New York: Grossman, 1970.

Hillman, James. *Insearch.* New York: Charles Scribner's Sons, 1967.

Josephson, Eric, and Mary Josephson, eds. *Man Alone: Alienation in Modern Society.* New York: Dell Publishing Co., Inc., 1962.

Jourard, Sidney M. *Healthy Personality.* New York: Macmillan, 1974.

Kübler-Ross, Elizabeth. *On Death and Dying.* New York: Macmillan, 1969.

Lapp, L. *Death and Its Mysteries.* New York: Macmillan, 1968.

May, Rollo. *Psychology and the Human Dilemma.* Princeton: D. Van Nostrand Co., Inc., 1967.

May, Rollo, ed. *Existential Psychology.* New York: Random House, Inc., 1961.

Pearson, L., ed. *Death and Dying.* Cleveland: Case Western Reserve University Press, 1969.

Sartre, Jean-Paul. *Being and Nothingness.* London: Methuen, 1956.

Severin, Frank T., ed. *Humanistic Viewpoints in Psychology.* New York: McGraw-Hill Book Co., 1965.

Sutich, A. J., and M. A. Vich, eds. *Readings in Humanistic Psychology.* New York: The Free Press, Inc., 1969.

Tallent, Norman. *Psychological Perspectives on the Person.* Princeton: D. Van Nostrand Co., Inc., 1967.

Tillich, Paul. *The Courage to Be.* New Haven, Connecticut: Yale University Press, 1952.

Vonnegut, Kurt, Jr. *Player Piano.* New York: Avon Books, 1967.

Warner, Samuel J. *Self-Realization and Self-Defeat.* New York: Grove Press, 1966.

Wheelis, Allen. *The Quest for Identity.* New York: W. W. Norton & Co., Inc., 1958.

"What a Piece of Work Is Man"

*What a piece of work is man! how
noble in reason! how infinite in
faculty! in form and moving how
express and admirable! in action how
like an angel! in apprehension how
like a god! the beauty of the world!
the paragon of animals!*

(*Hamlet,* act II, sc. 2)

*we are
spectres and shadows waiting for form
corpses cadavers shrouded in skin
with death our only potential
we are the postures of pain
and the touchstones of soul*

EVERETT HOAGLAND
Assistant Professor of English
Southeastern Massachusetts University
Dartmouth, Massachusetts

William Shakespeare was Somebody! He has been claimed by so many people as their own, psychologists often referring to him as a marvelous psychologist, philosophers insisting that he was first and foremost a philosopher. He's been claimed by poets, theologians, mariners, and physicians. He may have been a dabbler at many things, or a very well-studied man, but one of the things he very definitely seems to have been was a human sort of man. He studied humanity, analyzing the mental life, the tortured thoughts, the hidden innuendoes, and the forgotten dreams of the people he wrote about. He knew the highs and lows, the glories and the follies, and he knew that all of these were simply parts of the whole which is *Homo sapiens.*

The excerpt quoted above has a touch of irony in it, as the student of Shakespeare well knows. When the writers of the musical *Hair* lifted these lines and set them to music, the irony became even more apparent. Man is considered to be the bearer of many wonderful gifts but a poor steward of his inheritance. No humanistic writer is blind to the fact of man's foolishness, his cruelty, his faithlessness. Yet, the words can be read and understood, apart from their irony, as fitting descriptions of the potential Self lying dormant in each human being. They are not myths or lies. They are simply too often unfulfilled. Man can claim wonderful inventions, ingenious insights, remarkable creations. Yet he is capable of the most supreme folly. The creature who can paint a Sistine Chapel ceiling is the same one who can turn Lake Erie into a cesspool. The same nature that can conceive of the most altruistic love can also butcher millions of his fellow men.

Contradictions? Possibly. More likely we will find as we explore the nature of man—our own nature—that the seeming contradictions pop up because we take limited glances. Our perspectives are fogged or fenced in by our needs, wishes, fears, and unconscious ambitions. Hatred can cause us to see only hate in people about us. Love can truly limit our vision to that of loving. Man is more than any one picture of him can portray, and he is more than all the pictures added together can say.

Humankind has been the subject of billions of words of fine poetry, literature, drama, music, and oratory. We have fashioned our images out of wood, marble, clay, oil, acrylic, soap, sand, wire, cheese, papier-mâché, and welded iron. We've dissected, analyzed, studied, and X-rayed ourselves in every way conceivable. Yet for all the experiences in recorded history of which man has been the subject, the one thing that can't be made or reproduced is that slippery something called his *essence,* his nature.

Even if we succeeded in setting down in words the most beautiful, or penetrating, or meaningful ideas ever used to try to describe human nature, all we'd have succeeded in doing is talking *about* it. It's like the Zen concept of what Zen Buddhism is: "That which can be talked about is *not* Zen!" This means that words are just too frail, too limited to capture a flesh-and-blood experience. Just as Zen and its goal of *satori* (enlightenment) are living experiences that defy being captured in words, so human nature is such an alive, personal, fluid thing that as soon as the words are dry on the paper it moves on to be something else.

It is possible, however, to talk about what human nature has been found to be by various persons at various times. History isn't just dry-as-dust, dead hulks of once-living buildings and nations. It often hides in its occasionally musty words real clues to what human experience is really all about. So, when we undertake to dig in the past through archaeology, anthropology, history, philosophy, or theology, we are often amazed to find frighteningly contemporary, pertinent, and relevant ideas. Humankind has only roamed this planet for a couple of million years—a drop in the bucket of life, when you consider living forms like the cockroach, certain fishes, and some mammals that have persisted so much longer.

Yet, man's most fascinating feature—one which may account for his uniqueness—is the persistent search for answers to the questions: *Who am I? What am I? How did I get here? What is life all about?*

In the Beginning . . .

At our most basic level of existence, we are *organisms*. This word tells us that human aliveness is described by the same fundamental characteristics found in any organism in nature: irritability of the protoplasm, need for nutrition, the capacity to digest food, reproduce, and move about. Whatever else we are, we begin in our understanding with our biological existence, and not only build on that, but also build *with* it. For it's a wondrous piece of equipment, this body each of us has. It is weaker and more fragile than the bodies of many animal forms and more prone to disease and decay than many. Its senses are less acute than those of many other animals. As a human being, you have a longer period of dependence on your parents than any organism in nature—nearly 18 years. And by no means do you live the longest. Your posture makes you among the least-coordinated organisms and makes your musculoskeletal structures and internal organs particularly vulnerable to all kinds of disease and disorder. Yet, the human brain and the rest of our nervous system are of a quality unduplicated in nature thus far. Our primitive dependence on instinctive behaviors has been replaced by learned and acquired behaviors, making us more in control of our lives than any other organism.

Thus, we can say we are first of all highly specialized organisms, organized systems of nucleic acids, performing vital functions, with sensory and neural mechanisms of a particularly selective brand. But what else? A porpoise is also an organism with a highly specialized nervous system. So is a chimpanzee. So also are millions of creatures further down the evolutionary scale. We could add to human traits the fact that our particular nervous system enables us to learn, but a fantastic array of other organisms can be conditioned, can profit from trial-and-error experiences, can imitate, can be instructed. Is it in the *kinds* of things humans can learn that a proper and meaningful distinction can be found?

René Dubos, in *So Human an Animal,* says that "as far as is known, only man can control and use fire."[1] Dr. Dubos, a microbiologist and experimental pathologist at New York's Rockefeller University, is also a humanist and, as such, is caught up in the holistic study of his fellow humans. He finds that in studies of human life, we've been differentiated from other animals not only because of our use of fire, but also because of our development of shelter, clothing, tools, weapons, complex social structures, and the practice of some form of magic or worship.

Even the complex social structures we build are somewhat different from those found in troops of baboons or colonies of paper wasps, however *similar* they may also be. Our social structures seem to spring not from instinct, but from *cultural* patterns built up around both biological and social needs. For instance, the patterns of family are designed to meet the bodily biological needs for sexual activity, touch-tenderness, nurturance, and protection. They *also* effectively meet the group needs for continuation through childbearing, for protection and instruction of the young, weak, ill, and aged, and for division of the labors of the society. The human family is much more than merely the springboard from which the young dive into adult living.

But is biology all there is to human beings? Are we only organisms, however finely developed, encased in the "clay" husks of our bodies? Is it not also necessary to pay attention to those other aspects of human experience—whether they are shared by our animal cousins or not—that have fascinated and inspired human beings since cave-dwelling days? What about the nonmaterial aspects of human experience? This leads us naturally (though not easily) into what has been called the "spiritual" dimensions of human nature. This has not been explored in psychological studies very much. William James, Carl G. Jung, Gordon Allport, and many others have done pioneering work in this area. But, for the most part, both behaviorism and Freudian psychology have ignored, even rejected, this aspect. Humanistic psychologists, though not always

1. René Dubos, *So Human an Animal* (New York: Charles Scribner's Sons, 1968), p. 34.

agreeing on terms or concepts, have shared a willingness to explore *all* dimensions of human experience—including the "spiritual."

Psychologists who have mentioned man's "spiritual" or religious aspect have often considered it to be superstition or illusion—irrelevant to their main concerns. Or they've considered it to be unscientific and therefore impossible to deal with as part of a scientific study of human psychology. Social psychologists have studied religious institutions such as organized churches and denominations, the social structure of synagogue life, or the importance of religion for perpetuating the values of the society. As important as these studies are, we don't feel that they get to the essential importance of the religious experience.

The human animal is human partly because he is able to relate to preexisting patterns. Human beings have delved into their own backgrounds, have linked themselves up with their primitive ancestors, have found the importance of certain enduring patterns in belief and thought. Every society ever studied has had some form of religion, in the sense that there was some attempt to tie the people to an ongoing pattern or process, an Ultimate Concern (as Paul Tillich defines God). The word *religion* itself gives us a clue: it comes from the Latin, *religare*, meaning to tie, to bind, to fasten. In other words, religion literally means the process of integrating (binding up into a whole) all facets of human life, all members of a given group, all groups in the Family of Life.

This, of course, may not reflect your individual religious experience or ours. Many people have been turned off by some of the forms and structures of organized religion and therefore see it as negative or meaningless or irrelevant. Yet, in spite of particular churches, temples, dogmas, or preachers, there is that which transcends us as individuals and binds us together. This is part of the search we must make and part of what makes us human. We will explore this in greater detail in chapter twelve.

Human Values

Among the human characteristics that we can't locate or identify in other animals is a concern with Value. In its simplest definition *value* means the worth of something. So far as we know, only human beings set up criteria of value by which to judge everything from pickles to abstract qualities like Goodness, Truth, Beauty, Justice, and Right.

Perhaps man began putting value labels on things when our early ancestors first found that they could keep, guard, or carry only so many objects and had to decide which were necessary, useful, vital for their survival and which were not. This evaluative process was expanded when these early people began grouping together and had to make judgments about which items and actions had survival value for individuals, group, and eventually for whole *societies*. Later, of course, as societies became more complex and simple physical survival became a less critical concern, "necessities"—and thus values—were redefined in terms of other needs, likes, and wants.

So, we are valuing creatures, and these systems of valuing have a deep effect on the way in which we live our lives and relate to others. To understand the importance of values in human experience, let's explore some of the value systems by which humans have lived. We will look at only some of the more important and notable Ultimate Values we've found in the history of Western humanity, though we've also been mightily influenced by similar values in Africa, Asia, and other parts of the world.

1. Pleasure

Pleasure is a value to many of us. The loudest spokesman for this viewpoint was Epicurus, who in the third and second centuries B.C.E. started advocating Pleasure as man's highest value. He defined good as the pleasure of the individual: "I know not how I can conceive of the good, if I withdraw the pleasures of hearing, and withdraw the pleasurable emotions caused by the sight of beautiful form. . . . All living creatures as soon as they are born take delight in pleasure, but resist pain as a natural impulse apart from reason." Even Plato, not usually considered an Epicurean (a follower of Epicurus' ideas), said: "Things are good insofar as they are pleasant."

In the seventeenth century, Thomas Hobbes wrote: "Whatever is the object of any man's appetite or desire, that it is which for his part he calleth good." Epicureanism came at that time to be called Hedonism. The philosopher Spinoza advocated Hedonism by stating: "We endeavor, wish, desire, or long for nothing because we deem it good; but, on the other hand, we deem a thing good because we endeavor, wish for, or long for it."

Hedonistic individualism gave way to Bentham's Utilitarianism, which promoted the idea that people should search not for individual self-pleasure, but for the greatest happiness of the greatest number. Good was whatever brought about large-scale happiness.

Long after this philosophical fire had become embers, Sigmund Freud added new fuel with his emphasis on the satisfaction of instinctive biological urges. Today, there are still philosophers and psychologists who believe that a person is most strongly motivated by a desire to gain pleasure and avoid pain.

What about this? We all are equipped with bodies that are capable of responding easily and readily to pleasure and turn away from pain as much as possible. The touch receptors contained in the body are far more receptive and sensitive to pain than to any other feeling, and thus avoiding painful injury is one of the most important tasks of our sensory equipment. The opposite end of the discomfort continuum is pleasure, total comfort, and thus human striving away from pain puts the attainment of pleasure very high on the priority list.

In the history of the Christian church we can observe, too, that people have been condemned again and again for their bodily desires and for seeking physical and emotional pleasure. Perhaps the medieval church, by placing such emphasis, albeit negatively, on the search for physical happiness, has forced many to experiment with something so obviously "important" to a very large segment of society. (There are some indications that the human mind cannot translate the word *don't* into action. Experimenters maintain that the mind translates whatever image succeeds the word, so that "don't take drugs" becomes, in the mind, "take drugs." All the facts are not in, of course, but the idea is worthy of consideration, particularly in relation to why *don't* so often seems to be a challenge or dare that is difficult to ignore.)

The ethic of seeking pleasure is far from dead. *Playboy* magazine has for twenty years made its publisher, Hugh Hefner, a wealthy man by capitalizing on and extending this ethic. The Playboy philosophy fits right into the notion that pleasure is good for its own sake. Sex is pleasurable and therefore good, though Hefner hastens to add that personal responsibility for one's actions is important. In recent years many imitators have come along—*Oui, Penthouse, Gallery, Playgirl, Viva*—and they all sing the same tune.

Though Hefner's viewpoint is pretty representative of that of most middle-class American and European males, it has been criticized from a number of perspectives. Moralists charge that he treats sexual activity as a free experience that exploits people for the sake of satisfaction. Women have charged that the publication and the philosophy behind them make women into mere objects of sexual and voyeuristic pleasure, into "things" rather than human beings. There are objectionable things about the Playboy philosophy, though we think individuals will continue to find pleasure in their own way; and it isn't our job to tell them what to read and what not to read. The Playboy philosophy, we feel, does have some values—among them that it has helped to free many people from guilt and complexes concerning their sexual needs and behaviors.

Hefner and his fans are not alone in their present-day hedonism. There are orthodox religions which fully approve of physical pleasure, though without making it a central emphasis as do the Playboy philosophers. Hinduism and other oriental religions recognize sexual pleasures as a very important part of the life of a fully enlightened man. In places the *Kama Sutra* reads like a manual of instruction in the sexual arts. Even in the Christian scriptures, many passages indicate that God confers suitable blessings upon sensual acts such as eating, drinking, and being merry.

2. Perfection

Searching in Christian scriptures for justifications for physical pleasure is straining those scriptures and their interpretations a bit much. Most scholars would agree that the major emphasis in Christian theology is not on pleasure but on Godlikeness, or more correctly, Christlikeness. The very urgent thrust of the New Testament and of most Christian writers in the centuries to follow was: "Man has wallowed in bad behavior long enough! God has sent an example, to be followed and to be worshiped as God's own Son. Strive to be like Christ, commit yourself to Him, and the sinfulness of your nature—because of Adam's fall from Grace—will be erased. You can, through faith and worship, become perfect!"

Theologians may not agree with this oversimplification, but they will have a difficult time proving that the search for perfection was not a very major emphasis in the Christian and post-Christian era. Even orthodox Jews, whose heritage produced the Old Testament, have not seen fit to carry the story of Adam and Eve to the conclusions that Christian theologians have. In this story Adam, the prototypical First Man, is created perfect. He is veritably the image of God. But for reasons that differ in interpretation by as many splinter sects as they have produced, Adam committed a disobedient act, "eating a piece of forbidden fruit," and was condemned by God to work and sweat and die, instead of living forever as the original plan dictated.

This concept has been called the doctrine of The Fall of Man, the Depravity of Man, and other similar names. It assumes that man, originally created to be perfect, fell from that state of perfection and must go through all kinds of rituals, ordeals, trials, and tests to regain some sort of tentative perfection, or, as it's often called, Salvation.

It seems clear to even a casual reader of the words of Jesus that attaining this Salvation was a matter of a rather complete change of heart, resulting in better behavior toward one's fellow men. Needless to say, the church has made Salvation-searching a bit more complicated! We can't expect all our readers to agree with this, but it is a very respectable and well-studied viewpoint.

Following in the wake of a difficult period, the followers of Jesus became a community of believers; and with the acceptance of Christianity by the Roman emperor, Constantine, the church became an institution. With institutionalization came the exclusive right to interpret the doctrines according to church law. It also brought the right to publish new doctrines. One of these, with very speculative scriptural basis, is priestly celibacy. The doctrine that priests should forsake the pleasures of sexual activity and family living did more than just make them a special category of people; it also elevated the idea of celibacy above that of enjoying sexual pleasures. This not only made ordinary people feel that their priests were superior beings because they could follow a vow of chastity, but also made many millions of noncelibate people feel a bit inferior, since they weren't forgetting their bodies and the drives built into them. Some have even felt extreme guilt for their "base, animal nature."

The systematic study of human behavior must include looking objectively at such long-held and "sacred" doctrines as celibacy. What do such beliefs do to human beings? Examples tumble forth: St. Anthony of Padua, under a vow of celibacy, lived alone in a cave to shut out the world and make meditation more possible. Being only a man, he dreamed dreams of sexual activity that woke him from his sleep. Disgusted and disappointed at his body's inability to see that his soul was in charge, he punished his body for responding so "naturally." He rolled himself in briar bushes, letting the thorns rip through his flesh and tear at the "so weak and fragile" body in which his soul was imprisoned.

St. Bernard of Clairvaux dreamed even "worse" dreams than did St. Anthony. His sexual dreams concerned the Virgin Mary. He, too, punished himself for such an offense.

St. Francis of Assisi, a kind and gentle man, was so convinced of the vileness of his physical body and its drives that he tried through flagellation (whipping himself) and fasting for long periods to force his body to give up its demands and release his soul. Martin Luther, while still a Catholic priest, also beat himself in his search for salvation for his soul, at his body's expense.

The search for spiritual perfection has left many a mark on our history, some positive and some negative. Out of Christianity's concern for other human beings has come the development of hospitals, both physical and mental. In spite of many abuses and colonial enterprises that were exploitative, much good has been done by Christian missionaries for people who needed to acquire certain academic skills and a better understanding of health measures.

On the other hand, many of the most infamous acts in history are traceable, directly or eventually, to attempts at perfection and/or salvation. The Crusades, holy wars, the Inquisition, and the persecution of witches in New England are but a few examples. When Christian nations go to war and religious leaders in those nations proclaim that it is a "holy war" carried on "in God's" or "in Christ's name," the most offensive extensions of this search occur.

3. Wisdom

A similar value, not always linked to religious belief, is the finding of perfection in the fullest development of our intellectual and rational capabilities. This thrust has been called by various names (Rationalism,

Age of Enlightenment, etc.), which, though differing in individual matters, all emphasized the search for wisdom and knowledge.

The sons of the Enlightenment—Locke, Berkeley, Hume, Voltaire—were sure that through rational means we could become masters of all, rulers of eternity. Noble as it was, this emphasis on intellectual and cognitive skills became the hobby of a select elite. To have the time, energy, and ambition needed for intellectual pursuits, one needed to be wealthy or living in a monastery or the "pet" of some wealthy patron. The large masses of people had more basic pursuits—getting enough to feed themselves and their families, keeping a roof over their heads, and fighting off the many obstacles to simple existence. For the majority of the population, rationalism and intellectual activity had no survival value.

The idea of an Intellectual Elite is still with us. We subsidize "think tanks" in various parts of the nation, where highly trained men and women come together to pool ideas, to explore rationally the urgent issues of our times. Yet, much of this valuable brainwork goes unshared by the "ordinary" mortals who may be just as intelligent, but who have more immediate personal obligations and commitments.

The worship of intellectual power, the predisposition to believe that all problems can be rationally solved, and the subsequent tendency to ignore such other aspects of human experience as emotion, joy, and fellowship create an imbalance in social attitudes that is ultimately detrimental to each individual's sense of significance. The Enlightenment period made us aware of our brains and the untapped potentials of human intelligence, and for this we are grateful. However, because of a continuing tendency to believe that we need only to accumulate information, to gather knowledge, to amass wisdom, with no need for feedback into the pool of human experience, we would ask the worshipers of Knowledge to consider the question "knowledge for what?"

4. Meaning

Though these different ultimate value-emphases do not follow a straight-line progression, it's interesting to see how they do form a pattern. As one search runs its course or proves to be a sterile course, another comes along full of challenge and promise.

After the Enlightenment period, philosophers pursued several variations on different themes, some again emphasizing perfection and morality, and others emphasizing the value of pleasure. But since there are always a few individuals who try to get above the concerns of their everyday existence, new ideas and new goals continually arise. Sören Kierkegaard, in a book entitled *A Concluding Unscientific Postscript,* gave many thinking and aware people a shock when he suddenly focused on the fact of human finitude. He told them what they had

CHRISTIANSON

"THE MEANING OF LIFE? GOSH, I DON'T KNOW. IF I KNEW THAT I'D BE RICH."

all known intellectually but had not really recognized emotionally: that they were going to die sometime. He told them something else as well: that they were not dead yet. He reminded them that something had to be done with the time and the life between those two points, that they needed to find meaning in their existence, for it might well be all they would ever have. And so, with Kierkegaard and Nietzsche and several others, the informal Existentialist Movement was fostered.

Kierkegaard was actually not the first existentialist or philosopher of existence. Pascal and even St. Augustine were dealing with existential issues. But Kierkegaard's pithy statements brought the widely scattered and often obscure statements into a coherent whole. Pascal tells us that we open a book, expecting to encounter an author, and we meet a man! This is what happens when we read and experience Kierkegaard.

Many thinkers before this melancholy Dane had stated and speculated about the proposition: "I exist." But Kierkegaard went one better. He said that his own existence is not at all a matter of speculation to him, but a reality in which he is personally and passionately involved. *Anyone* who chooses or is forced to choose decisively—for a lifetime, and thus for eternity, since only one life is allowed us—experiences his own existence as something well beyond the simple mirror of thought. He experiences the Self that he is, not the idea of that Self.

Once we begin digging into the meaning of our own existence, we find a problem. What do we mean by *meaning*? *Meaning* here indicates that we must find it possible and necessary to become intimately, passionately, subjectively aware of everything about our own existence. And we do this not with book learning or formal instruction, or even meditation. We do this by existing, so fully, so real-ly, that existence takes hold of *us*. The Rationalists, the Enlightenment people, all talked about grasping hold of knowledge. The existentialist talks about becoming one with his own existence: living fully, experiencing widely. Meaning, then, comes from existence.

Dr. Viktor Frankl, now director of the Institute of Neurology at the University of Vienna, is a leading figure in the psychological borrowings of Existentialism. His first important book on the subject, *Man's Search for Meaning*, was originally entitled *From Deathcamp to Existentialism*. Frankl was one of the several million Jews who suffered in Nazi concentration camps during World War II.

In his deathcamp period, Frankl saw many things happening to his fellow prisoners. In addition to the torturing, incinerating, shooting, and gassing, he saw the lives of those who survived undergoing fantastic changes. In some cases he saw Jews turning on other Jews, not for food or personal belongings, but to blame one another for their tragic state of existence. Frankl saw loyalties and faith dissolve; inhumanity began to dominate the lives of these people. Most of all, however, he saw defeat and despair. Sexual interest died in many prisoners, not alone from physical fatigue and disintegration, but from a loss of any kind of desire or need. Everything was sacrificed for the sake of simple survival.

Various psychological and psychoanalytic explanations have been given to explain what happens to a prisoner in a camp of this type. One theory is that under such hideous stress, the person simply regresses to a primitive level of functioning. Another view is that the person develops characteristics that resemble those of a schizoid character. He relates to reality only when it is nonthreatening, and to fantasy (by withdrawing from other people, for example) when reality is too burdensome.

Frankl's view, bringing him directly into the existential ranks, is perhaps simpler. He feels that in view of the limited and transitory nature of life itself, camp life could easily bring about "an existential loss of structure." From the deathcamp there was no exit and consequently no end to suffering—except through death. When a person cannot conceive of an end point, of a future, he is in danger of falling apart inwardly.

But for some—and this profoundly stirred Frankl—there seemed to be no apathy, no futility, no despair. A few among the thousands were able to sustain their hope, and to aid others in sustaining hope. Frankl observed them and noted his own attitudes. What he found was this: although every physical, material, tangible scrap of personal property had been taken, although the Nazis were able to strip the body bare and subject it to torment, anguish, humiliation, and shame, one thing could not be touched and was therefore *free!* This one thing—perhaps that which distinguishes man from lower animals—was his sense of Being, of Selfhood, his freedom of thought and attitude.

Being in barbed-wire camps does not automatically make a person a prisoner. "Stone walls do not a prison make, nor iron bars a cage." In the deathcamp—perhaps the most vicious test a human being could be put to—one was still free to decide whether he or she would *become a prisoner* or *remain a human being*—one who happened to be in prison. Most succumbed to despair and became "prisoners." But a few, enough to justify Frankl's observations, committed themselves to the fundamental choice of preserving their humanity. These served as examples to others, and a chain reaction was set off that inspired and perhaps saved the lives of many others.

Just what can we say happened? Asked to surrender their humanness at the gate upon entering, some turned it in along with their civilian clothing. Others allowed it to be taken away through the degrading acts committed upon them. But it would seem that a few said: "Wait! I am, even without belongings, dignity, privacy, and rank, a human being." What does that mean? It means I can keep a bit of my own Self tucked away in the corner of my mind. In that one little corner, where there is no SS guard, no barbed wire, no trench, no threat, I can experience freedom. No one can take that away! The only way I can lose it is to give it up, sacrifice it to despair!

So, in this way, a few people were able to find meaning in an apparently meaningless situation. For they kept a private reserve of the hope, the defiance, the decision-making, choice-making ability that is the right of every practicing human being. And being human does take continual practice!

Frankl and his colleagues helped thousands to practice their humanness in many different ways: by convincing them to objectify their fears and sufferings, by talking about them in the third person, or by imagining another time, another place. Frankl even managed to pull himself through a winter march on frozen, swollen, edemic feet by imagining that he was standing in a bright, warm, packed lecture hall, thrilling his audience with a lecture on "Group Psychotherapeutic Experiences in a Concentration Camp"!

He helped people to remember the joys they had known, the love they had experienced, the fulfillments that had been theirs. By filling their consciousness with times that had been meaningful, they were able to crowd out the seemingly meaningless present. And, by nurturing private hope, they were able to preserve their own meaningfulness by *giving* some of it to a totally absurd, meaningless experience.

Games! Fraud! Trickery! These are some of the terms you may have muttered as you read these lines. "That's not true meaningfulness! That's deceiving oneself!" Perhaps we should reiterate that each person has to give meaning to each of his own experiences; that, by themselves, some experiences are simply neutral, devoid of any quality. This is very subjective existence. But with the existential thinkers we must raise the question: how can one's own existence be anything *but* subjective?

There are other examples of this approach to being. During the same war, Allied soldiers in Japanese prison camps told of using similar tactics, though they didn't attach philosophical labels to them. Some men relieved the boredom and emptiness of their prison sentences by playing "mental games." We have accounts of men who worked out math problems entirely in their heads. Others played chess games, conceiving each move mentally and retaining an image of each piece's location on the board.

Others were able to picture wives, sweethearts, children, homes, and other meaningful and personal experiences. These reminiscences and attempts to re-create the happy parts of their lives actually pulled many of these men through times when the darkness that seemed to have no ending filled their lives.

Some would call this hope and tie it in, as Frankl did, with religious faith. Others would say that it is part of the most fundamental learning of the human animal: to anticipate, to recall, to choose, to commit, to follow through. Frankl liked to remember the words of Nietzsche, a dreadfully unhappy but thoroughly sensitive and concerned man: "He who knows a 'why' for living, will surmount almost every 'how.' "

5. Significance

Each of the values we have mentioned is important. Together with others they form the living, quivering, suffering, occasionally cracking mosaic of human experience. It is good and necessary to experience pleasure and joy, wisdom and learning, perfection or the search for it, and, of course, to be able to actualize the most potential aspects of our humanness by conferring meaning on our own existence. But there seems to be more. It is all well and good to find one's own existence meaningful, to know that one has an identity no one else can take away. But what seems to be emerging now is a search to establish oneself as significant.

Dr. Rollo May in his marvelous little book *Psychology and the Human Dilemma* introduces the concept of significance. Our dilemma is that, while individuals, we are born into a world of *other* individuals. We are born here and now into a world that has been here for perhaps 5 billion years, and the lives and creations and experiences of the countless numbers of previously existing human beings have left marks, stamps, impacts on the present and the future.

Simply by being born, you are a member of at least one social grouping: your family. You have an individual identity (with your own personal first name or nickname) and a group identity (your family name). At birth, you're given several statuses or positions: "firstborn daughter," "second son," "change-of-life baby," "illegitimate," "only child," "black," "white," "yellow," "brown," "male," "female." You often come into this world with a religious, economic, or class designation.

But you're also 1/3,500,000,000 of the human population of the earth—a statistic, a fraction, a decimal. This knowledge may eventually become apparent to you and with it may come a sense of insignificance that may obliterate or overwhelm the other identities and statuses altogether.

And this, too, is part of the newborn child's reality: you are a Somebody. Not Everybody, not Nobody, but Somebody. At times, you're made to feel that the sun and earth rotate around and because of you! At other times, you're reminded: "You aren't the only one in this house, y'know!" or "You don't want to eat that? Think of all the starving children in the world!" Parents expect you to learn to share, to give-and-take, to earn, produce, strive, achieve, win, compete, and do thousands of things that convince you not only that you're not alone in the world, but that in many cases it's an extremely difficult, dangerous and cutthroat world in which to live. So an individual has to compete with millions of others, and since there are so many of them, one solitary individual often feels that he just doesn't make much difference!

In this attitude is the beginning of what Rollo May and others are calling the feeling of insignificance. It is more than a feeling that our individual vote, voice, dollar, or presence doesn't matter much. It is much more than "getting lost in the gears" or fearing that a computerized machine is going to take our job or feeling that the world is getting too crowded. It's very much akin to what Frankl saw in concentration camps—a feeling that individually and as people we are fighting a losing battle to maintain our own uniqueness and that there appears to be no end in sight.

Let's look at the times in which we live. In the past seventy-five years, human creativity has produced more inventions than had accumulated throughout all the rest of recorded history added together. The human mind is capable of creating a limitless number of forms and processes. The numbers continue to grow, because each idea suggests other ideas, each machine contains the hint of yet another machine to come. No one has yet created a machine that can think, but we've come very close. No manmade machine yet can duplicate all the complexities of the human brain, yet some machines can outdo most humans in certain processes such as calculating and information retrieval.

Even if machines are limited, some of them perform so well, so consistently, so rapidly, that many of us feel threatened. We have to admit that we can't produce as much, as often, as rapidly, nor for as long a time, as can some of the mechanisms now in operation. Some of us wonder if there's any particular advantage in being a mere mortal!

Yet, our technology, which has put us on the moon, which has sent space vehicles out beyond Jupiter, which has replaced human organs, which has given more human beings a better standard of living than ever before in history, also threatens to overwhelm us. We face energy crises because our technology is a never-satiated beast, devouring our natural resources at a rate we find difficult to halt. Our environment is threatened because of this rapaciousness. Our involvement with other living forms endangers them *and* us. We've polluted the air, the water, the plant and animal life, and the very earth beneath us. Thinking back to Mary Shelley's *Frankenstein,* we find frightening parallels with our own times. Man, so mighty and creative, has set in motion a technology that threatens to take him over.

And where, in all this, is the individual human being?

It is good, indeed, to seek perfection, wisdom, pleasure, a better life-style for all people, to find meaning in existence, but what if we gain the whole world and lose our very Selves? Such is the problem.

The struggle for personal significance is with us. We've explored most of our planet. We've sought out and satisfied much of our curiosity about the moon. We've photographed and spectro-analyzed other planets. Much knowledge of outer space is now part of our understanding. What of inner space?

Some answers to these questions will be found in the pages making up the rest of this book. They aren't perfect or beautiful answers; rather, they are the clumsy, awkward, and feeble attempts made by human beings, sharing the struggle, putting down the ideas that have been found, that have been forged on the cold steel anvil of human experience. They don't always work—not even for us and the others who have found them. But they provide us clues, and they provide us some comfort. We aren't alone!

The matter of personal significance, of knowing that we have value as human beings, individually and as part of an ongoing process of human experience, will take us through many areas. We will look at the biological and social nature of human beings. We will consider the matters of work, creativity, play, humor, and recreation. We will find that human beings play games with Selfhood, that they wear masks and adopt roles that only give us partial clues to who they are. We will explore human emotion and consciousness. We will find that many of our enemies are inside us: the inner *Self* fighting it out with the outer self, the ego, the *mask*. We want to explore the ways people have found for removing the false faces, the partial identities, of exploring and bringing alive their fullest Selfhood. We must also spend time dealing with the spiritual, nonmaterial aspects of human experience. Finally, we must concern ourselves with the Way of fullest Self-Actualization, the matter of loving.

Humanistic Psychology

We've introduced you to a concept that isn't yet well known in this country. Humanistic Psychology isn't a separate brand of psychology (though its critics often say it is!). We want to share with you, the reader, what makes this concept important and "significant."

Psychology began less than one hundred years ago as a separate area of study. Those who began the science of psychology (literally, the study of behavior) were people coming from areas like philosophy, physiology, sociology, theology, political science, and anthropology. All of these sciences were concerned with some aspect of human behavior. Psychology alone intended to study the uniqueness of individual human behavior.

To gain acceptance in this period—toward the end of the Victorian Era of Rationalism and Enlightenment—the first psychologists tried to treat human experiences as if they were like electrical, chemical, or automatic experiences. A few of them permitted introspection (self-analysis or self-examination) as a valid tool of their research, accepting a subject's verbal or written report about what was going on inside him. Most, however, felt this was a source too subject to bias and error, too difficult to validate and replicate, as good laboratory procedure demanded. The writings of John B. Watson crystallized psychological research into the school of thought we call *behaviorism:* only objectively observed and measurable data could be accepted as valid and used in building theory about human behavior. So, imagination, thought, fantasy, dreams, beliefs, values, and other "nonobservable" phenomena were ignored. And, thus, psychology got on a scientific footing.

At about the same time (toward the end of the nineteenth and the beginning of the twentieth century), a Viennese psychiatrist began probing around in some less-understood areas of experience, finding dreams, word associations, slips of speech, and other bits of data to be quite valid in helping to provide a more complete picture of human behavior. The man was, of course, Sigmund Freud. He called his method of study *psychoanalysis,* and the theories he built gave us the second major force in psychology, after behaviorism, the psychoanalytic theory of human behavior. These two pioneering emphases dominated psychology for the next fifty years. The behaviorists conducted a wide variety of laboratory experiments, animal research, and some field observations; psychoanalysts gave us further insights into depths of behavior, especially the unconscious areas and the areas of emotional and mental disorders.

Psychology would not exist, nor would it be as respected as it now is, were it not for these two strong emphases through the years. But, in the 1950s, building on the work of William James, Gordon Allport, Carl Jung, Carl R. Rogers, and others, a newer emphasis began to grow. These psychologists, interested both in contributing to general knowledge and theory about human behavior, and also in human problems, began studying not the severely ill who had occupied most of the Freudians' time, but the relatively "healthy" people whose problem lay in finding meaning and fulfillment in their own experience. In their studies, they built on the work of the existential writers and therapists of Europe, who had been dealing with these matters for years, especially the ideas of Ungersma, Frankl, Sartre, and Kierkegaard.

The strong hold of the psychoanalysts and the "clinical psychologists" was being challenged. The cold, objective research methods of the behaviorists were being called into question.

In the late 1950s a group of men and women met for breakfast in Philadelphia, while attending a national psychological conference. These people formed a new group, the beginnings of what is today the Association for Humanistic Psychology. Such pioneering figures as Abraham Maslow, Charlotte Bühler, David Eitzen, James F. T. Bugental, Sidney Jourard, Carl Rogers, Gordon Allport, and many others, have tried to bring the new spirit of that group into their teaching, writing, and psychotherapy, and to turn psychology into a real science of human behavior. There is no real battle going on among the varying groups in psychology, although it often seems so. Those who use the term *humanistic* may be behaviorist or Freudian or Jungian or Maslowian or Rogerian or may avoid any of these neat labels. Their overriding concern and unifying force, however, is that psychology be a study concerned with people, that it be based on the study, observation, and self-description of human beings, and that it be geared to the resolution of human conflicts.

This emphasis, the humanistic, is called the third force in modern psychology. Humanistic psychologists, though they try also to be scientific and valid in their theories, nonetheless attempt to utilize *all* the experiences of human beings, not merely the measurable or observable.

This is difficult, since things like alterations of consciousness, intuition, dream content, and psychic phenomena are not readily observed by others. But these hurdles have not prevented humanistic psychologists from allowing them into the research as valid data.

For perhaps the first time, parapsychology (ESP, occult, spiritualistic phenomena) is being seriously studied. Religious and theological beliefs, consciousness alterations, drug experiences, Oriental philosophies are being explored to see if they contain keys which can be used to open more doors to human experience, to see if by combining many avenues we can arrive at some solutions to deep and broad human problems.

Strange bedfellows? Perhaps, yet the walls that have separated us for too long must be broken down if we are to share the rich treasures of human experience amassed around the world. Just in the past few years, behavioral scientists have begun to explore consciousness, and the area of biofeedback promises us fascinating (and "scientific") insights into that area, which for years was ignored or dismissed as "mystical." The American Psychological Association has formed a new division specifically devoted to humanistic concerns.

Now, perhaps, psychology can come out of the laboratory and the consulting room and find out more about the way people really live. By being more open, perhaps psychology can become even more helpful to people with emotional, mental, and existential problems.

The Manysidedness of Human Nature

Humanistic psychologists emphasize many ideas that are acknowledged but often ignored or rejected by other psychologists. We feel that many problems in living come not from physical ills, diseased brains, or faulty learning experiences. Nor are they simply the effects of repressed sexual or hostile tendencies. Instead, the root seems to be often one of estrangement—from nature, from other people, and especially from one's inner nature.

We emphasize these things because they are part of what we see in human nature, part of the multiplicity and complexity of the human animal. Human beings are animals, operating at certain levels on the stimulus-response principles of the simplest one-celled animal, but they are more than this. They are members of groups, small and large, but they are also more than this. They are taught most of the things that fill up the memory banks of their brains, but they are also more than this.

Human beings are somewhat predictable, but never entirely so. It is easier to predict what 50 million people will do in a national

election than to predict what any one individual person will do in that voting booth. Human beings can be generalized about, with some appropriateness ("sickle-cell anemia tends to be concentrated among blacks and southern Mediterraneans"), yet no individual exactly fits the generalities.

Human nature includes the capacity to cause Watergates, Watts riots, Nazi atrocities, Hiroshima, and Wounded Knee. But it also includes the tendencies to heal illness, resolve conflicts, discover cures to disease, invent lifesaving machinery, and "promote the general welfare."

Some human beings emphasize their brutishness. They are often (and properly) called "animals," "beasts." Yet, more, far more human beings emphasize their decency, their cooperativeness, their compas-

sion, and their humanity. Of this we are stubbornly, idealistically certain.

In the name of human decency, hospitals and schools are built, disaster victims are cared for, charitable institutions (however full of inconsistencies and inefficiency) are established, millions of dollars are given to promote scholarships, research, and institutions devoted to improving the quality of human life.

Humanistic psychology tries to see the Whole Person in every individual: its emphasis is Wholistic or Holistic. (It is interesting and important that etymologically, all these words are related: *whole, holy,* and *heal.*)

Art, music, theology, dance, drama, philosophy, Zen Buddhism, clairvoyance, Sufism, war, death, Hinduism, drugs, diet, ecology, mediumship, media, humor, work, creativity, play: all of the things people do, in which people are involved, these interest and excite us. To the degree that you prize and value all the aspects of the whole person, you are also a humanist.

When the Skylab III astronauts circled the earth in early 1974, astronaut William R. Pogue sent back this statement to ground control: "The long flight has given me a more humanistic view toward other people and toward myself. I now have a new orientation . . . of almost a spiritual nature." Astronaut Gerald P. Carr agreed. He said people in technical work too often tend to "move along with blinders on. I think this mission is going to increase my awareness . . . of what else is going on besides what I'm doing."

It is paradoxical that as we push the boundaries of space further out—theoretically widening our horizons and increasing the space around us—the population of the earth increases continually. The net effect of this growth and expansion is a greater need for developing workable ways of understanding our inner nature and of appreciating the relationships and global identities of all human beings. These concerns make up the central themes of humanistic psychology.

Summary

Human nature is an object of philosophical study, but it is of utmost importance to us in trying to understand how self-actualization for personal significance comes about. The study takes us to the matter of organic evolution as a beginning. Human nature is fundamentally physical, so it is there that we begin, as we will show in the next chapter. Our approach is basically naturalistic, but we know that many aspects of human nature lead us into areas of human experience that are confusing if studied only in naturalistic terms—if indeed they can be studied in that way at all! Among these are human *values.* Our review took us through some of the values held most dear by people in the Western world over the centuries: the searches for pleasure, perfection, wisdom, meaning, and finally, Significance.

The emphases of humanistic psychology are directly related to our view of human nature. Our own best interests, viewed in the light of a fuller understanding of our nature, are the criteria for the study and application of humanistic psychology.

Suggested Readings:

Baba Ram Dass. *Be Here Now.* Lama Foundation. New York: Crown Publishing Co., 1971.

Berelson, B., and G. Steiner. *Human Behavior.* New York: Harcourt, Brace & World, 1964.

Brickman, William W., and Stanley Lehrer, eds. *Automation, Education, and Human Values.* New York: Thomas Y. Crowell, 1969.

Bugental, J. F. T., ed. *Challenges of Humanistic Psychology.* New York: McGraw-Hill Book Co., 1967.

Bynner, Witter, trans. *The Way of Life: According to Lao Tzu.* New York: Capricorn Books, 1962.

Christian, James L. *Philosophy: An Introduction to the Art of Wondering.* San Francisco: Rinehart Press, 1973.

Deese, James. *Psychology as Science and Art.* New York: Harcourt Brace Jovanovich, 1972.

Dobzhansky, Theodosius. *Mankind Evolving.* New Haven: Yale University Press, 1962.

Dubos, René. *So Human an Animal.* New York: Charles Scribner's Sons, 1968.

Erikson, Erik. *Young Man Luther.* New York: W. W. Norton Co., 1958.

Frankl, Viktor. *Man's Search for Meaning.* New York: Washington Square Press, 1963.

Fuller, R. Buckminster. *Utopia or Oblivion.* New York: Bantam Books, 1969.

Goble, Frank. *The Third Force: The Psychology of Abraham Maslow.* New York: Grossman Publishers, 1970.

Hesse, Hermann. *Siddhartha.* New York: New Directions, 1951.

Huxley, T. H., and J. Huxley. *Touchstone for Ethics.* New York: Harper & Bros., 1947.

Janaro, Richard P., and D. E. Gearhart. *Human Worth.* New York: Holt, Rinehart and Winston, Inc., 1973.

Jung, Carl G. *Modern Man in Search of a Soul.* New York: Harcourt Brace Jovanovich, n.d.

La Barre, Weston. *The Human Animal.* Chicago: The University of Chicago, 1954.

Laing, Ronald D. *The Politics of Experience.* New York: Ballantine Books, 1968.

Lamont, Corliss. *The Philosophy of Humanism.* New York: Frederick Ungar Publishing Co., 1965.

Maslow, Abraham. "Our Maligned Animal Nature," *Journal of Psychology* 28 (1949): 273-B.

Montagu, Ashley. *On Being Human.* New York: Hawthorn Books Inc., 1966.

––––––. *The Biosocial Nature of Man.* New York: Grove Press, 1956.

Reich, Charles A. *The Greening of America.* New York: Bantam Books, 1971.

Sherrington, Charles. *Man on His Nature.* Cambridge University Press, 1941.

Teilhard de Chardin, Pierre. *The Phenomenon of Man.* New York: Harper and Row, n.d.

Titus, Harold H. *Living Issues in Philosophy.* New York: Van Nostrand Reinhold Co., 1970.

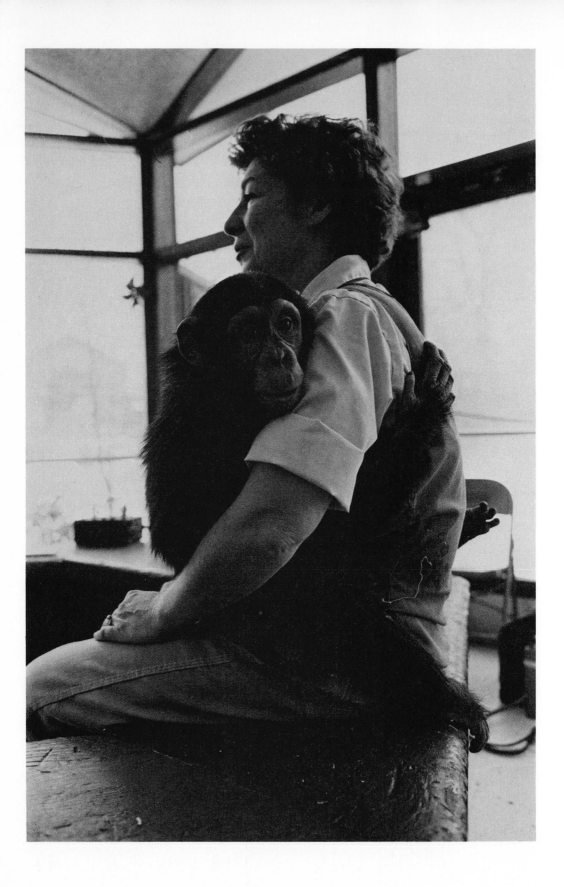

3

Neither Ape
nor Angel

*The curtain rises on a quiet country home in an English village. The first character in our cast is seen puttering about in his greenhouse and muttering about in his study. It was in this place and in this manner—apart from a famous voyage around the world—that Charles Darwin spent most of his life. Yet this uneventful life of this unassuming man in this unspectacular setting probably produced a greater impact on our world than that of the more flamboyant figures—the Caesars, the Napoleons, the Hitlers, the Churchills—who have stalked across our globe. After carefully collecting and collating evidence for 17 years, Darwin gently intimated to man that he was not a special creation of God with an exclusive soul but an animal on the same scale as his dogs and his cows. After the inevitable violent reaction—*Scopes v. State of Tennessee, Prof. Huxley v. Bishop Wilberforce—*man swallowed this bitter pill. Indeed, he now finds it not only palatable but sweet. Most of us feel better about being raised apes than fallen angels.*

W. LAMBERT GARDINER[1]

1. W. Lambert Gardiner, *Psychology: A Story of a Search* (Belmont, California: Brooks/Cole Pub. Co., 1970), p. 11.

In any discussion of the nature of humankind, we come inevitably and headlong into the fact of biology. This need not be a jarring crash. In fact, it shouldn't even surprise the fully aware person to discover just how much of his and her human existence is biological and physiological.

The word *organism* is used in virtually all contemporary sciences to describe forms of life composed of mutually dependent parts maintaining various vital processes. That describes a single-celled amoeba, and it describes the human animal as well. We share with all organisms these biological characteristics: we are made of the same essential substance, a protoplasm that is irritable (responsive to stimulation); we require nourishment for fuel and for rebuilding of cellular structures; we eliminate some form of waste matter; we possess motility (can move spontaneously); and we all duplicate ourselves (sexually or asexually).

In addition to the qualities described above, humans are a vital part of all that contains the other species of living things. We're in direct-line continuity with nature. Biologists use this taxonomic classification to describe humankind:

Kingdom: *Animalia* (organismic: motility, digestion, irritability, and reproducibility)

Subkingdom: *Metazoa* (many-celled)

Phylum: *Chordata* (dorsal central nervous system and axial symmetry)

Subphylum: *Vertebrata* (internal segmented skeleton)

Class: *Mammalia* (mammary glands, viviparous birth, warm blood, specialized dentition, differentiated vertebral column)

Subclass: *Eutheria* (possessing a placenta)

Order: *Primates* (generalized structure, prehensile hands, developed clavicle, nails, two pectoral breasts)

Suborder: *Anthropoidea* (eyes on frontal plane, stereoscopic vision, complete bony eye socket)

Superfamily: *Hominoidea* (no external tail, no cheek pouches, dental formula of 2:1:2:3, modified pelvis for upright posture)

Family: *Hominidae* (nasal bridge, philtrum, lumbar curve, bony chin, true upright stance)

Genus: *Homo* ("manlike")

Thus, if one can appreciate the findings of the Organic Evolution Theory, we can easily and fairly accurately be located in a direct relationship with other animal forms in nature. The arguments that evolution is absolutely opposed to and mutually contradictory to the Special Creation theory recounted in the book of Genesis are important, because they involve the beliefs and feelings of human beings; yet those arguments are nearly impossible to resolve. Proponents of Special Creation ("In the beginning, God created . . .") usually remain firmly rooted in tradition and religious faith. Proponents of organic evolution usually stick with the experts and the fossil evidence. Neither collection of evidence impresses the other group very much.

We, the authors, must take a position that is not rigidly or dogmatically held. Unless further evidence devaluates or disproves it, we assume that the theory of organic evolution best accounts for the presence and variability of living forms on earth. This includes Mankind, *Homo sapiens.*

In Continuity with Nature

The best explanation for the common characteristics held by both man and other animals is that there is a biological connection between them. There must also be important factors to account for the differences. Biology finds the best answers to both the traits in common and the different characteristics in the theory that living forms evolve from simpler to more complex, from generally similar to specifically different, because of the factors of adaptation and natural selection.

Mutations (deviations from the main form) occur by chance or because of environmental factors. If the mutations favor the organism by enabling the organism to adapt to its environment better or to survive its environment, then the mutant organism is "selected-for" by nature and will survive. Other organisms without the mutation die off. Surviving mutations will mate and produce variations, and so on.

The implications of this are important. It means that even though evolution is still going on (so slowly that we cannot observe it in ourselves), it's safe to say that characteristics that humans possess have just as much survival value as characteristics possessed by other animals. For example, if sneezing is "selected-for" by the evolutionary process, as is suggested by its universality among all humans and other animals, it must perform some function that is essential to the organic survival of man and the other animals. So it is with all other behaviors: blinking, shivering, sensing danger, feeling pain, sexual excitement, having five fingers, having an opposable thumb (it can touch the fingertips of each of the other four fingers), having abundant hair on only certain parts of the body, and so on.

Some of these factors may seem to belong more properly in a biology text, but we have put them here deliberately. We wish to make them so much a part of your thinking that as you deal with the rest of this book you cannot help but place the factors of selfhood and significance-searching against the background of biology.

You are an animal. That's what all the preceding information is saying. Each of us must deal with this. Part of knowing *who* we are must begin with acknowledging *what* we are. An important part of what we are is simply defined under the heading "Animal." Unless this fact is accepted, much of the following discussions will be both meaningless and incomprehensible.

If we are animals, then we must behave according to some of the behavior patterns followed by other animals. And even the stoutest opponent of evolutionary theory has to acknowledge some perfectly obvious similarities between man and other animals. Who, in mature awareness, can ignore the fact that there are many animals which propel themselves by walking, or have two eyes that convey electrochemical images to the brain, or have two ears that carry disturbances in the surrounding air to the brain, or are carried inside their mothers' bodies until they are born, or obtain milk from their mothers? Or that all animals require sleep, air, food, and exercise?

Even if the theory of organic evolution didn't answer most of our questions, or even if there was no such theory, we would have to call man some form of animal just to explain the obvious similarities in bodily structure and behavioral function. However, many people question it, doubt it, hem and haw around the issue, and protest that man is something else. Some back off from acknowledging man's animalness, even as a beginning point, when, in their own experiences, they have had pets to which they have "talked." Instead of using some kind of inductive process that would bring them to the conclusion that the things they shared with their "animal friends" made them all part of some big, happy "animal family," they do the reverse and use terms like "almost human," "so much like a person" to describe the animal behavior of their pets. Curious!

This tendency is part of a long-standing pattern among humans: to take rather excessive pride in being human, in being *not* animal. It comes, in part, from a strict interpretation of the Creation account in Genesis, which put the creation of mankind at the Grand Finale of Creation Week, with the added epilogue of "have dominion over" the rest of the creations. We have taken this literally by caging and controlling all kinds of animals, often including ourselves. In spite of all the fantastic progress we've brought about since we first harnessed fire, a great many parts of our own animal nature have yet to be tamed and put to nondestructive use.

Our pride in being something more than the other creatures has widened the gap in the understanding of many people. For in point of fact, we and our "animal friends" are much closer than we might think or want to admit. There are, however, important reasons for not only admitting our biological foundations, but actually rejoicing in them. There is comfort to be derived from our biological linkage with other life-forms: we have roots and a history and a very large "family" from which we can gain immeasurable insight and companionship. René Dubos, a microbiologist who writes more like a sensitive poet, puts it thus:

> All living organisms retain structural and functional evidences of their distant evolutionary past. Whatever the conditions under which they are born and develop, their responses to stimuli are always affected by the experiences of the past which are incorporated in their genetic make-up. The evolutionary steps through which man reached the level of *Homo sapiens* explain, for example, why the structure of his backbone can be traced to the early fishes, or why the salinity of his blood still reflects the composition of sea water from which terrestrial life originally emerged.[1]

On the physiological basis for human behavior, all psychologists tend to be in some agreement. Freudians and Watsonian behaviorists have, at times, made extreme statements about the importance of biology in human life, such as Freud's "anatomy is destiny." Physiologically focused psychologists have felt that the entire study of human behavior could be done in the microcosm, by the techniques of certain physical sciences which are able to isolate aspects of their subject matter, study them separately from the rest, and put them back together again, with no apparent harm done or anything missing from the study. Some pay no attention to environmental factors such as experience, learning, and social interaction in their studies of behavior. A few are "constitutionalists" in the sense that they attribute virtually all the behavior to the body's constitutional makeup. They do not have much following, and their studies have little real empirical documentation to their credit.

Others, not so extreme, still maintain that, important or interesting as environmental factors are, all that can be learned about people can be learned by simply studying them anatomically or physiologically. So much of our behavior can be analyzed in isolated (or nearly isolated) fashion that some scientists simply concentrate their time, energy, and foundation funds on such molecular research. It is, furthermore, fascinating study.

A former colleague of ours once boasted that he could teach the entire Introductory Psychology course, covering all the basic concepts,

1. René Dubos, *So Human an Animal* (New York: Charles Scribner's Sons, 1968), p. 70.

without once referring to human beings. It was not an entirely empty boast. Studies of lower and infrahuman animals have yielded valuable information about virtually every aspect of psychology, especially those basic concepts called learning, motivation, emotion, development, and social behavior. But is that what most of us want from a course in psychology?

Needs and Motives

The first thing that interests us in understanding the essential self is the question, "What makes us go?" What makes us tick has been the subject of countless books, but it all properly fits in the bio-psychological study of *motivation,* which begins with the physiological needs of our bodies. These needs are not always the most important, but they are fundamental to those that we acquire later. They are, as Maslow puts it, *prepotent.* Later in life, learned or acquired motives are vital, but if basic physiological needs are not met and the tension to satisfy them builds up, they assume urgencies that override the acquired motives. Probably the most obvious example is the physiological need for oxygen. A person strangling for lack of air cares very little about prestige, affection, money, or even food. At that moment, air is his greatest need; breathing assumes a prepotency over all other needs.

Primary Motives

The physiological needs are often called survival needs because they are vital for continuing physical existence. But since sex is included in any listing of physiological needs, we prefer to use the better term *primary motives.* For as important as sexual activity is to most human beings, it is not absolutely necessary for the individual survival of a human being.

The primary motives or needs are for:
1. Nutriment
2. Liquid
3. Oxygen
4. Rest and sleep
5. Elimination of body wastes
6. Regulation of temperature extremes
7. Avoidance of pain
8. Sexual activity or reduction of sexual tension

Some of these needs are based upon deficiencies in the tissues of the body, some upon stimulation from outside the body, and others on hormonal substances in the blood chemistry.

Secondary Motives

The next level of motivating factors includes those that are learned or acquired. Through learning, previously neutral stimuli seem to acquire the capacity to arouse motive states. Since these motives are probably not physiological in a direct sense, they are usually not included in any listing of needs related to survival. They are called secondary motives. Sometimes, because these needs involve other people to a greater degree than the primary needs do, they are also called social motives.

Examples of secondary motives are the needs for affiliation, social approval, status, security, and achievement. We are probably much more driven by these motives than by the primary needs, and they are far more complex. However, we are unable to find any way of separating the acquired motives from their grounding in the physiological makeup of the human being.

Maslow's Hierarchy of Motives

Abraham Maslow has helped give humanistic psychology a firm basis in scientific psychology. In his two books *Motivation and Learning* and *Toward a Psychology of Being,* he presents his theory of motivation and analyzes the motivational patterns of human beings. We illustrate his theory with the following diagram:

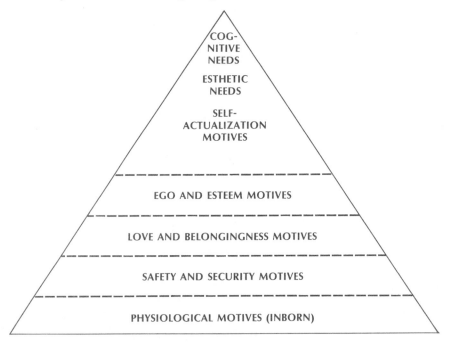

Basically, Maslow maintains that at various periods in your life you are primarily or predominantly driven by different kinds of forces. In infancy, inborn and unlearned survival needs are dominant (or "prepotent"). These are primary and are what we've learned to call the *physiological needs.* Your only job at birth is to survive, so you require food, liquid, air, avoidance of pain, elimination of wastes, and touch-contact. You may need other things too, but the major emphasis during this basic period of your life seems to be on the primary aspects of physiological survival.

In the chart shown above, the lines dividing the differing levels of motivation are broken to indicate that they aren't rigid and fixed. Physiological needs don't arise and subside at a precise point in everyone's life. They are always with us and continue through life, even though the motives "above" them may be dominating at a given time. We never "outgrow" any of the needs regardless of which level may be dominant.

If survival needs are met and regulated so that they no longer occupy all of your time and thought, a new set of needs emerges, assuming a greater urgency than mere survival. Obviously, survival needs are prepotent: they will always take priority! And again, millions of people in the world cannot move beyond survival needs because they barely survive—though Maslow finds it significant that even among starving or poorly sheltered peoples, many "higher" needs emerge and are met.

The second level of needs is that of *safety or security needs,* which are usually dominant in the young child. In this period, beginning at about age one, the child grows into a need for understanding and patterning of life. He begins testing out some of his own built-in resources: he learns how some of his parts work, how to make them function, how to control and coordinate them. This is the period when he begins to control large and small muscles, and walking and running develop. He also begins to control bladder and bowels, dress himself, pick up things, draw, and build.

At this stage, the child needs to know what happens when he does certain things. He does a lot of testing of the world around him, including testing the adults in that world. The child wants to know what the limits of things (including himself) are. So, in a sense, he develops security by experiencing insecurity—by testing things.

Most organisms operate at the lowest and easiest levels of existence. "Eat, drink, and sleep" is about all it takes to keep many simpler animals operating in balance—or *homeostasis,* as scientists say, referring to the tendency of an organism to maintain internal stability. What happens, we think, is that homeostasis occurs when a proper relationship is achieved between tension and ease, in any system. According to

Freud and others, humans act more or less like lower animals in this regard. These thinkers almost seem to expect human beings to find a comfortable niche, surround themselves with the basic essentials of survival, and then to go to sleep, never wanting anything more out of life. Freud found evidence for this position in the regressive behavior of many people, especially his neurotic patients. (Regression means to drop back to an earlier mode of gratification—like a forty-year-old man who throws a tantrum to get attention, as he had done as a child.)

Freud saw that when a person was rewarded by regressive behavior, he seemed extremely pleased with the results. From this Freud theorized that an individual does not willingly choose growth and maturation; they are forced on him by his external environment. Freud was impressed with the fact that some patients seemed genuinely shocked by demands to "grow up," as in accounts of resentment felt by some children at toilet training. He concluded that, left on his own, a child would remain at the most satisfying level of development, usually the one in which gratification came most easily.

In short, Freud felt that a child had to be forced to grow up, had to be evicted from the "home" he made at each level, and prodded into "going upstairs" to the next stage.

Maslow disagrees. His studies conclude that, far from being forced to grow up, the child who is growing in healthy terms, who has "made it" in the sense of acquiring a homeostatic balance of needs and tension-reductions, literally jumps at the chance to move up to the next stage. Maslow found that those who were kept at a level of satisfaction and need-reduction became bored, fatigued, resentful. From this, Maslow concluded that it is part of one's biological nature to seek continuing growth.

Homeostasis moves up, then, from the biological drive to a learned need at each level, following a pattern: discover a need, motive, or deficit, find a goal or incentive that will meet the need, and enjoy the satisfying tension-reduction for a period of time. Then move on to another field, for a different "ball game," of needs and their satisfactions.

After the child finds his basic needs being met in a regulated and consistent fashion, his built-in need to challenge the environment (sometimes called the curiosity, activity, and manipulatory needs) pushes him to experiment with the situation. It is during this period that his large muscle movements push him into explorations of the coordination patterns that enable him to stand, walk, run, and jump. Also, in this trial-and-error situation, he discovers that there are limits. Some of these are imposed by the built-in physical limitations of his young body. Others are imposed on him by the physical reality outside, like hard floors, force of gravity, walls, locked doors, and spankings.

Other limits come from the people in his world. He experiences the approval *and* the no-noes of the significant people in his life.

By testing and trying himself out with all these limits, he comes to some understanding of what he can and can't do. This enables him to arrive at some acquired patterns of thought, attitude, and action, giving him a sense of safety or security. He has learned how to stand, what falling feels like, what staying up feels like, and, in the healthy child, a preference for the feeling of staying up.

In later childhood, the predominant motive is to discover, seek out, and test the relationships of affection and belonging. In other words, *Love* comes to be a motive. As Freud, Erikson, and others point out, love is a pattern of response that takes time and effort. It's not inborn. The child can respond to love, and needs it and all that goes with it. But the newborn infant is hardly capable of loving or giving in the sense that we mean when we talk about mature love.

In the period roughly between 6 and 12 years of age, the child's predominant motives are to find out about love. It is partly an intellectual search, because he is usually in school at this stage. But it's also an intense emotional experience. His security now comes from finding out about the quality of his belonging, the depth of his affection and that of his "significant others."

Again, as before, the lower-level needs must be fully and satisfyingly met before the child can concentrate on higher needs. A child faced with the conflict between survival and safety needs will choose the prepotent survival needs.

At each stage there seems to be a necessity for choice. In the choice between staying at the level of safety and going on to the level of loving, the easiest choice is for safety, because it has already been experienced and is "known." Loving and belonging involve a lot of risk, for a child or for an adult. They involve putting oneself on the line, out on the limb of initiative. And that's scary! To take the chance of trying to love takes courage and willingness to risk. The risk comes from the possibility of failure and rejection. Nobody seems to enjoy rejection, excepting those called masochists.

In adolescence the predominant need is for identity, what Maslow calls ego or esteem needs. Once the child has satisfied himself that he is able to love and be loved, he begins to be strongly impelled to discover who or what this loved and loving person actually is. Is he loved because he is a "somebody" on his own, or just because he does what he is told? Is he loved for being himself or a reflection? How many adolescents discover that they aren't really loved and respected for their unique selfhood, but only for being "a chip off the old block," a good reflection of their parents?

In this age period somewhere between twelve and eighteen, the individual concentrates on differentiating, for others to see and ac-knowledge, that part of his behavior that is his own unique contribution, his Self. This differentiation may require radical breaks from the love patterns that were established in the previous age period. For identity formation often means breaking the mold, turning one's back on his family or tradition. All of this can cause pain and embarrassment. But the rewards of selfhood, in theory at least, more than make up for the pain and disadvantages.

Self-actualization needs

In young adulthood the predominating motivation is to put that newly formed self to the test. In this age period the drive is to realize and to make actual all the potential elements and facets of that Self-hood. During this period, one is involved in education, marriage, par-enthood, creative endeavors of many kinds, community activity, and career—all activities that *could* be Self-actualizing. However, for most of us, according to Maslow, these pursuits aren't Self-actualization. Maslow believes that the adults who are actually in the process of Self-actualizing make up only about one percent of the adult population. And we would tend to agree.

In our own experience, most people seem still to be working out their security needs, or love needs, or ego needs and are doing little, if anything, to realize their hidden potentials. Examples:

At a party, one of the authors engaged a young woman in conver-sation about her work. She said she disliked her boss intensely because he reminded her of her father, whom she hated. Asked what she liked about her job, if it gave her opportunity to discover new aspects of selfhood, or was satisfying in any other way, she could mention only the problems she had with her boss, the short lunch breaks, the lack of praise for what she did. Far from being Self-actualizing, she was stuck at the levels of Ego and Belongingness needs.

In a classroom, a young man was so involved in proving that he was masculine by talking about his athletic skills that he drove away young women around him who could have given him opportunities to show his masculinity far more effectively than any athletic event! Yet, he was not ready for girls: that took more masculine selfhood than he felt he had. His was more a Little League athleticism than a mature masculine self-concept.

The man who drinks to unwind and relax after a devastating day as a salesman, rather than going home and sharing his frustration and disappointment with his wife, very often is a person who is fixated (stuck) at the Security or Belongingness level.

Why can't people move up to a higher level of motivation? One of the major reasons is lack of encouragement from their environment to do so. For example, public education in the American society is geared toward conformity of behavior, not individuation, and pupils learn to prefer safety and security to risk-taking. There is, of course, much formal "teaching" about success, courage, and pride in accomplishment, but consistent urgings toward "behaving" or "not rocking the boat" indirectly encourage children to "fit in" and become "a part" of something else. Furthermore, the major educational emphases—direct or authoritarian teaching, rote memorization—often work *against* the Self-actualization of both student and teacher. These same emphases often occur again on the job. One's environment encourages him to stay at the Safety and Security level; too much Self-actualization or individualism may cause him to lose his job.

Maslow speaks of one group of Self-actualization needs as *cognitive needs,* and says they are commonly strongest in middle age. Many of us have strong needs to seek insight, information, knowledge, wisdom, rational experiences—and these experiences are satisfying in and of themselves. A lot of childhood and adolescence is spent cultivating the intellectual and rational powers, and once an individual has worked into a comfortable relationship with his early Self-actualization needs, he may find satisfaction in grappling with philosophical and abstract questions, rather than just the more practical questions of young adulthood.

In the period commonly called "the middle years," many people reach a level or plateau in terms of personal growth and significance. They have found work which may or may not express their Selfhood, but which at least meets their lower needs with some regularity. They may have formed love relationships and also possibly had children. They've arrived! Yet, they may feel a growing restlessness, a dissatisfaction (similar to that experienced at the upper reaches of each of the "lower" needs), a curiosity, a need to know more and beyond the confines of "practical knowledge."

For some, middle age is a crisis period. (Crisis, incidentally, need not be a negative experience. The Chinese word for *crisis* is appropriately made up of two pictograms, *danger* and *opportunity.*) Middle age is a fascinating but often frustrating and painful period, because the more an individual digs into understanding and awareness of his Selfhood, the more difficult it often becomes to settle for simpler and easier satisfactions. And a decision that higher needs are more important may result in giving up a job—or a spouse—to meet them. It's not for hormonal reasons alone that this period is often called one of "change of life."

Finally, Maslow tells us, in later years we are challenged by *esthetic* needs, needs for order, symmetry, consistency, cohesion, integration. This need may be met through religious involvement, meditation, art, by memory and recollection of a rich and satisfying life. Some people rediscover lost creative interests, but finding a hobby is not at all what this period of need is about. This stage actually represents a development from the Cognitive period: once we find out what life and the cosmos are all about, we find beauty and harmony and oneness in it. It does not only occur in the elderly (and it may not occur in most of the elderly!), for many young people are finding ways to experience this set of needs. More about that in chapter twelve.

Maslow's esthetic stage corresponds somewhat to what Erikson calls the stage of Ego Integrity. "Integrity" comes from the root word from which we get *integer*, a whole number, and *integration*, completeness. It means a congruence, a total combining of all aspects of the Self into one united and accepted Whole.

Human Sexuality

We dislike dealing with human sexuality as a separate subsection, for it should be seen in its proper perspective: as an integrated part of life and an aspect of human interaction. But humans have lots of cultural lags to overcome, and the contemporary attitude toward sexuality is one of them. So we set it apart, an object of special attention to be dealt with as if it were a caged animal instead of a normal part of everyone's life.

Each of us is a sexual being for the very simple reason that we are first of all bodies. Those bodies contain nerve cells (neurons) especially sensitive to certain kinds of stimulation. Their response to this stimulation is to start a chain of reactive responses along the peripheral nervous system to the spinal cord. Some of the responses simply activate a reflexive behavior, as a knee jerk or an eye blink. From the point of stimulation a neural message is sent back along another nerve network to a muscle, and it ends right there. Other messages go "upstairs" to the brain, where, depending on what's necessary, the message stimulates a gland or a part of the cortex of the brain.

Some of the messages go to a particular part of the brain responsible for the sensations of pleasure. Brain research has located at least five "pleasure centers" in the hypothalamus of the more primitive parts of the forebrain. Here, as far as contemporary neurological research can determine, the beginnings of the perception of pleasure take place. Apparently, then, any and all experiences of pleasure are communicated to our consciousness by the "pleasure centers." This would include the good taste of a hot pizza when hungry, the seeing of a fine painting (or, by combinations of perceptual matters, seeing even a poor painting by the "right" painter!), the comfortable feeling of stretching out in the soft folds of a reclining lounge chair, the soothing pleasure of basking in the sun at the beach, the exhilarating pleasure of riding a roller coaster (which may be heightened if one is aware of overcoming his own fear of roller coasters while doing it), and the "painful" pleasure of sexual orgasm. All of these, though vastly different in the properties of the stimulus, are perceived as pleasurable and apparently are mediated by these same centers in the hypothalamus.

If the experience of love is a pleasurable one, it too is a matter of hypothalamic responsiveness, although it's unlikely that in the popular mind the hypothalamus will ever replace the "heart" as the supposed seat of love. We don't expect any hot-blooded young Romeos to declare to their Juliets, "I love you with all my hypothalamus!"

Since pleasure can be communicated to the brain in so many ways and can be stimulated by so many different objects, persons, and situations, it's only a simple leap to the conclusion that pleasure and joy are general responses to a wide variety of specific stimuli: no one specific person, activity, or situation is always needed to bring about the feeling of pleasure. Obviously, we have to allow for some of the factors the person himself brings into the pleasure situation.

Each of our selves develops in patterns that are *simultaneously* almost identical with those of all other people, similar to others, and completely different from others. This is the beauty and the frustration of self psychology! For, as nice as general rules and principles and laws are, none of us fits neatly or completely into these general patterns. Something is always left over. This something or combination of something is what makes the Selfhood of each person unique.

Each person defines beauty, love, pleasure, pain, and all the other experiences in a way that is singularly his. He shares general interpretations and definitions with each person in his culture, but he narrows these down for specific situations. Even in one culture two men may choose entirely different-looking women to illustrate their individual definitions of beautiful or sexy. But somehow, their separate definitions of beautiful or sexy permit each of them to respond to properties of those two women and to communicate these interpretations, with emotional components, to the various areas of the nervous system. The two different messages get to the hypothalamic pleasure centers and the two men both experience the almost identical response we find described by the currently popular term "turned on."

Human beings are tremendously influenced by many things in their sexual experiences. Beginning with the innate factors of sexual activity, things like sexual hormones and the responsiveness of various areas of the body, we then have to look at the learning or acquisition of sexual attitudes, ideas, referents, notions, myths, fears, and interpretations that pick up where the physiological responses leave off. The responses don't actually *leave off*, either, since they are part and parcel of the other factors in an interactional three-dimensional process that is hard to describe with two-dimensional words.

Freud thought the erogenous zones were limited to the lips, breasts, genitals, earlobes, shoulders, and a few other parts of the body. When the last shred of evidence is in, we will more likely find that *any* part of the body that is equipped with sensory neurons in sufficient quantity and interrelationship can be a zone of receptivity that we can interpret as erogenous or sexually sensitive.

A lot of the misunderstanding about human sexuality could be eliminated if we substituted the clearer, more precise term "sensual" for the word "sexual." "Sensual" means just what it hints at: responsive to sensory stimulation. But that word too has been used and abused so much that it has taken on the same kinds of connotations that "sexual" has, some accurate, some wildly distorted and inappropriate. Thus, because communication involves using words or symbols that are shared by the largest possible number of people, we more or less have to use the word "sexual" but in its most general sense. Both by Freud's definitions and those of other more contemporary scientists, "sexual" must refer to feelings and behaviors that are physically pleasurable and/or gratifying, especially when the physical experiences are combined with emotional, cognitive, and spiritual experiences. That means, basically, that a physical experience such as having your back rubbed or stroked is considered a sexual experience if the person performing the act is associated in the mind of receiver with certain kinds of attitudes or relationships. If the back-rubber reminds the other person of a loved one or of an ideal of sexuality or love, then the act is sexual; that is, it is physically pleasurable to a greater degree than is the merely soothing experience of having the back rubbed.

Sexual Responsiveness

We can, after our brief excursion into the physiology of sexuality, now reaffirm our original position: *we are all sexual beings.* The broader definitions of "sexual" in no way diminish the pleasure and importance of the narrower or more limited definitions. They should, in fact, open up whole new worlds of thought and attitude. We should now be able to talk more effectively about human responsiveness.

If you had lived in Victorian Europe and heard a Freudian scientist or scholar say, "It is a sexual experience for a mother to nurse her infant," you would probably have put the heat on under a vat of tar and begun plucking chicken feathers, ready to give the speaker a new wardrobe! Similar Victorian reactions are still around, even in this enlightened day and age. But the term "sexual," newly and more broadly defined, should now be more acceptable. Breast-feeding is far from being the exciting or lustful experience that is commonly associated with the word "sexual." Several things are happening to both mother and infant:

1. The sensory neurons in the nipple *are* being stimulated and the response *is* one of pleasure.
2. The sensory neurons in the child's mouth *are* being stimulated and this response, too, is pleasurable.
3. The body of the mother, coming into contact with the body of the child, *is* experiencing pleasurable warmth and stimulation.
4. The same experience of warmth and stimulation *is* being felt by the child.
5. The mother's entire memory and ideational system *is* being stimulated by things she heard as a girl about the importance of breast-feeding for the child's health and security, about the importance of togetherness for mother and child, about the importance of skin contact for a feeling of comfort and security.
6. The mother *is* experiencing the pleasure of being important and significant to this helpless child.
7. The mother *is* reminded of the vital role she played in carrying and delivering this lively bundle of life.
8. The child may be a reminder to her of the love and sexual closeness she feels with its father.
9. The child is gaining attitudes and experiences about closeness (in addition to their immediate pleasantness) and a sense of physical belonging.

Many, many other things might be going on in both members of the mother-child unit, such as the pleasure of the warm, nourishing milk going down and satisfying hunger, the pleasure of relieving the tension of breasts too full of milk, and so on.

This definition of sexual may seem too broad and all-inclusive to you. Nonetheless, each individual element could be defined as sexual by any one person in the same circumstances. Combined, they serve to illustrate that love is more than just a simple emotion: it is a complex and interdependent relationship.

A child should learn to enjoy his body and its feelings. If the child is allowed to feel good about eating and drinking and moving and touching and stretching, he will develop into a person who appreciates the sensual aspects of behavior and can experience profound enjoyment in simple pleasures. If the child feels ashamed or guilty about physical pleasures, is scolded for eating too loudly, for example, with the result that he feels eating and enjoyment of food is "bad," he can develop into a person who is ashamed of physical body functions and needs and has a difficult time experiencing any pleasures that might even be remotely connected with physical gratification. One woman we know feels uncomfortable sitting before a nice, warming fire, enjoying friends, conversation, a drink, or the comfortable cushions! Hers is a complex discomfort, directly related to being told too often in childhood that comfort and pleasure were luxuries; that life is hard, and hard work was what each person needed to do; that comfort and pleasure take one away from the responsibility of life; that life is a "cross we have to bear."

The child who enjoys physical contact and closeness, is allowed the full range of touching and body experiences, is encouraged to find pleasure as well as what else life offers, is encouraged to give and receive affection and to experience the fullest array of emotional responses without shame or guilt grows into a mentally and physically healthy person who can enter into eating, drinking, work, conversing, sexual activity, play, and even sleep with a positive and fully involved attitude. This, reports Abraham Maslow, is a partial description of a self-actualizing individual; and though the number of people who live life this fully is rather small, it is growing. Maslow feels that Self-actualization is a goal toward which the human species is evolving.

The person who appreciates the fullness of his selfhood knows that the body is capable of many forms of expression. Sexual intimacy (in its many forms) is a way of expressing one's selfhood, of affirming the selfhood of another, and of uniting two selves into a unity that is, at one and the same time, two separate selves and one loving pair.

Many people view sexual activity as something to be used. Some young men are told by well-meaning but misguided older males that they aren't "men" until they've had sexual intercourse with a woman. Many young women are told the same thing: that it takes sex with a good man to make a female into a "woman." Such statements are unfortunate and are also rubbish! Sexual intercourse doesn't *make* either partner into a "man" or a "woman." The sexual relationship develops *because* one partner is a man and one is a woman: it's a full and satisfying way of expressing that manhood or womanhood.

Take the case of a young college woman who didn't consider herself a woman because she had never had intercourse. At the urging of friends, she got involved with a nice fellow who, out for a good time, didn't know he was being entrusted with the sacred responsibility of confirming or consecrating the girl's "womanhood." The sexual experience was satisfying for neither. He got only the release of orgasm: there was little responsiveness from the poor, scared girl. She had neither orgasm nor "confirmation." She experienced pain because she was tense and frightened. She experienced disgust because the boy's sexual organ was frightening and she thought the seminal discharge was messy. She was afraid because the boy's climax was loud and boisterous, and the emerging excitement and pleasure she felt were foreign and forbidden by her repressive background. She was disappointed because the aftermath didn't leave her with the high, spiritual transcendence she had been led to expect. She was shamed because she had not remained chaste as her parents and religion had taught her to do. She felt personally guilty because she had done something opposed to her own standards of conduct. She was angry because, instead of feeling more like a woman, she felt less, felt like she had lost something of her self. Add to this the anxiety and concern she felt as she worried that the act might lead to pregnancy, and a pretty tragic picture is added to the archives of sexual misunderstanding.

This is not a warning about the dangers of premarital sex. Many young people have perfectly wonderful and satisfying sexual experiences before marriage. It *is* a statement about the dangers of expecting sexual intercourse to do something to you, your lover, or the two of you, that isn't already present in the two of you individually. Sexual relating is a way of *experiencing* one's selfhood, not a way of getting it.

Any human being who has had a childhood that enabled him or her to acquire positive, accepting, enjoying, sharing attitudes toward self and relatedness, in the fullest extensions of those terms, can enter into sexual relations and bring to and gain from the experience a reaffirmation at every level of that selfhood. Your physical body is reaffirmed in its soundness by sexual relating: your body feels fine, is satisfied. Your emotions are challenged, stirred up, carried through, and finally experienced as "good," healthy, whole, human, by your sexual sharing. Your sense of selfhood, what may be called the spiritual aspects of the relating, is also reaffirmed in the sexual sharing: "I, a self-in-the-process-of-becoming, share this experience with you, another self-in-the-process-of-becoming; and in this sharing, we find, not our selves (or these we bring *into* the relationship), but the completeness that can come only from such sharing, blending, merging." This last concept goes far back into Oriental philosophy. It is the concept of *Yang* and *Yin,* familiarly illustrated by the following diagram:

It takes two *complete* halves to make a complete whole. In this conceptualization, the world, life, nature, people are made up of complete, but opposite, mutually complementary halves: Life and Death, Light and Darkness, Black and White, Male and Female, Beauty and Ugliness, and so on. Taoist folklore says of the male-female mating: "Before the beginning of Time, you and I were one entity. At birth, we became separate, living our separate, disintegrated lives. Now, in this coming together of the body, we reunite and become, once again, the unified Whole, male and female, that we were meant to be."

This poetic description speaks to the condition of many modern human beings who feel alienated and lost, or who feel they are living only a partial existence until they find a satisfying love relationship with at least one other human being. It also helps to make more meaningful Alfred Adler's concept of social interest: that we can best understand ourselves when we can get outside ourselves and into the life of another person.

Freud and Biosocial Selfhood

Among the many significant figures in history, Freud must take his place beside Machiavelli, Marx, Darwin, Nietzsche, and a few others who have told man what he actually *is,* not what he *should* be. They had courage, for too many people did not, and still do not, want to hear what they had to say. And for one reason or another, every name just mentioned is on somebody's List of Bad Guys, for one reason or another—Freud, too! Yet none of them is as guilty of shaking established patterns of thought or belief as he is of shattering weak or faulty foundations in the opinions man had of himself. Each of these people claims that man is not perfectly noble, heroic, saintly, perfect, rational, pure, altruistic, or loving, as he claims to be in the thousands of books, articles, art works, and speeches that men make for and about themselves.

When we have taken so much time to establish the humanistic base of our operations, the reader may well say that humanists are supposed to extol man's virtues, put man on a pedestal, see man as the be-all, end-all of existence, and to worship man. Some humanists do. But humanistic psychology is not interested in making gods out of men. It simply takes man as its basic unit of study and observes him, bases its findings on man-made rules and man-made goals, and puts man into his proper place in the nature of things. Humanistic psychology tries to correct the view that man is a worm, a nothing, a "zero with the ring knocked off." So in the attempt to see and describe human beings as they actually are, we have to pay attention to those who have been willing to "tell it like it is," not like we'd like it to be.

Freud told his Victorian students and readers that man was not the totally rational, reasoning, conscious, willing master of his fate (nor even of much of his day-to-day behavior) that the Enlightenment thinkers portrayed. Further, Freud said that most people were dominated far more by emotions and underlying conflicts than they were by reason, will, and their mental abilities. Not only that, but he said that sexual behavior began from the earliest moments of a child's life, not in adulthood as so many people chose to believe. Freud was getting less and less popular with every sentence!

When Freud began talking about the Oedipus Complex in the lives of 3- to 7-year-olds, many people were sure that the Devil had reincarnated himself in the form of a Viennese quack! Freud further stated that most of the problems we call *neurotic* are symptoms of repressed sexual or aggressive impulses in the unconscious minds of these sturdy, rational Children of Light!

Freud found little support or appreciation in his early years. His was an unpopular, thankless task but, like many such tasks, sorely needed. Most accepted theories of child development, psychosexual development, personality, and emotion are direct heirs to the findings of Freud. From Karl Abraham, a well-known embryologist and psychiatrist, Freud got the concept of *libido,* or the energy of the drives. The drives referred to are the basic physiological drives (hunger, thirst, sex, etc.). Each drive-state produces tension, or a buildup of energy, that needs reduction. Abraham and Freud both felt that in the life of each person there is an orderly sequence of stages of need/drive development. Briefly, here are the Freudian stages of development:

The first is called the *Oral Stage,* because most of the child's activity is centered in and around the oral area, the lips, gums, teeth. A child's first really meaningful contact with the world comes through this area as it is fed; and while sucking, swallowing, and feeling the warmth of food in the stomach are pleasurable, so is the contact with the world: the mother.

Second is the *Anal Stage,* which often overlaps the Oral. Here the child finds shifts in emphasis, though of course it still eats. Now the attention is directed to the matter of elimination of bodily wastes, as toilet training takes place. While this is an important task in our culture, what it also symbolizes is the control aspect of growing up. In addition to controlling bodily sphincters, the child has to learn to control the rest of its body as well, and parts of the outside world, too! In a sense, successful toilet training is a child's first recognition that he must conform to the demands of the outside world.

The *Genital Period* begins with the *Phallic* or *Infantile Genital Stage* (often called the *Oedipal Stage*). The genital organs are discovered and pleasure may be found in them. Infantile sexuality begins here as the child discovers that fondling and even masturbating the organs brings pleasure. Sexual curiosity is developing and sex play often comes during this stage.

An important part of this period is called the *Oedipus Complex.* This Freudian concept is poorly understood and has given a lot of people a lot of difficulty. Briefly, Freud felt that during this period of life (roughly from 3 to 7 years of age) the child becomes extremely attached to the parent of the opposite sex. "Daddy's girl" and "momma's boy" are terms we use to symbolize this. It may be a fairly simple, uncomplicated preference of the boy for his mother's time and attention, and the girl for her father's, or it may be a very fierce competition, seeing the same-sex parent as a real rival. Rarely is conscious sexuality involved (though Freud found this in a number of his adult patients), but it is believed that much of the unconscious emotionality during this period is definitely sexual.

When this period is ended successfully, the child realizes that it can't own or possess the opposite-sex parent, much as it might want to. Because it can't really compete, it represses some of the intensity (especially the sexual) of the attachment and begins to identify with the same-sex parent as a model, as a companion. If the resolution of this conflict period isn't handled wisely and well, the child can develop many sexual confusions and difficulties. Whether the Oedipus

CHRISTIANSON

"YOU CAN'T HAVE AN OEDIPUS COMPLEX, ADAM. YOU DON'T HAVE ANY PARENTS."

complex exists or not, an impressively large number of problems involving sexual maladjustment do seem to have their roots in this sensitive period of the persons' lives.

At this point, a break occurs. It is called the *Latency Stage*. From about 7 to 12, the child deemphasizes the earlier satisfactions, is less concerned about mouth, anus, sex organs, and possessiveness, and finds satisfactions in the outside world. Other people become far more urgently needed: playmates, school peers, teachers, other adults. The child is beginning to be a more socialized person. You may recall that it was in this period that you became quite interested in school, the playground, the kids and activities down the block, and your homelife had less importance, though you probably still enjoyed your family.

Many children begin religious instruction during this period, and the conscience which is struggling to emerge during the Oedipal Stage now begins to grow and develop.

At this age, the child's cognitive and intellectual skills are being developed and the rest of his body is slowing down a bit, prior to the eruptive period of adolescence which is looming round the bend. It's as if the body and emotions were relaxing a bit, letting the reasoning and intuitive and spiritual parts of Selfhood stretch their muscles!

Then comes adolescence, what is termed "puberty" in biology. The body comes alive—often painfully so! A growth spurt in all directions results when the pituitary gland triggers the gonads, the sex glands. Not only does the body become larger, more nearly adult, but the sexual organs grow and develop their capacities to engage in sexual intercourse and the reproductive functions. Adolescence is a very confusing period. It need not be as painful and frightening as it often is, but we're only beginning to learn how to prepare our children for the tremendous mixture of "agony and ecstasy" of adulthood.

Adolescence begins what Freud called the *Genital Stage* proper. It began in the Oedipal Stage, but it was an infantile, touching-but-not-experiencing stage. After the time-out of Latency, now the body enters the stage wherein the primary mode of gratification is in the genital organs. Freud, like all of us, oversimplifies, but here he says the major mode of pleasure comes from a mature and equal union of genitals in mutually satisfying intercourse and orgasm.

Erik Erikson has done much to break Freudian theory down into more contemporary and easily understood components. He has "translated" much of Freud's nineteenth-century concern and vocabulary into language that we in twentieth-century America can understand and appreciate, whether we call ourselves Freudian or not. The chart that follows is put together to show how Freud and Erikson describe the Freudian stages of development.

Our main emphasis here is the way in which Freud viewed man. Freud was a part of the deterministic and positivistic philosophy of nineteenth-century science, which said that all behavior is caused and the causes and effects can be charted, measured, and operationally defined. Thus, man is a *physical* being, subject to basically physical laws. The human organism is a complex system, getting energy from food and expending it on such activities as breathing, exercise, circulation, perception, thinking, feeling. Freud felt that the energy that powers our breathing and swallowing is the same (except in form) as that which we use to think and remember. Energy was defined in terms of the work it performs.

Freud also relied heavily on Instinct Theory. Instincts are innate psychological representations of inner bodily sources of activation. The psychological aspect was called a *wish;* the bodily activation, a *need.* Man's instincts could be summed up under two major headings: life instincts and death instincts. All the instinctive behaviors that enable one to survive and reproduce himself were catalogued under life instincts. All the self-defeating, self-destructive, and outwardly aggressive behaviors were part of the death instincts.

Chart A: Stages of Psychosexual and Psychosocial Development (Modified from Freud and Erikson)

Age	Stage	Psychosexual Stage	Pleasure Source	Psychosocial Crises	Significance for Personality Development
Birth to 1½ yrs.	Oral	Oral-Passive (Incorporative) Oral-Aggressive	Pleasure derived from sucking, eating, thumbsucking. Later, from biting.	Trust vs. Mistrust	Foundation for dependency on others. "Oral Incorporation" a factor in identification, learning, acquiring. "Oral Aggressiveness" a basis for sarcasm, verbal aggressiveness.
1½ to 3 yrs.	Anal	Anal-Expulsive; Anal-Retentive	Pleasure comes in expelling wastes; later thru muscular and parental controlling.	Autonomy vs. Shame, Doubt	"Anal expulsive character" is cruel, destructive, disorderly. "Anal retentive character" is stingy, compulsive, obstinate.
3 to 5 yrs.	Phallic; Oedipal	Infantile Genital Stages: Inclusive Intrusive	Pleasure comes from genital stimulation and associated fantasies. Oedipus Complex.	Initiative vs. Guilt	Identifications with parents emerge in resolving Oedipus Complex. Superego (Conscience) forms. Many important consequences for accepting appropriate age and sex roles.
6 yrs. to Puberty	Latency	Latency	With temporary repression of sexual interests, pleasure comes from external world, curiosity, knowledge, peer relations.	Industry vs. Inferiority	This period (elementary school age) very important for social development, for acquiring skills for life and work. Superego further developed.
Adolescence	Genital	Genitality	Pleasure comes from mature sexual relations with opposite sexed partner.	Identity and Repudiation vs. Identity diffusion	Self-love (narcissism) of earlier stages turns to love of others, altruism develops. Independence from parents.
Young Adults	Genital	Genitality	More of above.	Intimacy vs. Isolation	
Middle Age	Genital	Genitality	More of above.	Generativity vs. Stagnation	
Later Maturity	Genital	Genitality	More diffuse.	Ego Integrity vs. Despair	

Throughout his life, Freud remained firm in his belief that the *Id* (the primitive part of personality that contained the instincts) was supreme, was the most powerful. Though his followers later gave the *Ego* (the rational, reasoning, more conscious part of personality) more autonomy, Freud felt that it and the *Superego*, containing the "conscience" and the "ego ideal," were still under the dominance of the primitive, instinctual *Id.*

Summary

Homo sapiens is a part of the animal kingdom and is intimately related to it. His biological needs (and biological nature) have a tremendous impact on his behavior. Unless these primary needs (for food, liquid, air, sleep, and so on) are met, we are unable to go beyond them. But, according to Maslow, once such needs are met, we have an inherent desire to work toward higher levels of motivations. Different levels of motivation are strongest emotionally and physically in children of different ages. One can become fixated (stuck) at any of these levels if those needs are not met. At the top of the "ladder" are self-actualization needs—cognitive, esthetic, and integrative needs.

Freud did very little with the subjects of learning, cultural and social training, interaction, will (making the *Ego* more autonomous), motivation, significance, meaning, and so on, and studies in these areas have largely changed the picture of man to a more human one than Freud painted. Nonetheless, man's nature begins as a physical one, and the other aspects are simply elaborations and amplifications of his physical nature.

Man is more than just a passive responder to his drives. He learns and modifies and interacts with all his environments. And out of this, he attempts to experience effectiveness and significance by both acknowledging and transcending his physical limitations.

Sexual needs form a special category of drives that are difficult to deal with because society imbues them with so many taboos and unique meanings. *Sensual* and *sexual* are words that have much wider and more inclusive meanings than those commonly used. The need for touch (a sensual need) is present in all of us, for all of our lives.

There are many valid criticisms that can be, and have been, made of Freud's theories, his research, and his therapeutic techniques. The same is true of every theory, bit of research, and therapeutic technique ever used. Freud did all of psychology the service of pointing up the facts (tested and validated by many other scientists) that man's behavior is heavily grounded in his biological nature. Though "instincts" have been mostly thrown out in favor of more scientific ideas about "drives," we can concur with the Viennese giant that man does spend a great deal of his life answering the needs of his physical body.

Suggested Readings:

Allport, G. *Becoming.* New Haven: Yale University Press, 1955.

Boss, M. "Mechanistic and Holistic Thinking in Modern Medicine," *American Journal of Psychoanalysis,* 14 (1954): 48–54.

Comfort, Alex. *The Joys of Sex.* New York: Crown Publishers, Inc., 1972.

Dubos, René. *So Human an Animal.* New York: Charles Scribner's Sons, 1968.

Erikson, Erik. *Childhood and Society.* New York: W. W. Norton and Co., Inc., 1963.

Freud, Sigmund. *The Basic Writings of Sigmund Freud.* New York: The Modern Library, 1938. (There are many works of Freud, but this single volume is a good beginning source.)

Hesse, Hermann. *Demian.* New York: Harper & Row, 1965.

Katchadourian, H. A., and Donald T. Lunde. *Fundamentals of Human Sexuality.* New York: Holt, Rinehart & Winston, 1972.

Maslow, Abraham. *Motivation and Personality.* New York: Harper & Row, 1954.

Masters, W. H., and V. Johnson. *Human Sexual Response.* Boston: Little, Brown and Co., 1966.

Millett, Kate. *Sexual Politics.* Garden City, New York: Doubleday and Co., 1970.

Montagu, Ashley. *The Biosocial Nature of Man.* New York: Grove Press, 1956.

Olds, James. "Physiological Mechanisms of Reward," in M. R. Jones, ed., *Nebraska Symposium on Motivation, 1955.* University of Nebraska, 1955.

Stoller, Robert J. *Sex and Gender.* New York: Science House, 1968.

Watts, Alan W. *Psychotherapy East and West.* New York: New American Library, 1961.

Williams, R. J. *Biochemical Individuality.* New York: John Wiley & Sons, 1956.

Wooldridge, Dean E. *Mechanical Man: The Physical Basis of Intelligent Life.* New York: McGraw-Hill Book Co., Inc., 1968.

Once More
with Feeling

*I wanted to prove that human beings are
capable of something grander than war
and prejudice and hatred.*[1]

ABRAHAM MASLOW

*There is a new conception of man's capacities
forming within the scientific community.
During the twentieth century, academic
science has radically underestimated man
—his sensitivity to subtle sources of
energy, his capacity for love, understanding
and transcendence, his self-control.*[2]

DR. JAMES FADIMAN
Stanford University

1. Abraham Maslow, in
   Mary H. Hall, "A
   Conversation with
   Abraham H. Maslow,"
   Psychology Today, July
   1968.

2. James Fadiman, in
   Marvin Karlins and
   Lewis M. Andrews,
   Biofeedback, 1973.

Emotions. Feelings. Experiences that are incredibly difficult to communicate or even explain in words. Yet something happens—you and I have all experienced a feeling, a change, something going on inside your head, your stomach, your muscles. You try to tell about it. You select words, pull from your expressive "quiver" the straightest, truest arrows you can find, hoping your aim and strength and will are adequate, and you shoot the shaft toward a target—another human being, who might be listening, reading, hearing. What happens? Sometimes the arrows fall short—not enough strength, will, desire, intention behind your pulling of the string. Often the string is flimsy or breaks—the motivation is lacking or feeble. Or the arrows overshoot and miss the target—you're too forceful, tried too hard, or you're careless. Or maybe you just didn't *want* to hit it. Often when we miss in trying to communicate an idea, or a feeling, it's really because we are afraid of making contact, or actually being heard or understood.

Why Feel Anything?

Think how many times you've heard or even used the expression: "He's too emotional." What did this mean? For many it probably meant that the person was exhibiting emotions or feeling-states that were excessive or exaggerated. Others would interpret that description to mean: "He's using expressions or gestures or something that embarrasses others." Some people simply mean, "He's showing feelings that I've never seen before, much less experienced in myself." But others mean, "He's showing feelings that I've felt all too often. I'm uncomfortable because I'm being reminded of those feelings. I identify with this and it hurts!"

Underlying most of these statements is an assumption a lot of people make: emotions are strange, frightening, weird, odd. But what are the facts? The "facts," if we can rely on the work of those who specialize in the study of emotion, are confusing. Out of the various theories they propose, we can find only a few things that they all agree upon. But we can begin with the place at which many of them end: human nature includes a full range of emotional responses.

Each of us is equipped with the glands and hormones and brain centers to experience all of the emotions that there are. This is an important point, for it doesn't leave emoting to a few people whom we call "emotional," nor does it relegate emotions only to the ladies. Each one of us, young or old, male or female, is capable of experiencing any human emotion. The truth is we probably all do experience far more emotion than we admit or even realize. Some of us have fantastic defenses set up, enabling us to hide some of our feelings from even ourselves.

The word *emotion* seems to come from roots in Latin that mean "to move out." Here we get the idea that emotion is expressing or making manifest some inner experiences, which is definitely one aspect of emotion. Another important thing about "to move out" is that it points to the motive force of emotions. When you are feeling a particular way, you are going to do certain things *because of* that feeling, *in spite of* that feeling, or to *avoid* or *change* that feeling: emotions are highly powerful as motivating factors.

One way of looking at emotions or affective states is to view them as changes from the "normal" or "balanced" physiological state of the body. This definition is very respectable and is found in a number of expert opinions.[3] But it creates problems: who can decide what is "normal" or "balanced" so that we can figure out by how much or how far the behavior is different? Are the differences quantitative or qualitative? Yet we have to deal with the fact that each emotional state is experienced as a physiological change. Tensions are produced, directions sought, movements inhibited or energized. So we cannot completely avoid the physiological factors, especially in the light of the importance of man's biosocial nature.

So we can look at emotional experiences this way: the body is capable of experiencing any number of changes. Some of these changes come about because of things we perceive in the world about us. Some of them are based on memories, ideas, or other people. Whatever it is that is triggered by these experiences is felt, often strongly. Because some of these emotional states enable the person to survive, we can assume that emotions, in general, persist in human experience because they have some survival value, whether we understand them or not.

Normal and Abnormal Emotions

Many people experience emotional states they cannot understand and identify. They often wonder at the intensity, origin, explanation, and duration of emotions. They also worry about what they might do as a result of these emotions. They may even question whether the emotions are "normal" or not.

Of course, this happens to all of us at times. It is one of the risks of being thinking, sensitive people. We begin questioning, analyzing our own experiences. We also categorize them, because that's what our rationalistic, scientific society expects. And when we cannot find a neat explanation or pigeonhole for a particular experience, we either bend it to fit another category, deny it, repress it, or project it onto somebody else ("I'm not angry; you are!"). If we can't do any of these

3. Clifford T. Morgan and Richard A. King, *Introduction to Psychology* (New York: McGraw-Hill Book Co., 1966), p. 240.

things because we're too honest with ourselves, we may conclude that the feeling is a bad one or a "sick" one.

Consider the case of Shirley, who was raised to believe that nice people don't get angry, never feel anything like anger. But in the course of her life, things happened that irritated her. Frustrations would lead to aggression and at times she not only felt anger but hatred. Shirley often felt these things so strongly that she feared what she might do. She had dreams that often involved somebody getting hurt, mutilated, even killed. What brought her for professional help, however, was headaches. A medical doctor, after extensive testing, found no brain tumors, pinched or collapsed nerves or blood vessels, lesions, or anything else that might explain the severe headaches. In observing Shirley, he found her to be an extremely cautious and fastidious person. She was very careful how she sat, walked, and carried herself. She was even more cautious in conversation, selecting each word, unable to relax and let the words come out easily or casually. The doctor suggested that Shirley might be uncomfortable with some of the thoughts and feelings she had. When she finally admitted this might be so, he sent her to a psychological clinic where such things can be handled with patience and tolerance for the person's inability to deal with them right away.

In the course of therapy, Shirley came to see that her physiological tensions had been caused, not by anger, but by the attitudes she had been taught *about* anger. Having been told that anger was not a nice person's emotion, she felt that if she were angry, *she* must be bad. So she felt *guilt*. Guilt caused her to "walk on eggshells," to avoid doing or saying anything that might make her angry and expose her as the wicked creature she felt she was. The physiological tension resulted partly from the strain she was undergoing by her cautiousness. This, incidentally, is a perfect description of an "up-tight!" individual.

Another thing that was causing Shirley's tensions was her unconscious need to punish herself for having anger in the first place. The headaches were her punishment, her penance. Yet the body doesn't work that simply. The headaches made her angrier, at herself for both anger and guilt, and at others who made her angry or who reminded her of anger and thus her "badness." So she was caught in a vicious circle. Therapy exposed the circle, and through psychodrama, she was able to feel and experience the whole thing herself in front of accepting fellow clients.

The story's ending was only partly happy. Shirley began to realize the tension release of experiencing her angers, safely, nondestructively, and more importantly, with the full approval of therapist and other members of her therapy group. She learned to accept and like herself as a human being, a full, feeling person. But her family, with a long history of emotional suppression behind it, believing that anger was a "weapon of Satan," couldn't accept her open, honest expression of irritation or anger as her therapy group could. Since Shirley had discovered that certain so-called profanities were the only words that "worked" to express certain feelings, she horrified her family, who not only told her she should be ashamed for using "such language!" but also stopped her from continuing psychotherapy.

Hopefully, the release she has attained can be practiced in her own way, her own time, and she can continue to appreciate that her humanness includes such emotions as anger and guilt.

Was this girl abnormal? Was her anger abnormal? Objectively, we can say that the anger was not pathological, but since she felt it was, it had a pathogenic (illness-producing) effect. Further, according to the norms of a society that stresses control of emotions, her emotional expressions could be considered statistically abnormal. This is rather interesting, because all human beings experience anger, and not all of them express it openly. Some express it indirectly, or through some physical symptom, to the point where tension headaches, ulcers, lower back pains, and other physical complaints that are often converted rage reactions can almost be considered "normal" behavior. An interesting commentary on our way of life.

In the opinion of many such experts as Karen Horney, Erich Fromm, and Abraham Maslow, to name a few, some of the ways in which natural behavior is "controlled" are the really "sick" or "abnormal" behaviors. We become disturbed, ill, out of sorts, "not ourselves," neurotic even, because we are pushed to be what we are *not,* to act "unnaturally," in the name of social order, etiquette, propriety. Most of these disturbances are the result of some kind of *suppression* or *repression*—suppression is conscious blocking out, repression is unconscious—of natural, human emotions, especially the stronger ones like anger, fear, sexual passion, or greed.

What would happen to our social order if people were allowed full expression of strong emotions? We don't know, but imagination might paint a picture of wild, bloody lawlessness, rape, killing, plundering, rioting, singly or in combination. On the other hand, let's assume a society where children are raised to have a healthy acceptance of their full nature, to appreciate their emotions, to enjoy the tension reduction and experience of emotions. Guilt would be the emotion that any person in that society might feel when he violated one of the rules of his society, but he would not assume that he was a "bad" or "outcast" person. The guilt might simply be experienced as a total realization of having let down those expectations he had of himself, and could provide the motive force for him to "regroup" himself and try a new behavior. The socialization process of this ideal society would probably include showing the individual his kinship with every other member of society rather than instructing him in terms of obligations and duties. Thus, the child could grow up as a person who utilized reason and emotions in living a fuller life, knowing that he was one among many who were also doing the same things. In the process, he could develop the *kinds* of emotional expressions that would be satisfying, redeeming, and creative for him but not offensive or injurious to others.

If this utopian picture were broadened, the resulting social order might well be one of personal joy and self-expression, satisfaction of both individual and group needs, easy interaction, full experiencing of emotional states, and a creative style of life.

In our present society, however, to suddenly let everybody do as he felt might produce confusion and fear instead of creativity and peace. In other words, because many emotions are labeled "strong" or "dangerous," we react to them as such. We build up attitudes about them that aren't removed by suddenly telling people: "Okay, go ahead; do it!" We wouldn't expect, for example, should the rule of priestly chastity be lifted, that *all* priests, monks, and nuns would immediately rush out and find sexual partners, nor that those who did would feel completely free and easy about their sexual involvement even if they were married. Many would feel guilt about breaking a long-held rule.

Radical changes of any kind in long-standing social attitudes may disrupt the smooth functioning of societal organization. Nevertheless, we are convinced that the future development of human life demands a fuller acceptance and acknowledgment of human emotions with a freer experiencing and expression of those emotions.

Some people can open up, can relearn their emotional selves fairly easily, without hurting or hindering others in the process. These are the lucky ones! Most of us, loaded down by the cultures in which we are born and raised, have to shed these inhibitions and external controls as a snake does its skin, and this is plain hard work. The relative freedom of expression of many young people is both offensive to, and envied by, many older people. Rebelling students may be propelled by considerable anger against society's ills. But it's our experience that the rebels' parents are far angrier that they have been "cut out" of the freedom of expression their children enjoy. Of course, this isn't true for everyone in that generation. Some people up into their sixties, seventies, and beyond have been on good terms with their feelings, found nondestructive ways of expressing themselves for a good many years—either through their own efforts, or with the help of professionals.

Similarly, not all teen-agers and college-age people are loose and free with their feelings, either. Those who are the most vocal, most colorful are the ones we see and hear and who get our attention. The repressiveness of Victorian times has left its mark on many—perhaps most—of the younger generation, too. But young people seem more easily to find the keys to such emotional expression, whether it be through esoteric and exotic techniques, the music of today, the dress and hairstyles, or through alcohol and other chemical means.

Drugs and Emotions

Science knows very little about the effects of narcotics or hard "body" drugs on people's behavior, except for some information on those who die (physically or mentally) from overdoses, long-term use, accidents, or suicides. The "head" drugs—marijuana, LSD, mescaline, and others which aren't strictly narcotics—are even less understood.

Is this a drug era, a time of chemical affluence, a "dose-age"? The scantiest amount of research will uncover evidence that human beings in every culture, in every age have found chemicals locked up in plants, bark, leaves, roots, or in mineral compounds. They have utilized them as medicines with a well-known degree of success—indeed, many of today's highly refined chemical medications are based on ancient ingredients. Further, they have also been found to have used chemicals in preparation and preservation of their foods. But many uninitiated souls are surprised to discover that other chemicals have always been used to alter consciousness in one way or another, for one reason or another.

Chemical substances can have narcotic, soporific, and analgesic effects and as such have been used as medicines and anesthetics. They also produce changes in blood chemistry that affect the entire physical and mental process of living. Among the changes that chemicals can produce are alterations in emotion. Most people, having tried an intoxicant, can testify that among the first changes in emotionality is a dropping of inhibitions, a freeing of locked-up or held-back feelings. The intoxicants, whether alcohol or pot or whatever, *are* central nervous system depressants—meaning the chemicals act as "downers." But depressants may also have the effect of releasing barriers or learned limits on emotional expression. This is why many people incorrectly think of them as stimulants or "uppers."

You will have noticed by now that we aren't taking a strong judgmental stance regarding the use of these substances. Here we're interested more in opening up the relationship between various drugs and the emotional side of life, not in recommending or condemning their use. There are plenty of statistics and newspaper articles you can consult for this sort of thing.

We do notice, however, that many people seem to be able to learn their feelings, accept the emotional side of their nature, and live fuller, freer, more fulfilled lives *without* chemical means. Convincingly large numbers of people have learned—or seem to know "naturally"—how to get "stoned" on life, on their everyday experiences with things, people, with nature. Some of these people have tried chemicals and found them to be no better, and, in some cases, inferior to "natural" highs. Alan W. Watts, a philosopher who did a great deal to introduce Zen to the Western world, found, after trying LSD, that it seemed to produce the kind of enlightenment that Zen devotees spent years trying to achieve. For a while, he advocated that psychedelics could be "shortcuts to satori," but he later modified that view.

Timothy Leary, onetime "high priest of LSD," once advocated unlimited and full use of the psychedelics for everyone. In the past few years, while he still believes strongly in them, Leary has concluded that he "spoke too soon," that most of us aren't ready for chemical consciousness expansion. Baba Ram Dass (formerly Dr. Richard Alpert) once gave his guru, or spiritual guide, a dosage of 915 micrograms of LSD (a beginner usually starts with 60 mcg); he reported that the dosage had absolutely no effect. The reason, Alpert says, was that the man already had experienced everything the drug could give him in his meditative life. He didn't need it. It added nothing to his experience.

Today, LSD is almost a thing of the past. The numbers of those who still use it are dwindling to such an extent as to be negligible.

Marijuana use is about as prevalent as it was five years ago. Heroin use, while still alarmingly high, has apparently stabilized. Alcoholism still ranks up in the top five causes of death, and the number of alcohol abusers is huge. Alcohol use among young people has sharply increased. Some simply say they can get the same effects as from pot or acid without the side effect of being arrested or jailed for drug use.

All these chemicals have interesting effects on human emotionality. A usually quiet, friendly, shy person may open up deeply stored quantities of hostility and rage. An angry and uncontrollably aggressive individual may become a quiet, introspective lamb. Cautious people may become impulsive. Reserved people when stoned may cut loose with all sorts of behaviors they would consider "obscene," "disgusting," or "ridiculous" when they were "straight." Quite apart from the wreckage of lives and the criminally high expense of alcoholism and drug abuse, we must look at the emotions involved in their use.

Alcohol

Not just any alcohol, but ethyl alcohol, or ethanol, is what we're interested in. This is what makes up beers, wines, distilled liquors, and liqueurs. It is a depressant that acts on the control centers of the brain so as to reduce their activity. In time, with enough consumption, the reticular centers switch off and the drinker goes to sleep. We're primarily interested in what goes on between the first drink and the sleep.

Some people drink because they are thirsty. Any fluid, even water, is what they're after. If they aren't used to alcohol, don't like its taste, or have strong scruples against it, they won't usually touch liquor.

Some drink because it is socially desirable. They are people who find the pressure of their peers to be irresistible. They may or may not like alcoholic drinks, but they like drinking. It is a social experience; they can become part of the group of drinkers. So, their emotional need for acceptance, for belonging, for being a part of a group is involved. Any of us who've experienced rejection by a group we want to join can understand this need. It feels painful to be left out; it feels good to be included.

Some drink because they are bored. Nothing else to do. In such cases we can't really say what else is going on. Wouldn't drinking a glass of water or a soft drink give them something to do also? It might, for some. For others, feeling "bored" may indicate that they are not part of something, or have nothing valuable to do, or that they're not valuable themselves. In such cases, alcohol may help a person forget these feelings. The effects of alcohol may be to let him release other feelings, whether reality-oriented or not, to make him feel valuable, that he does have significance and important things to do.

One may drink because he is lonely. Either the socializing effects of being in a place where drinking is going on or the loosening-up effects of the alcohol may free him to make social encounters he might have been too shy to make when sober. Of course, the follow-up may put him right back in his loneliness when the effects of the alcohol wear off or the environmental factors change.

A few drink to block pain. As a depressant, alcohol can have that effect, physiologically, and many people drink to numb a toothache, back pains, cramps, or sore toes. Many others are experiencing psychological pain—anxiety, insecurity, depression, defeat, rejection, alienation, loss, fear, discouragement, or dread. We won't argue whether such feelings rightfully belong in the category of pain: too many people have testified that pain is the only word to adequately describe their feelings at such times, in such moods.

Alcohol, again, by depressing control functions of the brain, can produce changes in consciousness and the pain can be blocked or eliminated. "Drowning your sorrows" is an old but apt way of describing part of this.

Some drink because they want to "pass out." We don't have any idea how large this group is, but it is common enough. They know from experience that enough alcohol will put them to sleep. They can escape from boring or threatening social experiences by falling asleep, slipping off "in the arms of Morpheus." Sometimes people who are terrified to relate to others seek this channel of escape. If they get "ripped," they don't have to communicate because they know their speech is blurred, or nobody will take them seriously, or they don't have to be responsible for what they say or do. If they are "blasted," they don't have to make love—and making love for many such people is somehow threatening. Better to fall asleep than to fail their sex partners or be mastered or ridiculed by them.

There are countless reasons for drinking—and many of them are good reasons for *not* drinking. They all involve one's feelings about oneself and others. While a few people gain from drinking (such as getting "liquid courage" to do something they want or need to do), the long-range effects are disturbing. Over six and one-half million Americans are classed as alcoholics, people for whom alcohol has become a way of life and a problem. Probably ten times as many use alcohol as part of their daily lives, and we don't know how many of these actually have a drinking problem.

There is no simple answer, as short as this discussion is, to what can be done to straighten out the tangled relationship between alcohol and human emotionality. We hope, in this chapter, to suggest some alternatives.

Marijuana

"Pot," "grass," "weed," "Mary Jane," "tea," or any of the other names assigned to it, is a derivative of the drug cannabis, coming from the leaf and stem of the common hemp plant, *Cannabis sativa*. The active ingredient, as almost any student knows today, is delta-1-tetrahydrocannabinol, or THC for short. This plant, a weed growing everywhere, has been around for as long as anyone knows. For 4,000 years or more the Chinese have been making cloth and rope from it, but we aren't concerned with its rope- or cloth-making qualities. For nearly half that 4,000 years, the plant has been smoked or eaten for its psychotropic or mind-altering qualities.

In small doses THC produces a mild pot high, while higher dosages can give rise to hallucinogenic and psychotomimetic (mimicking psychosis) effects, similar to those found in LSD. Despite the similarities in effects, THC has no chemical resemblance to any of the psychedelic drugs, LSD, mescaline, DMT, STP, or psilocybin.

Hashish, the concentrated resin of cannabis, produces effects often ten times as powerful as marijuana itself. Researcher Ernest Barratt at the University of Texas found that monkeys, rats, and cats who were given chronic doses of THC developed a change in brain-wave patterning that persisted for weeks after the dosage was stopped. The type of EEG alteration observed was what one would normally expect in a drowsy individual. Continual smoking of marijuana often produces several days of drowsiness, lethargy, or "hangover." but usually this disappears after two or three days.[4]

Many people do not get high or stoned on their first marijuana experience, and some researchers conclude that, unlike alcohol, some pharmacological sensitization must take place first. Another explanation is that repeated exposure to pot reduces psychological inhibitions, as part of, or as a result of, some learning process. This means, as many pot smokers tell us, that set and setting (attitude and environment) are important aspects of the marijuana high.

Also, unlike alcohol and many other drugs, there is a reverse tolerance in marijuana use for many people. That is, as a person uses it more frequently, the amount of THC required to produce a high decreases.

Why do people use marijuana? Many answer, Why not? *For some people* the motives for using grass may be similar, or identical, to those for drinking alcohol. This has been borne out by multitudes of research studies. Others do it out of less dramatic motivation. Allan Y. Cohen lists the following motives for use of drugs (including drugs other than marijuana):

1. People use drugs because they *want to.*
2. People use drugs to *feel better* or to get high. Individuals *experiment* with drugs out of curiosity or hope that using drugs can make them feel better. "Feeling better" encompasses a huge range of mood or consciousness change, including such aspects as oblivion-sleep, emotion shift, energy modification, and visions of the divine.
3. People have been taught by *cultural example,* media, etc., that drugs are an effective way to make them feel better. [Note: aspirin, tranquilizers, pep pills, a pick-me-up drink are such examples.]

Cohen says that basically, individuals do not stop using drugs until they discover "something better." The key to meeting problems of drug abuse is to focus on the "something better," and maximize opportunities

4. Solomon H. Snyder, quoted in "Work with Marijuana: Effects," in *Psychology Today,* May 1971.

for experiencing satisfying nonchemical alternatives. The same key can be used to discourage experimentation or, more likely, keep experimentation from progressing to dependency.[5] Of course, one of the problems with such a listing is that it overlaps into the usage of other drugs (including alcohol) and isn't limited to marijuana use alone, though it does include marijuana use.

Emotions with or without Drugs

What we've tried to do in this section is to show that, whatever our personal feelings and judgments about alcohol and drugs, there is a very marked relationship between them and human emotions.

Many people need chemicals to feel anything; others to feel only certain things. What is important here is that feeling, whether we like it or not, is a big part of human experiencing. Carl G. Jung has pointed out that there are (at least) four main functions in consciousness:

1. Thinking
2. Feeling
3. Sensing
4. Intuition

Jung does not say that thinking is more important or that sensing is more important. While individuals vary, some emphasizing one or two at the expense of the two other functions, a healthy, Self-actualizing person is one who has learned to accept all four functions, to experience them all, and to find a workable balance in his or her life among the four of them.

Our current social emphasis, reflected in business, the military, most public and higher education, and even in theology, but certainly in scientific areas, is in thinking and sensing. In our society, observation and classification are far more important than wondering, intuiting, having opinions or feelings about things.

Yet, Maslow points out (as does Jung) that fully functioning, effective, and happy human beings know the world through *all* these modes of consciousness. Here is a lesson to be gained about chemical and other exterior "helpers" in consciousness alteration. Self-actualizing people more often than not have Peak or Oceanic Experiences, which involve a total involvement of the person at all levels of being.

> In the state of B-love (Being-love, in which the love is based on the person's experience of his own Being, not D-love, or Deficiency-love, where one loves to get something he hasn't got, or become something

5. Allan Y. Cohen, "The Journey beyond Trips: Alternatives to Drugs," *Journal of Psychedelic Drugs*, Vol. 3, No. 2 (Spring 1971), reprinted in John H. Brennecke and Robert G. Amick, *Readings in Psychology and Human Experience* (Beverly Hills, California: Glencoe Press, 1974).

he isn't), I found a particular kind of condition . . . which I have seen well described by certain writers on aesthetics, religion, and philosophy. This I shall call Cognition of Being, or for short, B-cognition. . . . The B-lover is able to perceive realities in the beloved to which others are blind, i.e., he can be more acutely and penetratingly perceptive. '

. . . the B-love experience, the parental experience, the mystic, or oceanic, or nature experience, the aesthetic perception, the creative moment, the therapeutic or intellectual insight, the orgasmic experience, certain forms of athletic fulfillment, etc. [are] moments of highest happiness and fulfillment [that] I shall call the peak-experiences.[6]

What is fascinating to consider is that people who talk about their acid-trips, or highs from other drugs, often do so in terms that are so similar to those used by Maslow and others in describing their "peak-experiences" or their "life-highs."

Peak-experiences are from this point of view more absolute and less relative. Not only are they timeless and spaceless in the senses which I have indicated above, not only are they detached from the ground and perceived more in themselves, not only are they relatively unmotivated and detached from the interests of man, but they are also perceived and reacted to as if they were in themselves, "out there," as if they were perceptions of a reality independent of man and persisting beyond his life.

• • • • • • • • • • • • • • • • • •

The emotional reaction in the peak experience has a special flavor of wonder, of awe, of reverence, of humility and surrender before the experience as before something great. This sometimes has a touch of fear (although pleasant fear) of being overwhelmed. My subjects report this in such phrases as "This is too much for me." "It is more than I can bear." "It is too wonderful." The experience may have a certain poignancy and piercing quality which may bring either tears or laughter or both, and which may be paradoxically akin to pain, although this is a desirable pain which is often described as "sweet."[7]

Compare these statements from Maslow with the commonly heard descriptions of drug-based experiences: "I was walking in space." "I didn't belong to my own body." "I stood outside and saw my own Self." "I and the people around me were all-together, like One." "It scared me to death, but I wanted it to go on anyway!" "Spaced is spooky!"

Our position in the drug debate is based less on medical or psychiatric evidence than on a philosophy of "Who needs it?" Everyone has the ability to get high on his own subjective experiences, without chemical help. Taking drugs is often the easy way. The hard way, without

6. Abraham Maslow, *Toward a Psychology of Being* (Princeton, N.J.: Van Nostrand Co., Inc., 1962), pp. 68–69.
7. Ibid., pp. 80, 82.

drugs, is what we really need to go through as a necessary part of the search for Self and significance.

Emotional Richness

Emotions are not in themselves good or bad, normal or abnormal, right or wrong. What puts them into categories is the way we interpret them, legislate about them, control or abuse them. Perhaps there aren't actually any quantitative differences among the various emotions. Anger may become a "strong" emotion simply because it's so often suppressed or repressed, in much the same way that caging an animal often makes it more aggressive. Also, hidden feelings frequently loom larger, stronger, more powerful than easily expressed feelings simply because they are made "special" by being hidden.

Human life is lived either minimally or maximally, depending upon what can be experienced. Merely responding to inborn physiological drives, getting those needs satisfied, turning over and going to sleep, would be living minimally—just surviving. But we can approach a maximal experiencing of life by noting and knowing what living consists of. It consists, for one thing, of learning. We can experience the world, inside us and outside, remember these experiences and

anticipate them the next time around. Learning is simply the acquisition of behavior as a result of experience. This includes formal, classroom-type learning as well as the learning from everyday involvement, what some have called "the school of hard knocks." But not all informal learning is hard knocks. One can learn what beauty is, for instance, by observing a sunset or the earth viewed from a moon module, by hearing music or other pleasant sounds.

In addition to learning, each of us can experience life fully through the development of his mind by reasoning and imagining—either associative thinking or "free-play" thinking like brainstorming or random ideation. Fantasy, curiosity, exploration, manipulation of the environment, trial-and-error problem solving, getting "lost" or deeply involved in a story, film, play, conversation, or intimate relationship are all within the range of opportunities presented to us by everyday life for utilizing our physical selves and enriching the experience of being alive.

We are advocating here the cultivation of a full, varied, free yet responsible emotional life. A person can be rich in economic terms, yet impoverished emotionally. Using Dr. David D. Eitzen's analogy: In addition to a monetary bank account, we also have an emotional bank account, a storehouse for feelings, or affective responses, that is available to us over the long haul of our lifetime. We are born only with the bank, the nervous system and brain: we have to make deposits into it in order to have emotional responses to "spend" or "invest."

From what, or whom, or where do these deposits come? Theory builders inform us that the child's earliest emotions, excitement and quiescence, gradually develop or change into other emotions, like distress, delight, anger, joy, fear, anxiety, affection, as he encounters aspects of the world about him. We cannot observe emotions in a newborn infant (which doesn't mean they aren't *there!*). When he experiences the pain of hunger or the discomfort of a wet diaper, he howls. The crying is probably just an innate response to internal physiological discomfort or to external pain and doesn't represent a true ·emotion. The one response we can call "emotion" with any degree of surety is a general *excitement,* which is the only apparent change from the infant's ordinary, general quiescence. But sometime during the first four to six weeks after birth, this diffuse excitement, even though it continues, takes on a different form, which we've come to call *distress* and to observe as tensed breathing and muscular tension that may or may not be accompanied by the crying response that was present at birth.

Another change occurs when something is done to remedy the conditions that produced the distress. When food satisfies the baby's hunger or when his diaper is changed, for instance, we notice the emotional response we've come to call *delight,* characterized by muscular relaxation, smiling, gurgling, or cooing. Thus, two emotional experiences have been deposited into the child's emotional bank account. In the normal, healthy and happy person, these early emotions (excitement, distress, delight) continue to be present, even though others have been added along the way.

As we grow we discover new ways of feeling, all made possible by the development of the inborn nervous system and by other emotions previously learned. *Fear,* for instance, is experienced quite early. Some researchers think they have discovered proof that some fears—particularly of falling and sudden or startling sounds—are inborn. But we do know and can demonstrate that in the average child fears are experienced by the age of six months. Fear has a definite survival value: it provides a response that motivates us, because of the endocrine gland hormone called epinephrine (adrenalin), to move away from a situation we perceive to be threatening or dangerous.

Anger serves to energize or motivate us to attack or act against some limiting situation. This conceptualization is based on Dollard and Miller's *Frustration-Aggression Hypothesis,* a theory which, briefly, assumes that one of the commonest responses to frustration is a *desire* or *inclination* to attack or somehow move against the frustrating situation. Often we do not act upon the desire, of course. We find a bully—inches and pounds bigger!—blocking the sidewalk as we walk to school. Our desire may be to punch him, but our fear of being hurt or our reasoning that we couldn't do it is usually strong enough to hold in that aggressive action and attempt other ways of solving the problem. There are, however, times when we do move directly against the source of frustration, like when we kick a box out of our path, shove a door out of the way, or assume it to be safe enough to throw a punch at a blocking bully!

If we can experience anger and accept it as a feeling we have as much right to have as any other, then we can find ourselves enjoying the aliveness of emotionality. Anger can be enjoyable, especially when it is not expressed in a way that produces guilt as an aftermath. There's a genuinely life-affirming experience to be had when you are in the midst of strong emotions.

One man, experiencing his emotions openly and acceptingly for the first time in many years, expressed it this way: "Before, when I was holding back, I often had the feeling that I was a zombie, a walking corpse. But, now, when I'm *good and mad,* my brain's alive, my heart's pumping away, and I can feel the blood zipping through my body, and y'know, I'm really alive! I can feel it!" This is not an unusual reaction in those who discover what experiencing within their own emotional range is really like. As the television commercial says, they "Come alive!" In terms of the "bank account" analogy, it's like discovering you forgot to record a deposit and have more money than your balance shows.

The person who is aware of the "wealth" of emotions he has at his disposal is one who feels capable of entering into a variety of experiences in life. He is also an infinitely more interesting person to be with, because his reactions spring from a wide repertory of emotional responses. How many people use only one or two of the whole range of possible emotional responses! They are the ones we call "cold," because you tell them you got an "A" on a midterm you expected to just pass and they can only say: "Nice." You tell them your grandmother died and it really leaves you empty, and possibly they can muster a "Gee, that's rough," or even a lump in the throat. You tell them you love them and they're the greatest people you've ever known, and they smile, or maybe blush. They are unable to experience or express emotions on any but the most lightweight levels.

There are all kinds of reasons for the inability to express deep or strong feelings, or to have a wide repertory of feelings. "Emotional poverty" is generally a product of learning, not inborn shyness or shallowness. It can be unlearned and a more effective emotional life learned. It's never too late to add to that "emotional account" and experience a richer, fuller, more interesting, more rewarding emotional life.

Emotional Education

A person who has been raised to believe his emotions are bad or that any emotional expression is excessive or immature has probably had this kind of attitude "positively reinforced" through rewards or through the use of related behaviors to avoid some kind of punishment. Possibly the learned attitude was more firmly entrenched in him because he learned it from his parents or his friends or another person equally important to him. Most young people hesitate to go against the teachings and beliefs of those whom they love and respect, tending to feel disloyal if they do.

Those who want to acquire a fuller, deeper, wider range of emotional responses must evaluate the learning that took place before. Do you hold to emotional restraint because you really believe in it, or because people you love, respect, or fear believe in it? The person who answers yes to the former may have an easier time changing his behavior than the one who subscribes to the latter reason, but both might well benefit from an experimental "emotional spending spree." If the other-directed experimenter feels tremendously guilty that he's let someone down, or is ashamed and fearful that others might find out and think less of him, he can try letting *those* feelings have their free run. It may be that just *having* whatever feelings are stimulated is the best practice. A case history serves as an excellent example of this type of "role playing":

A young man would like to learn to react strongly to great art. His parents, especially his father, are cold toward art (except "the great masters") and have negative attitudes toward artists and "arty" people. His mother wants him to become a doctor or an attorney; his father prefers that he follow in the family business. The boy has the aptitude for either business or some form of professional service career and, actually, is interested in both. He also wants to please his parents.

His friends tell him he is cold, colorless, unexciting, and he feels that they are right. He seldom experiences strong anger, fear, sexual passion, or excitement. He says he's never had an experience where he felt overwhelmed by the beauty or rhythm or symmetry of anything. A few friends are tempting him to "turn on" with marijuana. But he has a strong conscience and feels that the guilt would be overwhelming.

He talks his problem over with his psychology professor, who advises him to go into his room, lock the door, turn on the radio (preferably at a time when he is alone in the house), lie on the bed, and let his imagination go when the music plays. He's told to try instrumental music so he doesn't have any word associations interfering.

While listening to the music, the young man worries continually about his parents coming home and discovering him "wasting his study time." But his teacher has told him to experience whatever feelings he can, to know that they are *his* feelings and should be allowed to come out. He discovers that his fear of being discovered turns easily into resentment and anger that other people are telling him what he can and cannot feel. He sees his parents' faces as he's meditating on his feelings, and even the face of his teacher, who also is influencing his emotions. He experiences the anger and "talks it out," telling his parents off and his teacher too!

Concerned that he might be overheard, he looks up and listens for footsteps outside. He then feels foolish and doesn't like it, but he continues to feel the foolishness. Then he experiences guilt. He berates himself for feeling angry at these people: think of all his parents have sacrificed and done for him! And he's full of guilt at the anger he felt toward the teacher: after all, the teacher was the one who had listened to him, encouraged him to try his feelings out. In fact, the teacher would want him to work this guilt out as well. So, he lets himself go. The guilt causes him to think of ways in which he exhibited other ingratitude and pettiness. But he can't fix any kind of punishment for himself. He is puzzled. Why not?

He decides that he isn't really as guilt-ridden as this mental wandering had led him to think he was. He realizes that he'd been very grateful for all the help he'd gotten. He'd shown his appreciation in many ways. He didn't need to feel a deep, all-influencing debt of obligation. Again, he feels anger and resentment, but this time it feels better.

Suddenly, he finds his foot is beating time to the music. He has been caught up in the rhythm of the song being played, even while he was working through several emotional reactions. He decides to encourage this response and starts conducting the music with his hands, but his awkwardness and lack of knowledge about music embarrass him. He stops and lets the feeling of embarrassment flood over him. It burns. But he hears the music more deeply, feeling it, and with every new emotion he experiences, the music seems to mean more to him. He feels "caught up" in the music. Suddenly, he feels a chill as a particularly poignant chord sounds. This is strange to him, a sensation he can't identify.

After reporting this set of novel sensations, thoughts, and experiences to his psychology teacher, he asked if there were something wrong with him. The psychologist suggested that the only "wrong" might be the fact that the boy had never before experienced those feelings. For him they were new, different, strange, unusual. The psychologist interpreted the entire "session" as an esthetic event, even the guilt, shame, resentment, fear, and confusion. These strong emotions, strange to the boy, had cleared away the cobwebs that had kept the music from entering into his consciousness.

A major goal of all psychotherapies is to enable the client to experience more of his emotional life than before and to feel safe and accepted while doing it. Many clients come to psychotherapists for help in *blocking* certain kinds of feelings. They have been conditioned or trained to believe that restraint and denial of some feelings is of the utmost importance to their social well-being.

The Social Order and Emotionality

We know that our emotions can motivate us in many directions and with varying amounts of intensity. Writings from earliest times, including the Ten Commandments from the Old Testament and the Code of Hammurabi, indicate that people have always perceived the need to order and restrain certain human emotions and motivations for the greater good of the society. Anger, sexual passion, and covetousness are among those emotions whose expressions are universally structured. The emotions themselves are no more important or powerful than any others, but the fullest expressions of them have negative consequences for more than one individual. Anger, for instance, when carried to an extreme, can lead to such violent expressions as murder, assault, destructiveness. Sexual passions can in their extremes lead to rape, adultery, and similar offenses against others. Covetousness carried to extremes leads to aggression against the property of another person.

When human social life began, leaders found it necessary to form an unwritten "social contract," whereby in return for the benefits of group living, the individual had to agree to abide by certain laws and restrictions. Even Desmond Morris, in his speculative but fascinating book *The Naked Ape*, while insisting that man ("the naked ape") is instinctively aggressive, points to the necessity for inhibiting aggressiveness through ritualized actions:

> The phrase 'nature red in tooth and claw' was originally intended to refer to the brutal prey-killing activities of the carnivores, but it has been applied incorrectly in general terms to the whole subject of animal fighting. Nothing could be further from the truth. If a species is to survive, it simply cannot afford to go around slaughtering its own kind. Intraspecific aggression has to be inhibited and controlled, and the more powerful and savage the prey-killing weapons of a particular species are, the stronger must be the inhibitions about using them to settle dispute with rivals. This is the 'law of the jungle' where territorial and hierarchy disagreements are concerned. Those species that failed to obey this law have long since become extinct.[8]

Man is animal because of his continuity with nature, because he shares with all other organisms similarities in *ways* of existing: eating, utilizing oxygen, drinking, reproducing, and so on. Man's *humanness* consists

8. Desmond Morris, *The Naked Ape* (New York: McGraw-Hill Book Co., 1967), p. 159.

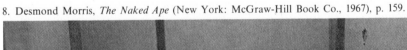

of the ways in which he has transcended his physical nature and its one-to-one dependence on the physical environment. He can profit from experience. And, having experienced the benefits to be derived from his social living, he can move in ways that enhance the group and thereby enhance his own existence. However, man doesn't quite so blithely give up his "instinctive" selfishness and follow the rules of other people. We have evidence that from the beginning of man's intellectual life there was as much survival value for him in cooperation and social living as there may have been in individualistic action and self-seeking behavior. While zoologist Morris and Konrad Lorenz, an ethologist, and Robert Ardrey, a playwright, and a few others have been insisting lately that man is primarily a beast, innately aggressive and instinctively a territorial animal, others have been struggling to show us the evidence for the opposite view.

One physical anthropologist, Ashley Montagu, has for several years been arguing that both man's nature and his nurture are much more inclined toward cooperative behavior than toward either competitive or hostile actions:

> The evidence as we are able to judge it, on the basis of field observa-
> tions among living primates, indicates the deep-seated nature of the
> cooperative drives which bind the members of primate societies together
> and preserve them. Among early men these cooperative drives were
> undoubtedly intensified for the very reason that every member of early
> human society was in an even more interdependent relation to his fellows
> than the members of any other primate group had ever been. The critical
> state of immaturity in which the human infant is born, and the long
> period of dependency which is characteristic of him, have from the first
> intensified and reinforced the cooperative organization of the responses
> from others upon which the human child is dependent for his survival
> and his development as a human being.[9]

Margaret Mead, in her monumental study of competition and cooperation, came to similar conclusions.[10]

On the other hand, people do seem to have "territorial" or "property" attitudes, and they do seem to justify attack and "self-defense"
and even armed aggression in the name of those attitudes. How do
we explain this?

Our earliest ancestors were wanderers, but not entirely nomadic.
They wandered about in search of food and, of course, to escape from
the dangers of their physical environment. When they found an area
that contained sufficient foods and access to water, they, like many

9. Ashley Montagu, *The Human Revolution* (New York: Bantam Books, 1965), p. 122.
10. Margaret Mead, *Cooperation and Competition among Primitive Peoples* (Boston: Beacon Press, 1961).

primates observed today, settled for a while. One of the main reasons for the settling was the need of women for a stable situation in which to give birth and rear their children. If there was sufficient food and water and the place was safe (or could be made safe) from animals that might attack them, the women probably preferred to settle. The settling usually involved some kind of laying out or defining of the boundaries. If attack came, whether from other humans or wilder animals, the defense usually took the form of rituals, rather than warfare. The rituals, observed in many wild animals and to some degree in modern primates, including ourselves, involved shows of strength, bluffing, dancing, loud cries and shouting. Armed fighting was a last resort. Within the small family or band other kinds of rituals would evolve, later extending to other groups. At first simple, the rituals became more elaborate patterns of social regulations which were agreed upon by all, for each person could understand his *own* desire to possess and keep that which was his. Those prehuman and human ancestors who selected cooperative and nonaggressive patterns of social interaction were the ones who survived.

There is more than just guesswork involved here. If the relations within families and tribes had been aggressive and hostile, or even begrudgingly tolerant, mating and the development of family life could hardly have taken place. Moreover, we have fossil and other physical evidence that cooperation and group living were the dominant social patterns for early man just as several universal patterns of cooperation and group living have been found in every society that has ever been studied: a family form, kinship relations, incest taboos, naming, birth and death rituals, and many others.

Emotions and Reason

If all the facts were in, we'd find that the so-called distinction between "emotion" and "reason" doesn't really exist at all, though existentially speaking, there *is* a real difference, because as most of us live our lives, we act, think, believe, and perceive in terms of one or the other. *That* is where the difference arises.

From India comes the statement of Samkara that in observing things we not only perceive our perceptions but something which is neither ourselves nor our perceptions. There is in the wisdom of the Taoist and Zen writers an attempt to communicate an important truth: that there is no difference, or rather, no distinction or boundary, between us and our experiences. We are part of all that we experience; all that we can experience is part of us.

The threshold created between Emotion (intuition, sensuality, feeling, or soul) and Reason (intellect, knowledge, cognition, logic or mind) was established because in Western civilization, there exists a strong tendency to make boxes, pigeonholes, categories, and blueprints. Into those boxes go our ideas, patterns of thought, reasons, relationships, and many other categories without which we're quite sure we'd be lost. For instance, it was necessary, thanks to the Zoroastrians, Plato, and others, to build a box labeled "Good" and another called "Evil." By thus categorizing what we thought were mutually exclusive opposites or polarities, we could easily sort our experiences by placing them into either one or the other box. We did the same with Truth and Falsehood, Beauty and Ugliness, Love and Hate, Right and Wrong, and hundreds of other things. All this is done in the name of somebody's need for conveniently obtained answers!

Among the convenient distinctions we've all made (one that existential and humanistic psychologists are trying to overcome) is that between Subject and Object. Behaviorists have tried to make this distinction the strongest of all by de-emphasizing any subjective aspects of an experimenter's work and forcing him to deal as objectively as possible with his data. The clinicians, beginning with Freud, were aware of the importance of the subjective experience but were careful to keep the subjective and the objective clearly apart. For example, most of the analysis that Freud insisted his psychoanalysts undergo in their own training was for the purpose of bringing the analyst's unconscious to consciousness so that he could clearly and purely interpret his patient's words without contaminating them with his own subjective wishes or fears. The analyst's mind had to be even more "sterile" than the surgeon's hands!

Humanistic psychologists would like to reunite "subjective" and "objective," to remove the artificial separation that Platonic and medieval thinkers have built between the two. Emotional, intuitive, "subjective" experiences are part of the process of knowing or perceiving any "objective" person or thing. We know from laboratory and field research that perceptions are greatly affected by what we bring to them. We know, for instance, that hunger can cause a person to think he actually sees food. We know, also, that if he is hungry a person will see more food, food words, or signs relating to food in his external environment than he does when his hunger is satisfied. This is called *perceptual set.* It's another way of saying what Samkara of India said: that the perceptual event is more than either the subject doing the perceiving or the object being perceived, separately or added together.

In similar terms, there is no difference between knowing something emotionally and knowing something rationally. Our feelings and our ideas are quite realistically and affectively interwoven. Take the following example, quoted from Eugene O'Neill's *Long Day's Journey into Night:*

> ... I was on the Squarehead square rigger bound for Buenos Aires. Full moon in the Trades. The old hooker driving 14 knots. I lay on the bowsprit, facing astern, with the water foaming into spume under me. I became drunk with the beauty and singing rhythm of it and for a moment I lost myself—actually lost my life. I dissolved in the sea, became white sails and flying spray, became beauty and rhythm, became moonlight and the ship and the high dim-starred sky. I belonged, without past or future, within peace and unity and wild joy, within something greater than my own life, or the life of Man, to Life itself! To God, if you want to put it that way![11]

The experience of delving deeply into subjective awareness is a total self-process, not just a mental exercise in book learning or logic.

Pitirim Sorokin recognizes three systems of knowing:[12]

1. *Sensate Truth:* obtained through responses of the sense organs.
2. *Rational Truth:* obtained through logic, reason, and the scientific method.
3. *Ideational Truth:* superrational and supersensory, obtained through direct intuition, revelations, and the sudden enlightenment of insight or the Buddhist experience of satori.

11. Eugene O'Neill, *Long Day's Journey into Night* (New Haven: Yale University Press, 1956), act IV, p. 153.
12. Quoted in R. G. H. Siu, *The Tao of Science* (Cambridge, Massachusetts: The M.I.T. Press, 1964), p. 79.

In a real sense, then, we're answering the question of the relationship between Emotion and Reason by throwing the question away! Yet, something must be done with the existential fact that, though in nature there may be no distinction, our "unnatural" minds have created the fiction of such a distinction and we live, most of us, with the fiction. Since we live as if emotion and reason were separate and not only exclusively separated but "mortal enemies," we get caught in several binds or dilemmas. As a scientist a man is expected to deal uncompromisingly with the facts of objective reality and never let his own "subjective reality" intrude into his research. The most important part of his subjective reality that must be kept out, or at least corrected for, is the man's own feelings. For example, a scientist with cancer should be capable of being "disinterested" in the results of his research on a cancer cure. He should be able to abstract himself out of his work, so that if the formula fails to cure cancers he won't feel disappointment or anger, and if it succeeds in curing cancers in his laboratory animals, he shouldn't feel anticipation or hope or joy that it might spare his own life.

In actual practice scientists are not capable of such superhuman abstraction. They are human. They experience the full range of emotions and acknowledge that there is tension in their research: they are aware of the strength of their emotional reactions and motivations and at the same time of the need to keep them from interfering with research.

An example from outside the field of science presents itself as these words are being written. One of the authors is missing a party he'd like to be at and is angry and resentful, but his reason tells him that the editor's deadline for this chapter will be reached only by working at this very time. Conflict! The emotion is strong and real because at the party are people he very much enjoys and would like to be with. But grudgingly he recognizes the validity of his reasoning: he is rushed in meeting his deadline because of his own poor scheduling of time. A rationalization ("poor timing calls for sacrifice of pleasure") is called forth to soothe the strong emotions which otherwise might interfere with his effectiveness at writing.

The Proper Synthesis

Western minds, dividing things up into dichotomies like subjective and objective, rational and emotional, have to solve the problems caused by such thinking. In the oriental mode, since there are no false divisions, there's no need for what the French call *rapprochement* or bringing together again. But Westerners, who set up polarities, have to deal with the gap. When a *Thesis,* like Reason, calls forth an *Antithesis,* like Emotion, we neatly dispose of the gap by delivering a *Synthesis,* a proper balance, a good or appropriate unification. Or in Taoist fashion, we bring the two back into a more natural relationship. This synthesis is precisely what humanistic psychologists are attempting with the concepts *Reason* and *Emotion.*

Part of the impetus for such synthesis will come from studying the works of people like Jung, who describes healthy, wholistic, satisfying Selfhood in terms of complete experiencing, of trying to understand and to actualize the total person. *Homo sapiens* is a label that says our species is wise (sapient = knowing, discerning). We have a superior brain. Superior has less to do with size (Neanderthal ancestors and some present-day gorillas have larger brains) than with functioning. We can rise above the instinctive and instinctoid urgings that characterized our primitive ancestry and present-day animal cousins and profit by experience. We can learn far more and far better than our closest relatives can. We learn, remember, associate, innovate, create, and transmit our insights and thoughts in written symbols. Clearly, this indicates something of a superiority!

Yet, as we evolved from creatures dependent on lower brain functions of an instinctive kind to creatures more dependent on higher brain functions of a learned and acquired kind, we may have forgotten that the whole person has to be carried along. None of us is "pure reason," whatever that may mean. Nor can we say actualizing Selfhood is pure emotion.

There may still reside, deep in our brains, in unconscious areas, instincts or instinctoid patterns of consciousness, emotionality, intuition, and communication. This isn't a statement about mysticism. It's a statement dealing with honest, valid, scientific concerns. The whole person, extolled by Rogers, Maslow, Jung, and others, is far more than we've yet discovered. Inborn and acquired behaviors must be blended and harmonized in each of us.

The proper synthesis may not be easily defined and most certainly is not easy to attain. Our technological, linear, objective, measurement-oriented, goal-seeking, and material society makes it difficult to find value in, much less to develop, the other aspects of human personality. Jung's ideal person, fully balanced among Thinking, Feeling, Sensing, and Intuiting, will require attitudes in our leadership that will help create environments that encourage and cultivate whole persons. Carl Rogers describes the "full-functioning person" in terms like these:

> Psychological adjustment exists when the concept of self is such that all the sensory and visceral experiences of the organism are, or may be,

assimilated on a symbolic level into a consistent relationship with the concept of self.[13]

We might paraphrase this by saying that all the experiences, sensory, intellectual, feeling, and intuitive are part of the consistent relationship that *is* the Self.

Maslow hints at this in different language:

> First of all and most important of all is the strong belief that man has an essential nature of his own, some skeleton of psychological structure that may be treated and discussed analogously with his physical structure, that he has needs, capacities and tendencies that are on their face good or neutral rather than evil. Second, there is involved the conception that full healthy and normal and desirable development consists in actualizing this nature, in fulfilling these potentialities, and in developing into maturity along the lines that this hidden, covert, dimly seen essential nature dictates, growing from within rather than being shaped from without.[14]

Apparently, we have to come to grips with the ongoing conflicts in our institutionalized way of viewing ourselves. Since we currently have some patterns of living that view people as Thinkers, they need to be expanded to recognize our needs to be Feelers, Sensers, and Intuiters. We have more tolerance and allowance for the Sensing function, since the world and universe abound with stimuli to attract our sensory organs. We provide museums, galleries, and other structured ways to provide stimulation and satisfaction for our sensory needs, but they are often considered merely as extras, as luxuries. Art has always been considered by many as less important than commerce, religion, education, and defense. Yet, the sensory functions of consciousness are as important as any of them. Without adequate stimulation, they atrophy.

Feeling is still a long way out in left field, too. Psychotherapists find that helping people to feel and to feel good about feeling is a major task, even today. Simple human emotions and values are still forbidden or disapproved of by many of us. It is still difficult to find males in our culture who can show compassion or affection openly and feel good about doing it. It is still difficult for men to cry, either in joy or sorrow.

> I'm in favor of women's lib in many ways because it liberates the male. He doesn't have to be the strong virile guy, which is strenuous. Maybe he feels like crying once in a while. He hasn't been allowed to do so in our culture. [Edmund] Muskie cried because his wife had been insulted. Apparently, that was enough to ruin him, as a presidential

13. Carl R. Rogers, *Client-Centered Therapy* (Boston: Houghton Mifflin Co., 1951), p. 513.
14. Abraham H. Maslow, *Motivation and Personality* (New York: Harper and Row, 1954), pp. 340–41.

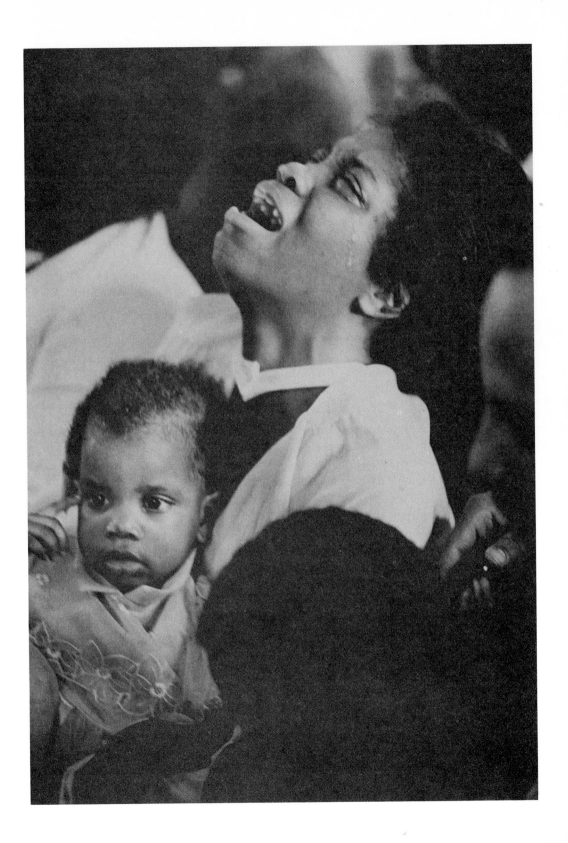

candidate, because it meant he was stupid and immature. Why not say he is an honest guy and he has emotions and he shows them?[15]

Things are changing, and any description of the emotional scene in America that doesn't acknowledge this is in error. Yet, we wish people had even more freedom to accept and acknowledge their feeling side. As men fear their passive or "soft" feelings, so women often fear their aggressive feelings. Women with the drive and talent to move into formerly male-dominated areas often hold back—though not as frequently as in former, less-liberated times—for fear they will come across as too aggressive (meaning, *unfeminine*) or that the males involved will not know how to deal with their honest feelings of initiative and drive.

The intuitive side of our nature is least understood and developed of all. This is the form of consciousness that deals with intangibles: hunches, guesses, "vibrations," the "strong feeling that . . . ," and other less-understood phenomena. Perhaps this is the realm of the psychic, the transcendental, which we will explore in chapter twelve.

Summary

"I think, therefore I am," said René Descartes. To this we add: "I also sense, feel, and intuit, and therefore I am fuller and more whole in my Being." If we were only emotional, we would simply *react,* as an amoeba does when touched by a probe under a microscope. But by combining the feeling side of our nature with the thinking side, we can modify our behavior, can mull things over, can experience more fully, when we bring *all* the aspects of our Selfhood into operation.

But emotions frighten many people. It's often easier to be just a brain, a Thinker, a human computer, than to combine those aspects with emotional responsiveness. At least partially because of this difficulty with feelings, we find that a large segment of our population requires chemical means to deal with emotions. Alcohol and marijuana are the most popular "chemical aids" to aiding and suppressing feelings. When drugs play too important a part in our lives, we give up much of our humanness and find ourselves functioning chemically, artificially.

Abraham Maslow, Allan Cohen, and others have pointed out that there are vast, untapped potentials within the human experience that must be explored if we are to correct this imbalanced dependence on chemistry for our "better living."

15. Dr. Ernest Dichter (psychologist), in an interview in *Penthouse* magazine, January 1974, p. 61.

Emotionality is not an enemy of reason. The social order will not collapse if human beings develop their feeling side. Rather, when emotions become a part of our ordinary experience, we will blend all the aspects of Selfhood more easily and readily into our daily lives, and the society (and its order) will be fuller, more flexible, more varied, and richer.

Suggested Readings:

Adler, Alfred. *Social Interest: A Challenge to Mankind.* New York: Capricorn Books, 1964.

Ardrey, Robert. *The Social Contract.* New York: Atheneum, 1970.

Baba Ram Dass (Richard Alpert). *Be Here Now.* New York: Crown Books, 1971.

Blackburn, Thomas. "Sensuous-Intellectual Complementarity in Science." *Science* 172 (June 4, 1971): 1003–1007.

Bylinsky, Gene. "New Clues to the Causes of Violence." *Fortune,* January 1973.

Castañeda, Carlos. *A Separate Reality.* New York: Simon and Schuster, 1972.

_____. "Coping with Depression." *Newsweek,* January 8, 1973.

Dollard, J.; L. Doob; N. Miller; O. Mowrer; and R. Sears. *Frustration and Aggression.* New Haven: Yale University Press, 1939.

Dubos, René. *So Human an Animal.* New York: Charles Scribner's Sons, 1969.

Fort, Joel. "The Drug Explosion." *Playboy,* September 1972.

Grier, W. H., and P. M. Cobbs. *Black Rage.* New York: Basic Books, Inc., 1968.

Jung, Carl G. "Synchronicity," in *The Interpretation of Nature and the Psyche.* Bollingen Series LI, New York: Pantheon Books, 1955.

Maslow, Abraham. *Toward a Psychology of Being.* Princeton: D. Van Nostrand Co., Inc., 1962.

Montagu, Ashley. *The Human Revolution.* New York: Bantam Books, 1965.

Ornstein, Robert E., ed. *The Nature of Human Consciousness.* San Francisco: W. H. Freeman & Co.; New York: The Viking Press, 1973.

_____. *The Psychology of Consciousness.* San Francisco: W. H. Freeman & Co.; New York: The Viking Press, 1972.

Schutz, William. *Here Comes Everybody.* New York: Harper and Row, 1972.

Siu, R. G. H. *The Tao of Science.* Cambridge, Massachusetts: The M. I. T. Press, 1964.

Today's Education ed. "Facts about Drugs." February 1971.

Watts, Alan W. *The Book: On the Taboo against Knowing Who You Are.* New York: Collier Books, Inc. 1967.

Zimbardo, Phillip G., and Christina Maslach, eds. *Psychology for Our Times.* Glenview, Illinois: Scott, Foresman and Co., 1973.

5

No Man
Is an Island

*The ante-natal life of the child is
one of purely natural combination,
bodily interaction and flowing from the
one to the other. Its life's horizon,
as it comes into being, seems in a
unique way to be, and yet again not
to be, traced in that of the life that
bears it. For it does not rest only in the
womb of the human mother. Yet this
connexion has such a cosmic quality
that the mythical saying of the Jews,
"in the mother's body man knows
the universe, in birth he forgets it,"
reads like the imperfect decipherment
of an inscription from earliest times.
And it remains indeed in man as a
secret image of desire.*

MARTIN BUBER
I and Thou.[1]

1. Martin Buber, *I and
Thou* (New York:
Charles Scribner's Sons,
1958), p. 25.

As we move further into the exploration of the world of significant selfhood, it becomes obvious that the journey isn't a solitary one. We aren't the only ones traveling through the highs and the lows, the hills and vales, the dark and the light. No, one of the most sobering facts we can present is that each of us must travel into realms of danger and delight, agony and ecstasy, victory and defeat. We are social beings, and each of us shares with every other human being the same kinds of goals and experiences. Yet, in the struggle to establish one's identity, no one can really help, no matter who he is or how many times he has made the trip. It is a solitary and often lonely route.

No matter how similar two people may be, each of them is unique. Even identical twins, having come from the same fertilized ovum, are only *close* to being the same. If an individual shares many things in common with one or more other people, we can say they are similar or alike in many respects, but we can't say they are, the two of them, *one.* Even the minutest differences between two people will cause certain significant experiences to take place, therefore producing two different people. This sounds obvious, but we tend to forget it.

Let's stay with identical twins a minute. Identical twins develop from the same zygote, the fertilized cell produced by the union of the male sperm with the female ovum. When a zygote divides into two cells, as in the case of identical twins, each cell separately goes on to form an embryo, a fetus, and finally, an infant. Since each cell has the same genes as the original zygote, the heredity of the twins will be *almost absolutely* identical. Of course, identical twins must be of the same sex, since each has the same sex chromosomes as the original zygote.

Because identical twins have virtually the same heredities, any differences between them must be explained on the basis of differing environments and experiences. Environment is an overworked and much abused term. We feel it deserves to be used correctly. Actually, it means the surroundings, the "neighborhood." In everyday speech we limit the term to the physical surroundings: air, residence, community. But in truth we have several environments, and each one is important for its own sake.

The individual's first environment is his *prenatal environment.* In the uterus, the baby's first world, he is highly protected as he undergoes the developmental processes that prepare him for birth and for the rest of life. The developing child is encased in the amniotic fluid-filled sac that is protected by the spongy flesh of the uterine walls, which in turn are shielded by the pelvic bones covered with the fatty tissues of the mother's hips. He will never again be so well protected. He will probably never again be so comfortable, so easily taken care of, nor so free to just grow and *be.*

In his prenatal world the child does experience, in microcosm, a foretaste of some of what he can later expect "on the outside." For, as protected as the child is, cushioned by so many layers of tissue and separated from actual physical involvement with the mother's body by the osmotic processes of the placenta, he can still experience a great deal. Many shocks and bumps will not be cushioned—for example, a severe twisting or wrenching of the mother's trunk during a fall or automobile accident. Certain substances, like morphine and possibly nicotine and caffeine, can be assimilated through the placenta and be absorbed by the fetus. Then, too, certain emotional experiences of the mother can produce changes in her body chemistry which will affect the development of the fetus. We are told that women who want to become pregnant, who eagerly desire the child, who enjoy the physical changes in their bodies, who love and are well-loved by their husbands often have less morning sickness, less excess weight, less severe labor, and healthier babies.

The second environment is the *physical environment* of the outside world. This includes the air we breathe, the earth, the geographical location of our birthplace, the kinds of trees, bushes, foods, buildings, cities, and all other physical factors in the world about us, each of which interacts with our senses and our nervous system. We experience the physical surroundings and they become part of our conscious and even our unconscious. Further, we become part of the physical world and attach meaning to items and experiences. In the interaction between our physical surroundings and ourselves there is created an event, an experience, not possible without the interaction of the two factors.

The physical surroundings provide us with many of the raw materials with which we design and build. They also provide inspiration and encouragement and goals and challenge. As we attach meaning to a chair it also gives some meaning to us, as sitters. We continually interact with the world within us and the world outside. We react and respond to the external world, and similarly, the physical world outside us reacts and responds to us. The pattern is called a *gestalt,* which means, roughly, a "holistic configuration." The Gestalt psychologists tell us— and this is basic to the phenomenological approach of the existentialists and humanists—that our perceptions take the form of figure-and-ground patterns. Each unit that we observe is seen as a "figure" in or against the "ground" of its context. For instance, if we look at a tree, it is the "figure." The "ground" is the earth below it, the sky behind it, the other trees around it, and the attitude we have toward trees.

The figure-ground relationship is an important concept, because it colors our perceptions. We never really just see the tree. We bring to the perception our whole mental set and emotional context. So, in truth, we are seeing a whole pattern of things, all in relationship. We can't say we're just looking at the moon, for example. We also see the sky behind it (which is just as much a part of the entire picture as is the moon), and we have a whole set of attitudes toward the moon and a concept of "moon-ness."

So the physical environment is affected by us and we by it. This relationship is probably a lot more important than we've previously thought. The new science of ecology is trying to tell us that our physical surroundings form an important part of our lives, and there is a symbiotic relationship—a state of mutual interdependency—between us and that environment. And when you consider the impact that smog and water pollution and pesticide poisoning have on our lives and the fact that they exist because of *our* impact on the environment, the "mutual interdependency" becomes a living reality.

The third environment is the *social environment,* the other people in our world. There are nearly four billion people on this planet, each of them struggling to live, to stay alive, and to find personal significance. We are related to each other human being first by sharing the same biological classification, *Homo sapiens,* the same basic physical nature. Secondly, we share the same physical and social needs. In spite of differences in skin coloration, hair texture and color, body build, and culture, humans are all biosocial animals. Thirdly, we have a mutual economic and cultural interdependency which has definite social consequences. Intergroup conflicts affect the life-styles and group relationships that are so important to our ongoing living.

The final environment to be discussed is the *cultural environment. Culture* is usually defined as an organized, handed-down style of life shared by a particular group of people. This life-style includes ways of thinking and speaking, idea-formation, attitudes, beliefs, and governmental, educational, economic, familial, and religious patterns. Although we draw national boundary lines around cultural groupings, one nation usually includes several cultural subgroups. There is actually no *one* "American culture," although we often talk and act as if there were. In reality, America is made up of hundreds of subcultures, each blending into the overall culture to a certain extent but retaining many of its own unique patterns. If America is a cultural melting pot, it's a pot in which ingredients have not been fully stirred or blended.

Some people think that each culture should give up its uniqueness and merge with the others, so that we can truly speak of one American culture. Others think it possible for each group to coexist, side by side, in a *cultural pluralism,* wherein each group can retain many of its unique features and do its own cultural "thing" without infringing on surrounding cultural groups. This latter pattern is the more difficult one. Some groups cannot tolerate the cultural differences they find in others and imply in one way or another that coexistence means "do it *our* way!"

In summary then, there are at least four environments that matter deeply to each individual. Identical twins are different because of these four differing environments. They may experience different prenatal environments, though this is rare. It's unlikely but possible that one twin and not the other would be harmed if the mother were to have an accident. Both twins would be born into the same physical environment, but each would have his own unique relationship to it. For instance, one twin could fall from the obstetrician's grip during delivery and be hurt. One twin could be given a slightly different feeding formula than the other. The mother (or father, or nurse) might react differently to one twin than to the other, thus providing slightly different social environments. If a mother really didn't want twins, as sometimes happens, she might favor the firstborn and subtly, but significantly, neglect the other twin. A situation we can describe might illustrate this difference better:

> Identical twin girls were born to a young and very poor family. The mother, fragile and poorly nourished herself, didn't have the energy to take care of both girls all by herself. So a division of labor took place from the beginning. When the babies cried in the middle of the night, the mother would feed girl A, and the father would prepare formula to feed girl B. The same thing occurred with diaper changing, holding, and playing with the twins. Gradually, girl A became much closer to her mother, and girl B became closer to her father.
>
> After the girls grew larger and were more autonomous, the earlier pairing-off wasn't forgotten, and girl A tended to be more like her mother, while girl B, in spite of the strong genetic pull of her "femaleness" and the similarity of genes to her twin, tended to identify more with her father.
>
> The twins, identical in every physical respect, soon differentiated, even in the clothing they wore. In spite of many similarities and many shared behaviors, there was a clear-cut difference between the two girls.

A final effect of the surroundings could occur in terms of the culture's attitude toward twins. In some societies, twins are bad fortune for the parents and are killed at birth. In others, twins are good fortune and are treated as special people. In America multiple births are rare enough that special treatment is accorded them. Twins, especially identical ones, are often confused with each other, dressed alike or not, and there can emerge an identity crisis in which neither twin feels he or she has a unique identity apart from the other. All of these factors can create the differences that do show up in the behavior of twins, no matter how close the statistical correlations between their behaviors may be.

Our Social Nature

A person is born into a social group, his or her family. Many forms of animal life develop something similar to human families, but few with such complexity or holding power. In all nature, no animal appears to come into the world so defenseless, so helpless, so dependent. The human family provides, first of all, a nest, a context, an atmosphere, a buffer against the rest of the world. In this family are virtually all the satisfactions for our basic survival needs. In addition to meeting these needs, the truly happy family offers affection, warmth, and security, which are essentials of a later stage of development. But if the parents satisfy the child's needs in accompaniment with the attitudes and behaviors of warmth, love, affection, and pleasure, the child nests into the family structure more easily and gains an attitude toward interdependency that serves him well at every stage of his development.

The family also provides legal and social status for the child. He has a name, legally given, with "all the rights and privileges appertaining thereto," and in the legal eyes of the society, he "belongs" to somebody and in fact *is* somebody. He has a legal and group identity. His social status (or more correctly statuses) contains several positions that the child occupies. Some of these statuses or positions are *ascribed* to or conferred on the child at birth. If male, he is given at birth a set of privileges and expectations that the society gives to each male. If female, she also is given both privileges and expectations for her behavior, all social and culturally prescribed.

If the child is the firstborn, he has certain privileges automatically: undivided attention from the parents, the first choice of family names, and the distinction of giving the father and mother their new status as parents.

The child may, in certain subcultures, be automatically a Jew or a Christian by virtue of being born into a particular family. Of course, the formal baptism or confirmation may take place later, but because the child is born into a particular family with a particular religion, he is raised in terms of that religion.

The child may be ascribed the status of racial group, socioeconomic group (called social class), nationality group, and so forth.

The child will have to reckon with other statuses as well. These are the *achieved* or *attained* statuses that he will have as a result of growth or some effort on his part. A boy will become a man, an adult male. He will become at a certain age a driver of cars, a purchaser of adult commodities like tobacco or liquor, a fully investitured citizen, a voter, a student, and in later life, a "senior citizen."

The child will *earn* the status of employee or employer, labels that come with earned promotions and advancements in his career, the status of spouse, parent, grandparent, and others. He or she will earn trophies, medals, ribbons, diplomas, degrees, certificates, as well as demotions, unemployment, retirement, traffic citations, and other "earned" statuses which he might wish he didn't have.

Each *status* or position in the social structure carries with it a set of behaviors that are expected of the person in that slot. The expected behaviors are called *roles* and can be pleasant or unpleasant. Additionally, they can come into conflict with each other, as when the role of student, with homework to do each night, comes into conflict with the role of friend or date, with social activities to participate in. The process of personal and social adjustment is concerned with the management of the various role conflicts that come with living the complex lives our society encourages.

So, the family provides the nurture nest and status for the new child. It also provides a definite context for the important education that each child needs. Even before formal schooling, all children are educated within the family structure. In fact, the development of the core of personality, with fundamental learning skills, emotional experiences, attitudes, preferences, and social patterns, usually takes place in our society before the child even enters kindergarten. Furthermore, there is scientific evidence to show that the experiences of the first five or six years can so condition the direction and temper of a child's life that he virtually becomes what he was raised to be. "As the twig is inclined, so grows the tree." However, as powerful as early experiences are, the child is capable of becoming his own person, even if it means throwing off the influences of those early, formative years. This isn't easy, but again, achieving significant selfhood is never easy. It *is* a struggle on which many don't follow through.

The education that takes place in these formative years is important: it's the only real learning some people will do. The attitudes, myths, beliefs, ideas, likes and dislikes that are learned, informally and subtly, may form the basic foundation upon which that child builds his entire life. We can see this best illustrated in racial attitudes. In a family where a child is told that members of certain minority groups are inferior or dangerous, and where he also observes that no members of those groups ever visit the home or participate in any of the fellowship activities of his parents, a negative (or at the very least, a neutral) racial attitude is formed. Further, if the child is prevented from experiencing members of those groups in informal associations, from enjoying their friendship, possibly even being prevented from attending school, club, or religious meetings with members of those groups, a very definite bit of learning has taken place. It's small wonder that an adult should have rather fixed attitudes toward those groups.

In keeping with our belief that each individual has the potential ability to become everything he or she can be, we feel that even a prejudiced person can change some of these attitudes, can be educated in the formal and the informal sense, and can develop a positive attitude toward members of minority groups. But, to reiterate, the unlearning and relearning is difficult, just as the unlearning and relearning of emotional responsiveness is difficult. Yet it can be done and, to editorialize, it *must* be done if we are going to try to bring order out of chaos, if the ideals of equality, brotherhood, and justice are to be actualized.

In terms of the educational process that the child experiences within the family, we must mention the learning of other social skills—not simply manners and etiquette, but the kinds of skills necessary for each child to learn to live in a world full of other people. Once again we point to the chart on page 99, which shows how psychosexual and psychosocial crises are experienced at various stages in a child's life. Powerful and fixed as these patterns may seem, they are not absolute.

Erikson feels that in the first stage the child acquires the social skill called *trust*. If the stage is mishandled, or the culture or poverty or other conditions cannot enable the child to experience the feeding-nutritive-contact relations fully, then he not only doesn't learn trust, he learns to *mistrust*. In the culture of poverty, trust becomes a virtual

luxury, and mistrust becomes the attitude that guarantees survival. It's a dog-eat-dog world, and everybody must be mistrusted, even those who call themselves "friend." Social workers, Peace Corps and VISTA volunteers, civil rights workers, and many others who have gone into areas of poverty tell about the attitude of suspicion and mistrust they face, and which they have the burden of relieving even before the poverty and squalor can be attacked.

In education and in psychotherapy, we have found that even the most mistrusting, suspicious, hostile-defensive people can unlearn that set of attitudes and relearn trust and cooperative interaction. It takes time, affection, determined effort, patience, empathy, understanding, and a lot of "tender, loving care," but it can be done.

We might agree with Erikson's chart that trust, autonomy, initiative, industry, identity, intimacy, generativity, and ego integrity are among the most important social attitudes and skills that can be listed. However, we don't agree that trust starts an irrevocable chain reaction, automatically leading to autonomy and the rest, any more than we believe mistrust bumps shame into guilt, and so on. At each stage of development, the person becomes more and more capable of choice, and as he becomes more proficient and confident he exercises that choice-making capacity and can become a truly autonomous, self-actualizing person.

Social Rules

There are many aspects of being a social animal that aren't as clear-cut as the psychosocial crises. Some of the vague and abstract situations involve the learning and following of the rules of the society in which you live. At the bottom, because they are the least clearly delineated, are the customs and traditions. These are often fuzzy and difficult to understand. For instance, no one seems to know, or bother to explain, why Americans shake hands when they greet each other. In his book *The Naked Ape,* zoologist Desmond Morris tells us we do this as a symbolic gesture of peacemaking, placating the stranger so he won't think we're going to attack him. Possibly this is the origin of the practice, but the evidence is still speculative. However, it's a good example of a custom that's taught but not explained other than with the statement, "Now, this is what you do when you meet somebody, Ralph." In this same class are things like opening the car door for a lady, walking on the curb side of a lady, and wearing particular types of clothing on certain occasions.

Anthropologists call these customs *folkways.* They are expected and strongly urged behaviors, but if you fail to perform them, you can expect only a mildly negative reaction. If you use the "wrong" fork with which to eat your salad at a fairly formal dinner, you probably won't be kicked out, although you may be frowned at. But there is another set of culturally prescribed behaviors and rituals having much stronger sanctions attached to them. These are the *mores* of a group or society. These are so important that two things come about because of them: first they often become part of the society's ethical behavior and we speak then of *moral* behavior; and secondly, many of them become codified and written down as laws.

Some of these moral rules involve the rights of other people and to violate them means to bring down all kinds of social wrath. Belching, spitting, passing gas, nose picking, or making sexual overtures in the full view of other people are good examples of unwritten but strongly sanctioned, immoral behavior. Negative mores are sometimes called taboos, from a Polynesian word meaning "behavior set aside as sacred."

Growing up and learning some of the rules for living that a society gives can become downright bothersome. Babies don't have to obey any rules but those of nature. But as they grow, natural behavior comes more and more under the control, direction, and sanction of the people who share the world with them. Actually, they become socialized.

Socialization is the process of becoming enculturated, or of absorbing the required behaviors of the culture of which the individual is a part. Kluckhohn and Murray, in their book *Personality in Nature, Society and Culture,* have illustrated the various aspects of life and experience that go into making an individual's personality. On page 120 we present the chart that they have developed to show graphically all that makes up human personality.

At the left of the chart are listed the four levels of the natural order that are involved, the *physical, biological, social,* and *cultural.* Along the top are the four determinants based on degree of involvement with the four along the left: from *universal,* meaning *all* humans experience these, to *regional,* meaning that people living in certain regions or cultures experience these, to *role,* only people in particular role situations experience these, to *idiosyncratic,* unique, personal, individual experiences.

To illustrate, look opposite *biological* and under *role.* Here you'll find those experiences at the biological level that happen, say, only to males or only to females, or only to adults or only to children, depending of course on the role that they play in their society. There is a blank opposite *cultural* and under *idiosyncratic* because none of us participates in the culture alone or by ourselves, nor do we, individually, create the culture.

This chart, as limited as it seems, helps us to understand the many elements that go into the development of socialized selves. Again, however, no one is an absolute slave or robot to this or any other

Chart B: The Components of Personality

Determinants Based on Degree of Universality Among Human Beings

Determinants based on Level of the Nature Order

	Universal	Communal (or Regional)	Role-related	Idiosyncratic
Cultural	Incest taboo, kinship systems, property, magic, religion, housing, time-reckoning, etc.	Special forms of kinship, property, magical and religious beliefs, appropriate to community or region.	Special roles culturally differentiated for status group within each society.	
Social	Group life, child care, leadership, etc.	Size, distribution, density of population, etc.	Play groups congeniality groups, cliques, etc.	Fortuitous experiences in social relationships.
Biological	Birth, death, hunger, thirst, metabolic action, skeletal-muscular structure, basic drives, etc.	"Racial" variations of universal traits, health conditions of the society, etc.	Age and sex differences, racially based class and caste.	Individual differences of stature, physiognomy, glandular functions, etc.
Physical Environment	Atmospheric pressure, gravity, earth, sun, moon, stars, clouds, water, wind, precipitation, etc.	Local climate, topography, air and environmental pollution, wild plant and animal life, other natural resources, etc.	Differential access to material goods by different status groups, etc.	Unique relations to flood, storm, lightning, and other physical phenomena.

Adapted from Kluckhohn and Mowrer, "Culture and Personality," *American Anthropologist*, XLVI, 1944, 1–29.

chart or scheme of things. We can, within the limits we must acknowledge, make or break our selfhood.

John Donne Redone

John Donne, a sensitive and perceptive lover of mankind, wrote a beautiful poetic passage that has been a favorite of men and women for years:

> No man is an island, entire of itself; every man is a piece of the Continent, a part of the main; if a clod be washed away by the sea, Europe is the less, as well as if a manor of thy friends or of thine own were; any man's death diminishes me, because I am involved in mankind; and therefore never send to know for whom the bell tolls; it tolls for thee.
>
> Devotions XVII[2]

Each of us is involved and interwoven delicately with his fellow humans. The analogy of a spider web may be useful. All of us in the world, but especially those grouped closer together in nation, state, community, school, family, and marriage unit, are tied together by delicate spider webs, webs of delicate resiliency. Each sensitive and responsive web tends to draw us closer or pull us farther to whatever side another person is drawn. Nobody dies without our feeling it; nobody rises without our also being pulled up. Each of us is responsive to and responsible for every other.

2. John Hayward, ed., *John Donne, Dean of St. Paul's: Complete Poetry and Selected Prose* (London: The Nonesuch Press, 1932), p. 538.

No person is an island, unless we look carefully at the geologic charts of our oceans. If we do this, we find that each island is the protruding peak of an undersea mountain range, but the range is connected and all of one piece, tied intimately and unmistakably to the earth below it. Islands don't *float* on the surface of the ocean. Individual people don't *float* on the surface of society, unconnected from any of the rest of us. A full realization of this is what must take place for any ideal of "global consciousness" or "oneness" to emerge.

If there were no ties connecting the people of this land, and no longer ties connecting people of all lands, then there would be no need for an elaborate plan of governing and interrelating. But there are. The designers of the Constitution of the United States, while only frail humans, full of personal flaws and inconsistencies themselves, wanted to put into effect a form of government based on the fullest participation of the largest number of the citizenry possible. Unfortunately, there are many ways of interpreting "citizens," and the abuses of civil liberties down the years testify to the problems of interpretation with which we live.

Yet the attempt is being made by people of conscience and good will to actualize the fullest meanings of the Constitution and Bill of Rights so that all men can participate in both the benefits and responsibilities of full citizenship. One of the most crucial areas is still civil liberties and equality, especially for who belong to minority groups: the poor, most women, and most members of ethnic minorities. Humans are not cruel or hostile by nature; there is a strong learning process through which each of us passes, which insists that distinctions must be made, setting race against race, class against class, and often pitting the sexes against each other.

This nation was founded on principles that were, at heart, spiritual: "liberty and justice for all." There is in this consciousness a realization that the good of all depends on our all receiving some of the good. We are, basically, the same in nature. The success of any nation, of any league or confederation of nations, depends upon that group's setting up conditions whereby all members of the group can actualize their fullest potentials, thereby returning such manifested development to the group in the form of work, shared responsibilities, mutual aid, and concern.

Many critics of this viewpoint (which they might call "socialistic" or even "communistic") insist that giving to the poor, for instance, means to take away from *them* something that they have rightfully earned. Such people, overly attached to their accomplishments and possessions, fail to see that if poverty, injustice, discrimination, and stereotyping can be minimized or even eliminated, that will mean more jobs, more wages, more tax receipts, more people taking a fuller and more creative part in the way the society runs. Everybody stands to benefit and prosper!

We can thrive and prosper in *all* the ways these things can happen if we can find and restore the relatedness we have with others in our upward climb. The world's population continues to soar, and the effects of this will continue to be felt. As the actual amount of square footage available for each human being is being computed, we need to deal with the many problems of sheer survival that face all of us—deal with them in a united fashion. Overcrowding brings about increased poverty, unemployment, housing shortages, crime, illness, and the biggest consequence of all: war.

There is a continual round of controversy in the history of nations and people. We find ourselves enmeshed in this conflict right now. In the frontier period of any nation, raw heroic, rugged individualism is the keynote. We sing the praises of the Daniel Boones, Jim Beckwiths, Jim Bridgers, Abe Lincolns, Teddy Roosevelts, and others who have done it for themselves, who have risen from poor or weak to successful or strong. This is part of the frontier history of any nation. However, most nations recognize that this period of emphasizing the solitary exploits of individual heroes must give way to the period of cooperative effort, group and family action. Even though our nation can show many examples of such cooperative programs (beginning with the Constitution, the doctrine of balance of power, the League of Nations, the National Recovery Act and its "New Deal," the United Nations), we have to a large degree continued to promulgate the success story to our children.

We do not feel that either the loss of personal identity that often accompanies socialist or communist programs or the loss of group cohesiveness and group relatedness is necessary. Rather, we liken any group endeavor to Fromm's definition of love:

> Love is union under the condition of preserving one's integrity, one's individuality. Love is an active power in man . . . which breaks through the walls which separate man from his fellow men, which unites him with others; love makes him overcome the sense of isolation and separateness, yet it permits him to be himself, to retain his integrity. In love the paradox occurs that two beings become one and yet remain two.[3]

It's not only possible, but highly desirable, to see any human cooperation as more important and productive than singlehanded or solitary effort when the goal has mostly social implications. This is true whether the effort is in the family, friendship group, work group, management group, legislative, judicial, executive, or any other kind

3. Erich Fromm, *The Art of Loving* (New York: Harper Colophon Books, 1956), pp. 20-21.

of activity. Physicians and surgeons still rely on the consultative skills of fellow doctors before making important final judgments. Even in the surgical arena, there are many hands doing the work, even the work of the greatest surgical brain around.

To rephrase John Donne: "No man is of necessity an isolated entity; he achieves his humanity by virtue of his interaction with others; he shares his humanity and it comes back to him multiplied many times over."

The Social Processes

In looking at man's social life, we're struck by several patterns that seem to be always present. One of the first of these is *cooperation*. The early years of sociology (the study of man's social life) were heavily impressed with the work of Herbert Spencer. Spencer followed in the tradition of those who were applying, in an oversimplified manner, the writings of Charles Darwin and Thomas Huxley to the social experiences of man. Darwin's *Origin of Species* hit the Western world like the atomic bomb hit Hiroshima. One of the first things Darwin's theory of organic evolution did was to throw theologians into a frenzy, for he seemed to be challenging the account of creation written in the biblical book of Genesis. The other thing Darwin's work seemed to do was to emphasize the important place played in nature by *competition*. Darwin told us that those species survived best which could adapt to their environment, and he let loose a phrase which he later regretted: "the survival of the fittest." Darwin had to write another book, *The*

"Scram!"

Descent of Man, to try to correct the misunderstandings, but it came too late. The Social Darwinists—a name later applied to social scientists who applied the concept of "the survival of the fittest" to human social interactions—had already begun their work.

These men insisted that, as everywhere else in nature, people were forced to compete with other people, and even to overcome them in the "natural" struggle to survive. This unleashed all the justification some people needed to perpetrate their competitive activities. Men became rich because they knew how to compete better and were therefore more "select" and "superior." Others lost their fortunes or were poor, lived in squalor and died, because they couldn't demonstrate their "superiority," and were, therefore, "inferior." To this day, racism thrives because it is believed that one race is on top by virtue of "natural superiority" and others are on the bottom because they are inferior.

Darwin's work dealt primarily with lower forms of animal life. He felt, even at the end of his work, that lower forms of life, unequipped with a cerebral cortex and selectively developed nervous systems, did have to compete for survival, *primarily with their physical environment,* and secondarily, with other species of life. But seldom, even in the lowest forms of animal life, was there a competition or conflict within the same species. The exceptions are certain species of ant, the hyena, and a few birds.

The general rule, then, was intraspecies cooperation. The simplest form of life, the single-celled microorganism, demonstrates the necessity of cooperative activity in the way in which cells, after splitting off, cluster together to form colonies.

On up the evolutionary scale, the rule is "divide (or reproduce) to live, but come together to survive and grow." The beginning of human life is a further example. After all, an infant is a result of the greatest cooperative act in nature: sexual reproduction. The coming together of two loving people, each bringing the necessary halves of a complementary whole to the relationship, is an action of supreme cooperativeness. No competitiveness is allowed.

One of the most frequent problems encountered in marriage counseling is an overly competitive attitude on the part of one or both partners in the marriage. This is disastrous at any level of a partnership. At the sexual level, it's a tragedy: one spouse trying to be "the better lover" of the two; one or the other spouse trying to see who can "hold out" longest, or exhibit the "best technique." This isn't loving sexuality; it's a sideshow wrestling match!

After sexual union, the sperm and the ovum further the cooperative process, joining together to merge forces and produce a new life form, the zygote. After the zygote is formed, it makes its way along the oviducts until it finds its home, the place prepared for it by processes in the mother's uterus. There, nestling into the soft, blood-enriched walls of the womb, the zygote literally becomes part of the environment of the womb: another cooperative act. A stubborn or resisting zygote passes out of the birth canal and no new life is developed.

The entire nine-month period of prenatal development is one tale of mutual aid after another. Not only does the mother's body provide for the developing embryo, but the embryo does wonderful things, in turn, for the host environment. With healthy, love-inspired zygotes, where the mother really wants to be pregnant and to deliver a healthy baby, the pregnancy can give her a radiant, happy, satisfying feeling of wholeness and creativity. Many women attest (and their obstetricians confirm it) that they've never been healthier than when they were pregnant and strongly desired the pregnancy.

At birth, the child is thrust out of the wonderfully satisfying warmth and protection of the womb into the cold, unyielding environment of the physical world. There, if left unaided, it would die. Humans, alone of most of the animals in nature, need someone else to help them survive. Other animals move about and can forage for food almost immediately, or can in some other fashion survive virtually unaided.

But to counteract the cold, physical environment, we've evolved a clever and beautiful pattern: the family. The typical mother, due to the training and the encouragement she's received since girlhood, *wants* to be a mother, *wants* her baby, and *wants* it to live and thrive and grow and develop. This is not an instinctive thing. There appears to be no "motherhood instinct"; it is a learned behavior, and because it's so well learned, most mothers do everything they can to provide the necessary social environment for their newborn.

The milk flows, the child eats, the family gathers protectively around, and the new life is encouraged to enter into the cooperative activity of becoming "part of the family."

Darwin knew this; the Social Darwinists didn't choose to acknowledge it. Darwin knew that the natural selection process had enabled man to develop the cortical matter of his brain over and above the primitive, reflexive parts. Because he could develop this cortex and profit from his own experiences and become aware of himself as a living being, man differentiated from the lower animals and freed himself from the rigid dictates of the "survival of the fittest." Our brain, complex nervous system, memory, ability to learn and build were all evidences of our *fitness*. We had only to compete with those other forces in nature that might harm us or impede our development. It was in the evolution of a superior brain that we became able to show our fitness eventually to master the physical environment.

But the Social Darwinists had other axes to grind. Many of them were playing the game of supermen. Some men had to be superior because there was only so much room "at the top." Others, in accordance with the biblical doctrine of original sin, believed that Darwin had shown that *Homo sapiens* was, after all, only a beast, and as such, still subject to the natural laws of "tooth and claw." Of course, salvation would transform the beast into a "child of God," but that came later.

Others, in the world of industry and commerce, needed the doctrines of the Social Darwinists to justify their business expansions and the exploitations of human labor, particularly women and children. Slavery, too, since it was still practiced in America for a few years after Darwin, was justified in terms of racial superiority and inferiority.

Competition, however, is a part of human life. Let's look as realistically as we can at this social process. In any context, nature or the neighborhood market, we find a fairly limited supply of goods and resources. Thomas Malthus, nearly two centuries ago, started us thinking about the population problem when he presented a gloomy mathematical forecast: as resources increase arithmetically, population increases geometrically. People got worried, and well they might! Freud and Marx and Darwin were three people who read Malthus and did some serious thinking.

Malthus' answers to the problem of population demands outstripping the resource supplies were that: 1) war, famine, old age, disease, and so on, would help; 2) moderation in sexual activity would take care of the rest. Things have not worked out that way.

Malthus didn't anticipate the technological revolution that would come. He couldn't know that our understanding of agronomy and other agricultural sciences would enable us to increase crop yields and virtually match the geometric increase of human population.

Malthus also couldn't predict that we would conquer many of the diseases he knew and expand the life-span of people to nearly double what it was in his day. So the problem became even more complicated: not only was life-span increased, but health and fertility were increased; so population continued to grow. Today, we face a problem of overcrowding that he could never have anticipated.

Competition exists whenever supply is outstripped by demand. It has always been so, even when supply could match demand. There is no innate factor that makes us compete, but our physiological needs are strong enough that when two or more persons want the same gratification for their needs, they will vie for it, competing and even fighting to obtain it. People call this the law of the jungle, though the real law of the jungle is cooperation and mutual aid.

Competition is the process of attempting to meet needs through activities that make individuals contenders for rewards or goals. The contention is usually with another person, as when two people compete for the attention of a third party. The competition is usually nonviolent, more often taking the form of verbal or skill contests. Two girls compete for the attention of the same man, not by fighting, but by trying to be more seductive, interesting, intelligent, and so on.

Is competition good or bad? This is a difficult question to answer. Those of us who attempt to analyze the society will find that American life is based on a strong system of competitive attitudes and behaviors. It seems to fit, or be demanded by, the economic structure. Of course, the Social Darwinism mentioned before is a very powerful factor even today and makes competition unnecessarily important.

We have to acknowledge that the social and economic life in this country is very rich and well developed; competition has apparently been "good" for us. If economic affluence were all that we had to worry about, this would be a satisfying answer. But we're interested in a deeper problem: our feeling of loss of significance. We share the feeling of numerous other social scientists that the economic competitiveness that has built America into the most powerful nation in the world, with the greatest productivity in the world, has contributed to the breakdown of many personal values, including the personal sense of worth.

This is a hard saying. It seems like an attack on the style of life that we've all lived with. We are not doing that, directly. As any analyst does, we find things within the system that are unworkable, maladaptive. These things need fixing, changing. When any aspect of a system works against the best interests of the people whom the system is supposed to serve, then that aspect is malfunctional and needs remedying.

The competitiveness which in the past enabled one person to contend with another for customers, land, position, privilege, and a mate has too often become the dog-eat-dog viciousness which says, in effect, "it's everyone for himself." This attitude is not only morally wrong (since it denies the sense of community which our social system needs); it's also bad science. It forgets that the very basis for survival, throughout our recorded history, has been the ability to work cooperatively and to take an interest in the welfare of others. This can work in complementary fashion with the necessary competitiveness that carving out a way of life may demand.

What about the "fallout" from this excessively competitive way of life, the losers in the contest? Too often in the competition, the "winning" of the struggle means a "conquest." The winner doesn't just get a point, or a goal; the loser is vanquished, defeated emotionally, made to feel completely worthless. Thus, in many modern forms of competition (especially in the commercial and business world), the "game" moves over into the third type of social process, *conflict*. And conflict is a desperate, no-holds-barred matter.

Conflict is probably as old as life itself and some would say that it's just as right. Our understanding of human behavior should enable us to make some distinctions between those kinds of natural phenomena that are necessary and those that we've outgrown as human beings. Conflict, in the sense of fighting and warfare within our species, is an outmoded and certainly dysfunctional social process. *Dysfunctional* means "not serving the survival needs of the organism or the structure."

So we have three basic social processes: cooperation, competition, and conflict. Of the three, cooperation and some forms of competition seem to be functional, while vicious competition and conflict can be shown to be devastatingly dysfunctional.

The proponents of instinctive aggression (cf. Lorenz, Ardrey, Morris and others) claim that competitiveness and conflict have just as much natural origin, are just as functional, and have just as much survival value as cooperation. However, Pëtr Kropotkin, Ashley Montagu, and many others feel that a full evaluation of the biosocial nature of man will point up the dysfunctionality of continued hostility in a world growing daily more crowded.

Dependence and Independence

At birth, you are the most helpless and dependent of all the animals. You're born with needs, and with little in the way of built-in methods or techniques for meeting those needs. But you are born into groups that care about you; so your needs for survival and nurturance are met and you flourish. You also acquire attitudes and feelings about that first group—the family—that are crucial for the development of other attitudes and feelings you'll have in your social life. One of the first attitudes to develop is trust; so a child learns fairly quickly to depend on mother, on father, on siblings, on the family unit, and then, hopefully, on other people.

This attitude-feeling of dependence is important for survival, for it consists of trust, affection, belief, hope, expectation, anticipation, and many other important social attitudes. Trust *does* start an important potential sequence of psychosocial attitudes moving.

There are, however, some negative side effects that must also be considered in this situation. Dependence may become a clinging, parasitic kind of relationship-attitude. One of the most common problems found among alcoholics and addicts is a dependency conflict. This doesn't mean they *do* or *don't* depend on anything. It means that they seem to have an intrapsychic conflict over their dependency patterns. "Intrapsychic conflict" means that within their own personalities two or more parts or aspects of the personality differ in some response or perception. In long term psychotherapy with alcoholics and addicts manifesting such a dependency conflict we've found many situations like the following (a composite of several actual statements):

When I was really small, I remember how wonderful it was to be around my mom. She always took time out from whatever she was doing to talk to me, to play with me, to make or do something for me. I was the most important thing to her.

Then my little sister was born. I found my mom giving her some of the time and attention that I had always gotten. I resented the little brat! But I know that's wrong. You shouldn't hate an innocent little kid who isn't doing anything but being alive. But I did! At times I still hate her. Sometimes I hate my mom for not being two people, or for not being able to give all her time and attention to me and my sister.

I tried to find another mom in my teachers, but everytime I did what was necessary to make special friends with one of them, they withdrew, or another kid teased me and called me "kiss-up!" I wish those kids would drop dead. Aw, but that's not a nice thing to feel either.

Take my wife now. You'd think she'd be glad for all the attention I give her. I only want her to know how much I need and love her. But sometimes she spends so much time with the baby that I never get to her until she's so beat and exhausted. . . . Well, she thinks I demand too much of her sometimes. Not that she isn't a great little woman, my wife. But sometimes I hear her complaining about me or the kids' making too many demands, and I swear I can hear my mother's voice. Funny thing!

In the above excerpt are several examples of the dependency conflict. The most common example is in the excessive attachment to the nurturing figure, usually the mother. Also there is some kind of guilt or shame because of a realization of the attachment. We also find resentment at having to share the mother, hostility toward the ones with whom the sharing must be done, and then self-recrimination for the hostility. These are usually extremely sensitive people who feel many emotions quite keenly and are often aware of how other people may feel. Frequently the dependency cycle is repeated with teachers, aunts, older siblings, policemen, clergy, Sunday school teachers, dates, and eventually spouses.

A man with a dependency conflict of the type mentioned above will often marry a woman who has a strong need to be a mother. She may complain and berate her husband for his clinging, yet unconsciously be very glad for it; it gives her the necessary assurance that she is needed and important. If the man attempts to solve his conflicts with alcohol, she frequently plays a complementary role, either accompanying him on his drinking route or buying him the necessary supplies. She justifies her actions by saying that he works so hard that he needs or deserves to unwind and relax. Even when she complains that he's drinking excessively, or that he's a rotten husband and father because he spends all their money on booze, her unconscious need may be for him to continue in this pattern. It again reinforces her need to be needed: when he's at his most intoxicated, she is the most important person in the world to him. She is then his protector, guardian, mother, confessor, pal, and provider of comfort and support, even if it comes across as derogatory curses and deprecations.

It's very difficult to treat this symbiotic—"mutually beneficial and reciprocally stimulated"—relationship, because the alcoholic is "the identified patient," and the role played by the spouse is seldom brought to light. Too often in situations just like this, the therapist is frustrated to find the wife complaining about the changes in her husband as he goes through therapy. He's no longer the same man; so she can no longer be the same woman. This upsets her expectations and she often cannot tolerate the changes. Frequently, as the husband in such a situation begins improving, his wife gets "worse." Often the wife will remove the husband from therapy, claiming that there's no improvement, that therapy isn't working, or that he's improved enough and she can take care of things from then on.

One way of handling this awkward situation, one that is becoming a more frequent method of operation for many therapists, is to insist that in such a relationship both husband and wife be seen together. Possibly the treatment program would consist of husband and wife together with the therapist or in a group of couples, and individual sessions for husband and wife alone with the therapist. In this way, the entire symbiotic relationship can be explored and the wife's role in her husband's "drinking problem" can be explored and modified. The husband must resolve his conflicts over his own dependency, must learn to depend more upon himself and to accept the nature of the interdependency he and his wife can have with each other. The wife must learn to resolve her own conflicts, explore her need to be "Big Mama" to her own husband, and learn how to involve herself in a healthy, mature, appropriate relationship of mutual interdependency with her husband. This is fairly easy to describe; to bring these changes about is exceedingly difficult.

So while we come into the world ready to enter into a very deep and involved dependency relationship—just to survive—one of the major tasks in the socialization process of each of us is to learn to become *independent*. This independence must be a matter of increasing self-reliance and autonomous decision-making. Healthy, self-actualizing adults are those who know who they are, what they can and cannot do in a realistic and appreciative way. They set realistic goals for themselves, pretty much *by* themselves, though they acknowledge freely and gladly the contributions of others in their decision-making process, and they are willing to take the consequences of their decisions. How we achieve this growing Selfhood is a difficult matter. Ideally, the process of growth from dependency to mature independency could be charted like this:

Yet there are so many things that interfere with this ideal growth: limitations in the individual person, like physical, mental, emotional, or social handicaps and deficiencies; resistance on the part of parents to let go and permit and encourage the growing independence of their child; a culture that encourages dependence and welfare mentality; and many chance or freak occurrences.

Too often parents, especially mothers, make the mistake of holding on too tightly to their children. They either overprotect them or retain control of them far past the point of the child's maturity. Some parents fasten on to their children through building in them a sense of obligation or duty to take care of their parents. In some cases, a parent can retain control "beyond the grave," by setting up conditions for inheritance. One of the best explanations for why parents will do this is not that they are selfish or cruel but are simply frightened or unthinking. To see a child grow up is to be reminded that you are growing old. To see a child become independent may mean to feel unneeded, unnecessary, worthless. In a society that encourages mothers to live for their children, many women literally "die" when their children outgrow their strong need for them anymore.

A healthy relationship to dependency is to recognize that all of us are going to be totally dependent on other people for a few things all our lives. Goods and services, love, sexual satisfaction, respect, appreciation, companionship and affection are things that we must get from others. Other activities and situations may or may not require other people, but this depends upon our own attitudes in the matter. If, for instance, a man wants to paper his living room wall, he could do it by himself. But many people enjoy the companionship of shared labor and would invite friends or relatives to help in the papering task, more for their social value than for their actual necessity in the job.

Dependency, independency, interdependency: three words with overlapping relationships. They are important to us and we must individually work out our own attitudes toward them if we are to attain some measure of significant selfhood.

Individualism: Luxury or Necessity?

The world's population is approaching four billion. The number of people making demands on you and your resources is increasing at alarming proportions. Formerly, an individual stood alone, partly out of choice, partly out of necessity. Today, time to be alone is at a premium.

Individualism is a word that puzzles many of us. We hear the cry from all sides: "Stand up for your individualism!" We also hear the word contrasted with the word *conformity*. If you see your own unique qualities, your own unique abilities and tastes no matter how much they are conditioned by culture, you are recognizing your *individuality*. As an individual, you have uniqueness and stand apart in distinctive ways from the nameless, faceless masses. Attaining this recognition is a vital task in the search for significant identity, and most of us accomplish it to some degree. Individualism, however, is a different matter, though the difference may be difficult to appreciate. Individualism is the attitude that holds individuality to be more important than sociality, group memberships. Some people, out of fear that they will lose their identity by group membership, de-emphasize any allegiance or membership in social groupings and go to dramatic extremes to emphasize their solitariness. They may disavow any need for anyone else and may even go so far as to alienate themselves completely from any relationships and become hermits or isolates. These people have made solitariness or uniqueness a new religion (cf. Ayn Rand's book, *The Virtue of Selfishness*).

Others perceive a threat in the headlong rush to join and to belong. They see it as a repudiation of individual identity. Without denying their need for others, they attempt to maintain that in addition to their group identities—the Smith boy, Mrs. Smith's oldest kid, Jim Smith's brother, employee Smith, citizen Smith, and so forth—they also have an individual identity: John T. Smith, human being. This is not individualism in the sense we've described it above. It's more an attempt at *individuation,* at saying that a person is *many* things, that he has several identities, and that he doesn't want to lose his personal identity in the group push. Carl Jung makes individuation the goal of his form of therapy.

Individualism, when it takes the form of denial of sociality, of standing alone and often against the masses, when it ignores the needs

and rights of others, *is* a luxury. It's a selfish attitude that leaves the person out of the important social roles he can and must play. It cheats him of the benefits of being a full member of society and it cheats the society of the benefits of knowing him and interacting with him.

Conformity, the process of submerging some desires and wishes for the sake of a larger benefit, is often a necessary act. Yet, some people actually lose their personal identity by overconforming to group norms and behaviors. Some of these people *want* to lose it; others find it taken away. However, it's important to remember that there may be some benefits coming to a person from participation in certain conforming behaviors, even though those benefits may at times be hard to see. A person who gives up most of his personal preferences and consistently "goes along with the crowd" may very well be meeting a greater need, like being accepted or avoiding rejection. People still tend to do what meets their important needs.

Self-actualization is a process of discovering important needs and goals, both personal and social, and finding creative and enjoyable ways of meeting these needs, of reaching these goals, so that the individual is fulfilled and able to feel significant, without taking away the same satisfactions from any other person. "I am," says Albert Schweitzer, "life affirming itself in the midst of other lives affirming themselves."

If we were driven by instincts alone, we would meet only our personal needs, heedless and unresponsive to those around us. But because of having the higher centers of the brain, the massive network of thinking and learning we call the cerebral cortex, the sensitive and aware person will always experience a tension between personal needs and group needs. This is the agony and the ecstasy of being a human being. This is the struggle for significant selfhood. But as one anonymous thinker put it: "I'd rather be a man in pain than a cabbage in ecstasy!"

Summary

The human social experience plays a vital part in the discovery and development of our feelings of significance. We are intimately involved, each of us, with four separate (but overlapping) environments: *prenatal, physical, social,* and *cultural.* The Gestalt psychologists have shown us the need for a complete and holistic view of person-interacting-with-environment. Our social experiences provide us with a whole host of positions in the social structure (called *statuses*) and definite expected behaviors (called *roles*) that go with them. In addition, we are given a set of rules or limitations that are placed on our personal and social behavior. These become quite confusing at times!

Our selfhood is complicated by our social interactions and interconnections. Among the social processes that aid and hinder us are *cooperation, competition,* and *conflict. Dependence* and *independence,* two more important elements of human biosocial nature, must be integral elements of what significant Selfhood is all about. Finally, we must distinguish between *individualism,* the divisive and often dangerous notion that we are unrelated to each other, that we stand alone— and often against the other—and *individuation,* the Jungian concept that says we must find our uniqueness, our personal identity, or self, and see it as part of a larger Self, thus giving us a global consciousness, a sense of unity with all of life.

Suggested Readings:

Ardrey, Robert. *The Social Contract.* New York: Dell, 1974.

_____. *The Territorial Imperative.* New York: Atheneum Press, 1966.

Brennecke, John, and Robert G. Amick. *Psychology and Human Experience.* Beverly Hills, California: Glencoe Press, 1974.

Buber, Martin. *I and Thou.* New York: Charles Scribner's Sons, 1958.

Darwin, Charles. *The Descent of Man.* New York: Modern Library, 1949; first published in 1871.

Eitzen, D. Stanley. *Social Structure and Social Problems in America.* Boston: Allyn and Bacon, Inc., 1974.

Erikson, Erik. *Childhood and Society.* New York: W. W. Norton & Co., Inc., 1950, 2nd Ed.

Fromm, Erich. *The Art of Loving.* New York: Harper & Row, 1956.

Glass, John, and John Staude. *Humanistic Society.* Pacific Palisades, California: Goodyear Publishing Co., 1972.

Hill, A. David, et al., eds. *The Quality of Life in America.* New York: Holt, Rinehart and Winston, 1973.

Kluckhohn, Clyde; H. A. Murray; and E. Schneider, eds. *Personality in Nature, Society, and Culture.* 2nd Ed. New York: Alfred A. Knopf, 1953.

Kropotkin, Prince Pëtr. *Mutual Aid.* Boston: Porter Sargent, 1955.

Lask, Angela, and R. Roe, eds. *This Is a Sociology Reader.* San Francisco: Rinehart Press, 1973.

Levy, Ronald B. *Self-Revelation Through Relationships.* Englewood Cliffs, New Jersey: Prentice-Hall, Inc., 1972.

Lorenz, Konrad. *On Aggression.* New York: Harcourt, Brace & World, 1966.

McNeil, Elton B. *Being Human.* San Francisco: Canfield Press, 1973.

Montagu, Ashley. *Darwin, Competition, and Cooperation.* New York: Schuman, 1952.

_____. *On Being Human.* New York: Hawthorne Books, Inc., 1966.

_____. *The Biosocial Nature of Man.* New York: Grove Press, Evergreen Original, 1956.

Morris, Desmond. *The Naked Ape.* New York: McGraw-Hill, 1967.

Rand, Ayn. *Anthem.* New York: The New American Library, 1961.

_____. *The Virtue of Selfishness: A New Concept of Egoism.* New York: Signet, 1965.

Schutz, William C. *Here Comes Everybody.* Harrow Books, New York: Harper & Row, 1972.

6 As Ye Sow, So Shall Ye Reap

Then a ploughman said, Speak to us
of Work.
And he answered, saying:
You work that you may keep pace
with the earth and the soul of
the earth.

. . . .

Always you have been told that work is
a curse and labour a misfortune.
But I say to you that when you
work you fulfill a part of earth's
furthest dream, assigned to you
when that dream was born, . . .

. . . .

Work is love made visible.
And if you cannot work with love but
only with distaste, it is better
that you should leave your work
and sit at the gate of the
temple and take alms of those
who work with joy.

KAHLIL GIBRAN
The Prophet[1]

1. Kahlil Gibran, *The Prophet* (New York: Alfred A. Knopf, Inc., 1967), pp. 25–28, selected.

This chapter is about many things: work, productivity, labor, creativity, and "blood, sweat, and tears." It's also basically about *responsibility*. There are conflicting views being bandied about these days concerning work and labor. As human beings in the process of finding out the most about ourselves and acting on that insight, we have a definite obligation to understand this important area of human experience.

The quotation from Gibran's *The Prophet* sounds on the surface like the typical "party-line" most of us have heard from the cradle to the grave: a responsible person is one who does his work and does it well. This viewpoint is in keeping with the Protestant (or Puritan) ethic. According to Gibran, work is far more than just a system devised by economists or managers to keep things going. It's a part of the very nature of things, just as the earth turns. Too often we find work to be a chore, a burden, an unpleasant thing to be avoided. Nonetheless there are important implications in Gibran's words. It is as natural for us to take part in the responsibilities of life as it is to breathe.

Why do we often find ourselves unable to appreciate the "beauty and glory" of work? Why is it that even the most glamorous and stimulating work can at times seem like drudgery? Is it because we are basically lazy? Is it because we consider work to be foreign to our nature, foreign to our desire to seek pleasure and avoid pain? We feel that leftover vestiges of the work-sin ethic and the loss of personal significance resulting from increased technology are responsible for some people's increasingly negative attitudes toward work.

The Work-Sin Ethic

The system of thought and action called work-sin ethic is the underlying philosophy of the capitalistic economy of the United States and most nations in Western civilization. It deserves some attention.

Oddly enough, a cursory exploration of this system takes us into the realm of theology and Christian church history. One of the ultimate strivings we surveyed in chapter two concerned the search for perfection. Based on the Old Testament account of the fall of man ("In Adam's Fall we sinned all," says a colonial proverb), a strong notion grew up in medieval times that man should seek salvation and thus restore himself to Adam's original perfection. By the fifteenth century, secular affairs—economics, wars, feudal estates, monarchies, art—had become heavily entrenched in European life and the church found itself no longer the monolithic leader in the lives of the people. The Renaissance opened people's minds to the idea that they might be not just animals but fallen angels. They also possessed abilities and could enjoy the fruits of achievement.

The Protestant Reformation, usually credited to Martin Luther in 1517, added to the disunity of the Catholic world. Not only were secular affairs interfering with spiritual strivings, but nationalistic power plays broke up the "one world" that had been led by the church of Rome since the fifth century. Further, Luther told people that no amount of good works would save their souls; it required only a simple faith in God. One of those directly influenced by Luther was a Swiss reformer by the name of John Calvin. The Evangelical, Reformed, Dutch Reformed, and Presbyterian churches are all direct-line heirs of Calvin; American and European capitalism owes much of its widespread development to Calvinist theology.

Calvin had a unique theological system. It insisted that the paternal God of Luther was unrealistic. The stern, autocratic God of the Old Testament was truer. This God had determined—predestined—before the beginning of time just who would be saved and who would be damned. "Working out" salvation by Catholic means and "believing" it by Lutheran faith were both futile. Only the grace of God was involved, nothing done by a person. So, there were the "elect" and the "damned."

Calvin met the desperate queries of his followers by saying that the elect knew intuitively of their foreordained salvation, just as the damned knew of their lostness. Furthermore, said Calvin, the elect must participate in the affairs of this world. Thus, he gave the concept of work as a vocation a theological base. *Vocation* comes from a Latin word meaning "calling," and the term is still used when Roman Catholic clergy speak of their work as their vocation.

This set of beliefs aided the economic system in Switzerland and, as it spread into Germany, did much to reinforce economic forces there. Calvin had told people that one sign that a man was one of the elect of God was his success in this life. Similarly, the damned were the failures on earth. In fairness, the economists and historians do not blame Calvin himself for this interpretation so much as they do his secular followers.

Economic success, then, came to be viewed as direct evidence of the hard work, sacrifice, and self-denial found among good servants of God. The Calvinist theology found its way into the lives of the people we call Puritans. The takeover of Puritanism in Europe is a bleak, cold period of history, where art, literature, decoration and beauty were sacrificed to the harsh dictates of the stern religious teachings. The Puritan emphasized sacrifice, hard work, ambition in work and social position, temperance, and worship.

The Puritans made their way to the new world, and the colonial period of American history is a continual study in the gray, harsh, rigid life pattern we still refer to as Puritanism. It was in this period that children were taught that "the devil finds work for idle hands."

Play was not only a luxury but a sin. Work was man's highest virtue, and the man who got up before the sun and worked until he dropped, having little or no time for relaxation, creative avocations, play, or leisure-time pursuits, was the hero of colonial times. Even children were included. From the time she could hold a needle, a young colonial girl had to sew. She learned her lessons and her morality by stitching the samplers many people today collect as relics and antiques.

Carving out a new Europe in the hostile, forbidding colonies was considered by many to be a new Crusade. Setting up churches and converting the pagan aborigines was God's will, the colonial theology insisted. Only incidentally were the economic exploitations acknowledged. They were justified, when someone brought them up, on evangelical grounds. Colonialism was conceived (and has been interpreted by historians ever since) as part of a God-inspired program for proving the hardihood of his elect, for enlarging his churches' membership, and as The Great Adventure.

During this time the concept of work grew into an enlarged version of the theological notion of vocation. Work became the privilege of the elect, since it provided opportunities to demonstrate salvation through economic success and achievement. Even for those who weren't too sure they were elected, there were the examples and lessons of the successful for them to follow. Workers were told not to despair if success eluded them; it was sure to be just around the corner.

Even for those who drifted away from the religious teachings of the Puritan leaders—and to do so too dramatically was to court the charge of witchcraft and heresy—the *divinity of work* persisted in their thinking. Work was considered noble and godly. The morality of the times developed alongside this perception. Good people worked hard and steadily and bad people were idle or unemployed. Many of the so-called blue laws, still on law books in many eastern states, made it a crime to engage in any kind of recreation or frivolity on Sunday. Sunday for the religious was the day for worship, not just for an hour in the morning, but by Bible reading during the afternoon and church attendance in the evening. Sunday for the less religious was a day of rest, deserved by the hardworking, and given some biblical justification by the verse in Genesis telling how God had rested on the seventh day after six days of hard work creating the world.

We are heirs to this Puritan tradition, called the *Protestant* or *Puritan ethic* by historians and economists. It gives all virtue to hard work, ambition, thrift, temperance, and personal piety. Since many of those who follow this philosophy are in no way connected with Puritan religions, we prefer the newer labeling, the *work-sin ethic.*

Partly due to its religious background and partly due to its traditionally being practiced, it has taken firm hold in American life: man

must work to demonstrate his manliness and his productivity and to justify his being on earth. Not to work is to be a parasite. The analogy of a large rowboat is frequently used. Each citizen is part of the crew of this ship of state, and each one must pull his own oar if the vessel is not to founder. To stop rowing is to endanger your own and all other lives in the vessel. The choice was between working and being baggage, between being a "good" man and being a "sinful" man.

Today we see this attitude not only in older people who were chronologically closer to Puritan times, but in their children and grandchildren. We find attitudes toward work that approach a worshipful level. This ethic has, of course, resulted in a tremendous vitality and upsurge in economic productivity in this nation. It has also resulted in feelings of worthlessness and guilt in people who couldn't keep up with the pace, who couldn't produce, or who had to retire before they were ready to do so.

The Industrial Revolution in the eighteenth and nineteenth centuries brought a new crisis. In colonial times a person who was productive felt worthwhile. There was pride in work, not only because he felt he was demonstrating "goodness" but because people needed and appreciated his products. Handmade goods, like furniture, wagons, guns, homes, and clothing, were usually well made. Even today, antiques have survived this long because of the superior craftsmanship that went into their making. Suddenly, with the advent of machinery that eased the burden of work, cutting production costs and producing more units faster, the worker faced a new realization. He was no longer the producer who used tools. The worker was now the one used by the tools, the machines. In previous times the worker determined how the tool would be used. Suddenly the tool was determining the course of construction and coordination of the work.

Additionally, the mark of success shifted from the satisfaction felt by producer or consumer to the emphasis on profits. It was the merger of technology and capital that produced capitalism and made the capitalist the new leader of the society.

In addition to their animal needs, human beings have social and human needs. The need to belong is an important one, but so is the need to feel worthwhile. The artisan or independent worker suddenly became the mass producer, the tool helper, the manager of an enterprise. The sense of personal involvement and worth was being undermined. By now the theological promise of eventual salvation was a dim hope, as there were too few "successes" to encourage the worker. Also, in the industrial era the workers had little idea of the real value of their work, since they were paid by the hour or day instead of by the unit.

When a system needs to keep itself going, and the people led by the system begin to question it, the system's leadership seeks to develop new myths or ideologies to accomplish that aim. The older myth of divine election needed to be replaced subtly in the minds of the dissatisfied populace. A popular myth that has always worked to rally support from common people is the one which maintains that what's happening is helping to bring them freedom. Freedom is a banner that has appealed to people for centuries, whatever the cause or movement. In this case the myth was that industry was freeing workers from the bondage of long hours of drudgery. To that was added the myth of Social Darwinism, to convince workers of the validity of the system. We've made mention of this before, but we'll briefly sketch it again. Charles Darwin, in *The Origin of Species,* theorized that species survived because they were fittest and therefore superior. Herbert Spencer and others applied the theory also to those who lived in the economic jungle: the organizations and individuals who survived the economic competition were the most fit. Captains of industry and entrepreneurs were obviously superior because they were demonstrating the most "fitness." By extension, the worker was inferior because he wasn't an industrial giant.

Working people have had little to say about the conditions or the outcome of their labors; they have often been treated (and have been content to be treated) like children. So long as industrialists and managers have viewed workers as children, little more than animals, they have tended to treat them as such. The worker was considered to have only the "animal needs" that children were long believed to have: food, shelter, fresh air, occasional rest. Employers and entrepreneurs were willing to meet only *these* needs when they considered their workers.

There have been attempts at reform from time to time, when it became necessary to say or do something about the inequities being worked in business and industry. Industry was chided for forgetting workers' *human* needs. Managers were cautioned and counseled to remember that their employees were people with souls, with families, with rights, with something like dignity lying latent in their beings. Many reforms were brought about through the efforts of labor unions and sociologists in the early years of the twentieth century. However, many of them, as beneficial as they were, only began to do the reform work that was needed. Better wages and working conditions were significant steps forward, but just steps.

In the economic system that has been based on a view of human nature that calls the worker an "animal," there has been little consideration paid to other aspects of the laborer's humanity. When a worker's age begins to affect his stamina, endurance, speed, and productivity, the economic system calls for his retirement. Like the workhorse, even the racehorse, he is "pastured out." The average worker has long believed that he is valuable only as long as his physical body holds up to make him productive; he also believes that at retirement his value is gone.

Although we are concerned with these problems, better trained economic minds than ours have wrestled with them for years, and we feel that other aspects of the problem can be better dealt with here. The attitudes of employers toward workers can be improved through re-education in business training. Workers can be brought together with employers to better the picture they currently hold of the "boss." Sensitivity training of many kinds is being utilized with varying degrees of success in trying to improve labor-management attitudes, relations, and policy. As workers gain better education they too will gain a better picture of themselves as human beings and will not settle for being treated as animals. Increased humane treatment can produce happier and more productive workers who in turn can increase their output, making profits available for all concerned.

More importantly, the workers must gain a picture of themselves as persons who have value in more than just one aspect of their lives. Having had no choice in the matter of being born, we need a belief in our *intrinsic* worth. "Intrinsic" means basic to nature. Most of us have been raised to believe we have only *instrumental* worth, value

when we do or produce something. Humanistic psychology says that human beings are valuable simply because they are human beings. If we can cultivate that sense of worth, reinforcing it both by our treatment of others and by our attitudes toward ourselves, we will find happier, more productive, more contributing human beings.

The value of such treatment and attitude hasn't been tested only in industry or business. Promoting a sense of individual worth is basic to effective psychotherapy and counseling, to effective public education, to marriages and other love relationships, and certainly to child-rearing. People who are accepted, loved, and treated as worthwhile have a greater tendency to develop more fully in their selfhood, to engage themselves more fully in their tasks and chores, and, if production is any kind of measure, to turn out more of whatever we might like from them.

Like sexuality, work is an expression of selfhood, not a means of gaining it. Painstaking and tremendously rigorous research by Dr. Frederick Herzberg of Western Reserve University has yielded fascinating facts concerning this subject. First his researchers gained objective and statistically valid results on a survey of both job satisfaction and job dissatisfaction. Asking their subjects to describe times and events of both satisfaction and dissatisfaction on the job, they gathered a body of material which is graphically analyzed in Chart C. The factors reported for job satisfaction did *not* correlate either positively or negatively with those reported for job dissatisfaction, suggesting that job satisfaction and dissatisfaction are two separate factors. This means that the opposite of job satisfaction is *not* job dissatisfaction; it's *no*

Chart C: Statistical Comparison of Satisfiers and Dissatisfiers

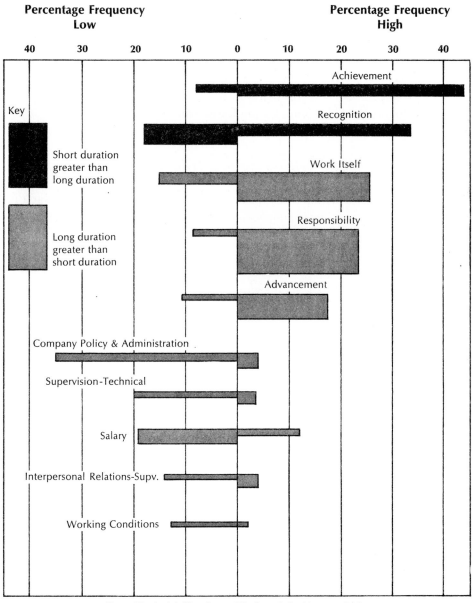

From Frederick Herzberg, *Work and the Nature of Man*
(Cleveland: The World Publishing Company, 1966), p. 73.

job satisfaction. The opposite of job dissatisfaction isn't job satisfaction, but *no job dissatisfaction.* It's like finding as we often do that happy isn't the opposite of sad: it may simply be not sad, and happiness may have nothing to do with it.

The factors that produced more or less job dissatisfaction had to do with environmental and maintenance conditions: company policy and administration, supervision, interpersonal relations, salary, and working conditions. Improvements in these areas didn't necessarily produce job satisfaction; they simply decreased *dis*satisfaction.

In terms of job satisfaction, the researchers found that factors like achievement, recognition, the work itself, responsibility, and advancement had to do with motivation and encouragement, stimulating the worker to better performance and effectiveness. Decreasing these factors didn't produce job dissatisfaction, either; it merely lessened the satisfaction.

The situations listed as producing job dissatisfaction are called by Herzberg and his associates *hygiene* factors, since the medical meaning of hygiene deals with "preventative and environmental" factors. Another term is *maintenance* factors. On the other hand the things the subjects associated with satisfaction were termed *motivator* factors.

It appears from the work of Herzberg and of several others[2] that human beings are strongly motivated to avoid unpleasant environmental factors, but rarely call such avoidance "happiness" or "satisfaction." In addition to simply reducing stress, tension, pain, discomfort, or the things aided by salary and working conditions, we seem to need what Herzberg calls motivators. Seeking growth and challenge and self-realization seems to be required to produce real satisfaction or happiness.

The work-sin ethic usually deals only with a small aspect of this problem. It tells us that if we want to avoid the pain of sin, the discomfort and guilt of being unfruitful, then we must work and work hard. Seldom does it talk about the built-in rewards of feeling good about being involved in the world's work, only about "pulling your own oar."

Schooling

Most of the readers of this book are involved in an important phase of work, gaining academic and proficiency skills for future employment and creativity. Schooling is work. There are few dissenters from this viewpoint. In addition to its often being just plain drudgery, like the carrying of buckets of water from a well and the digging of

2. F. Herzberg and R. Hamlin, "The Motivation-Hygiene Concept and Psychotherapy," *Mental Hygiene* 45 (1961).

a ditch, it qualifies as work in the sense described by Gibran at the beginning of this chapter: love made visible. This definition is possible only if you accept our concepts dealing with love (spelled out in chapter eleven), that it is a relationship of mutual regard, involving the giving and taking of aspects of selfhood, without any consequent loss of individual integrity or identity. In our opinion, schooling qualifies as love made visible under certain ideal conditions.

Schooling is not only preparation for work; it *is* work. The student who marched bravely off to kindergarten on that first big day of a school career may not recall it later, but it took a great deal of courage, determination, self-confidence (and often a push from mother) to take that first step. The child who stays with it, who is nurtured and nourished by it, who finds fulfillment of the developing aspects of selfhood, and who in turn puts much back into the schooling is a small but far from insignificant percentage of the total. Many children are discovering their schooling to be more a place to stretch and grow than a place of drudgery as it was in years past. And improvements are still being made in the educational system in order to encourage this kind of attitude in *all* children.

For many students a school represents the place where they are given facts, given a chance to exercise those facts through workbook or examination, and promoted on to challenge a larger, more complex body of facts. The process may be called schooling or anything you wish; but it is *not* education. Education comes from a Latin word, *educare*, meaning to draw out. You draw little out of a person by cramming something else in!

For far too many students schooling consists of a program of assimilating or acquiring stated and strongly reinforced viewpoints. The proper term for this is, of course, *indoctrination.* Very little of the individual's self-expression comes to the surface when he is bombarded with the single viewpoint of a particular instructor or text or orientation. Some people defend parochial instruction on the grounds that conflicting or confusing viewpoints are not presented and the child has a simpler time assimilating the facts. In Herzberg's terms, this is emphasizing hygiene or maintenance factors at the expense of motivator factors.

Schooling, if it is going to be effective in exposing individuals to the various kinds of information available, has to take into account many more needs than simply the animal ones, though it must not forget them. As animals we do need food, shelter, clothing, transportation, and other satisfactions of our physical needs, and consequently we need to acquire the necessary skills and insights to seek gainful employment. But as *human* animals we also need to seek the motivator factors, to find ways of stimulating our growth and selfhood.

Schooling needs to include information but also illumination, the means for gaining insight into selfhood and casting a brighter light on latent potentials. Schooling can and must provide illumination *for* the pupil and *within* him.

To the three Rs of readin', 'ritin', and 'rithmetic, which are very important, we could add the Rs of reality, realization, reaching-out, re-creation, response, and readiness to enjoy. Education for living ought to be the name of the game of public instruction. Not only would it then include courses that really prepared people for the world outside of school; it would include methods, situations, and experiences of reality and realization that would enable the child to test himself out on the world within the relatively protected atmosphere of the school.

A good example is in the area of vocational choice. Many children are asked in the junior high school to select a career or college major so that they can be programmed into a series of courses appropriate to their vocational choice. Nothing we know of in developmental psychology gives us confidence that children of 12 to 15 are emotionally, mentally, physically, or experientially ready to choose such an important thing as their life's work. It takes a few more years of experience with age-appropriate tasks (like fighting acne, choosing clothes, settling disputes with friends, learning to dance, and so on) before adolescents gain the kind of confidence in selfhood needed to select a vocation. Our experience in teaching and counseling has shown us that many students are not ready for final vocational selection until well into their college life. Nor is this particularly bad or tragic when it happens. Possibly arriving at graduation from college with a major you've only been into for a year or two gives you a better idea of who you are and where you're going than the person has who's been in a pattern for so long he may have forgotten to assess whether or not he's still interested in his original work choice. A job choice needs to be made on the basis of knowing pretty well who you are. A vocation will bring more satisfaction and happiness if it represents an honest reflection of personal identity.

In all situations where choices must be made, an individual *can* select those courses that are easiest, reduce stress, are most comfortable, and bring in the best money fastest. These choices would fit into Herzberg's concept of hygiene seeking. Maslow speaks of the tendencies to so choose as part of *deficiency-motivation,* wherein the individual tries primarily to acquire what he does *not* have or to be what he is not. In contrast are those who make choices that challenge their potential, that give them something to reach or stretch out for. Such choices are not always painless (nor are they always painful), nor do they guarantee salary increments or more comfortable working conditions. They are based more upon your desire to express something about yourself, to check yourself out in a new situation, to seek growth and personal achievement of your own goals. Herzberg calls this motivator seeking. Maslow speaks of it as *being-motivation,* or growth-motivation.

You can develop an idealistic and general set of attitudes about yourself that will spill over into many other areas of life, but especially into the two that even Freud recognized as most sensitive in terms of self-expression: love and work. He defined mental health roughly as being able to demonstrate a harmonious balance among ego, id, and superego through the activities of loving and working. We feel this is an important insight. In no other areas are we called upon to be more, to be more authentic, to give more, and to show more output and benefit.

The school years form the longest period of time some people will ever spend on the same job. In our culture we assume the maturing process takes until about 21 years of age. We set up laws in most states to keep children from 6 to 16 years old in school, where they are to grow physically, mentally, emotionally, and to develop the necessary skills for social interaction and some kind of career or work training. No child is ready by the time he enters school at 5, 6, or 7 to pick out a life's career work. But any child who has come from a home situation where he is loved and respected, appreciated, and involved in the life of the home is ready by this time to express some of the selfhood he's developed. In a warm accepting, integrated home, where each member is loved for himself intrinsically, where each person gives and takes according to what he's capable of, the emphasis is on the full and free development of people who are the fullest, most real, happiest people they can become.

But what of vocational choice? What if the child wants to become something other than what the parents might choose? Does the environment still support this choice?

A young man discussed with his psychology teacher the following problem. He is the son of a schoolteacher father and school counselor mother. Because both parents have masters' degrees and are intimately involved with education as a life's work, they have unthinkingly assumed that their children would follow in the same path, at least to the extent of college training.

The student is a bright young man, getting Bs in most of his subjects, with occasional As. But his best work does not come from the social science courses or the courses he might need to move on to the state college. His interest lies in cars. It began in junior high school when be bought himself a small motor scooter. He learned to take the scooter apart and do all the repair work. In high school he and his father teamed up to build a dune buggy out of the mother's old Volkswagen sedan. He has his own car now, paid for with money he earned from fixing cars for other people.

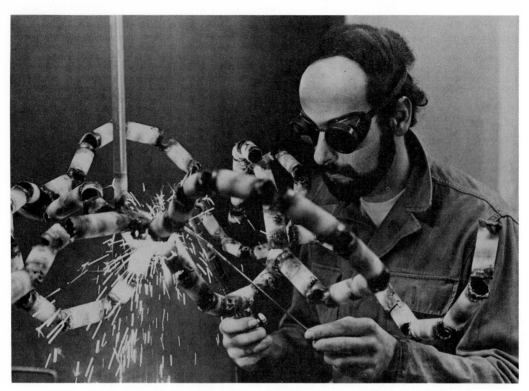

He feels strongly that he would like to drop out of junior college, go into the army, and take training in mechanics. He knows he could satisfy both his own interests *and* his parents' desires for him to be a college student if he would remain in junior college and take a number of courses in the school's fine auto mechanics program. The young man feels that this would be a compromise, since he really doesn't enjoy the other coursework nor is he particularly interested.

The psychologist noticed the student's embarrassment at saying he wasn't interested in psychology, and this prompted the teacher to push a bit further. He felt that the student was under a great burden of guilt because he did not share his parents' enthusiasm for education. That turned out to be the real problem.

In a few sessions, the student came to see that the psychology teacher was accepting him regardless of what he had said about the man's field of activity. The student gained some confidence and began to formulate plans to sit down with both parents. He told them that he loved them both as parents and as people, but that he had interests other than theirs. He appreciated all they had done for him, all the acknowledgment they had made of his interests and capabilities, but he wanted them to know that he was considering going into the army to learn mechanics.

The parents were shocked, not hurt. They had had no idea that their son's attitudes about college could be any different from theirs. They both realized that they hadn't paid too much attention to what he wanted and had merely assumed that their interest would be his.

The mother admitted she would have some trouble, because of personal pride, in accepting the fact that her son would not graduate from college, but having admitted it she realized it wasn't as important as his doing what he honestly felt was a better expression of who he was.

The father admitted that he had hoped the son would also go into teaching, but knew that the boy's interest in mechanics was more than just the hobby it was with him.

Cultural emphasis on higher education for everybody doesn't always take into account that some people cannot express their selfhood best in academic pursuits. Many people are mechanically or artistically or commercially or socially oriented. Although colleges are offering training in all these areas, some people will actually gain more from "field experience."

Another example of a supportive environment comes from the case of a young woman who had a different situation:

The girl's father was dead and she was helping to support her younger brothers and sisters. The mother worked very hard to operate a small gift and stationery store, and the girl helped her after classes, on Friday evenings, and all day Saturdays. She enjoyed the work, had a warm and open relationship with her mother, and yet was troubled. She had a boyfriend whom she had dated for over two years. They were in love and wanted to get married. But since he had received his draft notice, to marry him would mean to move and live near the base.

The mother needed the girl's help in the shop and with the children in the home, but she also knew that her daughter was a person in her own right and needed to live her own life. The mother developed a deep fear that her future son-in-law might get killed and that her daughter would be as hurt as she had been by her own husband's death. She became aware that her fears were keeping her from letting the girl go, and when she discovered this and worked it through with the help of her pastor, she was able to tell the girl to go ahead and do what she felt she must.

Of course, these are somewhat idealistic situations. Not all parents are able to see that they often try to meet their own frustrated needs through their children. But increasingly parents are learning how to be persons in their own right and to release the persons in their children. They may *hope* that their children will follow in their steps, will make them proud of them, will provide them with grandchildren and other long-term goals, but if the parents are whole persons who want their children also to be whole persons, they will have no desire to live through their children or want their children to live through them. Secondhand or vicarious experiences are never fully satisfying.

In school you typically find yourself pitted against another challenge. Since the school system, even into college, is heavily geared toward grade attainment, many students find themselves having to work for marks and transcripts. Often they would like to take subjects in which they have a real interest; but because they don't have the time to take courses outside their majors or they have to worry about their grade point average, they cheat themselves of the chance to explore and widen their range of skills. Educational institutions are only partly at fault. In stating the requirements for success and advancement, society cautions you not to play around in your schooling, but to get your diploma, certificate, or degree and get out into the working world. This attitude produces narrow specialists. As Joseph R. Royce puts it, contemporary people are faced by encapsulation: ". . . the dilemma of contemporary specialism, that is, specialism in living as well as specialism in work. . . . I mean the narrowing down of vocational tasks brought on by the industrial revolution and resulting in 20 different 'experts' making a shoe rather than one master shoemaker."[3] We have become so impressed with specialized skills, deep but narrow knowledge in one isolated area, that we've forgotten the pleasure that comes from discovering things in fields other than our own. Why do we look at the manifold achievements and involvements of Leonardo da Vinci with such wonder and awe? Here was a man who could (some would say "should") have stayed within one field and perfected himself in that area. Instead, da Vinci perfected himself as a painter, writer, scientist, inventor, and many things totally out of keeping with narrow specialism.

The problem then is one of letting education do its job. If we could permit teachers to do their best work, or works, in helping a student draw out all his hidden potentials, we would be going further in the direction of promoting and aiding self-actualization. To do so would require a wholesale change in society's attitudes if only because it would require funding and program development. The student should be able to feel his value first of all as a person, then as one interested in knowledge and learning for its own sake, and then hopefully as a person who has proficiency in one or two important areas and general knowledge in many others.

The grading problem will be a difficult one to solve. Again it would be necessary to institute a change in the attitudes of a society which thinks that competing for grades prepares the student for the competition to be faced in getting a mate, getting a job, advancing in the job, and many other facets of living. Certainly we must prepare the student for the competitive ethos in the world off campus, but

3. Joseph R. Royce, *The Encapsulated Man* (Princeton: D. Van Nostrand Co., Inc., 1964), p. 3.

that knowledge could be balanced by the recognition that selfhood, personal value, is not totally dependent on good grades.

Schooling is not only preparation for living; it is part of living. In school the student is exposed to the whole range of problems and pleasures of life. More than being a laboratory *for* life, it's a laboratory *of* living. In the microcosm of the campus are people who exemplify the employer, the employee, the husband or wife, the competitor, the helper, the protagonist, the colleague. Education is only part of life, but a very important part. Performance during this period is dependent on your individual self-concept, your picture of personhood, and the values you hold concerning yourself and life in general.

Productivity

When we think of work, whether schooling, employment, hobbies, or any kind of goal-oriented behavior, we are faced with the concept of productivity—output, results, consequences. The industrial world has some fine measures of worker productivity, usually mathematically grounded, which can point at a glance to the number of units or hours or cases dealt with by the worker. Our economic system makes these kinds of figures important, for profit and loss sheets are based upon them. But what of the individual and his own personal productivity? Maslow and others who are utilizing self-actualization theory feel that rather than judge a person's adequacy or worth in number-units of production, it is more fair, more humane, to consider the person as adequate or valuable first of all as a person. Then the person is acknowledged and the outcome or productivity of his personhood follows easily. In other words, giving you acknowledgment of your selfhood encourages you to stretch yourself, not to prove it, but to demonstrate it. You can find work or tasks or situations that give you a chance to become more of what you potentially can be.

"Day after day, trying to be the damn early bird--that's what'll get you."

The student who wanted to be a mechanic will demonstrate more of his self in mechanics, because it is an area of his own competence and interest as well as one of pleasure to him. If he had followed his parents' wishes and gone on to finish his degree, it's possible that he still could have done something of value for himself. But he might also have felt strongly that he was doing what his parents felt important, not what he himself valued. His resentment, no matter how rationalized, could have interfered with his personal effectiveness and satisfaction. It could have limited the pleasure he got from his work, and this could have stifled his productivity.

One of the interesting things we find in surveying vocational attitudes is that people who feel their work limits them (either because they didn't pick that job or because they had other competing interests) tend not to find as much satisfaction. Resentment at the limitations of work too often creates physical problems. The following is a case in point:

A young marketing major went to his physician because he couldn't seem to sleep nights. The physician found no organic problems, so he had the boy tell him about his work and schooling. The boy wanted to do well in marketing; so he studied hard and put in long hours on a part-time retail sales job.

The boy's father was a construction laborer who was semiretired because of a work accident. The boy admitted he didn't want to get stuck in his father's "bag," because it was a dead-end street. He admitted that he was somewhat ashamed of his father's lack of education and physical disability, and he compared himself unfavorably with friends whose fathers were all successful businessmen.

The boy was motivated, in other words, to succeed in business more out of need to prove something, or to exceed his father and a brother who was currently working in the same construction firm that had employed his father. The doctor asked the boy if marketing was really his interest. The boy said he really enjoyed history and wanted to teach it, but there was not enough money in teaching. He needed to succeed in a field more down to earth than teaching because his father was skeptical of academics. So he had shelved his interest in history.

His underlying feeling that he was cheating himself, that he was doing something out of a need to prove himself, to excel his father and brother, made him tremendously anxious. His anxiety was reduced by medication prescribed by the physician, who also referred him to a psychologist for counseling.

The young man remained in marketing, but he came to see that his motivations were not as pure as they might be. He learned to accept this conflict and to do something about it. He took courses in areas he enjoyed more and at one point even considered changing his major, but his student deferment would not permit it, so he stayed in marketing.

At present he is doing well in school, has a more open and honest relationship with his father, enjoys his "side" course, and has reduced his anxiety level to the point where insomnia is nearly gone.

Wouldn't this young man be better off going into history? Not necessarily. He knows he has an aptitude for it, but he also knows and appreciates his aptitude for marketing. He doesn't think he wants to teach as much as to be in business; so for him history is going to offer only avocational benefits. He still has the economic motivation that will be better met by the business world than by teaching. His output will be affected by these considerations. He is less anxious and more accepting of himself, has a better relationship with the significant people in his life, and probably will do better in business than he would in teaching history.

Maslow feels that his research points up the high productivity and creativity levels of self-actualizing people. They tend to be involved in work that demands much from them, like leadership, education, literature, and art. Because they feel so much better about themselves than the average deficiency-motivated person does, they get much more done, show much more for their efforts.

Creativity and Work

A dictionary defines "creative" as: "1) having the quality or power of creating. 2) resulting from originality of thought, expression, etc.: *creative writing.* 3) originative; productive."[4] In terms of human behavior, "creative" refers to being innovative, coming up with new or novel ideas, actions, or constructions. You are creative when you can take the already existing elements, ideas, thoughts, experiences you find in or around you and put them together in new and different ways. Inventors and artists are usually mentioned as good examples of creative people. However, they are far from being the only ones. You're creative when you discover a new way of getting to work that may save time or money or energy, or one that merely enables you to experience different things along the route. One may be extremely creative in finding new ways to get housework done or in enlisting the help of one's children. A student who tries out several study techniques and finds one that works well for her—even though she may not have invented it—is creative. In fact, it would be a rare person who has never engaged in some creative act and produced something new and valuable for at least one other individual.

4. *The Random House Dictionary of the English Language* (New York: Random House, Inc., 1967), p. 341.

What then is creativity? Is it a quality or a circumstance? Is it something you're born with or which you can develop? Is it a gift or a curse? The answers are "still in process," but the results of some studies can be used as guidelines. One study, for instance, shows us that creativity is much more a matter of potentials being unfolded or developed than being an inborn trait or gift.[5] This study found that certain people displayed higher than ordinary amounts of originality, adaptiveness, and realization, the ability to bring an original insight to full elaboration and development.

A person who is defined by himself and by others using rating scales as being creative shows several interesting traits:

Is an effective leader.

Takes an ascendant role in his relations with others.

Is persuasive; tends to win other people over to his point of view.

Is turned to for advice and reassurance.

Is efficient, capable, able to mobilize resources easily and effectively.

Is active and vigorous.

Is an expressive, ebullient person.

Seeks and enjoys aesthetic and sensuous impressions.

Is natural; free from pretense, unaffected.

Is self-reliant, independent in judgment; able to think for himself.[6]

This is but one of many lists of traits that have a high positive correlation with creative productivity.

If all people can develop creativity, and this seems to be the case, how do we foster it? What are the environmental conditions that nurture it? How is it stifled?

Creative people generally were given many opportunities for self-fulfillment as children. They were encouraged to explore, not only their physical surroundings, but their own ideas and feelings. They were given guidance and instruction when it was requested, but the initiative was seldom taken away from them except when they were in danger. For instance, one parent of an exceptionally creative and self-reliant child told us that when the girl was learning to walk, they encouraged her, helped her to stand up, set up all the conditions necessary for a successful effort, and let her go. When she started to totter or fall, neither parent rushed to catch her. They knew she would fall on a soft carpet, that there were no hard objects for her to hit, that she would learn from the falling. In the process, she also learned that she was

5. D. W. MacKinnon, "The Nature and Nurture of Creative Talent," *American Psychologist* 17 (1962):484–95.
6. R. S. Crutchfield, "Conformity and Character," *American Psychologist* 10 (1955): 191–98.

loved and paid attention to, that her right to try was freely given, and her right to fail also. She knew that she was loved for herself, not for succeeding, or in spite of failing. The same kinds of learning occurred in most tasks that she undertook.

Creativity, then, seems to have a lot to do with autonomy and self-reliance. Many studies confirm this. It also has much to do with a certain degree of nonconformity. As we've said earlier, self-actualizing nonconformity isn't "adolescent rebellion" or stubborn resistance to what is asked of a person. It is more a matter of willingness to try a different approach, deviate from the usual, easy, or traditional way of doing things. It calls for what Dr. David D. Eitzen calls "living experimentally," a willingness to run the risks of failure, of being rejected, of alienating others, and of losing one's direction. However, you may be willing to run these risks—for what in life isn't risky?—because intrinsically you have self-confidence, have known much love and acceptance, value freedom and expression, and respect yourself and therefore have courage to be.

What of those people who don't have the emotional bank account upon which to write checks for experimental living? Some can use what they do have and hope that it will get them by. Others can profit from education and example: patterning behavior on that of others and by identification and experiencing small successes adding to the bank balance. Some will require professional help. Sensitivity training

is one avenue. Encounter groups in school, church, business, or privately can be a source of great help. Psychotherapy, from simple counseling by a clergyman or school counselor to intensive ongoing psychoanalysis, may be the most effective approach.

Whatever the method, the journey is long and hard. After all, it took many years to damage or kill that creative spirit, that curiosity manifested by all healthy youngsters. But to revitalize it is well worth the effort spent. More and more people are discovering that it's not an entirely lonely quest, that their lives were empty and meaningless before the attempt. That knowledge gives them the courage and incentive to continue trying.

This sounds very much like what was said earlier about the difficulty of the search for significance. It is. Significance as a human being includes all of these things. As different as they all are, creativity, emotional richness, self-realization, courage, and meaningful experimental living are all aspects of living fully that are present in each of us in the potential sense. They are readily uncovered and developed in a few people, but in the large group they have often been discouraged, neglected, deprecated, put down, crippled, or badly damaged.

Parents often unwittingly stifle the creative impulse by the way they communicate, by the way they try to teach and instill values and skills. Never allowing a child to experiment or "do it himself" is one of the ways. Often unconsciously, parents perceive danger where danger is only remotely probable, or they attach importance to actions that from a child's viewpoint are of no consequence. Similarly, behavior that is socially unacceptable for an adult is discouraged in the young, even though that behavior (for example, playing with feces) is totally outside the social realm *in early childhood.* The advocated, even necessary, parental attitudes are nearly impossible to achieve, for they involve, as sensitive educators and psychologists will maintain, perceiving as a child perceives. About the best we can do is to strike a balance.

Nobody is going to advocate putting a child into a dangerous situation unnecessarily. But sometimes a stubborn, pertinacious child can be taught the meaning of "hot" by guiding (and controlling) his hand toward a hot oven or iron. A slight but memorable burn is often excellent protection against more dangerously "free" actions. Somehow, to strike the balance, parents must be watchful, objective, and permissive—but all to a point. Parenthood is probably the most difficult function an individual ever faces.

Creativity is fostered by encouraging children to try themselves out in a variety of tasks. Success in the task may add to their self-esteem and also provide them with a monument to their own selfhood. But failure need not be a mark of worthlessness; it can be a chance to discover where self-resources were lacking or in error. The experienced artist does not worry about messing up his canvas, since he knows both that he can correct the mess and that it shows him something about his technique.

Schooling can provide actualizing students with opportunities to try themselves out in a number of different situations. They can interact creatively with the instructor, who (we hope) responds to this kind of interchange, by the kinds of questions and answers they make, by the kinds of projects they undertake, by the kinds of papers they turn in, and by the sorts of roles they play in class and in co-curricular activities. Actualizing students can interact creatively with the subject matter through the ways they study, by the kinds of sources they use (not everything is in the encyclopedia), and by the openness with which they view the subject areas. They can interact creatively with their peers, their classmates, and with the others with whom they live and work, on and off the campus.

The commercial work scene is a lot like it's always been, but there are subtle and encouraging signs of change, of opening up, of not only permitting but encouraging workers to experience themselves more creatively, fully, and more satisfyingly in their jobs. It didn't begin with suggestion boxes, but these are a small example of this change. Conferences among employees, middle management, and employers are increasing, enabling all participants in the life of the business or the plant to give and take more openly. Employers are also finding new vitality and creativity arising from employee participation in encounter-group experiences. This isn't a panacea for all the problems people have with their work, but it indicates, at least, that some people are showing more sensitivity to the full range of human needs of everyone working together, labor and management.

Creativity is a much-needed experience in the lives not only of individuals, but of the entire society. Creative people, innovative and experimenting people, who act courageously to explore new ideas and ways of doing things, build a society that can meet changing conditions, avoid much of what Toffler calls "future shock," and become most of what that society is capable of becoming.

Attitudes toward Changes in Work

Any change can be disruptive, whether it be the death of one's wife or husband (listed among the most stressful changes) or being given a thousand-dollar raise. But because so much of our selfhood is wrapped up in our work experiences, many of us suffer the most stress and trauma when we undergo changes in our work.

Many things can force such changes. Looking around today, at the labor crises being caused by energy shortages and economic cutbacks, we have examples on every hand. In Great Britain, in early 1974, hundreds of thousands of workers were laid off as industries cut to shorter production schedules or closed down altogether. Because of fuel shortages, in America as well we've experienced the shutdown of service stations and truckers being thrown out of work.

But other changes occur and these too must be faced: slack periods when there may be little work to do, layoffs for other (often unexplained) reasons, earlier retirement, changes in work schedules, cutbacks from a 40- to a 30- or even 25-hour workweek, changes in personnel, in functions, in the organization of things on the job. The workers, whatever their levels or ranks, have to deal personally with the meaning of these changes to them, as well as with what they mean to their families and associates.

If you are working at the peak of your performance, in a job that you feel represents your own best self-concept, you then may experience such changes most severely, particularly if you've wrapped yourself up in the job to the degree that it stands for the maintenance of your self-concept. However, if you can see your job as only one among many ways of experiencing and expressing your Selfhood and your worth, then changes like this may not bring such shock.

If you lose work, get fired, are retired, these things can affect your sense of security in a world where you must maintain yourself economically. But real security doesn't reside only in your work. If you really know who you are, and accept this, you can view your work, important as it may be in meeting your economic needs, as only one way of meeting your growth or motivator needs. If you've developed confidence in yourself, have developed *many* aspects of your Selfhood, then changes don't wipe you out, emotionally or economically. This is not an idealistic statement to be making in times that are as tight economically as we know them to be. Each of us *is* more than our work, more than the tag or label or role we're playing. Of course, such recognition demands courage. Yet, as scarce as good jobs are, significant people are still accepting changes, and some are even going out to meet them.

If you put all your security eggs in the one basket of any particular activity, be it a job, a project, your wife or husband, your children, or some anticipated windfall, then you're limiting yourself and your holistic Selfhood. You must know that you are more than just a worker, an opportunity, a parent, or any one thing. You are a person, potentially and actually, who can do many things.

The problem of employee displacement by automation is one that also needs looking at in depth. Not only are workers being laid off

or retired; they are being replaced by mechanical contrivances. To lose one's job because a tool, an implement, a machine can do his work better, more cheaply, more quickly, and with less need or cost of maintenance, repair, or replacement, undermines that individual's sense of personal significance. And since automation is here to stay, the solution to the problem may lie in changes of attitudes. Counseling is being done for those who are currently being displaced, but it's costly and often comes too late in the life of the worker. Hopefully, however, the young who take their place in the working world will recognize that much of the manual labor of years past will be done by automatic means. It may mean an unfair competition for man to pit himself against machinery. Young workers need to recognize these possibilities and plan their lives around them. First of all, they must conceive of themselves in terms of their potentials. Besides being workers, they will have other interests, aptitudes, and areas of emphasis. Family, friendships, recreation and leisure, social groupings, social projects, hobbies and avocational pursuits, all must be given a fair share of time and energy.

If many of the people now being retired had developed their potentials earlier and had not been so impressed with the work-sin ethic, they could approach their retirement with anticipation. They would be coming into the time when they could shelve one aspect of their selfhood—their working status—and emphasize some of the other parts of their being. Many retired people are discovering new vitality in living as they realize that retirement does not have to mean worthlessness and death.

So many things about work and other responsible situations in life are changing, it's hard to keep up with them all. In the past several years, because of the insistence of ethnic minorities and of women, both racial and sex discrimination in employment is being overhauled. We have an enormous distance to go before full equality will be found in the field of employment, but we cannot ignore the strides that have been made. Though it is causing disruption, the legislation behind affirmative-action policies is trying to open all doors of employment to all qualified, *and qualifiable,* people.

Just this past year, women have begun working in coal mines, in heavy industry, in every branch of the military, have gained admission to formerly all-male academies and training programs. It is a time of change. And, of course, some people cannot meet these changes. Their patterns have been set so long and so hard that they resist. The movements for equal rights have made many enemies, and have hurt some of the individuals within the movements, but the gains being made seem to encourage people to keep trying for change.

A woman's role, heretofore determined not only by biology but also by the men in positions of leadership, is now being seen as not just a single role: sex object, girl friend, wife, mother, or homemaker. Biology only determines the physical structure of a woman's body and sets forth only a small number of specific roles. Each woman is potentially a childbearer, but she is also potentially anything else her brain, nervous system, and body build can allow and encourage her to become. The rest of the opportunity must come from a society, dominated by males, rigidly sexist in its philosophy and even its language.

Women in their late thirties and forties often come to psychotherapy. They come in, not because they are "sick" or "crazy," but because they feel trapped by roles laid on them by others. They feel unfulfilled, untapped in terms of their potentials. They've seen their own mothers, as the children "leave the nest," suddenly become depressed, feeling used up and worthless, and they are determined not to let this happen to them. They want to discover what else they are, in addition to wives and mothers. They want to develop some of these other potentials so that, if they are mothers, they can turn their attention to many other activities and creative endeavors once their children reach a stage of autonomy. This is self-actualization for many. It is a movement toward health. The liberation of "oppressed" women and ethnic minorities can result in the liberation of men and all those in positions of majority status.

Self-actualization requires that as we individuate, find, and develop our own Selfhood, we explore all the avenues of creativity and productivity and work that we have within us.

Summary

We work for many reasons. In *The Prophet*, Kahlil Gibran reminds us that we work to keep in step with life itself, that we make our love visible in our works. We may view work as God's punishment for sin. We may view work as the thing we do to prove we are human. We may see it as a necessary demonstration that by our good work, we are the elect of God. We may see it as "man's curse and burden."

Work of all kinds confronts us continually. Some of it is necessitated by the life-styles we have. Work is required to keep things going. In this chapter we have tried, at the risk of some idealistic attitudes toward economics, to see work as a necessary part of the cycle of living and fulfilling our existences. One oriental view has it that we work to keep death away, both in the form of starvation and mortality itself. Many work to build something that will remain behind, thus giving them some small measure of immortality. We do not say that any one of these attitudes is right or wrong. Our attitude is that we work because most of the good things that we are and that we have require it. We work not to prove our worthiness, but to demonstrate it. In the two areas of love and work we best demonstrate our selfhood. In this crucial area, in an age when technology threatens to take work away from us, it becomes necessary to recognize the importance of fulfilling and actualizing our selfhood prior to the time we begin our labors. In this way, we already have a concept of who we are, independent of whether we can do this job or that. If the labors do not present themselves, we are not diminished. We must then find other ways of experiencing our selfhood.

Suggested Readings:

Bardwick, Judith; Elizabeth Douvan; Matina Horner; and David Gutman. *Feminine Personality and Conflict.* Belmont, California: Brooks/Cole Publishing Co., 1970.

Bendix, Reinhard. *Work and Authority in Industry.* New York: John Wiley & Sons, 1956.

Brown, George I. *Human Teaching for Human Learning.* New York: The Viking Press, 1971.

Burke, J. G., ed. *The New Technology and Human Values.* Belmont, California: Wadsworth Publishing Co., Inc., 1966.

Drucker, Peter. *The Age of Discontinuity.* New York: Harper & Row, 1968.

Dubos, René. *Man Adapting.* New Haven: Yale University Press, 1965.

Eitzen, D. Stanley. *Social Structure and Social Problems in America.* Boston: Allyn and Bacon, 1973.

Fromm, Erich. *Escape From Freedom.* New York: Farrar & Rinehart, 1944.

Goodman, Paul. *Growing Up Absurd.* New York: Vintage Books, published by Random House and Alfred A. Knopf, Inc., 1960.

Gross, Bertram M. *Space-Time and Post-Industrial Society.* Syracuse, New York: Maxwell Graduate School, Syracuse University, Comparative Administration Group Occasional Paper, May 1966.

Henderson, Mary S. *Managerial Innovations of John Diebold.* Washington: The LeBaron Foundation, 1965.

Herzberg, Frederick, et al. *The Motivation to Work.* New York: John Wiley & Sons, 1959.

————. *Work and the Nature of Man.* Cleveland: The World Publishing Co., 1966.

Illich, Ivan. *Deschooling Society.* Harrow Books, New York: Harper & Row, 1972.

Kubie, L. "The Forgotten Man in Education," *Harvard Alumni Bulletin* 56 (1953–54): 349–53.

Lask, Angela, and R. Roe, editors. *This Is a Sociology Reader.* San Francisco: Rinehart Press, 1973.

Lee, Alfred M. *Multi-Valent Man.* New York: George Braziller, 1966.

Lynd, R. S. *Knowledge for What?* Princeton: Princeton University Press, 1939.

May, Rollo. *Psychology and the Human Dilemma.* New York: D. Van Nostrand Co., Inc., 1967.

Mayo, Elton. *The Social Problems of an Industrial Civilization.* Cambridge: Harvard University, Division of Research, Graduate School of Business Administration, 1945.

Mills, C. Wright. *White Collar.* New York: Oxford University Press, 1956.

Royce, Joseph R. *The Encapsulated Man.* Princeton: D. Van Nostrand Co., Inc., 1964.

Saleh, S., and J. Otis. "Sources of Job Satisfaction and Their Effects on Attitudes toward Retirement," *Journal of Industrial Psychology* 1 (1963).

Schon, Donald A. *Technology and Change.* New York: Dell Books, 1967.

Selye, Hans. *The Stress of Life.* New York: McGraw-Hill, 1956.

Tawney, R. H. *Religion and the Rise of Capitalism.* New York: New American Library, 1955.

Wernimont, P., and M. Dunnette. "Intrinsic and Extrinsic Factors in Job Satisfaction." Paper presented at Midwestern Psychological Association, St. Louis, May 1964.

Yablonsky, Lewis. *Robopaths.* Baltimore: Penguin Books, 1972.

7

All Work and No Play . . . ?

Framed in a drugstore in Beverly, Massachusetts, are these Drugstore Rules, 1854:

Store will be opened promptly at six A.M. *and remain open until nine* P.M. *the year around. Store must not be opened on the Sabbath day unless absolutely necessary and then only for a few minutes.*

Any employee who is in the habit of smoking Spanish cigars, getting shaved at a barber shop, going to dances and other places of amusement, will most surely give his employer reason to suspect his integrity and all-around honesty.

Each employee must attend Sunday school every Sunday. Men employees are given one evening a week for courting purposes, and two if they go to prayer meeting regularly. After fourteen hours of work in the store, the remaining leisure time must be spent in reading good literature.

Boston *Globe*[1]

1. Gerald Kennedy, ed., *A Second Reader's Notebook* (New York: Harper & Brothers, 1959), p. 346.

A great deal of human experience does not seem to "make sense." The rules to which the Beverly Drugstore's employees were subject may seem humorous or tragic to you. And yet, they represent not only the limited perspective once found widespread in this country, but also some of the attitudes still prevalent in our thinking about work. Theoretically, if you sleep eight hours a day and work eight hours a day, you have eight hours left in the day for something else. Also theoretically, we should have no trouble with those eight "free" hours. Yet, the simple fact is we do. Most of us have not gotten thoroughly used to the idea that leftover time is *our own!* A case in point: a colleague of ours finds his teaching day ends at noon on Fridays. He is a hard-working man who puts in more hours during the week than his contract calls for. He is always prepared for his classes, spends plenty of time in conferences with students, serves on many committees, takes paperwork home almost every evening. He earns his salary and then some! Yet, because of his upbringing (presumably under the work-sin ethic) he has a difficult time when Friday noon comes around and he finds an entire afternoon at his disposal. He confesses that he often feels like volunteering for some assignment that would fill up his Friday afternoon. He invites students to confer with him after 12 o'clock on Friday, but those who are finished with their classes at 12 head for the beach or the billiard parlor or home. They are not troubled by any such deep guilt at finding free hours.

"I Work Eight Hours . . ."

The person who rigidly works a scheduled eight hours a day for five or six days a week probably doesn't sympathize with our colleague. J. V. Langmead Casserley, in his book *The Bent World*, describes a common attitude:

> I remember hearing a bishop eloquently, and in his case sincerely, telling a working-class audience in England that he worked at least sixteen hours a day and asked for nothing better. "If I were a bishop," said one workshop foreman in the audience, "I would work sixteen hours a day, too, but eight hours of my kind of work a day is quite enough for anybody.[2]

The assumption here, more prevalent than most people might suspect, is that people who don't punch time clocks do not work. This assumption is irrational and, individual variations on work habits to the contrary, simply invalid. The dictates of individual, corporate, vocational,

2. Ibid., p. 347.

and/or social circumstances support an infinite number of work-habit variations. Nine-to-five-ism may be the lot of the majority, but this is just one more example of why occasionally the majority does *not* rule, although it might like to. Our colleague, who may work "odd" hours by a laborer's standards and "erratic" hours by most people's habitual, routinized system, does his job, earns his salary, and in comparison with many people far exceeds what is expected of him. By these modern-day standards alone, he deserves every moment of leisure he can come by. (Granted his compulsion is more complex; we hope to have him straightened out by the time this book is published!)

Very well, we are attempting to make a strong case for a life of balance. The puritan attitude of work or sin should be an object of euthanasia, allowed or helped to reach oblivion. It's an ethic that denies humanness and makes workhorses or machines out of organisms that have the potential for being something much more than that—something irreplaceable in a sense that can't be applied to any machine.

"And I Sleep Eight Hours . . ."

Of course, nearly all of us have to work. Even those whose workday is cut down to less than eight hours still devote a large part of their day to work. But the doggerel we're using as headings here says:

> I work eight hours;
> I sleep eight hours;
> I have eight hours to play!

What about sleep? No matter how much you get, your body (including all the hard-pressed nerve cells in the brain and nervous system) requires rest. There is no fixed amount, though eight hours tends to be a fairly accurate average for people in the Western world. Each individual body system determines how much rest and rehabilitation it needs in order to operate at its optimum level.

Without going into the blood-chemical mechanisms and the functioning of the reticular activating system in the brain, we can still discuss here the biological necessity for rest and sleep.

Sleep does many things for us. One obvious function of sleep is to rest the tired cells of the body. During sleep, the cells are not called upon to fire and react as much as during the average day; they go through a longer period of what we call absolute refraction. In this period they build up potentiality for future use more easily and efficiently than when they might be called on for quick reactivity with short periods of rest. Also in sleep we have the chance to escape from conscious and direct involvement with the world around us. We can shut out some of the pressures we face in a waking state.

Another definite function of sleep seems to be to give us a chance to dream. Recently, dreams have been the subject of much research, and we now know a bit more than we used to about them. Dreams seem to play a very important part in preserving our mental health. When we are dreaming we are involved in what is called rapid eye movement sleep.[3] REM sleep, as reported by Kleitman, comes right after a period of deep sleep during which no dreaming seems to take place. There may be four to six stages of REM sleep each night, lasting for only a few minutes. During this period the eyeball is actually moving underneath the closed eyelid, much as it does when it follows the ball in a tennis match.

Subjects who are awakened when the recording instruments indicate they are in REM sleep report on their dreams, but they also give evidence that they are irritated by the interruption, leading dream experts to speculate that the dreaming is very important to them.[4]

Whether we are aware of dreaming or not (and evidence suggests that we all do dream every night), sleep is an important part of our lives. We know from many studies that subjects will experience fantastic changes at all levels if they are deprived of it. Subjects who have been kept awake experimentally for long periods of time report physical sensations they don't ordinarily have. Some subjects report tingling or numbness in the limbs. Some report headaches, nausea, dizzy feelings, and soreness in muscles. Others report mental confusion. A few have experienced hallucinations and delusions. All report a lowered threshold of tolerance for various stimuli. They have less patience, less ability to stand tension, less tolerance for bothersome noises.[5] Obviously, we need sleep and we need sleep that is relatively uninterrupted. But because sleep is a function of both individual needs and cultural attitudes toward it, the amount needed varies with each individual. The *average* or the mean is generally expressed as eight hours.

If the average workday is eight hours and the average sleep time is eight hours, what do we do with the remaining eight hours a day? In many cases they are most important of all, for the person may use them in such positive ways that they not only give him enjoyment, but also enhance his work and enable sleep to come more readily.

"And I Have Eight Hours to Play!"

What do you do with the time in which you are neither working nor sleeping? If we are going to talk about fully functioning persons,

3. Kleitman, N., "Patterns of Dreaming," *Scientific American* 203 (1960):82–88.
4. Vinacke, op. cit., p. 635.
5. Clifford T. Morgan and Richard A. King, *Introduction to Psychology*, 3rd Edition (New York: McGraw-Hill Book Co., 1966), p. 654.

if we're going to emphasize that significant Selfhood means deriving the most from life that we possibly can, then we must look at the remaining eight or so hours that is left to us after sleep and work are done.

Dr. Dwight Hanawalt, a recreation educator, likes to spell the word *recreation* with a hyphen: "re-creation." He believes, as do most people in his field, that the nonwork periods of our lives need to be periods of rebuilding and restoring, reenergizing and refreshing ourselves. The re-creation experience can include *any*thing that accomplishes this for us.

Most forms of work, be it trash collecting, accounting, ditch digging, teaching, preaching, or deep-sea diving, require the expenditure of physical and psychic energy, as well as a certain amount of emotional and mental involvement. We find it hard to believe that those who knock themselves out with twelve to sixteen hours a day of hard work—of whatever kind—who only sleep and then get right back at it, can be living very full lives. Often these people carry their work home with them in one form or another, even working on it in their sleep.

There are exceptions, but in general, we think the person who is doing mainly one thing—be it work, play, sleep, lovemaking, eating, or meditating—may be forming imbalanced perspectives and attitudes. Of course, no one has the right to define your behavior or thinking as "imbalanced," but we ask that each person study his or her experiences with an appreciation for the value of balance and variety.

A good balance between work and relaxation and an appreciation of both as valuable produce harmonious operating within the physiological as well as the emotional processes of the body. The result, usually, is a more optimum performance level, but also a more "alive" and aware sense of being. This, in turn, has the effect of helping us to feel better about ourselves, others, and life in general.

This emphasis on balance and wholeness may seem conservative, even old-fashioned. Yet, it represents the best insights of humanistic people as well. *"Be Everything that you can be!"* says a current commercial. We'd also add, "Do everything you can do!"

According to some, we must choose between being only *Apollonian*—living a rationalistic, logical, well-regulated life—or only *Dionysian*—experiencing mostly emotional, ecstatic, sensory lives. Not true. You can experience *both* of these patterns, thus rounding out your full human potential. Full-functioning, to use the terms of Carl Rogers and Gordon Allport, means development in *all* the aspects of your selfhood.

"Mental health" consists of many things, but at the very least it involves *feeling good!* If you can utilize the "free" eight hours in ways that you fully enjoy without feeling guilt, you will be contributing to your own mental health. If in your spare time you can engage in activities that fully express your self-concepts, you add to your storehouse of mentally healthy attitudes. Another way of saying this is that you can make substantial deposits in your emotional bank account.

However, the work-sin ethic still prevails. Many of us seem unable to relax and enjoy or acknowledge that we might have the right to leisure time, a time which is our own, a time when nothing important *must* be done because of external commitments or pressures. There should be no obligations attached to this time. Karen Horney speaks of "the tyranny of the *ought*," and refers to the sense of duty or obligation too many of us feel to relatively unimportant matters. The man who is ashamed of his front lawn because he hasn't mowed it in two weeks may brood to the point where the pressure to remove shame interrupts his sleep, his work, his mealtimes, and any leisure time he might accumulate. We can picture this man, putting in eight long hours over a metal lathe, feet hot and tired, coming home and wanting and *needing* to lie down and nap or relax with a cool drink. Granted, homeownership carries with it the responsibilities of yardwork, but here is a hardworking man who is tired. Cutting the grass does not represent a change in labor for him as it might for the man who sits at a desk all day. The man deserves to relax his physical self or balance his exertions with mental ones. But his well-being need not be sacrificed by the tyranny of shame over an uncut lawn. It will get done when the balance of his labor habits allows. Or he can pay to have it done, or he can wait for the strong sun to kill it. By comparison with his own body needs, tall grass is unimportant.

When anything takes on a compulsive quality it defeats the purposes of real selfhood. If you say "I *must* be the best-loved person at the party," you're saying volumes about your personal loss of significance. You're likely to check yourself in every mirror and store window, just to make sure you still exist. This is a tremendous tragedy. When your work or even your play takes on compulsive tones, it defeats your humanity. You're not the one doing the work. The work is *doing* you. You aren't the one playing. The play is in control of you.

Compulsiveness is not a characteristic of a self-actualizing person or of any definition of positive mental health that is currently being used. It implies that the individual is at the mercy of an obsessive idea or thought, that he himself is not living his own life.

You can no more gain re-creation of lost or fatigued selfhood through compulsive recreation than you can relax by saying: "I *must* relax!" If you've ever had a bout of sleeplessness, you may have tried to "force" yourself to go to sleep. You lie there, telling yourself that if you don't get some sleep you won't be worth two cents at school or work tomorrow, so *get to sleep!* What do you do? Hold your breath and squeeze? Clamp your eyes shut? Turn off the thoughts? The harder you try, the less you relax, and without relaxing, sleep doesn't come.

If play or leisure time activities are forced, if they are artificial and don't come out of your own selfhood, then they are usually more work than play. What more comical—or tragic—thing than to watch someone who doesn't want to do it attempt to skate or dance or play charades or enjoy himself.

What we hope to communicate here is a sense of spontaneity and naturalness in play that cannot be forced or even planned. When the spontaneous, exuberant experiences we call "happenings" were in vogue, how ludicrous it was to attend a "happening" that someone had been *planning* for two weeks. Structured spontaneity just doesn't make it. This doesn't mean one cannot engage in planned play activities and benefit greatly from them. Planned recreation can be quite re-creative if you are doing something that really expresses your own sense of being. If you hate snow and cold and are afraid of heights and speed, then skiing, whether planned or spontaneous, is not re-creative or relaxing for you, though it can become so, with time and practice.

When attempting to structure leisure time, the lightest touch possible is required. A heavy-handed and highly structured weekend may bring you to Sunday night so exhausted and resentful that you need the following three days to rest up. Re-creation should involve whatever

it takes for you to relax, enjoy, regenerate, and discover newness in your self, even if it means simply doing something different, no matter how hard or difficult it is.

Play frightens many people, possibly because they associate play with childhood and a state they think they've outgrown. Yet, one of the beautiful insights of effective psychotherapy is that we are all children. Freud felt that the child in us is expressed by the *id* impulses. Eric Berne, in *Games People Play*, points to the fact that many of the spontaneous, impulsive, sensual, and even silly, things we do are due to the Child each of us has inside.[6] Too many of us are so impressed with the fact that we've attained adult stature that we don't want to be reminded that we ever were anything but tall, strong, self-sufficient, capable, and wise. Some of us repress every childlike thought, feeling, impulse, and desire, and thereby cheat ourselves out of some of the most pleasurable, charming, fulfilling, and exciting parts of our being. It is the Child in us that enjoys sweets, driving fast, seeing beauty, making love, and telling jokes. The Adult in us is the objective, data-processing, rational, socially conscious part. Our Adult self gets and holds jobs, carries on intelligent conversations, plans ahead, gets things done, and gets us out of burning buildings coolly and calmly. The Parent in us, which is remarkably like Freud's *superego*, tells us we are good or bad, and enables us to evaluate our performances. All three of these aspects—*including the child*—are necessary and valuable for a whole healthy person.

Play frightens, offends, embarrasses many people. Because of this, they have trouble unbending and enjoying it. The popular understanding of Freud's theories about "regression" has damaged an important part of human experience. Freud may have meant something immature or even unhealthy by "regressive" behavior—that is, when a person reverts back to an earlier form of thinking or acting when confronted by frustration or stress—but we know that the motives for doing something are far more important than what is done. If my desire to squat down on the beach and make sand castles is motivated by my desire to enjoy myself, to replay some of my childhood pleasures, is this necessarily regression? Can anyone say it is unhealthy or pathological? I hope not.

Too seldom do therapists tell patients to learn how to play. Physicians often come closer to healthy, self-actualizing prescription giving when they tell a hypertensive or sleepless patient to take up a hobby or sport to get his mind off his work and onto something relaxing. Many of these same doctors fail to take their own advice. There are high rates of hypertension, alcoholism, and ulcers among doctors and

6. Eric Berne, *Games People Play* (New York: Grove Press, Inc., 1964), pp. 23–28.

their wives. Instead of clucking our tongues and saying, "Physician, heal thyself!" we'd rather just urge the whole group to "come out and play."

Playing comes in so many different forms that it's strange that each of us can't find at least one way to play that he can accept. Even for those who believe their dignity to be at stake, there are "dignified" forms of play, like chess, reading, extension courses, swimming, polo, and spectator sports. (We question, however, whether "dignity" is the real reason for not playing.)

Of course, physical limitations that prevent active play must be respected. However, many heart patients have improved their heart conditions through judiciously supervised physical exertion. Others have found that their imposed limitations were unrealistic. Theodore Roosevelt was a fragile and sickly boy who might have been consigned to a life of sickbed activities and occasional badminton. He tested his physical potentials and discovered that his activities had been unrealistically limited. He built his body up and increased his physical health, overcame respiratory weaknesses and eventually went hunting in Africa, rushed up San Juan Hill, and literally jumped into the White House. By stretching his potential resources much further than they had been extended before, he was able to lead a far more active life than anyone had expected.

Play is re-creative because it always seems to add something to the player. It's like an investment in selfhood. Even when the play activity is physically exhausting, we feel fuller, more complete than before. It is a curious fact, since physical principles would indicate that such expenditure diminishes rather than supplements. But the play principle here is similar to the one that is applied in love relationships wherein giving produces the feeling of actually receiving. As we give ourselves over to play activities, we receive an increment in our selfhood, in our estimate of our capabilities, in our perception and regard of who we are. This regenerates, restores, reenergizes us. Thus, play is re-creative.

Playfulness in Work

One of the faults in the way most of us think is the strong tendency to dichotomize, to divide things up into mutually exclusive opposites. If work is viewed as a curse, not working is viewed as a blessing. Mainly we view work as a necessary evil and our leisure time and days off as the necessary and balancing "good." Partly because we still hold onto the work-sin ethic and partly because of this dichotomous way of thinking, play takes on the interesting character of being something earned, a reward for working so hard.

Most of us do not know how to use leisure time or play in a creative and restorative way.

For some the "reward" comes from sleeping late on days off, refusing to do anything in the way of labor, avoiding chores or tasks, and resenting people or things that interfere with just lying about the house. A few people occupy themselves with eating or drinking or smoking too much on these days off. Reward mechanisms take many forms, and for all that people may resent childish behavior, they fail to recognize that their methods of rewarding themselves and the fact that they perceive their work as rewardable at all is a childish attitude. Work in the general sense need not be such a drag as to engender this necessity to escape into activities that are merely different without necessarily being pleasant or fun. Therefore, in order to discuss attitudes toward play, we must first consider attitudes toward work as play.

There are lots of examples of work that must be considered nothing more than drudgery. But it is possible to note that there are many people who are capable of finding enjoyment, even "fun," in the most menial or tedious kinds of work. How? Possibly the answer, complex as it is, lies not in the nature of the work experience, but in the person doing the work. If you bring to your work, whether ditchdigging or macramé, a sense of personal expression, you're likely to enjoy it. To actually be able to see work as an outgrowth of selfhood makes it more enjoyable. Many people report that their work is considered a chance to demonstrate their personal sense of selfhood. They find work that enables them to test out certain skills or that gives them an opportunity to explore other, often hidden, skills. They take on new tasks, or do old tasks in new ways, because it is a form of self-expression. Any job, no matter how insignificant, becomes a challenge in some sense.

Aware people have an increasing tendency to seek out work that is meaningful to them and to their employers. Many are unwilling to take just *any* job simply to earn money or job security. They recognize that in a complex and highly varied society such as ours there are thousands of different kinds of work, with some less traditional newer jobs offering individuals new chances to explore and express their selfhood.

But how does playfulness enter into working? It can be "artificially" inserted by those who try to find aspects of the work that are enjoyable, stimulating, "fun." Or the work or the particular task may be visualized as a game. One of the advantages of playing at work is that overly self-absorbed people can learn not to take themselves quite so seriously, to be so concerned about how they are doing, how they look, what others think or feel about them that they literally sit in judgment on themselves. People who do this are demonstrating a lack of confidence or self-liking. They are too dependent on external validation of their selfhood to be in the same category with self-actualizing people.

Better than artificially creating games or play is attitude-changing. "Work" and "play" are *not* absolute polar extremes. Most jobs are situations that include relaxation and drudgery, challenge and monotony, delight and disgust, exhilaration and tedium, inspiration and irritation, fulfillment and frustration, self-satisfaction and service. The creative, self-actualizing person is capable of experiencing all of these and growing from them.

Humor

In the face of the tensions and pressures each of us faces every single day, a sense of humor is a saving grace. The ability to laugh is crucial to our fullest development, to our "mental health." If we can laugh at ourselves, we're further along the road of self-fulfillment than if we're constantly self-critical.

Paradox? Not quite. As important as it might be to stand back and evaluate myself critically at times, that must only be a periodic thing if I'm to develop a healthy self-concept. If I continually expect too much of myself, tear myself down, and am dissatisfied with anything I do, this can hardly lead to self-respect and appreciation. It's not only a great tension reliever to be able to kid yourself; it also promotes a necessary objectivity. There is a delicate balance between extremes of objectivity (when you never get involved in anything) and subjectivity (where everything is directed at you or everyone is pointing at or talking about you). Like this:

Gordon is nineteen and he's trying very hard to become a singer. He has a good voice, is a good musician, and has sung in public a number of times, doing well each time. But he's very subjective about his abilities. For instance, if his voice coach tells him to practice a particular section a few more times until he gets it right, he falls apart, absolutely certain that the coach is implying that he isn't any good and has no future in music.

He mentioned this sensitivity in a paper he wrote for a psychology class. The psychology professor called him in, ostensibly to talk about the paper, but hoping to allow the boy to open up about it. This teacher rarely tells her students what they *ought* to do, but she felt Gordon should know that such hypersensitivity would make for a miserable experience in the entertainment field, where hecklers, stage personnel, critics, and fellow performers often are very hard on new talent. She asked Gordon if he had the firm commitment to follow through in such a competitive and difficult business. He was being asked to stand back from his extreme sensitivity and evaluate some realities.

Three days later, Gordon came back to the teacher, pointed a brave finger at her, and told her she was "dead wrong" about him. Further, Gordon asked, what could she possibly know about music and the pressures of the profession? The teacher stood up and turned Gordon around, right in the middle of a sentence, telling him to continue, but to watch himself in the mirror on the back of the office door. Gordon tried to continue, pointing and gesticulating, but suddenly seeing the expression on his face as he did so.

As he rampaged on, he nervously glanced in the mirror, and turned to confront the psychologist. As he got to the phrase ". . . and I have guts enough to stick with it," he noticed a grin beginning to form on the teacher's face.

At this climax in his "tantrum," Gordon burst out laughing. He stopped his tirade and asked the teacher if he looked that ridiculous all the time. The teacher shrugged and suggested that he might want to find this out from people who spent more time with him. Gordon continued to laugh.

Gordon displayed a great deal of growth when he discovered that when he took himself so seriously he looked like the stereotype of a pompous operatic prima donna, male variety!

In other aspects of our everyday life, the ability to catch ourselves being too serious, bearing all the burdens of the world, saving the human race, helps us relieve some built-up tension through laughter.

Laughter has other uses and meanings. For some it is the tension release chosen when they recognize the futility of trying harder. For example, you may beat your head against the symbolic brick wall in trying to communicate with another individual. You may have to acknowledge that the communication may not take place with this person, or with this set of words, or in this particular time or place. If you can then laugh it off, you find yourself better equipped to experience similar frustrations and, once the tension is released, you may discover a more successful tactic.

Laughing at the misfortunes of others is sometimes a form of sadism, wherein some pleasure is gained from observing the difficulties of others. Sometimes it's an acknowledgment of how much we identify with another person and how "close a call" we've had in not being the target or object of the misfortune. "There but for the grace of God go I" is an expression frequently uttered with amusement.

Most laughter is a kind of reflex behavior that occurs when we recognize the irony in situations. For instance, we can look at the following cartoon, a strip aptly titled "The Born Loser," and see some interesting things about ourselves and the values we live by.

THE BORN LOSER By Art Sansom

Reprinted by permission of NEA.

We can ask lots of questions about this situation. Why is the character being so reflective? Is he criticizing himself in an attempt to get his wife to express her love for him? Why *did* she marry him? Why does it only now occur to her to look at the situation? Where is she going?

Life is full of little ironies like this. Humor enables us to "safely" experience them, or vicariously to go through them a second or third time. There are many incongruous things about life, too. We laugh at them partly because there may be something objectively humorous or absurd in them, but mostly because we really don't know what else to do. They are "unmanageable." We can't *do* very much to change or utilize them. Like the incongruity of environmental pollution. We construct a society that depends on industry. The industry converts raw materials into products and waste. The waste is disposed of, and it often clogs the very environment we're trying to improve. We take a fishing pole and try to get back to nature during an afternoon of fishing. But the waters are filthy and the fish are diseased or dead. When we realize the vicious circle that has brought us to it, most of us have to shake our heads and laugh at the folly of man. This point can be illustrated by the fact that various New York City newspapers not long ago suggested in all seriousness that to force the city's electric power plant to consider cutting down on its air pollution everyone in the city should, on a specified night, refuse to turn on their lights and use candles instead. Many people were in favor of this dramatic boycott but almost no one saw the absurdity of over eight million burning candles cutting down on smog—even with "smokeless" candles!

Maslow indicates that this type of humor, the acknowledging of the absurdities of human behavior, is the healthy kind of humor that the self-actualizing person experiences. He doesn't enjoy the hostile humor that laughs at cripples, minorities, or the less fortunate. "Sick" and "cruelty" jokes don't make him laugh; there is too much tragedy or sadness in them. It's in the absurd lengths to which some people carry their behavior that he finds humor.

Some laughter is hostile. Many comedians today are capable of biting satire. They select a person or a stereotype of a person and make him the butt of their humor. When we laugh at them, we make a commentary on our own feelings about the objects of the joke, or how we feel about the situation in which we live, or about ourselves. Satire has always been an effective tool for directing hostility toward a person or group. And the satirist has a certain protection or immunity from retaliatory hostility. Jonathan Swift's "children's tale," *Gulliver's Travels*, is a biting satire on the British Empire and was protected only because it was put in fictionalized form. Many people have never been aware of its original purpose. Nor are we aware of the political satire in most Mother Goose nursery rhymes we all learned as children.

If the object of satire feels the sting and is tempted to retaliate or at least get angry, the satirist's easy response is "What's the matter? Can't you take a joke?" Being able to take a joke is an example of "good sportsmanship." Pity the satirist, though. He may be a person who is unable to come out openly with his hostility and deal with it, mature person to mature person.

This is not to say that satire isn't effective in terms of social change. Many political cartoonists get their point across to politicians better than all the constituent cards and letters could ever do. But it's obvious that the satire, however subtle it may be, is meant to express some kind of hostility or resentment toward what's being depicted.

Laughter is good for our mental health. Honest joy, open amusement, pure childlike delight are all aspects of well-developed selfhood. In Eric Berne's terms, we are letting the Child in each of us "come out to play." The Adult in us is too often serious, stuffy, objective, busy with the data processing of daily existence. The Parent in us is often busy judging what we do as right or wrong, good or evil, appropriate or inappropriate. The Child, which is the remnant of simple, basic, sensual, open personhood, is vital to our fullest development. It's in the "play" activities, like sports, hobbies, art, lovemaking, eating, and dancing, that we experience this very important part of us. Each of the three—Child, Adult, and Parent—is necessary, but none more than the other. Fortunate is the person who can watch a cartoon on TV and experience it as funny (Child), entertaining and diverting (Adult), and good (Parent).

Laughter is one of the ways in which we relax and re-create the self. The things we find humorous may vary, but the experiences of humor, of pleasure, of enjoyment are extremely important and must be cultivated for the fullest experience of living.

Social Re-creation

Since we are social beings, we need other people for sheer survival from the beginning of life. Once the physiological needs are met, we cultivate needs that still involve other people. These social needs are secondary motives in the sense that they're learned, not inborn. But "secondary" is not equivalent to "unimportant" or "peripheral." Most of us are heavily involved in meeting our social needs.

We need others for love experiences. Solitary people often do not even love themselves. People who love themselves in a healthy fashion are people who also love others. In fact they are people who love widely and deeply because they have been loved—by others and then by themselves—and are in a continual cycle of reexperiencing. Erich Fromm has been criticized by traditional psychotherapists for his emphasis on self-love, which they feel is diametrically opposed to loving others. Yet, in *The Art of Loving* Fromm says explicitly that true self-love is self-respect, self-appreciation, and self-knowledge. The self-love that grasps and demands and exploits others is a false love that Fromm calls narcissism.

Real self-love enables us to involve ourselves with others, fully, deeply, real-ly, and satisfyingly for all concerned. We do not possess all the resources necessary to satisfy ourselves. For supplementation we have to go to another person. It's this realization that makes social intercourse, and certainly sexual intercourse, possible. We often find ourselves in the situation of experiencing emptiness or shallowness. We may have been too long alone with our own thoughts or feelings. We may have had too limited a social situation, knowing and experiencing a too limited or small group of "others." At times we find it necessary to replenish our supply of social feeling or social interest. It's at these times that we are strongly pushed or pulled toward other people, new people, or familiar people in differing or new circumstances.

At times professional people find the company of colleagues to be tiring or uninspiring and are refreshed or stimulated by enjoying a meal or conversation with persons from other disciplines and academic levels. For those who may view this as "using" other people, we would clarify. We all "use" other people: we pick their minds, we ask their opinions, we ask them to appraise our work, our looks, our ideas; we curry their favor. They, in turn, use us, for the same kinds of things. This is simply wholesome, cooperative interaction. There is also "abuse." A synonym for it is *exploitation:* to take advantage, uncaringly, of another person. Slavery is an obvious example, but far more subtle examples occur every day whenever someone "takes" something from another and does not give much back. Think of the adulation a movie star may "take" from a fan, without really giving much back.

Psychotherapists often "take" from their patients the good feelings they have to give, and often don't give the patient something in return. This doesn't happen often, but there are good cases in point. Many therapists feel pleasure at the "godlike" role into which their patients put them, and a few succumb to this and allow the patients to literally worship their every word, their very being. Then the patient gets very little that is real in return.

When a healthy, self-actualizing individual goes to another person, it's because he has a strong need for the presence and fellowship of that person. If he gets something from the involvement, he usually gives as much back as he gets. No contract is signed, no concern that the dividends will be absolutely equal to the investment. Between two people in the love that friends or lovers have there is no worry or greed. It's a continual round of sharing. When this happens, re-creation of each person takes place. It's again like the *yang* and *yin* symbols of Taoist thought: two complementary halves making up an integrated whole.

Love is a re-freshment. It's a time and opportunity for newness and rebirth. There is so much to be gained from giving in the shared love relationship, not the least of which is a growth of selfhood and of social feeling. "One good turn deserves another" is a way of saying that when you have experienced the growth and wholeness that comes from being deeply involved with another human being, you want to repeat the experience, time and time again. This feeling has been reported by many people as a phenomenon of any wholesome, satisfying social interaction and certainly seems to demonstrate the necessity of frequent and rewarding social contacts.

Simple contacts like casual conversation with strangers apparently also have a beneficial and growth-producing effect. How many people get deeply involved in conversations with perfect strangers! Taxi drivers, fellow drinkers at bars, bartenders, waiters, newsstand dealers, door-to-door salesmen are often asked to be sounding boards or to talk with people, are literally invited into the lives of lonely people. It appears that there is a great hunger for human companionship or for listeners. A few years ago, a group of New York City bartenders asked a psychotherapist to give them lessons in simple counseling because they were so often put into the role of counselor by their customers. The therapist

reasoned that there might be some therapeutic advantage in helping these men to be effective listeners.

The social experience is rewarding and regenerating because we know—whether we fully acknowledge it or not—that there are strong ties among all human beings. Rugged individualists, cynical loners, bitter hermits may deny it, but most of us are more than willing to acknowledge that we feel a sense of kinship with other people, a fellow feeling with all of humankind, which is more like saying that all *Homo sapiens* are in the same boat. Some individuals identify so strongly with others that they empathically experience sorrow with those in dire circumstances and joy with their happier friends. All of these experiences of empathy are growth-producing. Cultivating a strong feeling of kinship adds to a personal sense of fulfillment and worth. In German, the word is *Gemeinschaftsgefühl.* It means "feeling-sense of community," in a poor literal translation. Social interest or sense of community with others is based on feelings of worth and is aided by growth-producing interaction with other people. It's a very productive and satisfying circle: from satisfying self-feeling to satisfying group feeling back to satisfaction with one's selfhood.

One of the best expressions of the importance of human social interaction is from Endleman's fascinating work, *Personality and Social Life:*

> Man is a creature and creator of man. Come into the world a mewling helpless little animal, driven by diffuse strivings of a peculiar body, he is totally dependent on human warmth and care to survive and be. At once he is enmeshed in social life, at once begins to learn and share in culture. Dualities and paradox pervade his life: instincts and culture, the separate being and the vital social ties, the truly felt and the way to be, uniqueness of oneself and the sameness with all mankind. . . . We are vastly various and laughably alike. . . . Helpless yet vastly powerful, driven by irrational passions yet open to gigantic rationality, able at Olympian detachment and prone as well to boundaryless immersion in depths of oceanic feeling, of oneness with the herd or with ineffable mysteries of the universe—all of these is man. . . . Bodily female or bodily male, a part of oneself is the other sex, or no sex at all. The world of others, one's ties with them, are ordered and chaotic both. . . .
>
> Man becomes a human personality only through the joys and pains of human contact, care and giving and taking, and only through learning the ways of that small portion of mankind that is his tribe or community or nation at a particular time in history. . . .[7]

Our need for others may at times be *compulsive* (where we are driven by needs or motives we can hardly control) or *impulsive* (as

7. Robert Endleman, *Personality and Social Life* (New York: Random House, 1967), pp. 3–4.

when a spur-of-the-moment sensation allows or unleashes certain be-haviors). We may plan our social involvements or we may just enjoy them as "happenings." The very fact that every culture ever studied has had to make a place for social intercourse gives us some appreciation for just how universal this behavior must be. The hermit, the lone wolf, the isolate, the alienated: these are the exceptions. We must assume that some painful interaction has caused their solitary behavior to become a way of life.

So we go out from our own centers of being to touch the beings of others, partly to reassure ourselves of our sameness, our bonds of likeness, and partly to restore some of the social feelings we lose in our work or play or states of fear. It takes a drastic or traumatic series of events to convince us that it's unsafe or unwise to seek out others. It seems unlikely that any one event could sever our ties with the rest of mankind. No single trauma or hurt can drive us away from each other. It must require dozens of intensely painful and frightening expe-riences of rejection to develop a hermit or a social isolate.

In our social interaction, then, is a play element. We use the social experiences to re-create aspects of our selfhood that we have lost, or that have become fatigued, or which we doubt. We go to another person to gain validation of our own selfhood, whether in conversation, love, affection, sexuality, argumentation, nurturance, punishment, or compe-tition. We play games with these people, not just to structure our time or keep them away from intimate knowledge of us, but to get them to declare something about us. In challenging someone to a game of chess or tag or political discussion, we hope that they will see in us some element of worth or challenge to which they can respond. Their response is a statement that we are worthy of their time and effort. It is a form of "stroking," or social response, to use Eric Berne's terms:

> "Stroking" may be used as a general term for intimate physical contact; in practice it may take various forms. Some people literally stroke an infant; others hug or pat it, while some people pinch it playfully or flip it with a fingertip. These all have their analogues in conversation, so that it seems one might predict how an individual would handle a baby by listening to him talk. By an extension of meaning, "stroking" may be employed colloquially to denote any act implying recognition of another's presence. Hence a *stroke* may be used as the fundamental unit of social action. An exchange of strokes constitutes a *transaction*, which is the unit of social intercourse.[8]

Each time we are "acknowledged" or "recognized" by another person it is as though we are being "patted" or told, "Yes, I know you are

8. Berne, op. cit., p. 15.

there and I acknowledge your being." You may think this is overdrawn, but then you might recall times when some people literally "looked right through you" and how you felt then. You may have had the eerie sensation of doubting that you were visible. You may have even felt diminished as a person, no matter who the other person was. If you're ignored or "looked through," it has the effect, whatever your ego strength, of making you feel smaller, less important, insignificant. That's how important other people are to us. You know how effective silence or nonhearing of a person's words can be in putting him down. If you agree or disagree with him, you have given him a "stroke." You have at least acknowledged his presence. But by not responding, or not hearing him, you say, in effect, "You're not even there!"

On the more positive side, other people do add to our dimensions of selfhood and in wholesome social intercourse this is a mutual, reciprocal event. We validate each other's existences. Though this is not necessary all of the time, it seems to be important for all of us at some time.

Personal or Solitary Re-creation

No matter how urgent our social needs are, all of us have needs for solitude, for times alone with ourselves. Again, the optimum selfhood experience includes a balance of solitariness, sociality, and peripheral interaction ("spectatorship").

The need for privacy and time alone isn't so much a rejection or repudiation of others as it is a need to go within, to get acquainted or reacquainted with our selfhood. We like to roam about our own house with no one to disturb us.

We can get next to our own within in sleep, in church, or in solitary walks in the country. Or we can attempt to commune with the universe. This is not a mystical experience in the Indian or drug-connected sense. It is more like a periodic need to "get back to natural roots." Sitting on the top of a mountain, watching the sun come up or go down, is a commonly favored method. Watching the sea from a seaside cliff, wading in the stream high in the mountains are other ways.

What is behind this need? Maybe at times we do get tired of other people—their opinions, their conversations, their directives. Or perhaps we tire of the necessity of relating to others. When this happens, we need to move out of the other-directed circle into the area of solitary or innerdirected thinking, feeling, and doing and reassure ourselves that we *have* something or *are* someone. Those who are able to move within know themselves to be significant and feel that they have a right to solitary experiences. They don't feel lonely when alone and actually feel their own company to be very congenial.

In early childhood, our first play experiences are solitary. We discover the pleasures of fingers and toes, of blocks and dolls, and we enjoy using newfound coordination to manipulate toys or the physical environment. We are engrossed with the involvement and seldom experience loneliness of those times. Next comes parallel play, where we still play by ourselves but alongside others, with minimal social interaction. Then we learn to play cooperatively, and sharing and exchanging and bargaining become important parts of our social experience. This evolution from solitary to parallel to cooperative play is not a matter of discarding one form for another. The entire history of an evolution is invariably present in the optimum development. Just as Berne and Misseldine insist that we all retain the Child as well as the Adult and the Parent, the need to play or be solitary is present along with the needs for parallel and cooperative experiences.

Many people can't be alone. For them, to be alone is to be lonely, isolated, exiled. They have no inner resources upon which to draw or which they can enjoy. When they are by themselves, they are literally *alone:* no one is there! This is a tragedy. These are the people who are compulsive about their social activity: they must be around others; they must have the opinions and the regard of others. These same people have no ideas or suggestions or direction of their own. Ask them what they are going to do for fun that night and they are just as likely to ask you what you're going to do and say, "I think that's a good idea. Mind if I join you?" Unable to count on themselves, they are devoid of positive self-esteem. A psychiatric designation for many of these people is *inadequate personality.* They have trouble getting or holding jobs, making and keeping friends, giving or accepting love.

But for the self-actualizing person, there are many times in his varied life experiences when he enjoys getting off by himself, to explore his root relationships with nature or to find out more about himself. He is able to experience newness and refreshment from these times. They re-create in him a sense of personal appreciation.

These times of solitary experiencing can do other re-creative things for us. We can experience our own physical being. Most of us have grown away from the sheer enjoyment of our physical bodies, and solitary self-experiencing puts us into direct communion with our physical nature. Whether we are sailing alone over the ocean or walking through the park, we become increasingly conscious of our bodies. Sailing, for instance, demands continual vigilance and the body becomes attuned to the slightest change in wind or the tension of the sheet or tiller. At a time like this we are dramatically reminded that the body is more than a container for vital organs.

The body-consciousness experience helps us to regain the understanding of just how deeply rooted we are in nature. It also helps us to see how important body functioning is to the functioning of everything else we do. We become aware that the body is capable of communicating its needs and desires to our mental consciousness and that we should learn how to pay more attention to this communication.[9]

9. W. Schutz, *Joy: Expanding Human Awareness* (New York: Grove Press, 1969).

How many times, when you are with others, do you get the message that you are tired, and yet ignore it. You feel it's rude to yawn or excuse yourself to go to bed, though this is precisely what your body and your knowledge are telling you to do. In times of solitary experiencing, you get back to holistic experiencing and sleep when you are sleepy, eat when you are hungry, walk when you are restless, rest when you are tired, and do things more "naturally." Afterward, your entire being is refreshed and more in tune. Why we don't take these clues more often to heart is one of the mysteries of cognitive life.

Another thing that solitude does for us is to give us more experience with the unconscious. We can enjoy our fantasies, our daydreams, our nightdreams. In our imaginations we can do or be anything we wish. And again, exploring our imaginations and the nature of our wishes and fantasies is an excellent way of discovering the reality that is our own being. The dividing wall between reality and fantasy is not as essential and impenetrable as superrealists would have us believe. Many psychologists know that a self-actualizing, mentally healthy individual is often one who is highly skilled at leaping back and forth over the wall. But make no mistake: he knows the wall is there, which side he's on, and how to get to the other side.

Fantasy has definite self-syntonic or beneficial aspects to it, just as dreams apparently have. We know too that much creativity is fostered by the imagination. Giving the fantasy life a free rein at times may be a very healthy, even "fun," experience for everyone; for the creative artist, it is a prime requisite for continued existence.

> Man is the most social of animals—out of desperate need and exuberant play. As they grow up, other mammals unlearn to play—man never does. In this, he is ever an infantilized ape—and one capable of a maturity of such richness, depth, and complexity as no other mammals can attain. Play, even in its most complex and esoteric manifestations—the brilliant leaps of the scientist reconstructing the universe, the soaring poetry of the creative artist, the fabulous beguilements of the master confidence man—draws ever from and ever renews the great and inexhaustible forces of the unconscious, linking man to his evolutionary past, projecting him into a future ever changing yet ever the same, and also lifting him beneficently out of the stream of time altogether into the joy of an unbounded *now* of total absorption. . . .
>
> Play can be found in, and thus confound, all of its supposed antitheses. It isn't work? But work can be the highest play, for the scientists we have seen through Roe, the artists through Schneider, the shaman through Roheim, the comic through Lenny Bruce, and any man who loves the tasks that bring his daily bread.[10]

10. Endleman, op. cit., pp. 415–16.

Summary

Re-creation and play, whether solitary or social, are essential and natural aspects of human experience. They have been de-emphasized or ignored in the past because we have never been too certain that they were "right," partly because of the work-sin ethic and partly because we couldn't put their benefits down on a balance sheet or productivity chart. From recent literature, clinical and laboratory studies, and our own personal experiences, we have been able to infer the existence of some survival value in these lighter experiences, like humor, pleasure, play, and laughter, because they have counterparts in every culture. In addition to mere survival value, they play a vital part in enhancing and enriching human experience. A healthy personality is one that is capable of experiencing the full range of human emotions and seeking out a full range of human experiences. Play, laughter, humor, and leisure-time activities are re-creational: they enable us to re-create and replenish the exhausted "stores" of human strength and self-respect.

Suggested Readings:

Berne, Eric. *Games People Play.* New York: Grove Press, 1964.

Caillois, R. *Man, Play, and Games.* New York: Free Press of Glencoe, 1961.

Denney, Reuel. *The Astonished Muse.* Chicago: University of Chicago, 1959.

Endleman, Robert. *Personality and Social Life.* New York: Random House, 1967.

Fromm, Erich. *The Art of Loving.* New York: Harper Colophon Books, 1956.

Hartman, E., ed. *Sleep and Dreaming.* New York: International Psychiatry Clinics, Vol. 7, No. 2, 1970.

Huizenga, J. *Homo Ludens: The Play Element in Culture.* Boston: Beacon Books, 1955.

Kleitman, N. "Patterns of Dreaming." *Scientific American* 203 (1960):82–88.

Larrabee, E., and R. Meyersohn, eds. *Mass Leisure.* Glencoe, Illinois: Free Press of Glencoe, 1958.

Maharishi Mahesh Yogi. *Transcendental Meditation.* Signet Books. New York: New American Library, 1968.

Missildine, Hugh. *Your Inner Child of the Past.* New York: Simon & Schuster, Inc., 1963.

Murray, E. J. *Sleep, Dreams, and Arousal.* New York: Appleton-Century-Crofts, 1965.

Neumann, E. *Art and the Creative Unconscious.* New York: Harper & Row, 1966.

Riesman, David; N. Glazer; and R. Denney. *The Lonely Crowd.* New Haven: Yale University Press, 1950.

Schneider, D. E. *The Psychoanalyst and the Artist.* New York: International Universities Press, 1950. Mentor Ed., New American Library, 1962.

Wolfenstein, Martha. "The Emergence of Fun Morality," *Journal of Social Issues* VII (1951):4, 15–25.

8

Beyond Fun and Games

The individual has many potential selves. He carries around with him the capacity to define himself as warm or cold, dominant or submissive, sexy or plain. The social conditions around him help determine which of these options are evoked.

KENNETH J. GERGEN[1]

To us, the man who adores the Negro is as "sick" as the man who abominates him. Conversely, the black man who wants to turn his race white is as miserable as he who preaches hatred for the whites. . . . The white man is sealed in his whiteness, the black man in his blackness. . . . How do we extricate ourselves?

FRANTZ FANON[2]

The important point is not that the role of homemaker is necessarily inferior, but rather that our society is managing to consign a large segment of its population to the role of homemaker— with or without a dead-end job—solely on the basis of sex, just as inexorably as it has in the past consigned the individual with a black skin to the role of janitor or domestic.

SANDRA L. BEM
AND DARYL J. BEM[3]

1. "Multiple Identity," in *Psychology Today,* May 1972.
2. *Black Skin, White Masks* (New York: Grove Press, 1967).
3. "Homogenizing the American Woman," in P. Zimbardo & C. Maslach, *Psychology for our times* (Glenview, Illinois: Scott, Foresman, 1973).

Fun and games: we wish it were all so simple. We could wish, with many of you, that life consisted of simple rounds of work, sleep, refueling, and play. How uncomplicated! How much like the paradise so many people dream of. Yet, how unlike life as most of us know it.

We've said in the preceding chapter that many people do not know how to play. Other people *do* know how to "play"—in deadly earnest. There are games of fun and re-creation and there are the Games of deception and hostility. The former are aspects of significant and healthy Selfhood. The latter are ways of keeping yourself and other people at arm's length.

The word *Games* as we're using it, of course, comes from the work of Eric Berne and the others in the transactional analysis camp. The TA model of human interaction finds that very few people really live their lives openly, honestly, and Game-free. This is consistent with Maslow's findings that only a small minority of adults are really living self-actualizing lives.

Why is this? Why, in TA terms, are so many people convinced that they are Not-OK and that very few others are OK either? Are we missing something?

> To say that the bulk of social activity consists of playing games does not necessarily mean that it is mostly "fun" or that the parties are not seriously engaged in the relationship. . . . A game is an ongoing series of complementary ulterior transactions progressing to a well-defined, predictable outcome. . . . Every game . . . is basically dishonest, and the outcome has a dramatic, as distinct from merely exciting, quality.[4]

Now, we may begin to find clues to our dilemma. In games, in the re-creational and healthy sense (what Berne would call Pastimes or Operations), we are playing because it is fun and good for us to do so—straightforward, up-front, honest. But, in the interpersonal Games TA confronts us with, there is deceit, hidden motive, a need or desire to avoid honest and full interaction, and an aim to "get" something, not only from another person, but often at that person's expense. This ulterior goal is called a Payoff. Whereas a game of tennis or Scrabble has a payoff, too (a victory for the better or luckier player, plus a good time while doing it), the Payoff in Games is much more complex.

Virtually every person making the attempt to describe "healthy" or "normal" people lists as one of the distinguishing traits a good feeling about oneself and warm open feelings about others. Maslow calls this the kinship feeling; Adler calls it social interest; Perls, Freud, Jung,

4. Eric Berne, *Games People Play* (New York: Dell Books, 1964), pp. 17, 48.

Fromm and others call it love or lovingness. Yet, according to TA research, vast numbers of us aren't ready, willing, or able to engage in the kinds of attitudes and interactions that permit or foster loving interaction. We fear intimacy. To be intimate doesn't mean simply to be involved physically or sexually, though that may be a pleasant and sometimes effective way of finding and showing intimacy. It means, more generally, "the direct expression of meaningful emotions between individuals, without ulterior motives or reservations."[5] *That* is the kind of intimacy many of us fear.

Do we have answers to the *why* forming in your minds? We are beginning to find them. We know that an honestly intimate relationship demands certain things from people: things that many of us do not have, or don't have in sufficient quantity that we feel we can share.

Part of what each person needs in order to engage intimately is a feeling of his own personal and social significance (*I'm OK*), a belief in the inherent significance and value of others (*You're OK*), trust, caring, knowledge of Self and others, interest in others, and dozens of things more, none of which is insignificant, but which we will discuss as we continue this journey.

The analysis of our interpersonal *transactions* (interactions) gives us a variety of directions from which to choose. We will explore, first, the obstacles of OK-ness and intimacy that seem to come from the people outside of us. Then, in the next chapter, we'll see how these feelings and attitudes also emerge from within us, complicating the picture even further. Help arrives—in the chapter that follows—when we look at how we can uncover the full, free, honest, open, and OK self that lies hiding within us.

Today's Gameplan Is . . .

What is it like, the dishonest, Game-playing way of experiencing and presenting ourselves? Let's look at some made-up samples of Games people play:

> It's been a hard day. You're tired. As you get home, you recall that after dinner you're supposed to go over to Carl's and work with him to rebuild his carburetor. Working on engines is fun for you, but working on engines with Carl *isn't*. Bad breath? Hostility? Ugliness? None of these. Carl is an open guy, likes to talk, and is free to tell how he feels. Last time, for example, he told you how he always gets tied up before and during a night out with a woman.
>
> You aren't all that sure of yourself with women either, but you're *damned* if you're going to admit that to another guy! He tells you how

5. Eric Berne, *The Structure and Dynamics of Organizations and Groups* (New York: Ballantine Books, 1963, 1973), p. 322.

it's such a hassle having to go visit his widowed mother and he fantasies himself being a rich executive at times, with big cars, plenty of money, and women to pick and choose from. Crazy nut! Everybody feels that way, but you don't talk about it.

So, because you can't be as open and honest as Carl—and won't admit that!—you must find a way to get out of such encounters—a relatively effective and permanent way. You phone him and discuss how much you're anticipating coming over, to work on the engine and drink beer with him. Oh, and would he mind if you brought your FM radio because there is this replay of Mick Jagger's last concert and you'd rather hear that than talk. Carl, his feelings hurt, gets angry and tells you to stay home and listen to the radio if it's more important. And, *voilà*, you're out of danger.

The Game is a variation on one Berne calls "Uproar," wherein the person playing creates a situation that has to erupt into some sort of outburst, angry exchange, door slamming, or other vehement reply, so that the players can deny their feelings by avoiding intimate encounters. Frightened, bored, insecure, or cheating spouses often play such a game just before bedtime so they won't have to get involved in the intimacies of lovemaking.

Games are played with words, glances, gestures, situations, inanimate objects, and other people all serving as props and pawns. People learn to play these Games early in life, when, according to the *scripts* they prepare for themselves, they will tolerate only so much of certain kinds of involvement. When TA practitioners use the term *script*, they do not mean any written-down playscript or scenario. They mean a life-style format, partly conscious, mostly unconscious, which the child

Christianson

begins developing early in his life. For instance, a girl's script may be to marry young, have lots of children, and "accept a woman's lot in life." Or it may be to follow in her mother's footsteps and become a famous research scientist—and so on. The script is based on "tapes" recorded in the individual's psyche, those of Parent, Adult, and Child—"information" that enables him to figure himself and the world out (wrongly or correctly), develop a sense of identity, expectation, purpose, technique, and expression. In other words, out of these early recorded experiences his sense of Selfhood is formed, his expectations of the world and its inhabitants, and his way of living his life in all aspects begin to be laid out. As part of the script, the individual learns to expect certain things of others and learns what others may expect of him or her. In these expectations are found the basic ground rules for the Games the individual will play. It takes a long time to learn these Games, and as we shall see later, it often takes a long time to unlearn them and to learn open, authentic, intimate Selfhood instead.

The Players in Your Own Repertory Company

To refresh your memory, here's a brief review of our earlier description of the TA "players," to make this section clear. Berne describes each human being as carrying around inside a "group" of participants or players. In each of us are the ego states called the *Parent*, the *Child*, and the *Adult*.

The Parent doesn't represent your own parents or those who parented you. It represents the internalized attitudes, instruction, teachings, directions, judgments, and "conscience" that you get from your father and mother and other people in authority in your young life—by direct teaching and/or by example.

> The name Parent is most descriptive of this data inasmuch as the most significant "tapes" are those provided by the example and pronouncements of his own real parents or parent substitutes. . . . Everyone has a Parent in that everyone experienced external stimuli in the first five years of life.[6]

Whenever you find yourself feeling or thinking that things "ought" or "should" or "always" are a certain way, this is a playback of the Parent tapes in your own consciousness. Your Parent can come out in a variety of different ways—everything from getting very angry at yourself when you fail to live up to your own (your Parent's) standards, to your ability to comfort or reassure a frightened or unhappy friend,

6. Thomas Harris, *I'm OK, You're OK* (New York: Avon Books, 1973), p. 40.

to your ability to look at a given situation and decide what action would be "right" or "wrong."

At the same time you are recording the Parent "tapes" into your internal data, your Child ego state is developing. The Child doesn't mean "childish" in the sense of immature. It has to do with the side of your nature that is curious, afraid, enthusiastic, insecure, intuitive, affectionate, sexy, or playful. It is the side that lets you cavort with a date on the beach, that gives you a sinking feeling in the bottom of your stomach when someone has been critical of you. So, like the Parent, the Child has "negative" and "positive" aspects. Every person has a Child ego state, though some people have so thoroughly repressed their Child that it can hardly be perceived—and sometimes formal therapy is required to "let it out."

Both the Child and the Parent are "recorded" in you by about the age of five. No matter how old you grow, these are parts of your personality.

The Adult begins at about ten months of age, when you first move about, pick things up, and begin to explore external reality and take in data and information about life.

> Adult data accumulates as a result of the child's ability to find out for himself what is different about life from the "taught concept" of life in his Parent and the "felt concept" of life in his Child. The Adult develops a "thought concept" of life based on data gathering and data processing.[7]

To summarize and simplify, the Parent consists of the learned "tapes" in your head about what is right and wrong, good and bad, and how you "ought" to act. Your Child is your feeling and intuitive side. And the Adult is the information-processing, decision-making, "computer" side.

None of these ego states is "bad" or "good": all three are natural and necessary. In a healthy, self-actualizing person, there is a rational, in-touch Adult that determines choices and behaviors, with a balanced input from the teachings residing in the Parent, allowing judgments to be made of good, bad, right, wrong, appropriate, inappropriate, and a Child that permits the person to feel things and experience emotions and pleasure.

But in many of us, the Adult isn't sufficiently developed to cope with the multiplicity of sensory, cognitive, emotional, and social cues we experience. When the Parent is too domineering, the teachings of tradition, habit, or authority rule the person's life and prevent him from being able to respond spontaneously. He may, because of Parent

---

7. Ibid., p. 51.

"contamination" of his Adult, treat others according to what he has been *taught* to expect or believe about them, rather than experiencing each individual as he or she actually is. This is a prejudicial Parent.

Or the Child may dominate. In a Child-contaminated Adult, feelings may take over, and fears, unwillingness to venture forth and take risks, angers, or petulance dominate, preventing the Adult "computer" from dealing effectively with a frightening situation. Games may emerge as the Child seeks to control situations that could be experienced rationally and openly, or where the Parent won't permit new information or experience to enter the person's consciousness.

Games may have the effect of preserving one's fragile sense of interpersonal well-being, perhaps by keeping others at a "safe" distance, but the price paid is a forfeit of love and closeness. Game-playing is probably a universal phenomenon. Indeed, Berne feels that the *socialization* process we all go through from birth to adulthood is but another way of saying that we learn the appropriate or most effective Games to play.

All the World's a Stage

Shakespeare, a perceptive observer of human nature, felt the stage provided a "screen" onto which human behaviors, in all their glory and folly, could be "projected." Drama has always performed this function for us. Further, Shakespeare felt that life itself could be seen metaphorically as a drama.

At times you too may have felt as though you were acting or being stage-directed rather than really *being*. In TA terms, you may have felt you were playing out the script you wrote as a child. Or you may have felt that you were a player in a larger production than one you've written yourself. There is some reality to this. We do play roles, socially prescribed behaviors and "parts" that are necessary for some of the ongoingness of society. And there isn't much wrong with this except that none of us is as simple or plays only the one role given out by the "casting directors" in society. Humanistic psychologists have fought against this notion for years, insisting that we recognize the complexities and varieties of roles within each one of us.

The human being, be he or she a policeman, teacher, helicopter pilot, "rich man, poor man, beggar man, thief, doctor, lawyer, merchant, chief," is multi-dimensional.

> All the world's a stage,
> And all the men and women merely players.
> They have their exits and their entrances;
> And one man in his time plays many parts.
> (*As You Like It*, Act 2, Sc. 7)

If life is a drama, in reality or in metaphor, it is one in which we find a constant shift between Game-playing and intimacy, between "being yourself" and being what others might need or insist upon at the moment. The message of humanistic psychology is BE EVERYTHING YOU CAN BE. Recognize the Parent, the Child, the Adult, the inner and outer dimensions of your Selfhood. Take your socially prescribed statuses and those that you attain and explore them fully; they serve you as opportunities for growth, as you play the roles involved in each status.

The word *role* is important. For each of the social statuses or "parts" we occupy in life, society provides a set of expected behaviors: the role for that status. It's possible to say that the socialization process, the training and rearing of children, involves letting them in on the various attitudes, costumes, lines, and relationships that go with each of the statuses they will have.

It isn't only royal children who are groomed and rehearsed to take on royal parts when they take on their titles or thrones. It is just as true for each and every one of us "commoners" that we are given certain "parts" and will attain to certain others as we grow.

The black child may be taught by protective and well-meaning parents to expect racist hostility and discrimination. Because survival is an important aim in life, and the child is very likely to encounter racism and hostile bigotry, this advice is often valuable. But such teaching may give the black child a one-dimensional view of the white persons he will encounter in life. And none of us is one-dimensional, not even the bigot!

Similarly a white child may be taught to view blacks as enemies, as stupid, as dirty, as treacherous and violent. This training, also given under the guise of Survival Training, may lead the white child to expect such behaviors from blacks that he meets.

In most homes in Western cultures, boys are socialized differently than girls. There may be no conscious teaching to the effect that a boy is better than a girl, but for many of us, for far too long, that is the message that has gotten through.

In a very real way it's as if we are groomed for our life roles, with one or two being given preeminence. The most important (most *socially* important) role may be set apart and the "actor" is made up or masked to play that one role most of the time, to preset scripts, and to the neglect of the other roles.

The mask we are assigned is then taken as our only face. It's similar to what frequently happens with entertainers who are forced to *be* their stage or screen self even in their private lives. We'll leave until next chapter the problem of a person's actually preferring to play a part rather than to experience and express his or her Whole Self.

What Is a Mask?

In ancient Greece and later in Roman regions, the drama was a major entertainment force. The amphitheaters whose ruins make us marvel were far from being the only arenas or theaters in which plays were presented. Before acoustical science developed, the actors had the problem of being heard by the auditors far up in the Peanut Gallery. So, an enterprising dramatist developed a small megaphone-like device to be inserted in the mouthpieces of the masks the performers wore (this was before greasepaint and wigs). The device amplified the voices, giving the spectators a better show. This device-fitted mask became known as a *persono* in Latin *(per* = through, by means of; *sono* = sound).

It wasn't long before the role, not the mask, was known as the *persona*. From this word, meaning a voice-amplifying mask, we get our present word "person." The word Persona is still used by Carl Jung and Eric Berne to describe our Public Selves, the face, role, or self we present to others, by which we may prefer to be known.

> This term (Persona) . . . is used by Jung to designate the role played by an individual in accordance with the expectations of society, as opposed to what the person is in reality. A man may become identified with his role to the detriment of his personality. Thus, a judge may be always a judge, a doctor invariably a professional healer, or a minister may never lay aside his robes. It is a phenomenon frequently encountered in social life. In the sense that it is partly society which demands role-playing, the phenomenon of the Persona may be labeled as a collective one. . . . Those who are identified with their social roles are generally those who are unaware of their own antisocial impulses and out of touch with their own inner feelings.[8]

In the Middle Ages, mask-wearing became a diversion of the well-to-do, with masquerade balls serving the needs of people who often had nothing very challenging or interesting to divert them. Even the poor enjoyed an occasional costumery. Carnival and Mardi Gras, filled with religious significance, served to give hardworking people a break in the monotonous and depressing routing and harshness of their lives.

Today, with the exception of Halloween (which also had a religious origin), the wearing of masks is relegated to the past. Or is it? What of the Persona? What of the enforced hidden or partial identities of people all about us, including ourselves at times? As we've hinted, much of the Game-playing that goes on in our culture takes the form of imposed mask-wearing: requiring others to act or appear to be something we need them to be.

8. Anthony Storr, *C. G. Jung* (New York: Viking Press, 1973), p. 54.

The Vocabulary of Masquerading

Many problems come together under this heading. Among them are "social problems"—such as racism, discriminatory hiring practices, group hostilities, sexism, poverty, problems whose social implications and foundations we want to explore here. Their personal and psychological involvements will come in the next chapter.

Prejudice refers to a shaped attitude. No baby is born with attitudes; he learns them from others, and then shapes them himself. However they become part of the cognitive cellular structures of our brains, they are shaped according to needs, our own or those of the people who give them to us.

> "I just know I'm not going to like her. I can't stand her parents. They're rich snobs!"

Here's a simple example of a shaped, prejudiced attitude. The speaker knows how he feels about the woman's parents, and this negative attitude toward them has fashioned a prejudgment about the woman, although he doesn't know her. On the basis of partial information about her parents, whether correct or false, he feels competent to make a judgment about the daughter.

> "Gay people are all the same. Just look at Mark, the owner of that kinky little boutique!"

Another example of prejudiced attitudes. Only this time, the speaker has had some involvement, however perfunctory, with a man named Mark, who may or may not have homosexual preferences. Let's assume he does have such preferences. The speaker, then, knows *one* homosexual by name and appearance. But he has gone on to make a generalized statement about *all* homosexuals. This is an example of a very common type of forced mask-wearing: stereotyping.

In stereotyped thinking, we project information that may (or may not) have partial validity onto any and all persons resembling the one we've encountered. On the people level, it's the equivalent of the California governor who was quoted as saying: "If you've seen one redwood tree, you've seen them all!"

Stereotyping goes on all around us: oversimplified generalizations, sweeping statements, broad brushstrokes that paint large numbers of people with the same brushful of the same paint.

The simple fact is that the 3.5 billion people on this planet at any given moment are 3.5 billion separate and unique individuals. Humans all share many, many traits and behaviors in common, and this commonality is important and valuable. But so are the unique and special characteristics that differentiate us. This always has been a problem, and it will continue to be: how to recognize and allow for an individual's unique Selfhood while at the same time allowing for and encouraging each one to recognize his or her collective membership in the human race.

Stereotypes are usually based on some reality. They are not just made-up fictions. What is "fictitious" is the extent to which a description of one or a few individuals is also descriptive of an entire grouping. For example:

> "Any girl naturally wants to grow into a mother and housewive."

Biologically, every female human being—like the female of any other mammalian species—is equipped with the organs for sexual intercourse, reproduction, and nursing, along with the hormones that provide the impetus and energy to do these things. This, of course, guarantees the ongoingness of the species. But the social elaboration of this simple biological fact has been that some people insist that *all* that a female is born to do is to reproduce and keep house, and that women who choose to do other things, either instead of or in addition to their "natural role," are "deviants," or going against nature.

Many women *do* enjoy pregnancy and motherhood, and they find a lot of self-fulfillment in these roles. Many others enjoy these biological roles and also find other kinds of fulfillment in a variety of other roles. In other words, they've rejected the stereotyping and refused to just wear one mask. They know that as human beings they are multi-dimensional, multi-faceted, that they can have and fulfill many personal and social roles.

We then come into another term in the vocabulary of masquerading: *discrimination.* Prejudice is an *attitude* of prejudging a person on the basis of partial or incomplete information; discrimination is the *behavior* that may result from such attitudes.

> "I'm sorry, lady; your résumé is great! But if we give this job to you, then some poor guy with a family to support will be out of work. You understand."

Discriminatory practices in hiring have worked against self-fulfillment for millions of people—and they often seem to work against the same people more than others. Stereotyping may be a mental shortcut, used by lazy nervous systems in lazy or hurried people, but frequently the behaviors that result cut into and affect the lives of other people and they are forced to don the mask painted by that stereotype.

The TA Picture of the Dynamics of Prejudice

The language of transactional analysis has provided us with easy-to-understand terms for making sense out of many behaviors, including

prejudice, stereotyping, and discrimination. The Parent ego state carries with it the attitudes given us by our parents and/or other people in authority, and some of these attitudes may be prejudice. For example, suppose a child hears his father say, "Damned Jews! They'll skin the hide off you if you don't watch out!" Be that child for a moment: you've just heard this from your father at the dinner table. You don't know what a "Jew" is; your Adult hasn't acquired any objective information on the subject. Your Child is unknowing, curious. Your Parent is gathering information to help you make sense out of the world around you. Your mother and father usually give you valid and correct information. They provide for your material and most of your psychological needs. In other words, you get good *"stroking"*[9] from them, so you are likely to accept their judgments.

Thus, though you don't cognitively know what a *Jew* is, your feelings are affected by your father's negative opinion and words. Thus, the word *Jew* may come to be associated in your own mind, consciously or unconsciously, with negative emotional tones. A "tape" is being "recorded" in your Parent ego state.

Later, playing with your friends, you hear one of them say that a new kid, Gordon, is Jewish. Your Adult isn't sufficiently developed that you can ask for and process the factual information about this boy. Instead, the "tape" starts playing back in your Parent: "Jew-skin-the-hide-off-of-you." You meet Gordon. Your eyes tell you he is a perfectly normal-looking child, much like you. But the evidence of your senses, which might record something different in your Adult, is blocked by the playback in your Parent, and what you actually perceive in Gordon is something negative. You find that you don't like him, and if you were pressed to explain it, you might not be able to, other than that it's just a feeling that you have.

Gordon doesn't act anything like the mask your father has described, and so maybe you ignore Gordon, or repress the "fact" that he's a Jew. However, you may find at some point in your development that one Jew will look or act very much like the stereotype, and the Parent tape will play and your Adult will record that what your father said about Jews does indeed check out: it now becomes not only a feeling from your Child, taught by your Parent; it becomes externally

---

9. Berne tells us that we all require "strokes." In tiny infancy, this means body contact: warmth, hugging, touch, petting, fondling, and all the necessary skin-to-skin encounters we can get. But as we grow, the need for stroking continues to expand rather than diminish. We always need physical stroking, but we also grow to need more emotional, mental, and even spiritual stroking. In other words, we need continued reassurance, demonstrations of affection, and acknowledgment of our own existence. *Anything* said or done (a glance, a glare, a glower, a smile, a pat, a hug, a spanking) will serve as a stroke, albeit a negative one. After all, being ignored is the same as having your existence disregarded, unacknowledged, and almost any kind of recognition is better than that.

validated data and your Adult records it. You may use or hear others use expressions making fun of Jews, though your Adult may contain other data that tells you such jokes, clichés, comments, or jibes are very inappropriate and may hurt the other person. Your deeper levels of learning may conflict with the more recent and shallow levels of objective fact.

And perhaps that information became part of your father's "data bank" in much the same way.

Assumptions or expectations we acquire early are often reinforced or validated sufficiently to make us believe them to be truth. It only takes one example of a stereotype (a hook-nosed or stingy or clannish Jew; a black person who loves watermelon, steals chickens, or acts sexually aggressive; a white who hates blacks and takes advantage of them at every turn) to convince some of us that the stereotype is indeed true for all members of a particular group. Actualization and individuation of Selfhood requires that we be able to sort through the realities of our world and correct those wrongly recorded "tapes" from our earlier learning, and adjust our assumptions so that we can more effectively perceive reality.

Places, Everybody!

Our metaphor that life is often like a drama and the roles we play often cause us to wear a single face or mask to the exclusion of the rest of our personality points to the complexities of life.

Stereotyping puts people into categories: "You're a man, and a man isn't supposed to show his feelings!" This means that the expectations, traditions, needs of others, and even society's laws may cause you to play a single role, and insist that you play it very well—whatever else you are also able to do well! "Keeping in your place" is a form of social segregation.

Of course, some "segregation" is voluntarily undertaken—as among many Orthodox Jewish communities, where residence is focused in and around the temple and kosher sources of food. Here, an individual Jew may be required to associate primarily with other Jews, often to inhibit the possibilities of marriage with outsiders. There is some security from being with "your own kind," and such self-imposed segregation may give rise to stereotypes that Jews, Orientals, blacks, and Spanish-speaking peoples are "clannish," that they don't want to live with outsiders, and that integration or forced desegregation is therefore wrong!

This problem intensifies when desegregation laws are applied and many people are deprived of their rights to associate and reside when and where they might wish. It may be just as discriminatory to tell a white householder that the neighborhood *must* be mixed as it is to tell a black or Mexican householder where "their kind" must live.

The key word in all of this is "voluntary." This implies choice. If any group of people, of whatever color, nationality, religion, or ethnic orientation, chooses to live together, from need or desire, it needs to be their choice, *so long as some equitable way of ensuring the same freedom of choice for all others can be maintained.*

If blacks, Mexican-Americans, Orientals, Puerto Ricans, or Afghans wish to become part of the mixture of American society, giving up whatever elements of uniqueness of their own subculture that may be necessary in order to assimilate, that is their choice. The majority often refuses them that choice: thus forced segregation develops, and in the Southwest, the Mexican-American tends to *have* to live in the *barrio* or *colonia* (Spanish words meaning "neighborhood area," *not* slums); and blacks tend to be clustered together with only blacks.

Ghettos are areas of forced segregation. Originally, the word referred to the areas in Italian cities where Jews had to live, regardless of personal choice. Today we use it to refer to any area of forced residence. The word *slum* is not a synonym for any of the above, though economic and social consequences of segregation and discrimination often turn these areas into "depressed" communities.

The examples of racist and sexist discrimination are dramatic and there is much in the news, the literature, on TV, and in the schools about them. However, they only serve as obvious examples of the larger problem of people forced into partial selfhood by role expectations.

If a person chooses to go into law enforcement, a ready-made set of expectations awaits him or her. Not only does the police officer have the rules and regulations of the society and the police force to follow, but there are also stereotypes and negative designations coming from the citizenry as well. *Pig* was the name applied to police in the late 1960s, and it served to describe a dominant attitude about police personnel: that they were animal-like, ignorant, greedy, brutish.

The stereotype of the police officer has a long history; there is probably no society where the citizenry has total love and appreciation for those who must enforce that society's laws. Unfairness of certain laws apart, there is nothing pleasant about imposing the authority of law onto another person. It is hard and often "dirty" work. While there are unquestionably some police officers who deserve the hostility and mistrust of the citizenry, the majority do not.

But, rather than get into arguments about police brutality and citizen reactions, we must confine our study to what such stereotypes (if unfairly applied) do to the individual officer. The officer is also a human being. He or she has the same motivating needs and wants

as any of us. The fact that a police officer is responsible for enforcing the law twenty-four hours a day, even when off duty, puts that person into a different category from the ordinary worker whose work is done at the end of the day. A teacher doesn't *have* to teach while at home, on the road, at a picnic, just because someone is there who needs teaching. A research scientist may forget her lab chores after hours and enjoy being responsibility-less. But the police officer must always be prepared to enforce the law wherever and whenever he finds it being broken. And he is always subject to the scrutiny of citizens, who expect him to act in certain ways, even after hours.

The job you hold may be very important to you, not only for the salary, but because you like the work and feel it makes an important contribution to other people. Yet, you may find some people snubbing you or ridiculing you because the job doesn't have the prestige that other jobs do.

Class is a social concept that *theoretically* doesn't apply in this country—or in China or the Soviet Union, either! Yet, there are far too many examples of class consciousness and elitist behavior in all three of these nations (though the information on China is sparse and often contradictory in this regard). While we do not have objectively drawn class lines in this country, sociologists find that there are very definite class attitudes and behaviors. These often serve to remind us that we aren't so very far removed from the overtly class-structured societies of feudal Europe in the Middle Ages or the caste structures of pre-Gandhian India.

And for each social label—be it race, sex, class, socioeconomic, educational, vocational, religious, or legal—there are expectations and assumptions, operating much like the simpler stereotypes we've been discussing.

For instance, people without much money often assume that the very wealthy are inordinately privileged and happy. While this is no doubt true for some, there are many people of wealth who are not. There are even disadvantages to being extremely wealthy, as the recent kidnapings involving the Getty and Hearst families will attest.

Semihumorously, many less-privileged people might joke that they'd trade places with the rich and take their chances with such "disadvantages," but the more sobering fact is that the person carrying *any* label, even one like "millionaire," is seen as something less than a full human being. Wealth does not automatically make you a more complete or whole person, though it might provide better for the basic needs and free you to develop the esteem and self-actualization needs. Self-actualization of your potential takes place among all classes, sexes, races, religions, and nationality groups.

In families, the roles are often as rigidly prescribed. The mother may have absolute power in all things domestic—but nowhere else. Or she may make herself exempt from some of the same rules she expects her children to obey. The father may be the head of the household, or he may have authority only outside the home. The point here is that parent and child and sibling roles are often laid out on a traditional basis, without regard to the personality and needs of the individual. The family is one of the basic units of our society; as much of our most important learning takes place here. There is tremendous evidence that most basic learning, the writing of one's "life script," takes place in his first five or six years. If this is so—and we think this first five or six years to be very important, though not absolutely!—then what goes on in the home cannot help but affect every aspect of our lives in the larger world.

The family is a microcosm of the neighborhood, the community, and the larger geographical, political, and social units. The kinds of attitudes you acquire in this early "world" will in most cases last you throughout your lifetime. They can be modified later, but such modification often requires schooling, psychotherapy, or drastic experiences. For many of us, these attitudes are never challenged, modified, or questioned. So, the abuses of racism, sexism, elitism, and all sorts of prejudices are perpetuated through the generations of time.

> Charlie's father feels it is beneath him to change a diaper or do anything in the kitchen—except when he occasionally barbecues a steak. Charlie, at ten, finds himself in a classroom where the teacher (a man of thirty) is teaching art. After painting, the teacher tells the children to take their brushes to the sink and wash things up. Charlie has refused to wear the vinyl aprons worn by all the others; "aprons are for girls." His clothes are splattered with paint. He knows his mother will be upset, but he's sure his father will be proud that he stuck to his guns and refused to put on a "feminine" apron.

You may think this is a petty example. But consider the ramifications for the Charlies when, in future years, they find themselves married or involved in other situations where their sex roles are so rigidly tied into traditional patterns of thinking.

What is the answer? As with the other complex personal and social problems, there is no simple answer. The younger generations *are* questioning some of the assumptions and expectations of their parents and the older generations. Some of this questioning is rebellion-for-its-own-sake, but much of it is based on new experiences and information. Many younger people—however radical and disturbing they may seem to the older members of the society—are intent on modifying such rigid and inflexible attitudes, on liberating the entire group so that they may find more reasonable and humanistic ways of living.

This sounds idealistic and even a bit worshipful of youth. It isn't meant to be blind to the abuses and errors the youth are also capable of making. We feel such changes in attitudes toward role-expectations will produce more humanistic societies—at least more human and happier families! We want to explore some of the changes in brief detail.

Human Is Beautiful!

During the 1960s the raising of consciousness became a major issue and focus. Homosexuals banded together to protest stereotyping and discrimination against them, and the Gay Liberation movements began. Women formed groups to raise consciousness about oppression among themselves and in the larger community. They have found some success in rallying their own energies—and the energies of males as well—in focusing on male supremacist and chauvinistic attitudes and actions.

When American Indians dramatized their stereotyped and abused conditions in sit-ins and take-overs, we first heard of Red Power. Mexican-Americans in the Southwest introduced the word *Chicano* to the Anglo public and publicized the bias and hostility they have endured for three hundred years. Other groups have joined the consciousness-raising and have found power in unity, even when their unity was tentative and shaky. The power-seeking tactics of community organization and the labor union movements were learned, practiced, and refined. Public complacency in general seems at last to be a little shaken and the angry, hurt, threatening, demanding, and stronger voices have begun to be heard.

Possibly the most vehement and outspoken voices have come from the black 11 percent of our population—22,000,000 people who have let the rest of the world know that the promises of liberty were still not fully being delivered, one hundred years after the Emancipation Proclamation. The Black Power movements, building pride and confidence within—with cries of "Black is beautiful"—have also created tension and unease among the rest of the populace.

The "Masks of Niggerhood," of servitude and inferiority and oppression, were being ripped off and thrown back into white faces, often shocking and hurting many who failed to recognize that whiteness itself, and all it stood for, was *their* mask, and thereby, their problem. Now, many whites have been labeled *honkies* and found themselves openly hated and treated contemptuously. The new black identity has made

many unwilling to wear the servile and inferior masks they had been given or expected to wear. "Shine your own damned shoes!"

Consciousness raising has had many results. Within the groups themselves there has often grown a greater understanding of the individual and the collective identities of the members. Self-pride and group pride has often developed, or expanded where it had been before. Group loyalty, a feeling that those in your group are "sisters" and "brothers," has emerged for many. And just as surely as these positive benefits developed (and they *are* aspects of self-actualization!), so did many of the less-positive and detrimental aspects emerge. Group pride, in any group, easily becomes ethnocentrism: the belief that "my" group is the best and others are not as good. This is often called chauvinism.

As a result, there has been a period of *polarization,* wherein some groups deliberately pulled away from others. The distance, mistrust, and enmity have been there all the time, but this newer trend has dramatized and intensified them. Newer consciousness may define the distance and differences more clearly, increasing the strength and pride in the opposing groups, but it is nonetheless divisive and dehumanizing.

The confusion, hassle, and hurt of the sixties isn't entirely gone. But out of the settling smoke from the fires of protest, rebellion, reverse racism and reverse sexism is emerging clearly a newer need: to recognize some larger loyalties and a newer consciousness. We are all in this nation and on this planet together. What one of us does actually does affect the other, now perhaps more than in previous times when we had more space, more time. My racism and sexism hurt not only the person against whom I discriminate: they also hurt me and people like me. Nobody really benefits. In fact, the entire society suffers.

Many of those who have lived in the oppression of such rigid and dehumanizing attitudes will laugh and say: "Now you know how it feels, Charlie!" But the fact is, as long as stereotyping and other limitations of actualization exist, none of us escapes the pain and divisiveness.

Merle Shain, a feminist with outspoken and ardent feelings, believes, as do many others, that sexism has dehumanized and oppressed women throughout history, often irreparably. But she recognizes that sexism, like any ism, is a two-edged sword, that men are stereotyped and dehumanized as well:

> "I'm not one of those women authors who feels that men are untrainable and let's forget them altogether. We are all each other has. I don't want to see women go it alone. . . ." Ms. Shain prefers to explore her own relationships and offer advice to men on how to understand modern women. Women like herself, who are not looking for traditional love affairs, but for growth relationships where both partners are individ-

uals who have opted for something better than the "nothin's more lovin' than something from the oven" stereotype.[10]

The rigid role requirements for the lives of women, men, people of a particular color, ethnic background, social class, educational or vocational grouping, and all the rest, are problems not only because they keep people in single-dimensional positions, but because they often lock the rest of us into positions in relation to theirs. Further, the single-dimensional role played by any of us ignores and does violence to the other dimensions of that person's Selfhood. The Struggle for Significance is the tiresome, painful, and heavy duty of seeking out and developing our fullest selves. Anything less is a handicap, a cutting-out or cutting-off of the rest of who we are. We are made to become total and whole persons.

> Men have paid enormously for the whole superiority thing. They are asking: Why change? They think with people like me writing they'll end up having to take the garbage out and do the dishes. They don't realize that they would be getting the benefit of having total people in their lives whom they can rely on and who can help them.[11]

10. Alan Cartnal, interview with Merle Shain, *Playgirl*, February 1974.
11. Ibid.

Having to be dominant, strong, successful, an achiever, not being able to experience or express your frustrations, weaknesses, or passivity, or tenderness *is* one of the burdens imposed on men by the sexist stereotypes. The reducing of males to a one-dimensional caricature, having generally larger and harder muscles, a penis, body hair, a built-in mechanism that makes them work, earn money, build a home, protect their families is dehumanizing. The same reductionism concerning women—that they are ready-made lovers, domestic slaves, baby-machines, and are automatically emotional—is just as great a crime against them. But times are changing. It may well be that men, too, will realize how oppressing sexism can be for them when it takes choice away.

If we sift through the stereotypes by which we live, we find that, as convenient as they are to believe, they have the effect of dividing us from each other. Having to wear a particular mask because others need or expect it keeps any individual from knowing his or her full Selfhood. This limited experience and expression deprives the society of fullness, richness, and the fascination of variety. Our differences, though surface in nature, make for variation and color, spice and excitement. American Indian writer Vine Deloria, Jr., makes this point vividly:

> If the attempted renovation of religious imagery is ever combined with the dominant schools of ethnic studies, the result will be the Last Supper as the gathering of the "All-American Platoon" highlighted by the contributions of each group represented. Instead of simple bread and wine the table will be overflowing with pizza, tamales, greens, peanuts, popcorn, German sausage, and hamburgers.[12]

While dramatic, the point is well made. Our society is more heterogeneous in its makeup than most of the world. But the myth of the Great American Melting Pot has not really been tried, because the only groups really mixed into the pot have been the easiest to blend in: the white, Anglo-Saxon, Protestant for the most part. The notion of cultural pluralism must be tried in serious and earnest fashion. This ideology says, "Men, women, people of all ages, sexual preferences, colors, religions, national and ethnic backgrounds, blue-collar, white-collar, or no-collar: bring your varying talents, roles, ideas, languages, foods, music, art, writing, and needs together so that the entire society can learn from you, benefit from your full and free involvement, give to you of its abundance. You are part of the whole and without you, the whole is unwhole, unhealthy, incomplete."

12. Vine Deloria, Jr., *We Talk, You Listen* (New York: The Macmillan Co., 1970), reprinted in Angela Lask and Richard Roe, eds., *This Is a Sociology Reader* (San Francisco: Rinehart Press, 1973).

Any single mask you wear of your own volition is of value to you and hopefully to the rest of us. If you are a truck driver, lawyer, weed puller, cook, teacher, wino, child, doctor, or whatever, this is part of who you are. If you are proud of that role, then do it gladly and well, and the rest of us will learn that you are far more than this role, even though we accept that role, too. If you are female and are learning that "sisterhood is beautiful" you must remember that the men around you need "sisters" too, and that working together, each sex can learn to appreciate the uniqueness of the other and the common ground on which both stand.

Dr. Charles Thomas headed a group of black psychologists in forming their own professional association—a temporary measure so that black psychologists could know some of the pleasure and pride of feeling good about themselves as blacks. But in an interview in *Psychology Today*, Dr. Thomas points out that this group, like other black-consciousness groups, is only a stage on the path to the larger consciousness that we are all part of the same overall group: Human-kind.

> When you find a brother who wastes all his time rapping on whitey, you know he's at the *first stage*. As he moves on to the *second stage* he is testifying to all the pain he has endured because he has contributed to the process of denying the self. Another part of the second stage is learning to express his anxieties about becoming black; he gets confused as to whether this step has to include burning down the city or grabbing a gun.
>
> In the *third stage* we get into information processing on the cultural heritage, not only the African background but the black contribution to our homeland, America. You go out of this stage into the *fourth stage*, activity, working through a particular group to find linkage to the larger black experience. You now live in the black world. The *fifth stage* is transcendental—through your unique blackness you lose your hang-ups about race, age, sex and social class and see yourself as a part of humanity in all its flavors.[13]

It's easy to get idealistic and oversimplistic when we are talking about the need to get through our polarized separate masks and reach out for each other in a sense of common humanity. But anyone who is able to raise his or her head from the muddle or the huddle of their particularistic activism or interest will see how close tomorrow is. We've used the metaphor that we are all traveling together on *Spaceship Earth*. As passengers on this spaceship, moving desperately fast into the future, we must find ways of learning group identity, cohesiveness, not just as blacks, men, women, whites, rich, or poor, but as fellow passengers.

13. "Different Strokes for Different Folks," T. George Harris, *Psychology Today*, September 1970.

The energy crisis, the employment crisis, any crisis involving the survival of any individual, also involves the survival of the whole group. Our personal roles are vital, but each of us is more than any single mask we may wear and we need to constantly explore the fullness of each other's Selfhood. The Games we play to preserve our inner selves are losing games. The human animal lives in *symbiotic* relationships with the rest of the human race, the rest of animal life, and the entire realm of nature. It hurts the oppressor to oppress, just as it hurts to be oppressed. Mask-wearing should be for fun and special times: not for the everyday business of discovering and developing our personal, social, and *global* significance.

Summary

We play Games with other people out of psychological needs. Eric Berne and others in the transactional analysis camp tell us that within us are many selves, many states of being. Three of these are the ego states called Parent, Adult, and Child. The Games we play are losing games in that they keep us from experiencing each other in meaningful intimacy.

In a metaphor describing life as a drama, we find that our inner needs and societal pressures often force people to display only one aspect of their inner selves, to wear a mask or a *Persona*. The language of such masquerading or dramatic Game-playing includes the ideas of prejudice, stereotyping, discrimination, racism, sexism, and other forced identities. Social problems emerge, affecting not only individuals involved, but the entire social structure.

Significance means knowing your Whole self and being able to express that, recognizing other people's needs for the same behavior. Cultural pluralism and various consciousness-raising movements among women, the poor, the ethnic minorities, homosexuals, and others, seek to enlarge the societal perspective to permit full and free functioning for all the integral parts of the society: the individuals.

Suggested Readings:

Bardwick, Judith M. *The Psychology of Women.* New York: Harper & Row, 1971.
_____. "Women's Liberation: A Nice Idea, but It Won't Be Easy," *Psychology Today,* May 1973.
Berne, Eric. *Games People Play.* New York: Dell Books, 1967.

_____. *The Structure and Dynamics of Organizations and Groups.* New York: Ballantine Books, 1973.

Bird, Caroline. *Born Female.* New York: Pocket Books, 1969.

Cartnal, Alan. "Merle Shain," *Playgirl* Magazine, February 1974.

Chesler, Phyllis. *Women and Madness.* New York: Doubleday and Co., Inc., 1972.

_____. "Men Drive Women Crazy," *Psychology Today,* July 1971.

Deaux, K., and J. Tayner. "Evaluation of Male and Female Ability: Bias Works Two Ways." Unpublished paper, Department of Psychology, Purdue University, 1971.

Deloria, Vine, Jr. *We Talk, You Listen!* New York: Macmillan, 1970.

Dixon, Vernon J., and Badi Foster, eds. *Beyond Black or White.* Boston: Little, Brown & Co., 1971.

Edmiston, Susan. "How to Write Your Own Marriage Contract," *Ms. Magazine,* Spring 1972.

Farber, J. *The Student as Nigger.* North Hollywood, California: Contact Books, 1969.

Farber, S. M., and R. Wilson, eds. *The Potential of Women.* New York: McGraw-Hill, 1963.

Foote, N. M., and L. S. Cottrell. *Identity and Interpersonal Competence.* Chicago: University of Chicago Press, 1955.

Freeman, J. "The Social Construction of the Second Sex," in M. Garskof, ed., *Roles Women Play.* Belmont, California: Brooks/Cole, 1971.

Friedan, Betty. *The Feminine Mystique.* New York: Dell, 1963.

Gaviglio, Gary, and David Raye. *Society as It Is.* New York: Macmillan, 1971.

Goffman, Erving. *The Presentation of Self in Everyday Life.* New York: Doubleday & Co., Inc., 1959.

Greer, Germaine. *The Female Eunuch.* New York: Bantam Books, 1972.

Grier, W. H., and Price M. Cobbs. *The Jesus Bag.* New York: McGraw-Hill, 1971.

Harris, Thomas. *I'm OK, You're OK.* New York: Avon Books, 1973.

Horner, Matina. "Fail: Bright Women," in Bardwick, Douvan, Guttman, and Horner, eds., *Feminine Personality.* Belmont, California: Brooks/Cole, 1972.

Kovel, Joel. *White Racism.* New York: Vintage Books, 1970.

Laing, Ronald D. *The Self and Others.* London: Tavistock Publications, Ltd., 1962.

Lasch, Christopher. *The New Radicalism in America.* New York: A. A. Knopf, Inc., 1965.

Lask, Angela, and R. Roe, eds. *This Is a Sociology Reader.* San Francisco: Rinehart Press, 1973.

Lewis, M. "Culture and Gender Roles," *Psychology Today,* May 1972.

McBee, M. L., and K. A. Blake. *The American Woman: Who Will She Be?* Beverly Hills, California: Glencoe Press, 1974.

Psychology Today, Editorial Staff. *The Female Experience.* Del Mar, California: CRM Books, 1973.

Pugh, Roderick W. *Psychology and the Black Experience.* Belmont, California: Brooks/Cole, 1972.

Ramparts Editorial Staff: *Divided We Stand.* San Francisco: Canfield Press, 1970.

Ríos, F. A. "The Mexican in Fact, Fiction, and Folklore," *El Grito,* Summer 1969, Vol. II, No. 4.

Salper, Roberta. *Female Liberation.* New York: A. A. Knopf, Inc. 1972.

Schrag, Peter. *Out of Place in America.* New York: Random House, 1969.

Shain, Merle. *Some Men Are More Perfect Than Others.* New York: David McKay Co., Inc., 1973.

Simmen, E., ed. *The Chicano.* New York: Mentor Books, 1971.

Steiner, Stan. *The New Indians.* New York: Delta Books, 1969.

Steinfield, M. *Cracks in the Melting Pot.* Beverly Hills, California: Glencoe Press, 1970.

Storr, Anthony. *C. G. Jung.* New York: Viking Press, 1973.

Toffler, Alvin. *Future Shock.* New York: Bantam Books, 1971.

Urban Coalition. *One Year Later.* Urban America, Inc., and the Urban Coalition. New York: Praeger Publishing Co., 1969.

Watts, Alan W. *The Book: On the Taboo against Knowing Who You Are.* New York: Collier Books, 1966.

Wright, Nathan, Jr. *Let's Work Together.* New York: Hawthorn Books, 1968.

9

The Enemy Within

*For a long time I toyed with the idea of writing
a novel in which a Negro, Bigger Thomas,
would loom as a symbolic figure of American life,
a figure who would hold within him the prophecy
of our future. . . .*

*The more I thought of it the more I became
convinced that if I did not write of Bigger as I
saw and felt him, if I did not try to make him a
living personality and at the same time a symbol
of all the larger things I felt and saw in him,
I'd be reacting as Bigger himself reacted: that
is, I'd be acting out of* fear *if I let what I
thought whites would say constrict and paralyze me.*

*As I contemplated Bigger and what he meant, I
said to myself: "I must write this novel, not
only for others to read, but to free* myself *of
this sense of shame and fear."*

RICHARD WRIGHT[1]

*I've been sort of dead in a way. I cut myself
off from other people and became shut up in myself. . . . You have to live in the world* with *other
people. If you don't something dies inside.*

—A SCHIZOPHRENIC PATIENT, quoted in
The Divided Self [2]

1. Richard Wright, "How Bigger Was Born," in Abraham Chapman, ed., *Black Voices* (New York: New American Library, 1968), pp. 551–52.
2. R. D. Laing, *The Divided Self* (Baltimore: Pelican Books, 1965), p. 133.

In each of us are many varied facets of our integrated, holistic self. Notice we don't say "varied *selves.*" One of our earnest goals is to get away from the analytic, pluralistic way of thinking that so many of us have developed. We are *not* many selves. We are human beings with emerging concepts of selfhood. In the selfhood of any one of us, multiple images or pictures or representations pop up. No one of them alone is all that we are. A whole diamond cannot be experienced by studying or seeing only one facet of that diamond; we must view the entire gem. Now, of course, we can't *see* all the facets of a diamond at one time, nor can we see or experience or know all aspects of selfhood at one time. Years or a lifetime may be required to experience *all* of the self of any one person.

This includes one's own self. None of us is completely aware of all that he is. None of us knows the complete answer to the question, *Who am I?* Part of the self is submerged beneath layers of time, experiences, feelings, and defenses, and even if some "know-it-all" machine or technique were devised, it's unlikely that *everything* could be uncovered. Furthermore, it might not be advisable to know everything about oneself—if it were possible. We have buried some parts of ourselves for very good reasons.

How, then, are we to understand and actualize our fullest selfhood? What are the things that make it difficult? In the excerpt at the beginning of this chapter, Richard Wright is describing some of the conflict he felt when trying to write *Native Son.* He wanted to portray the black man, and Richard Wright, as he really knew him. He wanted to make the picture skin-black and blood-red vivid! Why was this a conflict situation? He suspected in advance that the response of white Americans to his book might lead to difficulty. For one thing, many of the things he would portray in *Native Son* would reinforce the old racist stereotypes. Although stereotypes have elements of truth in them, they are generalizations that obscure details and realities essential to a true picture of the whole group being stereotyped. He felt that the reinforcement his book might give to these stereotypes would hurt his own image and that of the black American in general.

A part of Richard Wright, one aspect of his self, needed and wanted to write this book. Another aspect of Richard Wright's self foresaw difficulties. Another aspect fed memories, fears, defenses, social needs, and other information into the conflict. Still another aspect—the executive or arbitrator role that Freud called the *ego*—tried to mediate the conflict. It gave him this to work on: if you don't do this book, just as you feel it, you will be acting on another, more critical stereotype that white people have of us, that of fear and weakness. This may be more detrimental to you as a man and as a black person than the other consequences. Out of the conflict, and with the aid of this umpire part of him, Richard Wright brought forth a novel, a statement about himself and what was part of his people in his self.

The other excerpt leading off this chapter tells us of the insights of a schizophrenic patient of Dr. Ronald Laing's. This person knew that he could avoid the pain of his internal conflicts by withdrawing into himself, by locking himself in the closet of his Within-ness, but he knew that doing so meant splitting himself off from the living, alienating himself from life.

The conflicts we experience by being asked or forced to live partially or in a false fashion have already been described in chapter eight. Now, we must look at the conflicts that go on within us, inside our personalities, that prevent us from living fully, from experiencing joy and fulfillment. We want to explore that no-man's-land often called mental illness, abnormal behavior, psychopathology, or emotional disturbance.

The Jigsaw Puzzle of Self

Any of the theories of personality can be used: they have much in common. Even with their differing language and emphases, they all acknowledge the multiplicity of parts that make up the whole, whether they talk about separate structures of personality or merely separate processes.

The idea that the human personality is somehow partitioned and diverse has a long and poetic tradition. Primitive peoples portrayed their animistic beliefs in ways that indicate that they, too, saw human nature as multiple.

The major religions of the world, dualistic in terms of strong convictions about good and evil, have given rise to beliefs in forces or agencies for the Good and Evil—angels, devils, cherubim, demons, and goblins. Such beliefs have persisted through the ages—look at the astounding interest in and success of the novel and movie *The Exorcist*—and have been the most frequent explanations for bizarre, unpredictable, destructive, or frightening behaviors in people around us. In fact, demon possession is still with us—whether we *believe* in it or not!—in some of our language:

> "I don't know what possessed me!"
> "What gets into you sometimes?"
> "I'm not myself today."

The *demon-possession model* has a long history, but because of the work of alchemists and physicians through the Middle Ages, it was supplanted throughout Western civilization by the *medical model*, which assumes that, just as a fever or infection is caused by bacteria, viruses, or other external "agents" of disease, so emotional and mental problems are the result of essentially physiological causes. The etiology of these problems is considered to be part of one's biological nature.

While this view didn't answer all the questions, it did rescue thousands of people in the Middle Ages from the beatings, drownings, torture, and neglect that used to be the treatment when a demon was thought to possess a patient—to literally "beat the devil out of him." The physicians who began to convince people that insanity and lunacy were not the result of infestations of spirits, but illnesses like any others, found it possible to build hospitals and sanitary facilities for the patients.

The medical model is still dominant in Western psychiatry, where laws require that a psychiatrist be a medical doctor. But in the latter years of the nineteenth century, one man, Dr. Sigmund Freud, turned his psychiatric attention to a nonmedical model, a theory that is called psychoanalytic theory. Freud's model, in some ways a modernized demon-possession theory, sees three functions of personality: the *id*, the *ego*, and the *superego;* and three levels of awareness: the conscious, the preconscious, and the unconscious. Emotional disturbances, notably neuroses, were caused by repressive actions of the *ego* and *superego*, particularly of the sexual and aggressive impulses of the *id.* Though our statement that Freud's was a "modernized demon-possession theory" was somewhat tongue-in-cheek, there is some reality to it, too. Freud considered sexuality and aggression to be instincts, and he named them Eros and Thanatos, respectively. (Rollo May reminds us that Eros and Thanatos were daimons—demons—in ancient mythology and literally had the power to dominate or take over a personality.) Freud, a medically trained physiologist and neurologist, felt his theory was consistent with the prevailing medical model, though he couldn't always explain exactly *how* it was consistent.

Carl Gustav Jung was a Swiss psychiatrist who became Freud's favorite (if not most controversial) disciple. More than any other, Jung departed the most radically from Freud's basic teachings, which he saw as too mechanistic and medically rigid. Jung's work became known as *analytical psychology.*

Jung's model, too, finds a multiplicity of "parts" and "processes" in the human psyche. Drawing not only from his medical background, but also from anthropology, archeology, theology, mythology, sociology, alchemy, and the arts and philosophies of both East and West, Jung produced one of the most all-encompassing models of mental and emotional health and disturbance we've ever encountered.

The unconscious was the aspect most fascinating to Jung. In its hidden and mysterious depths lay not only forgotten and repressed memories (the personal unconscious) but also archetypal and symbolic

images and patterns of thinking, feeling, and acting shared by all human beings, regardless of their culture (the collective unconscious).

For Jung, emotional disorders were caused not so much by repressed sexuality or aggressiveness, or by strivings to overcome feelings of inferiority (as Alfred Adler taught), but by disintegration or splintering of the essential unity of the psyche. The *anima* (female) or *animus* (male), or the *ego* and the *self,* might be in conflict. The goal of analysis was to bring the fragmented portions of the psyche back into unification, into wholeness, and thus, into health.

Other thinkers have had a variety of theories, none better or worse, simply different. What we personally find important is the growing emphasis on the fact that a human being is essentially a Whole Unit. While acknowledging the important contributions of the medical model and the learning model of Freud, Adler, and others, we in the humanist camp attach the greatest importance to the existential and wholistic models. Many in this camp believe the essential nature of the newborn child is Wholeness, with all aspects functioning in unified harmony. But through life, beginning immediately, external and internal events change the functioning of the body's physiology. The blood chemistry and the neurological processes are often altered—sometimes such alterations are inherited or are caused during the prenatal period, and these chemical changes may affect our later behaviors. (Some evidence indicates this may be the case with schizophrenia and some behavior disorders.)

We are saying that our bodies mediate all experiences, internal and external. Just as the pupil opens autonomically to changes in light brightness, the nervous system responds autonomically to stress, conflict, pleasure, pain, fear, anxiety, and all the learned responses we experience.

Whatever learning is, be it the simplified conditioning processes of Pavlov or more technical learning exercises, learning operates to bring about changes in the structures of the essential chemistry of the nervous system, the DNA and the RNA. So, the medical model has something to teach us. But so do the learning models of the behaviorists and those concerned primarily with environmental conditioning of personal behavior. And so do a number of other models. The human being responds to the external world, and some of the responses can produce disturbed functioning. At times the disturbance seems to resemble the cracks in the earth after an earthquake, the splintering of a priceless ceramic vase, the fragmentation of a torn-up piece of silken paper. Somehow, the Wholeness, the integrity, the unity, the Oneness of the human being is cracked or entirely shattered.

And so the personality becomes battleground, ally, and enemy, all in one. The enemy, as we've said, is usually within. In many ways, we "are our own worst enemy." How does this attack, this tension, this pain manifest itself? What are the many guises of the inner enemy?

"What Is Truth?"—The Pain of Reality

In traditional terms, the enemy causing a split or inability to relate to reality has been called psychosis. This is the often frightening, always dramatic disorder or disturbance of function, the one most people think of when they hear the words "mental illness" or "mental disease." Such terms come from the medical model. We won't debate their validity here.

What apparently is going on is a generalized change in the perceptual and cognitive, as well as the emotional and integrative processes. There are split-offs of all kinds. The older layman's definition for the most common psychotic disorder, schizophrenia, was "split personality" (from Greek words, *skizos* = "split," and *phrenos* = "mind"). There is some small validity to this popular definition; many mental functions do appear fragmented and disintegrated in some schizophrenics, but this isn't the major characteristic. In most cases of schizophrenia, the person shows a strong inclination to split the mental (and emotional, sensory, and other) processes from their ordinary tasks: those of making contact with and sense out of the world in which we live.

Here the ideas get sticky, since nobody has a very good definition for "reality," but we have a pretty good idea what somebody else means when he tells us about certain aspects of reality: "The sky is cloudy today," "My face is sunburned," "It's a gorgeous sunset." So, what we've tended to do is to assume some common ground for our experiences of reality. When someone doesn't share this common ground experience, we question him, wonder about him, maybe even diagnose him as "crazy."

There is no one single cause for schizophrenia, and there is no single type of schizophrenia.

Diagnostic manuals list many varieties of schizophrenic reactions, including:

1. *Simple schizophrenic reaction:* Withdrawal from others, from external stimulation; noninvolvement with outside concerns, often including the individual's own health, appearance, and functioning. There may be hallucinations.
2. *Paranoid schizophrenic reaction:* Includes many of the above but with the addition of delusions, of either persecution or grandeur.

3. *Hebephrenic schizophrenic reaction:* Involves "bizarre" or fragmented ideas, words, actions, "silliness," some delusions and hallucinations.
4. *Catatonic schizophrenic reaction:* Involves rigid postures and lack of reaction to external stimuli.

Today we know that schizophrenia is among the most complicated disorders of the human condition. It is probably caused by combinations of inborn blood-chemical and externally caused psychological factors. We know, from LSD experiments, that there are definite physiological changes but we are not yet able to isolate them in such a way as to produce a pill or serum that will "cure" the disorder.

Of course, chemotherapy is useful in relieving some of the symptoms and enabling the person to experience "external reality" more comfortably, but a method of total cure is yet to be discovered.

To sell books and films, authors and screenwriters have often taken the most bizarre and dramatic psychotic experiences and distorted them to portray mental or emotional disturbance. As a result, the average person has mostly erroneous notions about such problems. To tour the wards of a typical mental hospital is not to take your life in your hands, or to find large numbers of howling, shrieking, laughing, or wall-climbing semihuman people. Even allowing for the sedative effects of modern drugs, most "residents" of these institutions would be found to be sitting or lying silently, or weeping, or working at tasks to keep their minds occupied. The percentage of violent patients (dangerous either to themselves or others) is minimal. As we have said, the typical "mental patient" is pretty undramatic and his or her story would hardly be a subject for filmed or written drama.

The psychotic reactions also include paranoid and affective reactions.[3] *Paranoid reactions* are those characterized by delusions. The "true" paranoid makes up less than 1% of all mental hospital residents. If his delusions are of persecution, he may be so frightened or intimidated that he will see another person as a threat. Often his defensiveness is violent. If the delusions are of grandeur, he will try to convince you that he is a famous or important person. The significant problem in dealing with paranoid reactions is that a therapist can rarely establish rapport with or gain the trust of the patient, and this makes psychotherapy extremely difficult.

Affective reactions are of three types:

1. *Manic type:* The individual experiences elation and "high" emotional reactions, regardless of the stimulating circumstances.

---

3. If you need a reminder of the meaning of any of these terms, check the glossary.

   2. *Depressive type:* The individual seems depressed or lethargic, sad and discouraged, most of the time without obvious cause.

   3. *Circular type:* The individual experiences alternating moods, including both manic and the depressive phases.

Like all psychotic experiences, these are only episodic; they come and go at times. There doesn't seem to be any "rhyme or reason" for the moods: during a manic episode, the person may laugh even when he's hurt himself or is told of the death of another. Depression—when psychotic—doesn't seem to have any observable or knowable cause. There may be long periods of time when the psychotic doesn't manifest any of the symptoms we've been describing. Here, the stereotypes break down. It's possible to visit the chronic wards of a mental hospital and see psychotic patients who have been there for a dozen years, and come away wondering why one particularly charming or seemingly happy person is locked up.

    Reality is harsh, however we define it. It's probably neither as harsh as many of us think during our pessimistic moods nor as wonderful as our optimism convinces us it is. It's a complex and challenging mixture of both, if our "doors of perception" are open and we are on friendly and honest terms with it.

    The psychotic, apparently, isn't able to find comfort in such a philosophical discussion of reality. Because of chemical mix-ups compounded by harsh experiences, many psychotics find their only way of dealing with reality is to withdraw from it, to trade in what you and I see as reality for an inner "reality" of their own choosing or making, one which may be safer or less confusing to them.

    The inner world of psychosis isn't different from our own inner perceptions, except in degrees of difference. We've all had moments when we "saw" something that wasn't "really" there: heat vapors on the asphalt road, looking like water on the highway; a mirage; a very real dream or fantasy; even a hallucination, if we've gone without food or sleep or sensory stimulation for too long. So, you and I are not unfamiliar with the kinds of experiences related by schizophrenics, or even paranoids or manic-depressives.

    The differences seem to lie in several important points. Most functioning people can have bizarre, frightening, confusing, or disintegrated experiences and yet maintain a comfortable relatedness to external processes, people, and things. We can take a "fantasy trip" and then come back "home" to our own reality-bound life. One of the commonest warnings given out by regular users of *psychedelic* drugs (which often produce psychoticlike experiences) is that they are for "together" people only—for those who are functioning effectively and comfortably in the "real world."

Many of the terms we've used in this section are intensely difficult to define. Perhaps Ronald Laing is more correct than many believe when he says the psychotic is living in his own "real world" which is simply another aspect of his own reality, not a made-up or wrong perception of reality at all.

"The Dark Night of The Soul"—The Pain of Selfhood

Descriptions of psychotic disorders make for fascinating reading, and the 300,000 or so patients admitted each year to mental hospitals know the "reality" of such disorders. But for most of us, the problems are not so dramatic, and they require no hospitalization. The number of people hospitalized, incidentally, is decreasing each year, thanks to chemotherapy, outpatient clinics, better attitudes toward counseling and other therapeutic help, and improved health standards.

There *does* seem to be an increase in problems that have less clear-cut causal factors, ones for which medication and even psychotherapy can promise no immediate release. There are some labels for these (neuroses and character disorders), but we will view them in terms of *dynamics*—that is, what seems to be *happening* within the person, and between him and others.

When Freud was starting out in the late 1800s, most of his patients were crippled by neurotic reactions, not psychoses. They got along fairly well in society, got and held jobs, married and had children. But they often suffered deeply within. Occasionally (as with psychosomatic and conversion disorders) there were physical problems along with the emotional ones. But essentially, their suffering was internal and emotional.

Today, therapists most often see people who are having difficulty with self-concept and resulting problems in getting along with other people. We will explore several of these types of problems.

"Poor Me"—Inferiority Feelings

To feel inferior is to feel unequal to those whom one considers to be *OK*[4] or functioning adequately. If these *OK* people are my parents, I may conclude that they are better than I am, not only in the specific things they can do that I cannot, but in general as well. They are superior, I feel, and I am then inferior. They are Top-Dogs and I

---

4. *OK* and *Not-OK* are terms that come from transactional analysis theory, especially that found in the works of Thomas Harris, M.D. (see bibliography).

am an Underdog.[5] There is usually no conscious attempt on the part of parents or any others to make themselves feel superior at others' expense—though this does happen occasionally—but my perception of the situation may be that these people "usually win." It may seem to me that they have all the power, the looks, the money, the fun, so I may conclude that they will always win, and because I don't have these things, I'll always be the loser.

This isn't a new idea. Alfred Adler parted company with Freud over the latter's insistence that adult neuroses were always the result of conflicts and anxiety over repressed instinctive sexual and aggressive impulses. Adler felt that far more primal and basic to the cause of adult neuroses and interpersonal disorders was a conflict based on feelings of inferiority.

> The feeling of inferiority rules the mental life and can be clearly recognized in the sense of incompleteness and unfulfillment, and in the uninterrupted struggle both of individuals and of humanity.[6]

5. This concept comes from Dr. Frederick "Fritz" Perls, and is found in his "Four Lectures," in Joen Fagan and Irma Lee Shepherd, eds., *What is Gestalt Therapy?* Perennial Library Ed. (New York: Harper & Row, 1973), p. 13.
6. Alfred Adler, *Social Interest* (New York: Capricorn Books, 1964), p. 102.

One must remember that every child occupies an inferior position in life; were it not for a certain quantum of social feeling on the part of his family he would be incapable of independent existence. One realizes that the beginning of every life is fraught with a more or less deep feeling of inferiority when one sees the weakness and helplessness of every child. . . . This feeling of inferiority is the driving force, the starting point from which every childish striving originates.[7]

We might question whether *any single* concept, be it the notion of repressed sexuality or aggression, feelings of inferiority, notions of existential helplessness, or any other one idea, can cause *all* adult neurotic and social difficulties. We can agree, though, that most if not all of us have been in inferior positions relative to parents and other "big" people early in life. We also can recognize how persistent such feelings are.

But, in most of us there are other self-evaluations recorded along with these inferiority feelings, or recorded after them. We have successes, achieve goals, find ourselves petted and praised, and begin to experience life as more pleasurable, less a striving to *compensate* for our inferiority feelings. So, we can outgrow these early learned feelings by acquiring feelings of self-worth, through the individuation process, by learning, and by experiencing ourselves as *OK* at times.

In a large part of the population, however, such OK-ness is never learned. Such a person may have one or two such experiences, but his overriding feeling is one of being *Not-OK*. When defeats, beatings-down, failures, frustrations, limitations persist, he then finds himself laboring under a massive feeling of inferiority, what Adler called an *inferiority complex.*

When the *Not-OK* feeling is this generalized and all-inclusive, when the individual can't admit anything acceptable or *OK* into his self-concept, when he has to "spell his name only in lowercase letters," he is feeling the fullest weight of inferiority. He may feel about his appearance, dress, speech, walk, or performance on almost any task that he *is* an inferior being, a mere grub and inconsequential nothing!

Wilhelm Reich found this to be one of the dominant problems in Western humankind, and he spent much of his psychiatric career trying to help people get out of the "poor, little insignificant me" syndrome. The existentialists have found this problem to be endemic among us as well, and the attempt to solve it has pervaded much of humanistic psychology today.

Carl R. Rogers proposes that everyone develops a self-image of himself (like the "script" described in TA theory) which serves to guide and maintain his adjustment to the external world:

7. Alfred Adler, *Understanding Human Nature.* A Premier Book (Greenwich, Connecticut: Fawcett Publications, 1963), p. 65.

Harsh, rejecting judgments prevent the individual from accepting himself and therefore cause him suffering. Even though they may be ignored or denied expression, they continue to have a subverting effect by producing underlying doubts of worthiness and competence.[8]

Erich Fromm, too, indicates that early doubts and inferiority feelings prevent one from emerging as a full-functioning, autonomous adult:

. . . If he does not feel confident of his views and expressed position, he may forsake independence. By joining and conforming to a group he enjoys the shelter and privileges they provide, but also obligates himself to their authority.[9]

So, humanistic psychologists also bear out the TA position and Adler's views that in his earliest years one may assume the *I'm Not OK–You're OK* position by developing feelings of inferiority.

The Mask of Nigger described in chapter eight is one of assumed inferiority. It is enough to *feel* you are inferior, but if others beat it down at you, soon you may *act* in an inferior way. This is the self-fulfilling prophecy of much stereotyping and forcing of identity. Others' needs in trying to make a "Nigger" out of another person are not as important here as the fact that some people actually respond by becoming "Niggers."

One of the hardest things we black people have to deal with is our inferiority feelings. Oh, we don't like to talk about it! I've brought this up in a class—especially a class with whites present—and had some of the "brothers" and "sisters" glare at me with hatred, or look away as if all this was just too much "garbage," or get up and walk out of the room. But, face it: so many of us have been brought down for so long we've come to believe it! It's one of the biggest problems we've got to overcome, and all the blowing out of hair, of wearing African shirts, of "Gimme Five!" and talking jive isn't going to remove the fact that many blacks feel totally inferior.[10]

Feeling inferior is not what the concept of "Nigger" is all about. It's in *acting* the part. It's in permitting somebody else to do a put-down on you and play the part of one who deserves to be put (and *kept*) down.

Do all people feel the same way when they are treated as inferior? Research indicates that the reactions are similar. To have minority

8. Carl R. Rogers, *Client-Centered Therapy* (Boston: Houghton-Mifflin Co., 1951).

9. Reported in Stanley Coopersmith, *The Antecedents of Self-Esteem* (San Francisco: W. H. Freeman, 1967), p. 34.

10. From personal interview with Ernest Gregoire, Dean of Special Programs, Mt. San Antonio College, Walnut, California, 1974.

status is to be put in an inferior mask, to be a "Nigger," regardless of your color. Blacks outnumber whites in South Africa by nearly four to one, yet blacks, in the statistical majority, actually have minority status: they do not have the same rights of citizenship as do whites.

Women in America are in the statistical majority by a ratio of 100 to 94, according to the 1970 census, yet women everywhere occupy minority status. Studies of women's reaction to sexist pressures indicate that until these reactions of inferiority are changed, many of the changes being made at the institutional levels will have no effect.

The human species is biologically divided into two discrete and definable groupings: females and males. Yet, sexism has taken a few anatomical and hormonal distinctions and elaborated a whole set of sex-role expectations and assumptions that have dictated life for both males and females for centuries. Yet, the psychological burden constantly is borne by the women.

Balzac said:

> A woman who is guided by the head and not the heart [as the sexist stereotypes insist she should be] is a social pestilence: she has all the defects of a passionate and affectionate woman, with none of her compensations: she is without pity, without love, without virtue, without sex.[11]

Can reading such a description do much to enhance a woman's sense of self-esteem? We doubt it. The evidence indicates that women and girls suffer greatly from feelings of self-doubt and inferiority.

> [Women] get higher test-anxiety scores than do the men. Eleanor Maccoby has suggested that the girl who is motivated to achieve is defying conventions of what girls "should" do. As a result, the intellectual woman pays a price in anxiety. Margaret Mead concurs, noting that intense intellectual striving can be viewed as "competitively aggressive behavior." And of course Freud thought that the whole essence of femininity lay in repressing aggressiveness (and hence intellectuality).[12]

Test anxiety and conflict over intellectual performance do not necessarily indicate inferiority feelings, but they correlate highly with such feelings.

Phyllis Chesler notes that significantly more women than men are hospitalized for emotional problems. She also found that "most female 'neuroses' are a result of societal demands and discrimination than the supposed mental illness of the individual. Therapists and husbands

11. Honoré de Balzac, quoted in Phyllis Chesler, *Women and Madness* (New York: Doubleday and Co., 1972).
12. Matina Horner, "Fail: Bright Women," in *Feminine Personality*, ed. by Bardwick, Douvan, Guttman, and Horner (Belmont, California: Brooks/Cole, 1972).

alike, however, persist in encouraging women to take the blame for their unhappiness—thus, to be 'cured.' "[13]

People of color and people of ethnic "uniqueness" have been put into the position of *Not-OK-ness,* and many of them have described their feelings of inferiority status, but perhaps the most inferior you can feel is to feel "invisible":

> I am an invisible man. No, I am not a spook like those who haunted Edgar Allan Poe; nor am I one of your Hollywood movie ectoplasms. I am a man of substance, of flesh and bone, fiber and liquids—and I might even be said to possess a mind. I am invisible, understand, simply because people refuse to see me. Like the bodiless heads you see sometimes in circus shows, it is as though I have been surrounded by mirrors of hard, distorting glass. When they approach me they see only my surroundings, themselves, or figments of their imagination—indeed, everything and anything except me . . . you ache with the need to convince yourself that you do exist in the real world, that you're a part of all the sound and anguish and you strike out with your fists, you curse and you swear to make them recognize you. And, alas, it's seldom successful.[14]

Feelings of inferiority create many conflicts in us. You may have external evidence that you are *OK,* and this information is being noted, but perhaps the early Adult tapes didn't record enough of this kind of information, not enough to counteract your Child's *Not-OK* tapes.

So, Games result.

> All Games have their origin in the simple childhood game of "Mine Is Better Than Yours. . . . When the little person says, "Mine Is Better Than Yours," he is really feeling, "I'm not as good as You." . . . When "Mine Is Better Than Yours" is pushed far enough, the game ends with a hard shove, a slapped face, or devastating evidence of some sort that "It is not: *mine's better."* This then puts the little person back in his place; it has been proved again that I'M NOT OK, and in the maintenance of this fixed position there is a certain miserable security.[15]

So, many people handle their inferiority feelings by presenting themselves in inferior or inadequate fashions, donning a mask of their own choosing.

13. Phyllis Chesler, "Men Drive Women Crazy," *Psychology Today,* July 1971.
14. Ralph Ellison, "The Invisible Man," from Nathan Wright, Jr., *Let's Face Racism!* (New York: Thomas Nelson, Inc., 1970), p. 16.
15. Harris, op. cit., p. 147.

"But I *Couldn't!*" —Inadequacy Feelings

Among the self-defeating behaviors or Games that one can play based on low self-esteem is that he is *inadequate* to do things. "Poor Me" may be the Game. The player may seem to be saying he or she is inferior, but the *payoff* is that nothing heavy will be expected of the player.

> George had been in a therapy group for over a year. He continually felt inadequate to get or maintain a job, to seek warmth and love from people of either sex, to make or hold onto any material possessions. The first day the therapist brought in his co-therapist, a bright and attractive young woman, George let her know by word and gesture that he posed no threat to her. "I'm impotent," he announced before introductions around the group had even finished.

CHRISTIANSON

"GOOD HEAVENS! YOU'RE NOT *THE* MR. NOBODY?"

Strange behavior, many men reading this will say. A man doesn't parade around his sexual inadequacies. If he has them, he ought to keep quiet about them; or if he has to talk, let him bluff his way through, as schoolboys (of all ages!) do. Yet, in George's script there was such a heavy and loud resounding of *Not-OK-ness* that his inferiority feelings had to be expressed in terms of inadequacy. By declaring himself "impotent," and therefore harmless, to the woman, he was putting her into a position of OK-ness that might "turn on" not her sexual Adult or Child, but her protective Parent. She'd never be able to get *him* into a sexual encounter! Further, because his *Not-OK* feelings needed stroking, he preferred the relatively negative strokes of being patted or treated like a helpless child than the more positive strokes of being seduced or loved as an Adult.

That sounds like *masochism*—preferring punishment and rejection to love. But remember, *any* stroke, be it positive or negative, is preferable to no stroking at all. A small child may actually make a pest or a brat of himself to get yelled at or smacked, in preference to being taken for granted or ignored, and adults may do similar things.

> Though there is misery, there is *something*. As the comedian said, "It's better to have halitosis than no breath at all." It's better to be roughed up playing games than to have no relationship at all.[16]

Goffman reminds us that even as others force masks and limited roles on us, we also wear single masks and present ourselves in specific ways, depending on how much of our real Selfhood we are prepared to have others know.[17]

In all interactions, one of the basic themes (scripts) is to somehow guide and control the responses made by the others present, whether beneficially or in a manipulative fashion to stroke his own childish needs.

Back to what may appear to be masochism. Many people end up playing losing Games because their inferiority or inadequacy will not tolerate their winning. To win means to face responsibility, if for nothing else, than the responsibility of being consistent. The "Fastest Gun in the West" had a terrible burden in maintaining that reputation; the only way to lose it was to die. Similarly, many people refuse to run the risks of winning or achieving, because they do not want the burden of having to *continue* to achieve and be responsible adults.

> Helen came to her psychology professor with a problem. She was a very bright and competent person in every area of her life. Her good brain betrayed her far too often for her to hide it. Yet, in his class, she consistently got Ds and Fs on exams that were as fair and valid as exams can be. She could read the book and understand it, engage in fairly competent dialogue with her peers, but when the teacher asked her a question or gave her an exam, she blew it.

Helen's was an extremely complex script to live by. As she and the psychologist discussed her feelings, it came out that he reminded her of her father, a stern, judgmental, never-satisfied man. (This was not characteristic of the teacher at all.) When she was in his presence, her Parent tapes started playing and she was reminded of her *Not-OK* position as a child. She had to fail in his presence, to bolster her inadequacy feelings: it was the only position she knew how to take in reference to what she perceived to be a stern, unloving parent figure!

16. Ibid.
17. Erving Goffman, *The Presentation of Self in Everyday Life* (New York: Doubleday & Co., 1959).

People who feel inadequate often find it safer to present only that mask, and they thereby escape the tension involved in breaking or disrupting familiar patterns. (It feels *familiar* to be Not-OK.) To present the negative side of themselves so much, so exclusively, may cause them social difficulties, and even intrapsychic tensions, since they also have other roles, other masks. Perhaps they sometimes felt *OK* and presented themselves that way, but at other times the hassle was just too much for them.

Masochism in its deepest sense is the deriving of pleasure from some sort of pain. The pain need not be physical; mental, emotional, and "spiritual" pain will do just as well. But in making some sort of peace with other early-learned patterns of self-feeling, masochistic people will undergo all sorts of humiliating, self-effacing, self-defeating experiences. To them, this pain brings a sort of "relief," even a form of "pleasure."

"I'm Such a Heel!"—Guilt Patterns

Underlying many behaviors that come from feelings of inferiority and inadequacy (and others besides) is the feeling of *guilt*. *Mea culpa* is more than a way of beginning to say your confession; for many people it is the dominant way in which they present themselves in everyday life.

Early patterns are formed, and they often stick tenaciously, in spite of overwhelming experiences and much evidence to the contrary. How many of us find forgiveness for actual crimes or "sins" we've committed, and yet continue to feel guilt-ridden? We don't know the statistics. Our own psychotherapeutic experiences convince us that this is still a major problem among humankind. A healthy human being, having made a mistake, wronged or hurt someone, feels normal guilt reactions. His early learning has rightly taught him to feel ashamed, to be aware of the interdependency existing among people, and to want to make amends somehow. This interdependency, or kinship feeling (to use Maslow's term), makes us aware that each of us is affected by what happens to the other: if I hurt you, it hurts me and possibly others as well!

But others do not first feel such "normal" guilt and then, forgiven by those they have hurt, forgive themselves. Even if such a person does seem to forgive himself, he can't forget his "crime," can't "let it go." He consciously or unconsciously flogs and defeats himself, often without knowing why. One quality of healthy people is their ability to accept their own—and others'—human weaknesses: to forgive and forget.

"Ain't I Somethin'?"—Narcissism

An individual may walk about, acting as if he were wonderful, putting on a good front, while knowing or suspecting deep inside that he isn't all that OK at all. This "knowing," of course, is really a feeling, but it's such a dominant theme in many of us that it never leaves us.

Narcissism is a term we can apply to this behavior. It often (but not always) describes people who flaunt their good looks, their strength or sexuality, their clothes, money, cars, brains, or other accomplishments. While such a person often appears confident, accomplished, or happy, he is frequently empty and miserable inside. His hope—often quite desperate—is that if enough other people are convinced of his worth, validity, or OK-ness, based on these surface manifestations, then he too might believe it.

Jan had a really gorgeous face and figure. She knew this was important to people who told her how beautiful she was; so she spent a good hour each morning making up and dressing. She just *had to* present the most attractive picture she could to those she met each day.

But something about their praise was hollow and unsatisfying, though she couldn't put her finger on it. She went out almost every night, enjoyed the attentions and the favors of an assortment of attractive men. She was also aware of the stir she created among the women: especially those who found her a threat and a competitor.

Yet, after each event, after each bit of flattery and flirtation, she felt an emptiness inside her, which seemed to grow rather than diminish. She felt depressed. She spent even more time, attention, and money on her appearance. But the extra effort didn't seem to help, and she began to be afraid. Because she felt her looks were the "most valuable" attributes she had, she began to realize that they would soon run into that scourge of narcissists, time.

We didn't make Jan up for this study. She and her counterparts of both sexes are legion! Our society is partly to blame, emphasizing youth and beauty, often to the exclusion of many other more worthwhile traits and behaviors.

Narcissism is an age-old problem. In its simpler elements, it has to do with letting a surface or single talent "stand for" your whole being, because you have little or no confidence in the rest of yourself. The most frequent cause is self-dislike, even self-hatred.

Narcissism isn't self-love. It is an "appearance" of loving and appreciating yourself. It's another mask, a Game we play. It is similar to the ploy of wearing only one mask or role and not letting the others be seen. Many of us can only handle one role, one bit of our own selves. We've never found the integrating center of Being that not only allows us to accept and value the whole Self, but insists on it. Once wholeness has been tasted, we find it difficult to settle for anything less. If you've had even the slightest, most superficial experience with seeing yourself as an integrated, fully functioning wholistic person, you know the pleasure, the thrill, the real appreciation you can have for yourself. This begins to approach authentic self-love, the love and respect for your whole self.

What has been called "self-love" or conceit is more often this pale, insipid, unsatisfying playacting called narcissism. As with any of these patterns of accepting part and rejecting the rest, it is still true that "a house divided against itself cannot stand."

"Castles in Spain"—Withdrawal and Fantasy

Another problem we find in these self-defeating patterns is the tendency to give up, to withdraw from the fight. Many of us feel so badly about ourselves that we just "lie down and early-retire." This retirement may mean becoming marginal and alienated. Of course, in these as in other problems in living, there is more than one side. Some people are kept in marginal status—as we outlined in the previous chapter—by stereotypes and discriminations of all kinds. In most communities, some jobs and roles are accepted out of necessity, and the

individuals playing them are masked with that one role and are seldom known for anything else they are or can do. Prostitutes, police, trash and garbage collectors, mayors, dogcatchers, teachers, and others may share a similar marginality in the interpersonal sphere.

But most marginality is motivated from within. It's safer to stay away from others, to remain on the periphery, just coming close enough, and for just long enough, to obtain the necessities of life. Hermits and loners of all kinds abound, some feeling the rest of us are Not-OK and preferring not to contaminate themselves with our presence, but most feeling we are OK, while they are not.

Or the withdrawal isn't physical, but is into fantasy. The person who prefers dreams to reality is an example of what we're describing. Or one's fantasy-life may become the only world he wants anything to do with. Now, as we've said before, dreams and fantasies are perfectly natural and OK experiences, part of the richness of human consciousness. A healthy Adult keeps us aware of our fantasies and also involved with reality. We know we can find value in both. The person whose Parent so dominates the Child that the Adult is excluded is a person possibly on the road to psychosis, where virtually all Adult data is left out and fantasy becomes the only reality.

Chemical Withdrawal: Alcoholism and Drug Abuse

Recent studies indicate that definite personality patterns seem to predominate in people who are abusers of alcohol or certain drugs. Without getting into the clinical aspects of these addictions or habituations, we can elaborate on a central focus: most of these people are acting out *I'm Not OK–You're OK* positions.

In the life scripts of many people with chemical addictions can be found a parent who set the stage for the child's later picking up the mask of Drunk or Addicted.

> The . . . situation is found over and over again in the case histories of alcoholics and other drug abusers who describe their parents' dismay when they discover their offsprings' drug abuse after years of encouraging the use of alcohol or other drugs to deal with stress, and of condoning drug abuse in themselves and others.[18]

Dr. Steiner's work with alcoholics and drug abusers convinces him and many others that TA principles can be applied in understanding

18. Claude Steiner, *Games Alcoholics Play* (New York: Ballantine Books, 1974), p. 50.

and treating these problems. The Games we find in people who abuse alcohol and drugs are the same self-defeating and self-punishing Games we find in other people playing out an *I'm Not OK–You're OK* script.

The chemicals provide an escape, a shortcut to consciousness change. Consciousness changes, as we'll see in chapter twelve, are in themselves usually healthy aspects of human experience. But too often, with the help of powerful chemicals, the individual experiences aspects of consciousness and of unconsciousness that do not enhance his Selfhood, but destroy it.

The ultimate enactments of withdrawals and fantasy can be the "trip" of hospitalization or imprisonment. These may seem harsh comments, but in the sense that institutionalization provides full "custodial" care for one's Child, giving strokes as he's learned to get them, hospitalization may indeed be a form of withdrawal.

"Living in a Bubble"—Autism

One of the sets or patterns of behaviors that has perplexed and troubled therapists for years is *autism,* sometimes considered to be the same as childhood schizophrenia. Other psychologists see it as similar to, but basically different from, schizophrenia. An autistic person withdraws into a shell—a clear plastic bubble, it seems. We can see him, but we can't seem to otherwise interact with him. He won't talk or respond, and seems not even to listen. Is such behavior the result of an inborn (genetic) problem, or is it a learned reaction to harshness in his environment? The arguments rage, and the scanty evidence lines up about evenly on both sides. In recent years, due to work by behavior modification specialists, there is a growing tendency to see it as mostly genetic.

An autistic person may talk only in rhyme, or echoing the person with whom the "conversation" is going on. He may never learn to speak or read or write, or he may reach a level of literacy and verbal ability that enables others to penetrate a bit into his private worlds.

Dr. Harris feels that while there may be a genetic component to autism, it is primarily the result of a child's learning extremely early that he is *Not-OK* and others are also *Not-OK:*

> If the state of abandonment and difficulty continues without relief through the second year of life, the child concludes *I'm Not OK–You're Not OK.* In this position the Adult stops developing, since one of its primary functions—getting strokes—is thwarted in that there is no source of stroking.[19]

19. Harris, op. cit., p. 70.

"How Do I Know You're Harmless?"—Mistrust

There are many neurotic and frightened people in the world. Among the most frequently encountered patterns is that of *mistrust.* This is another expression of the TA position of *I'm Not OK–You're Not OK.* It is also one of the greatest tragedies of human interpersonal life.

All right, you might say, it's a hostile and rough world. Trust can get you into trouble, especially if you trust the wrong people: con artists, robbers, murderers, rapists!

There's truth in this position. Yet, in spite of these real risks, if one does not feel trust very early in his life, and build it into his life patterns of thinking, feeling, acting and reacting, he never learns the courage he needs to try liking, loving, full-functioning and significant selfhood. Without these experiences of trusting (no matter how painful and risky they may be at times, especially when the trust is betrayed) we find ourselves out on the edge of human warmth and relatedness. As Erich Fromm says, without trust, love is so difficult to learn as to be nearly impossible.[20]

In the social world, apart from love relationships, we find that mistrust is at the very least a losing Game. If I mistrust, I not only lose out on intimacy and closeness, but I also find the simplest transactions to be difficult. How, for instance, can I conduct a business transaction—be it over a pound of pinto beans or a Stutz Blackhawk!—if I cannot trust at least minimally? Without trust, what do you believe? Do you read the literature, attend to the other media, and disregard it all? And what of confidences people "entrust" to you? Can you handle them? Are you strong enough? Are they?

The mistruster often can't find help. For help in the form of casual advice or intense psychotherapy means believing and trusting, if not in the therapist as a person, then in the counseling relationship.

In the world of ethnic relations, mistrust abounds. Survival in a hostile world often creates the need for mistrust, especially of the one perceived as "the enemy." Blacks who are taught that every nonblack person is no damned good may survive vulnerable times because they never let themselves get put into helpless positions such as friendships or patient or client relations. But they never quite get over the script of *I'm Not OK—Neither Is the Man!* Black psychiatrists William H. Grier and Price M. Cobbs say in *Black Rage* that the typical black in America learns mistrust of whitey during his first few months, and this mistrust, often called "paranoid" by white social scientists, is actually a means of survival, and hence, it should be considered a Black Norm.[21]

20. Erich Fromm, *The Art of Loving* (New York: Harper & Row, 1956).
21. W. H. Grier, and P. M. Cobbs, *Black Rage* (New York: Basic Books, 1968).

But Grier and Cobbs note, too, that for all the health and energy Black Consciousness has given black people, it, like other drugs, can also make people sicker, even emotionally sicker. They recount the case of Roger, who suffered feelings of inferiority and racial hatred for the first twenty years of his life. Then he discovered his blackness and came alive, both within and without.

> He spoke knowingly about black culture and developed a way of challenging anyone, black or white. All whites were summarily accused as racists, and most blacks as "Toms." His words took on a life of their own. There emerged a ranting, liturgical quality in his indictments. The genocidal conspiracy of whites, "the killer white man," became a close, immediate threat and dominated his thinking. He was thus able to justify carrying a gun for self-protection, and he exhorted others to join him in the organization of an armed cadre for the defense of the black community against the soldiers who were sure to come. When the blacks declined to join, Roger assumed that they were all in the pay of the enemy. He retreated further and further into an armed, crablike defense, secret and alone.[22]

Such tragedies have happened for thousands of years as the prejudices and discriminations of others have created the most violent forms of mistrust and projected hostility in people.

Women who have felt the pressures of male-dominated social patterns have also felt similar conflicts and inner disorder. Yet, as in the case of people of color, women too often find that help is in the hands, and at the whim, of the very people who have helped them feel Not-OK in the first place: white therapists and technicians outnumber minority professionals by outrageous odds, and most of them are males.[23]

My People Is the Enemy—The Pain of Interaction

Finally, we come to a third set of problems usually originating with our "enemy within." For some, as we've seen, the reality of others is their foe. For many others, it is conflicting elements of their own self-concept. For this third group, the pain comes from "You, Me, and the rest of Us."

Here too the lines cannot be drawn too rigidly or too inclusively. We are talking about people in conflict with people. Some are in the half-world of psychosis for at least some part of their waking lives.

22. W. H. Grier and P. M. Cobbs, *The Jesus Bag* (New York: McGraw-Hill, 1971), p. 118.
23. Phyllis Chesler, op. cit.

The whole pattern surrounding the Charles Manson "family" and its violence leaves you with a confusing picture: were the "family" members "crazy," or were they simply conscienceless psychopaths? We honestly do not know.

Some antisocial actions originate in neurotic, self-conflicted feelings being acted out against the environment in general, or against certain people in particular. As with psychosis, autism, and other problems in living, there is mixed evidence as to the cause. There may be very real genetic factors, such as hormonal imbalances, chromosomal anomalies, brain tumors, neurological lesions. And in some cases, as the TA model puts it, the person who has acquired this antisocial patterning is one who has had the stroking taken away very early in life, but who has learned how to stroke himself. ("Licking one's wounds" is an apt phrase here.)

There are many psychiatric labels for these problems—"character disorders," "personality disorders," and others—but the labels do not help us in trying to understand the dynamics at work within. In a large number of cases, these are people who have done drastic things to survive physically, but who have died psychologically.

Psychopathic personality is a general catchall label, and even if it's a loaded term psychiatrically, the roots of the word indicate a "soul-sickness" or "psychic wounding" that we cannot ignore. If the antisocial feelings are acted out against others, the term *sociopath* is often used.

Why is it that for many of these tragic human beings there is appearance of "behavior without conscience"? If the antisocial feelings lead to a violent crime, often the individual will claim to feel little or no remorse, and often won't or can't come up with a very valid reason for his behavior. However it's expressed, it often assumes the form of the TA position of *I'm OK-You're Not OK.*

Is the person really without a conscience, without a sense of right and wrong? This is hard to say. We find it difficult to believe, whether we take the view that conscience is inborn or learned: most of us do learn such values and distinctions, even if the lesson doesn't stick. It's more likely that so great a conflict exists within the person, especially regarding others and their behaviors, that his sense of morality gets lost in the shuffle, and the question of right vs. wrong becomes clouded.

Is antisocial behavior inborn? This is part of the ongoing debate about the innateness of aggression.[24] We feel that it is possible for any individual, whatever his learning experiences, to commit a violent

---

24. This question is dealt with in such works as René Dubos' *So Human an Animal;* Ashley Montagu's *The Biosocial Nature of Man;* Konrad Lorenz's *On Aggression;* Anthony Storr's *Human Aggression;* Robert Ardrey's *The Territorial Imperative;* and J. D. Carthy and F. J. Ebling, eds., *The Natural History of Aggression.*

and aggressive act, even murder. The potential is there, along with the potentials for loving, creativity, and health. In a few cases, chemical pressures or neurological tensions have forced an individual to act violently. The facts are not all in, and we *are* faced with an alarming increase in antisocial crimes in virtually every society in the world.

The Need for Reintegration Within

The internal conflicts, the enemies within, are serious, as any of us who have suffered from them can attest. The feelings of being a battleground for an internal warfare are devastating and painful, no matter how we experience them: in symptoms of physical illness, psychosis, neurosis, or antisocial expression.

If conflict and disintegration of the working and creative harmony of the inner forces and structures of selfhood form a key to the problem, we can then move forward to putting "our houses back in order." If people with emotional and mental disturbances, with self-defeating and self-punitive behaviors, are split off from their Wholeness, then we can appreciate the necessity for moving into dimensions of restoration of wholeness and unity.

It's a gigantic problem, for—in TA terms—the *Not-OK* feelings in many of us far outnumber the *OK* feelings: integrated and fully functioning persons are a definite minority. Attacks on our essential Wholeness and health come from so many sources that it's easy to forget that for most of us, the pain-giver, the attacker, is present in our own minds and attitudes most of the time.

THE ENEMY

He and I are old friends,
For I have known him many years.
We have met countless times
  on the field to do battle.
Never have I been able to
Repel his first assault,
So great his strength.
He strikes with the lust that a
  man feels for a woman.
With viciousness that only a fire of
  passion can create.
It would appear my foe knows every
  weak point, and begins his attack there.
If in my lifetime I am ever able to
  defeat him, the victory would make me whole.
For this is the enemy that every mortal knows,
Few have truly defeated.
For my enemy lurks within a fortress
  I cannot breach:
He lives within me.

—GOMELIA BAKER, 1971

Summary

Each of us carries around within him his own worst enemy: the disintegration and disharmony existing among the varying aspects of his selfhood. Animism, demonism, medical models, Freudian, Adlerian, Jungian, and behavioristic models of personality can be studied and compared, and in all but the last we find the emphasis on the essential unity of the human psyche. All these approaches recognize how easily the inner "parts" get mixed up, lost, or opposed to each other.

We looked at how the pain of this inner disorganization can be felt and expressed: in psychotic reactions like schizophrenia, paranoia, and the affective reactions; in neurotic and existential disorders like inferiority, inadequacy, guilt, mistrust, narcissism, and other withdrawal behaviors. And we found, too, that for some there is a playing out of these inner conflicts on the lives of others. We see and appreciate the need for restoration of the Wholeness of our being.

Suggested Readings:

Adler, Alfred. *Social Interest: A Challenge to Mankind.* New York: Capricorn Books, 1964.

———. *Understanding Human Nature.* A Premier Book, Greenwich, Connecticut: Fawcett Publications, Inc., 1963.

Arendt, Hannah. *The Human Condition.* Garden City, New York: Doubleday Anchor Books, 1959.

Berne, Eric. *Games People Play.* New York: Grove Press, 1967.

———. *The Structure and Dynamics of Organizations and Groups.* New York: Ballantine Books, 1973.

Blatty, William Peter. *The Exorcist.* New York: Bantam, 1972.

Chesler, Phyllis. "Men Drive Women Crazy," *Psychology Today,* July 1971.

Coopersmith, Stanley. *Antecedents of Self-Esteem.* San Francisco: W. H. Freeman, 1967.

Fagan, Joen, and Irma Lee Shepherd, eds. *What Is Gestalt Therapy?* Perennial Library Edition, New York: Harper & Row, 1973.

Freud, Sigmund. *A General Introduction to Psychoanalysis.* Garden City, New York: Garden City Pub. Co., 1943. (First German edition, 1917.)

———. *The Psychopathology of Everyday Life.* New York: Random House, 1938. (First German edition, 1904.)

Fromm, Erich. *The Art of Loving.* New York: Harper & Row, 1956.

Gergen, Kenneth J. "Multiple Identity," *Psychology Today,* May 1972.

Goffman, Erving. *The Presentation of Self in Everyday Life.* New York: Doubleday and Co., 1959.

Grier, W. H., and P. M. Cobbs, *Black Rage.* New York: Basic Books, 1968.

———. *The Jesus Bag.* New York: McGraw-Hill, 1971.

Hall, Calvin S., and Gardner Lindzey. *Theories of Personality.* New York: John Wiley and Sons, 1957.

Harris, Thomas, M.D. *I'm OK—You're OK.* New York: Avon Books, 1973.

Horner, Matina. "Fail: Bright Women," in *Feminine Personality,* ed. by Bardwick, Douvan, Guttman, and Horner. Belmont, California: Brooks/Cole, 1972.

Josephson, Eric, and Mary Josephson, eds. *Man Alone: Alienation in Modern Society.* New York: Dell Publication Co., 1962.

Jung, Carl G. *Modern Man in Search of a Soul.* New York: Harcourt, Brace, 1933.

———. *The Integration of Personality.* New York: Farrar and Rinehart, 1939.

———. *The Undiscovered Self.* New York: Mentor Books, New American Library, 1959.

Kierkegaard, Sören. *Fear and Trembling: The Sickness unto Death.* New York: Doubleday Anchor Books, 1954.

Laing, Ronald D. *The Divided Self.* London: Tavistock Pub., 1960; Penguin Books ed., 1965.

_____. *The Politics of Experience.* New York: Ballantine Books, 1967.

_____, and E. Esterson. "Sanity, Madness, and the Family," in Vol. 1, *Families of Schizophrenics.* New York: Basic Books, 1965.

Maslow, Abraham H. "Emotional Blocks to Creativity," *Journal of Individual Psychology* 14 (1958):51–56.

_____. "Neurosis as a Failure of Personal Development," *Humanitas,* 1967.

Menninger, Karl. *Man against Himself.* New York: Harvest Books, 1958.

Miller, D. R., and G. E. Swanson. *Inner Conflict and Defense.* New York: Schocken Press, 1966.

Rogers, Carl R. *Client-Centered Therapy.* Boston: Houghton-Mifflin Co., 1951.

_____. *On Becoming a Person.* Boston: Houghton-Mifflin, 1961.

Steiner, Claude. *Games Alcoholics Play.* New York: Ballantine Books, 1974.

Stephen, Karin. *The Wish to Fall Ill.* Cambridge, England: The University Press, 1960.

Wright, Nathan, Jr. *Let's Face Racism.* New York: Thos. Nelson, 1970.

10 Will the Real Self Please Stand Up

I believe I caused the illness myself. In my attempt to penetrate the other world I met its natural guardians, the embodiment of my own weaknesses and faults. . . . In my case the personal self had grown porous because of my dimmed consciousness. . . .

I wanted to enter death without going mad and stood before the Sphinx: either thou into the abyss or I! . . .

Then came illumination. . . . A larger and more comprehensive self emerged and I could abandon the previous personality with its entire entourage. I saw this earlier personality could never enter transcendental realms. A new life began for me and from now on I felt different from other people. A self that consisted of conventional lies, shams, self-deceptions, memory images, a self like that of other people, grew in me again but behind and above it stood a greater and more comprehensive self which impressed me with something of what is eternal, unchanging, immortal and inviolable and which ever since that time has been my protector and refuge.

KARL JASPERS
General Psychopathology[1]

1. Karl Jaspers, *General Psychopathology* (Manchester, England: Manchester University Press, 1962), pp. 417–18.

In the last chapters we explored some of the ways in which the Self becomes obscured, hidden, and how it often fights itself. This inner battle is often the worst kind of war that can be fought: the victor and the vanquished are the same! When the internal battles are waged, the struggle often takes its toll, as in all battles, on the battlefield itself. The battlefield is the person. Christians will recall St. Paul complaining that he was often at odds with himself. "I do not understand my own actions. For I do not do what I want, but I do the very thing I hate. . . . I can will what is right, but I cannot do it. For I do not do the good I want, but the evil I do not want is what I do."[2]

The conflicts that go on inside each of us are the mixed motives we have, the competing needs, the differing ideas and attitudes. They aren't differing *selves* slugging it out. We are whole persons, but there are many conflicting elements in each of us. Sometimes the rational part of us is in fierce competition with the emotional or the physiological parts. The result often seems to be a disintegration of the self, or behavior that seems to point to disintegration.

To settle the conflicts, we often compromise parts of our selfhood. At times we play as if there were no conflict. "I'm all right, Jack!" and "Stiff upper lip!" are some of the terms our British cousins employ to portray a stolid, unperturbed façade, while inside the battle goes on.

Be Everything You Can Be

One of the goals of significant Selfhood is that all the "players" play together. When a person is living authentically, one of the things that comes through is that "all his systems are Go" and that they work in some sort of integrated, total fashion. This sounds so mysterious, so mystical or magical. Is it? Sidney Jourard, among a growing number of others, says it's nothing magical at all. It's living your authentic existence, being truly, fully, real-ly all that you actually are:

> Authentic being means being oneself, honestly, in one's relations with his fellows. It means taking the first step at dropping pretenses, defenses, and duplicity. It means an end to "playing it cool," an end to using one's behavior as a gambit designed to disarm the other fellow, to get him to reveal himself *before* you disclose yourself to him. This invitation is fraught with risk; indeed, it may inspire terror in some. Yet, the hypothesis of the book is to the effect that, while simple honesty with others (and thus with oneself) may yield scars, it is likely to be

2. Romans 7:15–19.

an effective preventive both of mental illness and of certain kinds of physical sickness. Honesty can be literally a health-insurance policy.[3]

As you will no doubt have noted in this and previous chapters, we take the widely shared position that what is often called "mental illness" is not something that *comes from* being dishonest and alienated from your fullest experience of self; "mental illness" *is* being dishonest and alienated from self and others.

When you are split off from who you are and thus from others, *this* is psychopathology ("sickness of the psyche or behaving self"). If you are playing false with yourself and if this causes you to play false with others, you aren't effectively functioning or actualizing your Self. You're living a lie, and it's just not very satisfying.

The Self in conflict often displays behaviors that other people can't understand or predict, and which may alarm them. Sometimes, the behavior takes the simple form of forgetfulness. At other times, it may resemble the anxiety-possessed behavior described in the various neurotic classifications. In a number of cases, the person acts out behaviors

3. Sidney Jourard, *The Transparent Self* (Princeton, New Jersey: Van Nostrand Insight Books, 1964), p. 153.

that resemble the stereotyped "crazy" behavior of those who are labeled psychotic.

If the person living falsely, inauthentically, in continual self-alienation is labeled "mentally ill," then what do we call the person who is functioning fully, experiencing maximally, living and loving in the most satisfying manner possible? Jourard, Bugental, and others use the term "authenticity" to describe the reality-oriented personal and social life of the healthy person.

Each of us is born to certain situations or statuses in his life, and acquires others. Attached to each of these statuses is a set of behaviors. People expect certain things, say, from a teacher, a carpenter, a doctor, a welder. Those expectations make up the "roles" of social interaction. Among the many things we do, then, is to perform certain expected behaviors. The authentic, fully functioning, self-actualizing person is one who tries to concentrate on playing only those roles that are consistent with who he is. That is, the healthy person is one who is able to sort out the various roles he may play, select for concentrating on those that are personally meaningful to him and expressive of his selfhood, and act out the role-behavior well and satisfyingly. Self-actualizing people try *to be everything they can be.*

Another way of putting this might be to say that such a person feels so *OK* about himself that he is willing to take risks, to risk being more of what he's already shown of himself. This risk-taking ability doesn't mean foolhardiness or playing games with death or destructive experiences. It does mean putting yourself on the line when it's necessary, either because you need to be authentic and whole in a given situation, or because the situation requires your participation and intervention.

> Harriet enjoys the company of different sorts of people. She finds each person to be a unique human being and while she enjoys the similarities and kinship she shares with others, she also enjoys and appreciates the differences between them. She can't enjoy jokes that poke cruel or degrading "fun" at those differences.
>
> One day with her neighbor, Gloria, Harriet went shopping. As they rode the bus, the two men sitting in the seat in front of them, aware that Gloria was Mexican-American, began to talk in obviously loud voices about how passionate Mexican women were. Their humor got fairly crude. As Gloria burned with embarrassment and resentment, Harriet leaned forward and tapped the man talking on the shoulder. "Do you really enjoy making people feel silly and uncomfortable like that?"
>
> The man shrugged and both of them stopped talking. She knew she hadn't done much to change their mental attitudes about Mexican and Mexican-American people, but she hoped they might get the message eventually. At least for now her friend's discomfort might decrease a bit.

This woman wasn't playing any Games: she was feeling her friend's anger and hurt, and this kindled empathy in her—a realization of how she might feel in a similar situation. To be authentic, she knew she'd have to express her anger. There are never any guarantees that doing this will change the situation at all, but if nothing else the expression of feeling relieves the tension.

Harriet's Child was experiencing a bit of Gloria's pain, and the Adult in her had to make a decision how to handle this, to get strokes for herself, to get some strokes for Gloria's hurt Child, and so she replayed a bit of her Parent tapes and spoke in a criticizing fashion.

None of this is easy or foolproof. But individuated people, knowing who they are and appreciating themselves, dislike behaviors that hurt or belittle or dehumanize others.

Life is far more than simply playacting. It involves a constant round of choice-making experiences. In playacting, there is a more or less rigid script to follow and no matter how creative you may think you are, you aren't encouraged to deviate from it. Your own Life Scripts, on the other hand, are products of your own writing. You aren't obligated to stick faithfully to a script that is un-Self-actualizing, especially if you have learned differently. It's your prerogative and obligation to write new scripts for yourself as you discover more and more about yourself.

Individuated people, those who are in the lifelong process of actualizing their fullest, freest, realest Self, try to live authentically, being aware of life and by not dodging the sticky problems that confront them because they are fully alive.

How can a person be authentic, real and unpretentious, when for much of his childhood he is taught to be otherwise? In the absence of a wholesale change of social attitudes to encourage authenticity, the only hope at present apparently lies in the freedom of the person to become more fully what he is. Suppose a person doesn't know he's free? Most of us don't. We get caught up in the bag of thinking of ourselves as determined by *something*—biology, destiny, God, culture—and one of the most difficult things to do is to convince someone that he is a free, moral agent, that he can live his life in his own terms, that he has choices which may be hidden but which are nonetheless freely his. If a person will conscientiously study his own life, his choices, his preferences, he will find, we believe, that a startling amount of what he has done is his own "thing." Most of his preferences, he will find, are products of his value systems; thus preferences are automatic choices as unique to an individual as his value systems are. To believe otherwise is to deny the richness and variability of life and to limit man's freedom to make choices based on his individual character. The trick is, of course, to enable a person to develop and operate on the basis of his own value system. This may involve changing his behaviors.

Behavior Change for What?

How do personal value systems develop? How do we get to Wholeness? Are some people born fully functioning or does that take work, training, therapy? What is the behavior change process we call psychotherapy?

If all psychology did was to describe human behavior and build theories about it, it might have scientific and academic respectability, but it could not hope to be of much use to the large numbers of us struggling with the inner and outer battles of living.

In our struggles and searching, we are encouraged to recognize that not only in this age of crises, but from its beginning, psychology has been as interested in "applying" its findings as in "researching" them.

The methods and tools of applied psychology especially that part involved with behavior change, are varied—too much so to grasp in a simple fashion. To make the situation alive and "real," we can explore the behavior change processes in terms, first, of the *orientations or approaches* which motivate and guide the people practicing the process; second, in terms of the *settings* involved; and third, in terms of specific *techniques or methods.*

But before we get into the analysis of the various ways of changing behavior, which involves contrast and comparison, thus emphasizing *differences,* it would be important to urge your attention to a viewing of the *common ground* found among them all. For, regardless of viewpoint being expressed, locale of the process, or *modus operandi,* most attempts at behavior change share some common goals—though not all of them would agree that the following does anything like a complete job of stating their purposes or goals.

> [The goal] is the experience of becoming a more autonomous, more spontaneous, more confident person. It is the experience of freedom to be one's self.
>
> In the relationship with an effective therapist . . . the client moves gradually toward a new type of realization, a dawning recognition that in some sense he chooses himself. This is not usually any sudden burst of light—it is a groping, ambivalent, confused and uncertain movement into a new territory. The client begins to realize, "I am not compelled to be simply the creation of others, molded by their expectancies, shaped by their demands. I am not compelled to be a victim of unknown forces in myself. I am less and less a creature of influences in myself which operate beyond my ken in the realms of the unconscious. I am increasingly the architect of self. I am free to will and choose. I can, through accepting my individuality, my "isness," become more of my uniqueness, more of my potentiality.[4]

4. Carl R. Rogers, "Learning to Be Free," in *Conflict and Creativity,* ed. by Farber and Wilson (New York: McGraw-Hill Book Co., 1963).

Essentially, then, these behavior change processes involve freeing the person of dehumanizing, crippling, enslaving, fear-producing (or fear-caused) ideas, feelings, attitudes, self-conceptions, and interpersonal orientations. Obviously, the differing problems vary in intensity, extent, and duration. So, the program of change must be suited to the severity and type of problem.

The Problem, as I See It! (Therapist's Orientation)

Any practitioner of behavior change will be affected by his or her own personality, needs, background, and experiences. This is so obvious as to not merit mention. Yet, we must mention it, to explain why there are so many different "schools" of thought in psychology and in the applications of psychological insights.

Those who hold fast to a demon-possession model of mental and emotional disorders will probably view their roles as exorcists, as shamans (conjurers, healers, medicine men), or possibly as priests. There are elements of this in the work of some pastoral counselors (though not in the strict sense of exorcising), and often in the work of primal therapists.

Those who believe in the medical model will primarily work as physicians, treating the organic problems of the entire body, assuming the problem to originate in the blood chemistry, the metabolism, the endocrine system, diet, fatigue, or neurological damage. Medical doctors working with people in emotional or mental stress often utilize their basic medical skills, though recognizing the importance of the "talking it out" techniques of conventional psychotherapies. These behavior-change specialists are usually psychiatrists, working in private practice, in community centers or mental hospitals.

Those who view the problems from the psychoanalytic model (the Freudian approach), mostly M.D.s, undergo long training procedures to prepare themselves. They basically view the problems in their patients as symptoms of unconscious conflicts between two or more elements of the psyche: the *id,* the *ego,* or the *superego.* They view their role as that of a tireless guide who helps the patient confront these conflicting patterns in a protected and relaxed environment, by drawing them out, pointing out and interpreting what lies hidden. Their goals include not only psycho*analysis,* which involves dissection of the varying components of the psyche, but a thorough investigation of these components, including an acknowledgment of their origins (etiology), and finally a careful and painstaking synthesis, or putting back together the pieces of the psyche, this time with fuller awareness and acceptance, and a sense of control by the ego of the patient. The *id* and *superego*

must find newer, less painful or damaging, ways of getting satisfaction, and the ego is schooled in ways of doing this so that the ongoing flow of psychic life can continue more freely and more acceptingly.

This orientation, which dominated Western psychology for nearly fifty years, is basic to the work of such people as Erikson, Greenson, Stekel, Fenichel, and in modified form, in the therapeutic writings of Horney, Fromm, and Sullivan.

If the practitioner finds more promise, or more answers, in the existential model, he will accept in his behavior change programs to bring the client to a fuller realization of the meaninglessness in his life, of anxieties about existence, of fears of making decisions, commitments, of following through on the consequences of such crisis points. The existential therapist tries to engage the client in a here-and-now orientation, to keep past history in its proper perspective, and to help the client to decrease the attempts to "cop out" by blaming parents, society, genetics, or anything other than himself and his anxieties, his indecisiveness, and his unrealistic fantasies. Such orientations are found in varying degrees in the works (and among followers) of Viktor Frankl, Ludwig Binswanger (originally a Freudian), Sartre, Rollo May, Gordon Allport, and to some extent in the work of Carl Rogers, Fritz Perls and other Gestalt therapists.

If the practitioner views the primary problem as originating in poor psychic developments of one sort or another (the ego psychology model), his work will consist of helping the client to accept himself, develop his strengths, accept and, if possible, incorporate his weaknesses into the new self-concept, converting or transmuting them into beneficial forces. Many orientations include some of this in their therapeutic programs: certainly Rogers and other client-centered therapists, many of the Jungians (analytic psychology), many of the Adlerians (individual psychology), Nathaniel Branden and his self-esteem psychology, and in varying degrees the followers of Wilhelm Reich, Harry Stack Sullivan, and many people involved in a variety of human potential programs, like Perls, Bindrim, Simkin, Janov, Pesso, and others.

If the orientation involves a belief that human conflicts originate in our psychosocial development (the encounter model), the behavior change practitioners may utilize group experiences of a wide assortment of types: encounter groups, sensitivity groups, human potential groups, nude encounters, and many others in the more recent, often more radical, growth centers, such as Esalen and the Center for the Study of the Person.

The wholism model (our term) covers a lot of ground, often overlapping many of the others already mentioned. Its followers find inner psychic disintegration to be the main problem. Often the emphasis is like that of psychoanalysis, in getting the various aspects of the psyche back into harmonious and wholistic functioning, such as definitely characterizes the work of the Jungians. But it may include more *esoteric* attempts, such as reorienting the person to a mind-body wholism, as is found in the psychosynthesis, bioenergetics, structural integration (Rolfing), macrobiotics, and other orientations.

Then, because they defy easy and simplistic classifications (as indeed do most approaches!), there are those that are too divergent to be lumped together: transcendental meditation, Zen Buddhist therapies, Janov's primal therapy, and many others.

Finally, because they share some common assumptions, there are several approaches to behavior change which avoid the use of psychiatric labels (like "neurosis," "symptoms," or "therapy") and view the problems in living as functions of environmental conditioning. These can be said to follow the reinforcement or behaviorist model. Social learning is the main emphasis, and what others call "sickness" or "psychopathology" the behavior modification specialists call maladaptive or dysfunctional learning. Since problems are learned, they say, they can be unlearned, and in their places can be substituted new learned behaviors. Behavior modification works in areas such as modifying the effects of phobias, autism, mental retardation, alcoholism, addiction, sexual difficulties, and habits such as smoking, overeating, gambling, and so on. It is easy for non-behaviorists to be critical of this model, but it is indisputable that many of their techniques are working and helping great numbers of people to change their behaviors for the better. They never talk of "treatment" or "cure": instead they simply talk of modifications of problem or maladaptive behaviors.

Is there a humanistic model? Not as such. Any of the models or approaches can be considered humanistic if the attitude of the practitioner is to actualize the maximum amount possible of the potential of the subject or client. To attempt this, the "therapist" must believe that such potentials do indeed exist in the client and that the client can, somehow, be helped to find, develop, and maintain his own autonomous controls over his own life.

"Step into My Parlor" (The Setting of Behavior Change)

Our stereotypes of psychotherapy cause us to conjure up a picture of a doctor's office, richly furnished and paneled, with a leather couch, on which the patient reclines, looking up at the ceiling and telling all to the therapist (usually bearded like Father Freud), who sits out of view, taking down copious notes, and mumbling, "Mmm, I see!"

Like any stereotype, this one has some basis in fact. Psychoanalysts (and others) often do utilize an office and a couch. Though this has changed drastically, there are some who still insist Freud had the best setting for his work.

Regardless of where the therapy is conducted, setting is very important. It must be easily accessible for the client; the light and ventilation must be adequate and noninterfering; the seating (if utilized) must be comfortable, to enable the fullest involvement of the client or clients. Privacy must be assured, for many people who bring long-standing concerns to a psychotherapist are full of guilt or shame about them. They may find it difficult enough even to divulge some of this to the therapist himself; if others are present, such communication is made more difficult. So, receptionists and secretaries and others in waiting rooms must be out of earshot.

There must be a guarantee of freedom from interruption; so traffic must not be allowed to intrude on the therapy session, be it the noise of vehicles on the street or the flow of people from one room to another.

Many behavior change practitioners have a private "practice," utilizing an office of one or more rooms, some in which individual therapy can be conducted, and larger rooms where group therapy can proceed. In working with children and adolescents, some therapists have a "playroom," where toys, dolls, clay, paints, darts, and other media can be freely employed.

Some behavior change goes on in special rooms set aside in schools and colleges (as is the case with many behavior modification programs). Here, a variety of instruments for measurement and specially designed implements (like tachistoscopes, pupillometers, shock devices) and conditioning techniques can be used.

In community mental health centers, there is often a suite of offices, where individual, group, play, and occupational therapies can go on. Often, such a center utilizes a converted house, storefront, or suite of medical offices. A center of this type is usually under the direction of a psychiatrist, though the director may be a clinical psychologist or clinical social worker. It will employ a variety of specialists: apart from the three groups mentioned just above, there will be clerical help, recreation, occupational, and nursing specialists. Students doing graduate work or completing internships are often brought in to learn while doing, always under the careful scrutiny of certified and experienced therapists.

Your authors have worked in several centers of this kind, and can attest warmly to their success in helping people to meet crisis situations and work out rocky marriages or alcohol or drug problems, often preventing the necessity of hospitalization. These centers are often screening centers for those who must be hospitalized, however. And they provide a valuable service as "halfway houses" for people leaving the mental hospitals and returning to their communities.

The psychiatric unit of a general hospital is usually a single ward of five to fifty beds. For acute cases of psychosis, suicidal attempts, alcoholic binges, overdoses, and other emergency problems of a short-term treatment duration, such units provide important help to the people in the community. A psychiatrist usually serves as chief of psychiatric services, and the treatments usually involve those found in most inpatient hospital settings. But they may also provide the rehabilitative programs or crisis intervention that are also carried on in other communities by the mental health centers.

Finally, let's look at the mental hospital itself. Even though we emphasize that many problems in living do not fit neatly into the medical model, there is no denying that some persons are so damaged psychically that they must find help in a setting far removed from the more threatening aspects of community life.

In short, some people are simply frightened of the outside world, or seem on the verge of doing harm to themselves or to those around them. The function of the hospital, usually far removed from the noise and fast pace of the city, is to provide a retreat, a rest, a time apart.

The so-called asylum took the place of the prison and the general hospital in the 1600s and 1700s. It offered protection and sanctuary for those troubled in mind and spirit. Being a medical facility, it provided physical medical treatment for bodily distress, but it also began the practice of psychiatry as we know it today. Medicines have always been a part of the treatment programs, and more is said about them under the topic of chemotherapy later in this chapter.

For those whose violence is uncontrollable, restraint methods may have to be used, some chemical, some mechanical: like hot, wet sheets into which the patient can be rolled (like a hot dog in its bun), or wrist bonds, or warm water baths. The strait jacket and padded cell, though still found, are being replaced by other procedures less reminiscent of the medieval torture chamber.

"Now, Watch Closely" (Techniques of Treatment)

As the orientations and settings vary, so will methods of behavior change. There is much common ground: many programs involve talking things through, with emphasis placed on the feelings, not on the concepts; many involve medication to reduce anxiety or psychosis or to fight depression and elevate mood; many involve acting the conflicts out, as in role-playing or sociodrama, primal therapy, Gestalt therapy, and others.

But to give you some idea of the variety of methodologies, we now present an alphabetical listing of many behavior change procedures.

Behavior Modification Techniques

The behaviorists conclude that most problems in living are the result of faulty or ineffective learning experiences. The need to apply their research efforts to the problems of human existence has led some behaviorists to develop techniques for modifying problem behavior. Basically it involves *assessment, deconditioning,* and *reconditioning.* The assessment is in terms of how adaptive or maladaptive the person's (subject's) behavior is for his life. No psychiatric labels (neurotic, psychopathic, schizophrenic, and so on) are used.

Once the subject's conditioning needs are understood by the "therapist," it's necessary to help the subject to decrease the maladaptive behaviors so that adaptive ones can be learned instead. One technique is *aversive conditioning.* K. Freund treated 67 male homosexual subjects by giving them a drug that caused vomiting and then showed them slides of dressed and nude men. One treatment a day was given up to a period of 24 days. In other words, the subjects learned to associate the emetic drug with pictures of nude men, so that they would become averse to the idea of male nudity. Then the subjects were injected with male sex hormones, and they were then shown films of nude or seminude women.[5]

Such procedures have not been tremendously successful except with less deeply ingrained attitudes and problems, like bedwetting, smoking, drinking, and a wide variety of phobias. Perhaps the most significant contribution of behavior modification is in the treatment of autism, especially in young children. Dr. Ivor Lovaas at UCLA's Neuropsychiatric Institute and other behavioral specialists around the country are utilizing conditioning techniques to break through the "autistic barrier" of these children and condition them to respond to the world around them.

We all use conditioning techniques every day and so they are a very real part of our lives. The behaviorists are helping people to achieve adaptive and effective lives by using these techniques in the behavior modification process.

Body Awareness Techniques

Body Awareness Techniques is an inadequate term to describe dozens of techniques, but it seems to fit these many approaches to Wholeness, which will emphasize the healing aspects of reuniting us,

5. K. Freund, "Some Problems in the Treatment of Homosexuality," in H. J. Eysenck, ed., *Behavior Therapy and the Neuroses* (London: Pergamon Press, 1960).

in one way or another, with our physical bodies. Not only are we disintegrated within and among our personal and social roles, but our very concept of selfhood is disintegrated: we may see ourselves as a body, a mind, a soul, or "all heart." We tend to separate these various functions from the essential wholeness and unity of Being.

Among these techniques (and we must just mention them and leave their greater depth exploration up to you) are *Bioenergetics* (which emphasizes breathing and exercises); *Rolfing* or Structural Integration (a bodily massage and touch-awareness technique developed by Ida Rolf); *body movement and awakening* techniques (Bernard Gunther, Judy Aston, Ann Halprin, Charlotte Selver, and many others); *psychomotor therapy* (tying Jungian concepts in with dramatic bodily activity—developed by Albert Pesso); *hatha-yoga* and *kundalini-yoga* (utilizing the wholizing principles of Indian yoga practices—developed by Joel Kramer, V. G. Rele, C. W. Leadbeater, A. Avalon, and others); *Tai Chi Chu'an* (Chinese bodily/spiritual exercises and dance—Gia-Fu Feng, and others); and many others.

Psychologists often hesitate to include these forms of wholeness development with more traditional forms of therapy. However, humanistic psychology believes in the whole person and recognizes the truth that feeling *OK* or having a sense of well-being (which is part of "mental health") definitely involves the body as well as the psyche. Most of these techniques cannot be found by finger-walking through the Yellow Pages. You will have to check in the Suggested Readings section of this chapter for contact names. The Esalen Institute is a primary source of information for a great number of body awareness techniques and growth centers.

Biofeedback

We will elaborate more on this procedure in chapter twelve, seeing its relationship to studies of consciousness alteration. However, biofeedback techniques are being widely used in the reduction of tension, anxiety, and working with individuals plagued by migraine headaches, epilepsy, insomnia, muscular tics, muscle cramps, high blood pressure, and some forms of heart disease.

Essentially, *biofeedback* refers to any communication from your body that you pick up and utilize in modifying your behavior: such as observing your own knees shaking or palms getting sweaty. Specifically, it refers to electronic measurement of internal states, such as those recorded on EEG (electroencephalogram) machines. Observing brain wave patterns, for instance, enables you to attempt to condition yourself to "produce" certain patterns at will, and these are associated with desirable physical and/or mental states.

Chemotherapy

Basically, we are talking here about the use of chemicals to treat or alleviate emotional or mental problems (though technically a physician prescribing medication for the flu or pneumonia is also using chemotherapy). There are several aspects to this.

Narcosynthesis involves the use of certain drugs, like sodium amytal or sodium pentothol, so-called "truth serums," which release some unconscious materials into the conscious for an inhibited or repressed patient to deal with.

Tranquilizers, the well-known "mother's little helpers" of song and story, have been around since time began in natural herbal, root, and bark forms. For instance, rauwolfia (snakeroot) was used for centuries in India as a general medication, but patients suffering psychotic symptoms were often aided by ingesting this drug. A derivative of rauwolfia, reserpine, was found to have value in treating hypertension and some symptoms of psychosis as well. Other tranquilizing drugs are chlorpromazine, perphenazine, meprobamate, librium, and others.

Energizing drugs, or "mood elevators," are generally used with people experiencing depressive states. They are iproniazid, phenelzine, imipramine, amitripthyline, and others.

Ours is close to being a "chemical age" and many people put their fullest confidence in the use of such drug combinations. However,

> Chemotherapy is not a cure-all. Psychotherapeutic drugs are welcome adjuncts to the total treatment program, but it would be unrealistic to assume that mental disorders based on the gradual development of faulty frames of reference and response patterns could be permanently cleared up by such limited methods. . . . Tranquilizers and energizers tend to mask symptoms rather than to come to grips with the actual causes of mental disorders.[6]

LSD therapy is relatively new on the scene, though the chemical, lysergic acid diethylamide, has been known about for thirty years. The use of LSD as a therapeutic aid has met with quite mixed reactions, more because of media coverage than because of inherently controversial qualities of the drug itself.

One researcher (Coughlan) found that when an LSD user *expects* to have a rewarding experience, has good rapport with the therapist, and feels comfortable in the environmental setting, the "trip" is much more likely to be positive and therapeutic. Users experience some delusions and hallucinations, but also what has been called "humanity identification,"[7] all of which may aid the therapist in bringing the subject out into more humanistic patterns of interaction.

6. James C. Coleman, *Abnormal Psychology and Modern Life* (Glenview, Illinois: Scott, Foresman and Co., 1964), 3rd Ed., p. 563.
7. Ibid., p. 582.

Individuals with known histories of psychosis and some personality disorders are considered bad risks for LSD usage.

What is the present status of LSD as a therapeutic tool?

> When LSD was used for psychotherapeutic purposes a decade ago (before its use was limited to experimental efforts only), it was hailed as a breakthrough that promised an end to a variety of mental conflicts. In a ten-year follow-up study of such patients, however, it was concluded that no lasting personality, value, belief, attitude, or behavior changes were produced.[8]

Counseling

This word, much used and much abused, refers to the practice of working "therapeutically" with people in distress, emotional conflict, grief, or other kinds of trouble. We feel it is a valid part of psychotherapy. However, even when psychiatrists and licensed clinical psychologists use the term to describe their own efforts, they often feel that other less certified and "ordained" individuals who call themselves "counselors" are only paraprofessionals. This may be a problem in semantics, and it may also be professional snobbery.

Educational counseling often refers to the simple process of giving academic guidance. High school and college counselors are often untrained in psychotherapeutic procedures and they might more appropriately be called advisors or guidance workers. However, many of these professionals *are* trained in therapy techniques, some holding licenses as marriage, family, and child counselors. Their techniques differ little from those used by other psychotherapists in private practice or in clinical settings. Some have earned advanced degrees and credentials in psychometry and pupil personnel services, and many are going on to earn credentials as school psychologists, which is far from being a "paraprofessional" function.

Pastoral counseling refers to the counseling services provided by trained clergy. Many of these men and women, in addition to their theological training, have done advanced work in psychology and psychotherapeutic techniques, some even doing a year-long "clinical" internship. There have always been pastors, Jewish, Catholic, and Protestant, who had skills in developing wholeness among their parishioners, but only in the past twenty years have such psychological courses become firmly rooted segments of their seminary training.

Marriage counseling is a specialty profession. Those who do this work, trying to find root problems and effect wholistic changes in married couples, come from a variety of backgrounds. Some are clergy, psychiatric social workers, psychologists, psychiatrists, sociologists, and

8. Elton McNeil, *Being Human* (San Francisco: Caufield Press, 1973), pp. 81–82.

even attorneys. Their techniques vary as psychotherapeutic techniques vary, but in most states they must pass a rigorous examination, indicating training and breadth of experience before they earn their licenses to practice.

Encounter and Sensitivity Groups

Such groups emerged in the 1960s as part of humanistic psychology's human potential movement. There is no unified voice, dogma, licensing, or preparation. Most people who lead such groups do not claim to be psychotherapists (a licensing and legal definition is involved), but all report therapeutic results in many of the participants of such experiences.

Encounter training began in the late 1940s at the National Institutes of Mental Health, as a way of helping people get better in touch with who they were. Carl R. Rogers was one of the first professional psychologists to identify himself with training or T-groups.

The sensitivity group is similar, with the difference lying in the directionality of the awareness. In encounter groups, typically, the other members of the group serve as agents of insight, showing each member just how he or she comes across, wherein each might want to explore further, or might want to change. Of course, semantic differences have arisen and the two terms are often used interchangeably, which is no great problem.

William Schutz, Terry O'Banion, April O'Connell, Lawrence Frank, Max Gunther, and hundreds of other well-trained professionals are leaders and promoters of these programs, the most famous of which is still the Esalen Institute at California's Big Sur. Ida Rolf's structural integration grew out of these retreat experiences, as did many refinements of Perls' Gestalt therapy.

Gestalt Therapy

The Gestalt psychologists—Wertheimer, Lewin, Koffka, et al.—promoted the idea that a person had to be seen in the context of his or her whole configuration of meaning, the *gestalt*. This German word translates awkwardly into English, but roughly it means the pattern, configuration, whole figure-ground relationship. Their most important contributions were in perception studies.

Frederick S. Perls developed a psychotherapeutic process from these insights, stressing the wholeness of human experience. A psychiatrist, "Fritz" Perls came away from his one and only meeting with Freud a disenchanted and frustrated man, feeling that human experience had to be far more than Freud had described it to be.

In his work, Perls stressed the importance of helping his clients to learn to live in the here and the now. This was important, because traditional therapies insisted on playing what Berne called the Game of "Archeology," of digging into the wounds and traumas of the past, ignoring responsibility for dealing with the present.

Gestalt therapy utilizes free discussion between therapist and client—as other therapies do—but more attention is paid to nonverbal communication than to the form or contents of the words used. The therapist may draw the client's attention to finger drumming, deep sighing, foot tapping, inability to look the therapist in the eye, or points of hesitation in verbal contributions to help him understand what is going on inside him.

> The aim of Gestalt therapy is to develop more "intelligent" behavior; that is, to enable the individual to act on the basis of all possible information and to apprehend not only the relevant factors in the external field, but also relevant information from within. The individual is directed to pay attention at any given moment to what he is feeling, what he wants, what he is doing. . . . The process of increasing awareness enables the individual to discover how he interrupts his own functioning.[9]

Gestalt therapists utilize dream analysis, "hot-seat" techniques, inner dialogue, role-reversal acting-out, and body awareness experiences—anything to help the individual see just what he or she is doing that is inconsistent, fragmentary, gamelike, and inauthentic in ordinary behavior.

> The Gestalt approach is to integrate dreams rather than to analyze them. Integrating can be accomplished by consciously reliving the dream, by taking responsibility for being the objects and people in the dream, by becoming aware of the messages the dream holds. . . . Each part of the dream is likely to disguise a message about the person dreaming it. When the message comes through, he is likely to feel, "Ah ha! So that's the way I am."[10]

Gestalt therapy has become a large and well-known movement, especially on the West Coast. Perls' successors have tried to develop and refine the techniques outlined by Perls, Goodman, and Hefferline, to bring into focus the relevancies of this technique to the pressures of modern living. The curious reader is referred to Perls' works, the works of the above-named people, and an exciting book that combines

9. Joen Fagan and Irma Lee Shepherd, eds., *What Is Gestalt Therapy?* (Perennial Library Ed., New York: Harper & Row, 1973), p. 57. The excerpt is from the article "Gestalt Therapy: A Behavioristic Phenomenology," by Elaine Kepner and Lois Brien.
10. Muriel James and Dorothy Jongeward, *Born to Win* (Reading, Maryland: Addison-Wesley Publishing Co., 1971), p. 246.

Gestalt techniques with transactional analysis, *Born to Win*, by Muriel James and Dorothy Jongeward.

Hospitalization

The techniques of the typical mental hospital in this country vary from heavy emphasis on medications (chemotherapy) to heavy emphasis on psychotherapy and rehabilitative training. The physical body of the patient is given great emphasis. Diet, exercise, rest and sleep, occupational and recreational therapy are part of the regimen. In addition, there are also the various programs of restraint mentioned briefly before.

These are all medical procedures and this requires that the administration and treatment programs be under the direction of medical doctors. Clinical psychologists, nurses, nurses' aides, psychiatric technicians, social workers, and vocational nurses have all been added to the staffs of such hospitals in recent years. Chemotherapy has reduced the need for restraints in a vast majority of cases of violence or attempts to run away. Psychotherapy and physical programs have cut the duration of hospitalization for most patients in a remarkable manner.

Among the most controversial treatment programs are electroshock therapy (EST or ECT) and psychosurgery. The former, involving the administration of electric currents to electrodes placed on the patient's temples, produces a convulsion and immediate unconsciousness. After waking, the patient is showered and fed. There is often a short-term memory loss, but in many depressive and catatonic schizophrenic patients, the EST produces a readiness for the psychotherapy that usually accompanies the total treatment program. While many hospitals have given this treatment up, since patients often fear the shock or view it as punishment, others continue to find it highly effective. TA leader Thomas Harris says:

> In cases of severe depression, electric shock treatment is administered. The effect of shock treatment is dramatic. After two or three treatments the patient becomes cheerful, relaxed, willing to talk. The treatment temporarily knocks out the painful, archaic recordings, allowing the recommissioning of the Adult. With the Adult again functioning the patient can begin to learn P-A-C, to understand where the archaic feelings come from and how he can turn them off himself.[11]

Your authors, after studying this treatment modality for many years, are less enthusiastic. We are happy for those whom the technique has helped, but urge that much more research be done to discover alternative methods for producing similar results.

11. Thomas Harris, *I'm OK—You're OK* (New York: Avon Books), p. 133.

Psychosurgery involves operating on the brain of a patient, with the express purpose of alleviating neurological lesions and other complications. Where a tumor or lesion is producing epilepsy or violent behaviors, surgery is often effective.

In 1936, a doctor in Lisbon performed the first highly publicized prefrontal lobotomy, an operation during which neural pathways between the prefrontal lobes of the brain's cortex and the hypothalamus were severed surgically. This produced a reduction in the patient's hallucinations and other disturbing thoughts.

In recent years some have advocated that such operations be utilized on a variety of antisocial offenders, to reduce or eliminate aggression. Opponents of such operations claim they would form *1984-*like controls over individual freedoms—especially those deemed "offenders" by the state. There has been a lessened tendency to use such drastic and irreversible measures in past years, mainly because of a relatively high death rate among patients, frequency of postoperative convulsive seizures, and undesirable personality changes: the so-called "vegetables" produced by such techniques.

Hospitalization will remain one of the treatment modalities for a wide variety of emotional and mental disorders which the "outside" world still doesn't understand or accept. Community mental health centers, "halfway houses," and psychiatric units of general hospitals have taken some of the patient load; medication and preventive psychiatry have helped too. But for the chronic schizophrenic, paranoid, depressive, or senile person, such programs do not afford the same element of total or custodial care that the hospital does. A great deal of research is being done to consider what the future of such patients and such programs will be.

Meditation

The leap from hospitals to meditation seems an odd one, but such is the situation when techniques are examined alphabetically. In meditation, under a variety of names and labels, the individual attempts to get in touch with himself by altering his consciousness. It is done without hypnosis (though some autosuggestion is involved), without drugs, and without a therapist. A leader of sorts is often involved in the training stages, but meditation is basically a solitary and individual matter. With or without spiritual or transcendental emphases, meditation involves concentrating on a thought, an idea, a word or phrase (in meditation forms related to Hinduism, like transcendental meditation, this is called a *mantra*), or upon emptiness and infinity. Through deep concentration, the person becomes absorbed in a state of peace and clarity.

Many people—perhaps as many as 500,000—are involved in meditation of a variety of forms in this country. Without elaborating on their claims for "cure," we *can* document cases of reduction of anxiety, greater confidence, increased self-awareness, self-respect, and better waking and sleeping habits. These will be discussed in chapter twelve.

Psychotherapy

Now we come to a broad category of services, offered in private offices and clinics, and in hospitals and schools. Psychotherapy refers in general to techniques of "treating the psyche," or working to restore harmony to the contrary or antagonistic forces and partitions within the person in trouble. We will explore the major forms, doing violence to their wholeness by this brief treatment. You will profit more from further study in sources recommended in the bibliography.

Psychotherapy involves two or three major formats, whatever the orientation of the therapist. *Individual* therapy means the patient or client is in a one-to-one relationship with the therapist. *Group* therapy means more than one client (usually up to eight or ten) is involved

with the therapist (though sometimes two therapists are utilized). *Conjoint* therapy refers to the practice of some therapists to have a family or at least a couple involved together at the same time with the therapist. Your authors have utilized all these techniques and have tended to specialize in group therapy for the past twelve years.

Psychoanalysis is the name given to the classical form of therapy developed by Sigmund Freud, and also to modifications of this program developed by Horney, Erikson, Fromm, Greenson, Fenichel, and other Freudians and neo-Freudians.

Briefly, psychoanalysis considers the problem of the patient to be an expression of internalized and repressed conflicts between the *id, ego,* and *superego.* Usually, in a neurotic syndrome, the sexual or aggressive impulses of the *id* have been repressed by the moralistic or judgmental forces of the *superego,* or the reality findings of the *ego.* Such repressed impulses must be brought out.

Psychoanalysis involves the analyst and the patient working together to make conscious these unconscious conflicts. The analyst uses dream interpretation, free association, transference, and other techniques wherein the patient lets the long-repressed feelings out, often in violent or dramatic fashion. Then, together, they work to produce a synthesis, where the *ego* will be in control, allowing the *superego* and *id* to find safe and free expression. This technique is mostly a "talking cure," with the patient recounting as much of his life experiences as possible until he begins to see the whole pattern emerge.

Classical psychoanalysis is a huge undertaking, often involving the patient in treatment for an hour a day, from three to seven days a week. Unfortunately, most analysts are relatively expensive, and a person seeking psychoanalytic treatment must be willing to spend from ten dollars to 75 dollars per session. The minimum program runs a year, in most cases, with many programs continuing for two to five years. Very few community clinics provide this service at their reduced rates.

Existential Therapy, coming to this country from Europe through the work of Viktor Frankl and others, attempts through talking to help the patient discover the meaningfulness of his life experiences, even where such meaning is apparently absent.

> . . . Most existential therapists who stress the importance of *confrontation*—challenging the individual directly with questions concerning the meaning and purpose of his existence—and the *encounter*—the relationship which is established between two interacting human beings in the therapeutic situation.[12]

12. Coleman, op. cit., p. 594. See also the studies of Viktor Frankl ("Existential Dynamics and Neurotic Escapisms," *J. Existential Psychiatry,* 1963, 4, 27–42; *Man's Search for Meaning*); Rollo May, "Existential Theory and Therapy," in J. Masserman, ed., *Current Psychiatric Therapies;* and L. A. Pervin, "Existentialism, Psychology, and Psychotherapy," *American Psychologist,* 1960, 15, 305–09.

Hypnotherapy. This technique has been around a long time, though its initial users were often scoffed at or disregarded. Today, the use of hypnosis in changing a wide variety of behavior which patients see as problems is well accepted. Everything from smoking, drinking, or masturbation, to deeper neuroses and severe self-image problems is being treated. Some therapists use hypnosis effectively with psychotic patients.

While few therapists consider hypnotic experiences to be "curative" of deep-seated problems, most agree that they can be used effectively in overcoming inhibitions and resistances to therapy and in uncovering unconscious material.

Jungian therapy. Jung called his form of treatment analytical psychology. However, he felt his most important contributions weren't in the area of treating neuroses and character disorders, or even in the remission of symptoms of psychosis—all of which he did. Jung and his followers felt their techniques worked best with those individuals who functioned fairly effectively in the society, but who were troubled with inner turmoil, dissatisfaction, restlessness, boredom, and a lack of feeling of wholeness.

Jung called such a problem a "spiritual crisis." To Jung, modern human beings seemed to suffer mostly from estrangement from their full Selfhood. The inner workings of the psyche needed to be explored, the unconscious materials made conscious, and the individual needed to find more meaningful ways of experiencing his life. The most effective technique of analytical psychology is dream analysis.

In each human being, Jung said, there is both a personal unconscious—where past memories and repressed materials reside, and a collective unconscious—a repository of memories and experiences common to all people. Among these hidden treasures were the archetypes, the anima, the animus, the shadow, the soul, the ego, and the Self, among others. The ego is but the apparent self, the executive who is in charge and who is aware of things in the conscious. Dreams reveal, however, that other experiences and yearnings are present. Jungians almost always consider dreams as communications from the collective unconscious to the conscious mind of the dreamer. Some dreams, of course, refer to matters in the personal unconscious, dealing with family, work, sex, marriage, or early life. But there are countless dreams that seem to refer to nothing the individual can recall.

> In handling a dream or a fantasy I make it a rule never to go beyond the meaning which has an effect upon the patient; I merely strive in each case to make this meaning as conscious to him as possible, so that he can also become aware of its suprapersonal connections.[13]

13. Carl G. Jung, *Modern Man in Search of a Soul* (A Harvest Book, New York: Harcourt, Brace and Co., 1960), p. 66.

Jung's growth process (he avoided the term "therapy," seeing the healing of neurotic and other personality wounds as only a small, first step toward the fuller growth of the Self) involves full participation by the client, in contrast to many other therapies, where the therapist is the central focus, his interpretations often becoming "truth" for the patient. In Jungian work, it is a partnership. The analyst functions more as a teacher in the earlier stages, then as a guide and companion.

When a client begins Jungian analysis, his goal is clearly laid before him: to change the center of his personality, or psyche, from the conscious ego, or Child-self, to a point midway between the conscious and the unconscious. This new point, called the Self, provides the psyche with unity, equilibrium, and stability. In other words, the self grows up to become the Self. This part of the growth process is called the *individuation process,* wherein the various components of the psyche, such as the Persona, Anima, and Animus, are differentiated. Once this is done, the client has greater realization of his own uniqueness and autonomy. Then, the *transcendent function* begins to integrate the individuated "parts" into a new unity, building toward greater wholeness and a recognizing of one's place in the human family, time, space, and the cosmos.

There is much confusion about Jungian theory, primarily because Jung's writings are heavy with symbolism, references to mythology, and use of theological, philosophical, and even archeological terms. Jung's followers (notably Kunkel, Jaffe, Jacobi, and Wolff) have done a better job of "translating" his ideas. The psychological "establishment" has criticized Jung's theories and therapeutic processes because they involve "mystical" elements and are unscientific. Yet, few deny that Jung has been one of the most profound thinkers of the modern era. He, more than almost any other modern thinker, has been able to integrate widely divergent scientific areas in a more wholistic picture of human nature.

Play Therapy

Recognizing the re-creative aspects of play, many child psychologists and psychiatrists have long utilized play activities for therapeutic purposes, especially with children. Moreover, some therapists have found play to be an effective way of diagnosing a child's (and some adults') problems, especially since the usual vocabulary of diagnosis and treatment may be lacking with a child. So, art, drama, dance, dolls, Pla-doh, clay, and other media are used to help the child express what's going on inside, and to get some of his feelings out in safe and nondestructive ways. Most community clinics offer such programs.

Psychodrama

Children aren't the only ones who may require play or nonverbal methods to alleviate distress or uncover conflicts. Adults too can use such techniques for their insight and growth. Jacob Moreno pioneered the techniques we now call psychodrama (often called sociodrama when relationships are being acted out).

In such therapy, the individual is asked to "play" his or her part in a situation, and others are cast in supporting roles. Occasionally, role-playing (a variation of psychodrama) involves reversals: a wife portraying her husband and he taking his wife's part, so each can see how the other perceives that person's role in their marriage.

Psychodrama and role-playing have become part of the repertory of many therapeutic forms, including Gestalt therapy and TA.

Radical Therapy

In a sense, every new therapy is radical in that it represents some change from traditional patterns, but the first to insist that it actually sets out to be radical is radical therapy.

> It is new in that it appears to be a form of activism different from the protest movements of the 1960s—more interested in the relationship between personal change and political change, less preoccupied with demonstrations and civil disobedience as tools of change. It is old in that it represents a strong and persistent line of psychological thought: the idea that society is the root cause of all mental suffering and that a radical transformation of it is the only real and lasting form of therapy.[14]

The radical therapy movement isn't focused in any one leader or ideologist, having grown out of several diverse efforts. The roots are found in the works of Wilhelm Reich, Herbert Marcuse, Ronald D. Laing, Thomas Szasz, Frantz Fanon, and some of the works of Perls, Rogers, and Berne.

The movement is less a technique of therapy than a protest against conventional forms of treatment which the radical therapists insist only compound a person's problems. Claude Steiner, a founder of the Berkeley Radical Psychiatry Center in California, actually uses the TA model. It is trying to humanize and "deprofessionalize" the mental health professions (use lay people in therapy situations), a goal both admirable and frightening! Without judging this movement, or recommending it either, we simply list it here as a topic worthy of your interest and

---

14. Walt Anderson, "Breaking Out of the Establishment Vise," *Human Behavior*, December 1973.

investigation, with the hope that it *will* have some effect in giving health to more and more people.

Reevaluation Therapies

Though there is a definite therapeutic program calling itself reevaluation therapy, we are putting together several differing modalities that all utilize similar models and methods.

Albert Ellis' *rational-emotive therapy* works to help the patient see that his problems arise from faulty assumptions about himself and the world around him. These therapists try to help the patient unmask and recognize his self-defeating verbalizations, to rethink his situation, and to put his new insights into action.

E. L. Phillips does *assertion training*, helping the patient to discard his negative self-concepts, encouraging him to explore alternative assumptions, and discover the flexibility within him.

Others with similar approaches are Adler's *individual* psychology, George A. Kelly's *psychology of personal constructs*, Adolf Meyer's *psychobiology* (not to be confused with the more general term "psychobiology" which refers to the biological factors involved in behavior), and the work of G. A. Miller, E. Galanter, and Karl Pribram, who stress "changes in plans."

Rogerian Therapy (Nondirective, or Client-centered Therapy)

In the 1940s, Carl R. Rogers began trying out his own ideas of human personality and growth, launching the first "radically" new ideas in psychotherapy since Freud. Whereas the Freudians viewed human psychic problems as arising from repression of sexuality and aggression, Rogers saw them in more existential terms. The Freudians put the analyst at the center of the therapeutic process, and if change for the better was effected, the patient often came out thinking and acting more like the analyst than himself. Rogers put the patient—whom he called a *client*, de-emphasizing the medical model and stressing the contractual relationship between him and the person seeking help—at the center. He felt the best mode of treatment involved getting the therapist out of the way and allowing the *client* to formulate his own insights, to verbalize and label his own feelings and attitudes. The nondirective therapist simply mirrored the client's expressions, rephrasing them to clarify them in his own mind and helping the client to see that it was possible for another person, outside the situation, to understand such feelings.

This therapy met with opposition, but gradually it began to take hold and is now at the center of the humanist psychology and human potential movements.

Transactional Analysis (TA)

Psychiatrist Eric Berne began his "radical" movement in the early 1960s, studying the "Games" people play, the playacting, false, self-deceptive, other-fooling manipulations and protective lies. Out of this study evolved a method of helping people—helping them to understand the deceit, to gain insight into their internal conflicts, to recognize the role-playing, and to learn how to live more appropriately and honestly.

We have already examined, in previous chapters, how personality is formed (according to the TA model), with the development of patterns of feeling, thinking, believing, and expecting, called Life Scripts. We've learned that the personality develops according to playbacks of "tapes" recorded internally: of parental and judgmental attitudes in the Parent, of impulsive, emotional, and need-oriented feelings in the Child, and of rational, logical, reality-related ideas and insights in the Adult.

In transactional analysis, usually conducted in groups, but also highly effective in individual programs, the goal is educational. It is not as oversimplified as TA language often makes it seem. A wide variety of problems may be dealt with—not just patterns of deceit and trickery. Many emotional problems labeled by psychiatrists are also described and dealt with in TA terms and techniques. Schizophrenia is a real experience, and it is no less serious to describe it as a Decommissioned Adult than it is to describe it in Freudian or medical terms.

The person who has a Blocked-out Adult is psychotic. His Adult is not functioning, and therefore he is out of touch with reality. His Parent and Child come on straight, frequently in a jumbled mixture of archaic data, a jumbled replay of early experiences that do not make sense now because they did not make sense when they were recorded. . . . In the setting of a group, the psychotic patient feels supported, stroked, and reassured, and the stage is set for the return of the Adult.[15]

Treatment of severely damaged psychotics may require traditional psychiatric and medical programs, but eventually the rebuilding of a human being requires reeducation. TA tries to do such reeducating. The prerequisite for effective therapy in TA is that the patient or client develop some version of the position, *You're OK*, with the *you* referring to the therapist, even if his view of himself is, *I'm Not OK*. Without this rapport and belief and trust in the therapist, no educating can proceed.

In a typical TA session, the members' Games are analyzed and the personality structures of P–A–C are studied. The members of the group learn to use the terms *Parent, Adult,* and *Child* as readily as they do the pronouns *he, she, it,* and *you.* The individuals become quite adept at recognizing and analyzing intimacy transactions and Game transactions. Following is an excerpt of a typical TA session:

THERAPIST: Bob, you don't seem to want to share this thing with the group.

BOB: It's none of their damned business!

THERAPIST: *(To group)* Okay, what's happening here?

JANE: He sounds pretty defensive.

THERAPIST: Any idea why?

DICK: It's like a kid who won't show his little brother a comic book he's enjoying.

THERAPIST: Why would a kid do that?

DICK: Because he's got a good thing and doesn't want anybody else horning in on it.

JANE: Yeah, I've felt that way myself. I hated my little sister always having to butt into what I was doing, or wanting to go with me when I went shopping with my girl friends.

THERAPIST: So, this sounds like the actions of a child?

BOB: You people make me sick, all of you! What do you know about me? What makes you all so right?

THERAPIST: Nobody should make any kinds of judgments about you without knowing more about you, eh?

15. Thomas Harris, *I'm OK—You're OK* (New York: Avon Books, 1973), pp. 130, 132.

BOB: Right! You people don't know nothin', and yet you're all writing my life story.

THERAPIST: Let's see: I asked what people thought about your refusal to let us inside your life. Jane simply said you sounded defensive. Dick thought that defensiveness was like a kid not wanting to share something with someone, probably something he remembered from his own childhood. Jane admitted that she had similar feelings when she was a child. I wonder why their analysis of their own childhood experiences should make you so angry?

BOB: It doesn't! It's just the idea of judging people without getting to know them.

JANE: We aren't judging you! We're talking about what your behavior reminds *us* of, from our own past.

DICK: Yeah, pal. You're acting pretty damn' childish about this yourself.

The therapist in this kind of session tries to get the clients to understand that each action or reaction is related to whichever part of their personality is being stimulated. In the above case, the therapist would say that the Child in Bob was fearful of having to give up something (his secrets) and the Parent in him came to the Child's rescue by accusing the group of being "bad Children" by attacking him without cause. The therapist tries to do his bit in an Adult fashion, when that's possible or advisable. At times, the therapist may let his own Child enter the situation to dramatize a point, or the therapist's Child may come into the scene without his intending it:

THERAPIST: . . . and so, Judy, your need to push Dave away from you is probably . . .

HAROLD: *(interrupting)* It's probably her Parent telling her sex is naughty! Don't let that vile little boy get you dirty. Right?

THERAPIST: *(annoyed at being beaten to the interpretation)* Sounds like your Child needs to be paid attention to, Harold. You always have to jump in with interpretations.

MARY ANN: Hey, Doc, why does that bug you?

THERAPIST: Huh? Well, I . . . I guess the therapist's Child likes being King of the Mountain. *(laughs)* Sometimes the Child in all of us has to get his licks in. I'm sorry, Harold. The Child in me is going to have to learn to take turns!

Occasionally the therapist too—being only a human being—has to learn of his or her own Game-playing, and the TA group permits and fosters this kind of growth in *all* members of the group.

We could at this point mention that people become psychotherapists for all kinds of reasons, usually their own good experiences with therapy being a major one. Today, psychotherapists are able to recognize their own humanity more openly. The time of considering the patient to be "sick" and the therapist to be "radiantly perfect" is over. We expect therapists to be well on their way to Self-actualization, but not to be perfect. They must, first of all, be *human*. And human means fallible.

As a Last Resort

An advantage in living in the "Age of Anxiety" is that we are all more acutely and sensitively aware of the problems of living in a world as complex as ours. This has, for the most part, enabled far more people to seek out professional help when they are troubled than was the case some years ago. There is still a stigma attached to the word "insane" and the idea of mental illness in general. But more and more, people are able to recognize and accept human frailties and approve, even to encourage, the seeking out of help.

But most therapies cost money and money isn't always available. When it is, the "right kind" of therapist may not be. For many people, the "right kind" of therapist means somebody like them, or someone who can at least know and feel what they've been through. There are still far too few black, Mexican-American, Oriental, or female psychotherapists for the large numbers of people in those categories who might require somebody "like them."

There is help. The media have come of age. Television and radio industries are beginning to recognize how much influence they have and how pervasive their contact is. Programs relating to personal problems, to social adjustment, to mental health are being produced in ever greater numbers, with increasing quality.

The film industry, both in commercial "movies" and in educational films, is being utilized to explore the problems and to promote the wide variety of solutions available.

Medical insurance programs are extending their coverage (though at increased costs) to help people secure psychiatric and therapeutic treatment.

Education, too, is expanding, by providing courses for laymen in these vital areas of self-help and in making more available and understandable the other forms of treatment available.

Religious organizations, of all faiths, are recognizing that they too play an important part in helping their people to live more effective, healthy, and happy lives. Clergy are better-trained for counseling, and many churches and temples are providing counseling services of all kinds.

The "free clinic" movement of the 1960s has provided thousands of people with a variety of psychiatric, medical, and personal services, though always under the fire of the more "establishment-oriented" programs. Thousands of physicians, psychiatrists, psychologists, social workers, teachers, and drug-treatment specialists have volunteered millions of hours of their time to helping people heretofore unreached by the traditional programs.

Finally, there are books and magazines. We cannot begin to describe those that are available, some of doubtful help, but most immensely helpful. In the bibliographical section, we have listed many that you can use with confidence.

A Model of Wholeness

As you can see, there are a number of ways in which a person can be helped to cultivate a set of values that represent the fullest expression of who he is, and which are fairly workable within the limits of the society in which he lives. Abraham Maslow has suggested that there are motives that are universal to each member of the species *Homo sapiens*. At the core level are the physiological motives, those tensions created by tissue needs—hunger, thirst, elimination, air, and so on. Few humans and no animals ignore them. After these are put into proper perspective, into a relatively regulated process, humans are motivated by needs for safety, for love and belongingness, for esteem and ego-identity, and for self-actualization.

The self-actualizing person, our model of "mental and emotional health," is a person who recognizes first of all his animal nature as well as his human nature. He's a person whose value system is based on this recognition of his many-sided nature. He appreciates his natures, he tries to gear his life to the optimum meeting of all his needs, he recognizes these needs in others, and he tries to create a world in which he and all others can meet their needs.

One of the ways in which each of us can help another to realize his fullest selfhood is to begin with the common experience or recognition that we are *all* selves in the process of becoming. This acknowledgment should give us the ability, the perspective, to appreciate the common bond that unites each one human with all others, regardless of culture, color, creed, or social position.

In his research Maslow has found characteristics that represent a core set of traits of people who are in the lifelong process of attaining self-actualization:

1. *They have an efficient perception of reality and a comfortable relationship with it.* They can detect what is real and authentic and seem to gravitate toward it. They don't divide Reality and Unreality into mutually exclusive compartments. Rather, they know and appreciate the facts of existence without minimizing the importance of imagination, fantasy, dreaming, and fiction.

2. *They have an ability to accept themselves, other people and nature as they are.* They don't experience extended *morbid* psychological guilt, anxiety, shame, anger, or chagrin. The emotions are there as in any of us, but extreme degrees or prolongation are rare. These people know and appreciate their animal nature. They enjoy eating, drinking, sex, sleep, work, and physical activity of all kinds. Not particularly disgusted by bodily functions, they see them as normal and natural. They are less defensive than the typical person is, and care less than most about what other people might say about them.

3. *They seem to behave spontaneously and naturally.* Self-actualizing, authentic people often act on impulse, on the basis of "wanting to." Doing something because it feels good is not quite the same as infantile gratification-seeking or compulsive behavior. Self-actualizers experience each moment as precious and valuable, as something to be enjoyed merely because it exists. They "don the cloak of conformity" voluntarily and with good grace because certain conforming behaviors may be important to people who are important to and loved by these self-actualizing people, not because they care whether people will "talk" if they don't. Their ethics tend to be humanistic; that is, they value human life, human experience, and they define good and evil in terms of what benefits and what detracts from that humanness.

4. *They are problem-centered rather than self-centered.* Self-actualizing people focus their energies and attention on things outside themselves, although the opposite may *seem* to be the case. The truly egocentric (or egotistic) person is usually so hung-up on holding together a slipping sense of self-worth that he hasn't time or energy for anybody else's problems except insofar as other people and their problems can help define his sense of self. Self-actualizing people have such a healthy self-appreciation and self-respect that they have time and energy to deal sincerely and genuinely with matters outside themselves. They are usually engaged in the larger issues of human experience, appear to have a goal or mission in life,

and work on large-scale problems like poverty, bigotry, hostility, warfare, ecology, and so on. Maslow calls these individuals *Being-Motivated* (or Growth-Motivated), as opposed to being *Deficiency-Motivated.* They express their fullness rather than attempt to fill voids.

5. *They have a sense of detachment.* Self-actualizers like their own company and often enjoy privacy. Solitude doesn't disturb or panic them. They can easily transcend the petty demands of environment, yet remain completely part of the world and its people.

6. *They are autonomous.* B-Motivation enables individuals to strike out on their own and to live their own lives. D-Motivators are busy making up for deficiencies, compensating, or engaging in futile competition. Self-actualizing people need other people, but retain the right to make important decisions autonomously. When they seek out others for company, companionship, or advice, they tend to gravitate toward others with similar motivations.

7. *They have a continuing freshness of appreciation.* Maslow is most impressed with the fact that these people are seldom bored, stale, mediocre. They constantly find novelty, wonder, beauty, and delight in the world. Even repeated experiences are new and delightful. Sexual love, for example, is never just a routine; each coming together is a refreshing, re-vivifying experience quite unlike the experience of the D-motivated or self-alienated person who says of most experiences, sexual or otherwise, "Thank God that's over!" The self-actualizer is mature, capable of childlike delight in and appreciation of simple things: flowers, art, butterflies, people, a good cup of coffee.

8. *They experience more Peak or Oceanic feelings than the ordinary person.* The self-actualizing person is overwhelmed with a feeling of joy at being alive. He feels totally; all systems are involved—intellect, emotion, physical senses. One man described it thus: "I was a drop of water in the gigantic ocean, infinitesimal and insignificant, but totally aware that the gigantic ocean is made up of simple drops of water." Such a Peak Experience is a paradoxical sensation: being at once tiny and all-encompassing, being nothing and being everything, being helpless and being all-powerful, being weak and being super-strong. It is not a religious or supernatural experience, though it resembles the mystical experiences described by St. Francis, William Blake, and others. It also resembles the tran-

scending experiences reported by some people on LSD and peyote, though self-actualizing people generally have no use for drugs. It seems to be a fleeting experience; yet, during the few seconds the person is involved in it, centuries of time may seem to pass. Moreover, self-actualizing people report that a Peak Experience is a growing experience. They feel that they have become more real, more authentic, more of what they were before.

9. *They have a strong kinship feeling for other people.* Healthy, authentic people feel engaged with and related to other people. They seldom become hermits or ascetic monks. They are part of the human race and value the association. They feel a kinship to mankind as a whole and to individual persons in particular. They like and enjoy the company of others. Other people are drawn toward these people, too. The benefit derived from these kinship associations is not exploitive, at least not from the self-actualizer's side of it.

10. *Their interpersonal relationships are profound.* Because they trust more, empathize and associate more with other people than the typical person, they seem to develop greater love. They are able to disclose themselves to others and break down the barriers that we all build up. Their love is warm and comfortable, seldom clinging and possessive. They have many acquaintances and casual contacts, but usually a small, select circle of deep friendships. They tend to select friends who exhibit similar traits.

11. *They have character structures that are democratic.* Differences in class, color, creed, or personality are accepted by these people as part of the rich variety of humankind. There is a surprising lack of racist or ethnocentric prejudice among them. They value individuals as individuals and tend to emphasize the common bonds existing among human beings rather than the superficial differences. Their only prejudice seems to be in the direction of preferring other Being-Motivated people. Although they respect other people and their opinions, they tend to draw them out and try to enable them to become more of what they can become. Their relationships with others have a therapeutic quality about them; they do other people good by being with them.

12. *They are able to separate "means" from "ends."* The means is as enjoyable as the end. The doing is as satisfying as the accomplishing. "Getting there is half the fun" is a good cliché to describe their outlook. This again shows the impulsive rather

than the compulsive quality of self-actualizing people. They are more likely to take off for a weekend drive and enjoy wherever they go; whereas other people set a goal and if they don't attain it, feel that nothing was done or enjoyable.

13. *They have a philosophical, unhostile sense of humor.* The self-actualizer can appreciate the irony and the absurd in life, and especially in the behaviors of man in general, but he has no patience with ethnic jokes, "sick" jokes, "cruelty" jokes or those situations in which a particular person is made the butt of a joke. This sense of humor enables him to transcend unimportant concerns, and of course, enables him to laugh at himself when he becomes foolish or ridiculous.

14. *They display more than average creativeness, originality, and inventiveness.* These are not always artistic or mechanically oriented people, nor are they always involved in problem-solving occupations. They are often people in fairly ordinary lines of work. But in their work, they display innovative skills, they are more creative, and they tend to enjoy their work. Maslow's conviction is that creativeness is a fundamental characteristic of human beings, but that most of us lose it through the enculturation process of going to school and taking on the norms of the overall society. In self-actualizing people, there is apparently a strong encouragement for them to follow their own lead, as children, as teens, and as adults.

15. *They tend to resist blanket enculturation.* Self-actualizing people are not "well adjusted" in the naïve sense of being always approved of or totally identified with their culture. They are described as well adjusted personally—that is, congruent and authentic in and to themselves—but often they reject the ideals of social adjustment. As a result these people often appear to be "eccentric" or even somewhat "odd" when compared with the run-of-the-mill, conforming, look-alike people around us. Murray Burns, hero of Herb Gardner's play *A Thousand Clowns,* and Zorba the Greek are good examples of this kind of unconcerned, free, human person. These are not just irresponsible, rebellious nonconformists; they are usually responsible, often extremely productive people who need to be themselves.

16. *Their value system results automatically from acceptance of themselves and others.* Most self-actualizers are not petty moralizers. What most people are offended by, what most people consider moral problems, are usually of no concern to self-actualizing people. If, for instance, a self-actualizer hears of a

young couple running away to live together unmarried, one of his first concerns is likely to be: "I hope they'll be happy. I hope they can find fulfillment together, in each other, and in this new situation." The question of immorality isn't of paramount importance to the self-actualizer. Neither is the ethical-legal problem of how the two will support themselves. Belief in the flexibility and potentiality of the human being is so strong that he assumes that, unless interfered with, the couple can do just fine.

Because self-actualizers see life as a whole, and because they dislike dichotomizing, words like "selfish-unselfish," "work-pleasure," "right-wrong," "good-bad," and others seem to them unworkable, unusable and false categories. To most of these people, life's dilemmas and conflicts have more than two horns, or none at all. Life is an exciting, stimulating challenge.

17. *Drawbacks to self-actualization.* Many readers cannot identify with the theory of self-actualization because it seems to point to a state of perfection. Nonsense! Neither Maslow nor anybody else describing healthy human functioning uses words like "perfection." The self-actualizers are far from perfect. They are human. As a consequence of their kinship, deep feeling, sensitivity, and awareness, they suffer more of the pains of being alive. They also experience more of the joys! Because they find so much pleasure in being alive and being authentic, they often expect too much of the same kind of behavior from people who are less able to live the same way. This makes them frequently impatient, even somewhat resentful, concerning those they care about.

Lisa, for example, has been to the top of a certain hill many times, to sit and think, to meditate, to be alone, to watch the sun come up and go down. She is very fond of Gordon, who is still trying to prove himself, striving to appear competent and masculine, and disliking people who seem to have found themselves. Lisa takes Gordon for a climb up her favorite hill. In her eagerness, she runs on ahead. Gordon, unexcited by the prospect of seeing a sunset and winded from the exertion, pokes along. Lisa, who wants to share this experience with Gordon, taunts him: "Hurry up, slowpoke! C'mon! The sun's nearly down. Hurry up! What's the matter?" When he gets to the top, Gordon's self-absorption makes it difficult for him to appreciate something as "insignificant" or external as a sunset. He sits on a rock, panting and belittling the whole thing. Lisa, because she loves the hill and the experience, and because she wants Gordon to become more of himself than he is, expresses her disappointment in him, even shows how much she resents his attitude.

Lisa feels that her involvement with being part of humanity is important to her and wants some kind of response from other members of the human race. In her zeal and eagerness to experience life fully, she is intolerant of those who cannot or will not! Lisa is likely to be aware of her impatience or intolerance of Gordon and apologize to him. Because she feels deeply, and because she cares for Gordon, she will probably feel some guilt—it's a normal, human emotion. But she will not experience neurotic guilt; that is, she won't dwell on it, letting it devour her. She'll feel bad, apologize, and try to restore the relationship with Gordon. But she won't spend a great deal of time apologizing and feeling guilty. She'll have enough respect for the man that's latent in Gordon to let him work with what he has and with what she's given him.

Which leads us to the next drawback: self-actualizing people, in their zeal to share their insights and good feelings about life, often find themselves surrounded by the hungry, actualization-seeking people and by the neurotic and much conflicted people. Misery may love its own company for a while, but most miserable people flock to a person who seems to be happy and fulfilled and often seek to "get some of it" for themselves. They hang around, hoping something of the "health" will rub off onto them. They frequently ask: "You seem so happy, so sure of yourself. How did you get that way?" And, of course, the self-actualizer has trouble explaining it. He may say: "Just be yourself, man," which is far more of a clue than he may know. Sometimes the self-actualizing people are conscious of wanting to help other people find happiness; sometimes they just "get themselves into" situations like this, without knowing why.

Another difficulty many of them encounter is that their eagerness to live and live fully makes them impatient, even forgetful, of the details and trifles of everyday social experience. They are often absent-minded about dates, names, and places, preferring to emphasize experiences. They may forget to say "thank you" when it seems unnecessary to them; after all, throughout the event they have been communicating their feelings and their appreciation to the host or the person sponsoring the event. Friends or relatives despair of their ever learning the social niceties. Yet, how unimportant the "niceties" are compared to the exhilaration of living fully, freely, and feelingly!

Self-actualizing people, out of kinship and kindness, often let people take advantage of them, impose on them. This isn't out of masochistic need. It's more a feeling that they have so much and the other guy seems to need so much that it just happens. Close friends may tell the self-actualizer that he's being used by so-and-so and the answer is: Better me than somebody who can't afford to be used. *Affording it* harkens back to our discussion of "emotional richness," not to economic wealth. Self-actualizing people literally have an overflow of feeling, of affection.

Occasionally they enter into unequal relationships. Friends, acquaintances, relatives, and even loved ones may be *far* less actualizing than he is, but the self-actualizer enjoys the giving of himself with little thought of receiving something in return. The danger here is that this may become more self-defeating than healthy. Without some replenishment, even a self-actualizer's well can run dry temporarily.

You may be bothered by the dogmatic tone of the preceding list of characteristics. Please remember that Maslow himself is talking about a *process* of living, not a set of goals that can be (or should be) attained. Self-actualization is an ongoing experience, a way of life. Unfortunately, to describe people who are living their lives in this fulfilling, satisfying way is often to make it sound as if they had reached a *state of being*. Maslow is tentative about it: possibly 1 percent of the adult population is even geared into living in such a fashion. But he does feel a larger number of people are learning, or trying. When asked to give examples of such people, he has mentioned a few figures from past and present history to illustrate the concept: Eleanor Roosevelt, Walt Whitman, Henry Thoreau, Albert Schweitzer, Pope John XXIII, John F. Kennedy, and Winston Churchill. But the major point he makes is that for all their successes, they were very mortal, very fallible, very human individuals.[4] Such human qualities are the goals of most behavior change processes.

As you can discern from this long chapter, there are large numbers of people and a variety of programs aimed at helping people to know themselves, to learn to like and appreciate themselves, and to aid us in the painful and arduous tasks of growth toward significant Selfhood. We cannot pick and choose among them. If one known to you is not mentioned here, that does not necessarily mean we feel it is worthless or fraudulent. Although we have tried to include all the programs in which we have some confidence, many are developing as we write these words, and we may not be aware of them.

The significant thing is, that as severe as people's problems seem to be, there are those who care, who are working and sacrificing to make the lives of individual people and groups of people more effective,

---

4. The descriptions in the preceding pages are abstracted from Abraham Maslow, *Motivation and Personality* (New York: Harper, 1954).

more meaningful, happier, and less troubled. These people, these programs, these efforts do not always make the front pages of the newspapers, or the 11 o'clock news. They are nonetheless important and precious.

Summary

In trying to understand how people can learn to quit the Game-playing, the fraud, the self-deceit, and the "sickness," we've discovered a multitude of factors. We know that self-actualization can produce happier, healthier, more effective human beings. We know that very few people are fully actualizing. But we know that there are many ways of learning how to be everything we can be; how to make peace with those "enemies within."

In this chapter, we have looked at the helps offered by a variety of techniques: behavior modification programs, body awareness techniques, biofeedback, chemotherapy, counseling, in its variety of forms; encounter and sensitivity training. Gestalt therapy, hospitalization, meditation, mental health centers in the community, the various forms of psychotherapy, including Freudian and neo-Freudian psychoanalysis, existential therapy, hypnotherapy, Jungian analysis, play therapy, psychodrama, radical therapy, reevaluation therapies, Rogerian (client-centered) therapy, and transactional analysis.

Finally, we recognize that a changing attitude toward people in distress has launched programs on radio and TV, in news media, in medical insurance, in films, in educational programs, religious institutions, and finally in the books and magazines available to us all.

Suggested Readings:

General: These publications give an overview and comparisons of therapeutic and growth techniques.

Barron, Frank. *Creativity and Psychological Health.* Princeton, New Jersey: D. Van Nostrand Co., 1962.

Bennis, W. G.; E. H. Schein; D. E. Berlew; and F. E. Steele, eds. *Interpersonal Dynamics.* Homewood, Illinois: Dorsey, 1964.

Bergin, A. E., and S. L. Garfield. *Handbook of Psychotherapy and Behavior Change.* New York: John Wiley, 1971.

Buhler, Charlotte. *Values in Psychoanalysis.* Glencoe, Illinois: The Free Press, 1962.

Coleman, James. *Abnormal Psychology and Modern Life.* Glenview, Illinois: Scott, Foresman, 1964.

Frank, Jerome. *Persuasion and Healing: A Comprehensive Study of Psychotherapy.* Baltimore: Johns Hopkins Press, 1961.

Horney, Karen. *Self-Analysis.* New York: W. W. Norton, 1942.

Haley, Jay. *Strategies of Psychotherapy.* New York: Grune & Stratton, 1963.

Jaspers, Karl. *General Psychopathology.* Manchester, England: Manchester University Press, 1962.

Jourard, Sidney. *Disclosing Man to Himself.* Princeton, New Jersey: D. Van Nostrand Co., 1964.

Lasko, Alvin. "Psychotherapy, Habits, and Values," in J. F. T. Bugenthal, *Challenges of Humanistic Psychology.* New York: McGraw-Hill, 1967.

Leary, Timothy. *The Interpersonal Theory of Personality.* New York: The Ronald Press, 1957.

Martin, David G. *Introduction to Psychotherapy.* Belmont, California: Brooks/Cole, 1971.

Maslow, Abraham. *Motivation and Personality.* New York: Harper & Row, 1954.

Masserman, J., ed. *Current Psychiatric Therapies.* New York: Grune & Stratton, 1963.

Moustakas, Clark. "Honesty, Idiocy, and Manipulation," *J. Humanistic Psychology* (1962), 2, 1–15.

Paul, G. L. *Insight Versus Desensitization in Psychotherapy.* Palto Alto, California: Stanford University Press, 1966.

Schofield, W. *Psychotherapy: The Purchase of Friendship.* Englewood Cliffs, New Jersey: Prentice-Hall, 1964.

Shostrom, Everett. *Man the Manipulator.* New York: Bantam Books, 1964.

Strupp, H. H.; R. E. Fox; and K. Lessler. *Patients View Their Psychotherapy.* Baltimore: John Hopkins Press, 1969.

Walton, H., ed. *Small-Group Psychotherapy.* Baltimore: Penguin, 1971.

Watts, Alan W. *Psychotherapy East and West.* New York: New American Library, 1963.

Whitaker, C. A., and J. Warkentin. "The Therapist as a Prototype," in J. F. T. Bugenthal, ed., *Challenges of Humanistic Psychology.* New York: McGraw-Hill, 1967.

Wogan, M. "Effect of Therapist-Patient Personality Variables on Therapeutic Outcome," *J. Consulting and Clinical Psychology* (1970), 35, 356–371.

Specific: These publications illustrate the various individual forms and orientations of psychotherapy, in alphabetical order.

Behavior Modification, Behavior Therapy, Reinforcement Therapy:

Albert, R. E., and M. L. Emmons. *Your Perfect Right.* San Luis Obispo, California: Impact, 1974.

Bandura, Albert. *Principles of Behavior Modification.* New York: Holt, Rinehart & Winston, 1969.

Begley, L., and L. Lieberman. "Patients' Expectations of Therapists' Techniques," *J. Clinical Psychology* (1970), 26, 112–116.

Krasner, L., and L. P. Ullmann. *Research in Behavior Modification.* New York: Holt, Rinehart & Winston, 1965.

Lindsley, O. R., and B. F. Skinner. "A Method for the Experimental Analysis of the Behavior of Psychotic Patients," *American Psychologist* (1954), 9, 419–420.

Skinner, B. F. *Beyond Freedom and Dignity.* New York: A. A. Knopf, 1971.

Ullman, L. P., and L. Krasner, eds. *Case Studies in Behavior Modification.* New York: Holt, Rinehart & Winston, 1965.

Watson, D. L., and R. G. Tharp. *Self-Directed Behavior.* Belmont, California: Brooks/Cole, 1972.

Wolpe, J. *The Practice of Behavior Therapy.* New York: Pergamon, 1966.

Body Awareness Techniques:

Alexander, F. M. *Resurrection of the Body.* New York: University Books, 1969.

Assagioli, Roberto. *Psychosynthesis.* New York: Hobbs, Dorman, 1965.

————. *The Act of Will.* New York: Viking Press, 1973.

Baker, E. *Man in the Trap.* New York: Macmillan, 1967.

Fast, Julius. *Body Language.* New York: M. Evans & Co., Inc., 1970.

Feng, Gai-Fu. *Tai-Chi.* New York: Collier Books, 1970.

Fitzgerald, W. H. *Zone Therapy.* Health Research, Mokelninne, California.

Gallert, M. *New Light on Therapeutic Energies.* London: Clarke & Co., 1966.

Gunther, B. *Sense-Relaxation.* New York: Macmillan, 1968.

Keen, Sam. "We Do Not Have Bodies: We Are Our Bodies" (Bioenergetics), *Human Behavior.* September 1973.

Lowen, Alexander. *Betrayal of the Body.* New York: Macmillan, 1967.

————. *Love and Orgasm.* New York: Macmillan, 1965.

————. *The Physical Dynamics of Character Structure.* New York: Grune & Stratton, 1958.

————. *Pleasure.* New York: Coward-McCann, 1970.

Reich, Wilhelm. *Character Analysis.* New York: Orgone Institute Press, 1949.

————. *Function of the Orgasm.* New York: Bantam Books, 1967.

Rolf, Ida. *Structural Integration.* Esalen Books, Big Sur, California.

Schutz, William. *FIRO: A Three-Dimensional Theory of Interpersonal Behavior.* Reprinted as *The Interpersonal Underworld.* Palo Alto, California: Science and Behavior Books, 1966.

————. *Here Comes Everybody.* Harrow Books. New York: Harper & Row, 1972.

————. *Joy,* New York: Grove Press, 1967.

Structural Integration, Bulletin of. 16756 Marquez Ave., Pacific Palisades, California 90272.

Biofeedback Techniques and Research:

Barber, T., et al., eds. *Biofeedback and Self-Control.* Chicago: Aldine, 1971.

Bower, G., ed. *The Psychology of Learning and Motivation,* Vol. 6. New York: Academic Press, 1972.

Kamiya, Joseph. "Conscious Control of Brainwaves," *Psychology Today,* January 1968.

Karlins, M., and L. M. Andrews. *Biofeedback.* New York: Warner, 1973.

Shaffer, R. "Biofeedback," *Wall Street Journal.* April 19, 1971.

Chemotherapy:

Barsa, J. "Combination Drug Therapy in Psychiatry," *Amer. J. of Psychiatry* (1960), 117, 448–449.

Caldwell, A. E. *Origins of Psychopharmacology from CPZ to LSD.* Springfield, Illinois: C. C. Thomas, 1970.

Greenblatt, M., et al., eds. *Drug and Social Therapy in Chronic Schizophrenics.* Springfield, Illinois: C. C. Thomas, 1965.

Klein, D. F., and J. M. Davis. *Diagnosis and Drug Treatment of Psychiatric Disorders.* Baltimore: Williams and Wilkins, 1969.

Krakowski, A. J. "General Principles of Chemotherapy in Mental Illness," *Psychosomatics* (1969), 10, 82–87.

McNeil, Elton B. *Being Human.* San Francisco: Canfield Press, 1973.

Ray, O. S. *Drugs, Society, and Human Behavior.* St. Louis, Missouri: C. V. Mosby, 1972.

Stewart, M. D. "Hyperactive Children," *Scientific American,* 1970, 222, No. 4.

Encounter and Sensitivity Groups:

Egan, G. *Encounter.* Belmont, California: Brooks/Cole, 1970.

Gibb, J. R. "Sensitivity Training as a Medium for Personal Growth and Improved Interpersonal Relations," *Interpersonal Development* (1970) 1, 6–31.

Levy, Ronald. *I Can Only Touch You Now.* Englewood Cliffs, New Jersey: Prentice-Hall, 1973.

Lieberman, M., et al. *Encounter Groups.* New York: Basic Books, 1973.

Marshall, Bernice, ed. *Experiences in Being.* Belmont, California: Brooks/Cole, 1971.

O'Banion, Terry, and April O'Connell. *The Shared Journey.* Englewood Cliffs, New Jersey: Prentice-Hall, 1970.

Siroka, R. W., et al., eds. *Sensitivity Training and Group Encounter.* New York: Grossett & Dunlap, 1971.

Yalom, I., and M. Lieberman. "A Study of Encounter Group Casualties," *Archives of General Psychiatry* (1971) 25, 16–30.

Gestalt Therapy:

Fagan, Joen, and Irma Lee Shepherd, eds. *Gestalt Therapy Now.* Palo Alto, California: Science and Behavior Books, 1970.

————, eds. *What Is Gestalt Therapy?* New York: Harper & Row, 1973.

James, Muriel, and Dorothy Jongeward. *Born to Win.* Reading, Maryland: Addison-Wesley, 1971.

Perls, F. S.; R. F. Hefferline; and P. Goodman. *Gestalt Therapy.* New York: Julian Books, 1951.

Perls, F. S. *Gestalt Therapy Verbatim.* Toronto: Bantam Books, 1970.

———. *In and Out of the Garbage Pail.* Lafayette, California: Real People Press, 1969.

Polster, Erving, and Miriam Polster. *Gestalt Therapy Integrated.* New York: Brunner/Mazel, Inc., 1973.

Hospitalization:

Goffman, Erving. *Asylums.* Garden City, New York: Doubleday, 1961.

Hartlage, L. C. "Sub-Professional Therapists' Use of Reinforcement versus Traditional Psychotherapeutic Techniques with Schizophrenics," *J. Consult and Clinical Psychology* (1970) 34, 181–184.

Kesey, Ken. *One Flew over the Cuckoo's Nest.* New York: Viking, 1962.

Meltzoff, J., and R. Blumenthal. *The Day-Treatment Center.* Springfield, Illinois: C. C. Thomas, 1966.

Rapaport, R. N. "Principles for Developing a Therapeutic Community," in *J. Masserman, Current Psychiatric Therapies.* New York: Grune, 1963.

Shiloh, A. "Sanctuary or Prison?" *Transaction* (1968) 6, 28–36.

Meditation Techniques:

Baba Ram Dass (Richard Alpert). *Be Here Now.* New York: Crown, 1971.

Maharishi Mahesh Yogi. *Transcendental Meditation.* New York: Signet, 1968.

Mental Health Centers and Clinics:

Bellak, L., ed. *Handbook of Community Psychiatry.* New York: Grune, 1964.

Cowen, E., et al., eds. *Emergent Approaches to Mental Health Problems.* New York: Appleton-Century-Crofts, 1967.

Golan, S. E. "Community Psychology and Mental Health," in I. Iscoe and C. D. Spielberger, eds., *Community Psychology.* New York: Appleton-Century-Crofts, 1970.

Golan, S. E., and C. Eisdorfer. "Mental Health and the Community," in *Handbook of Community Mental Health.* Meredith Corp., New York: Appleton-Century-Crofts, 1972.

Hobbs, N. "Mental Health's Third Revolution," *Amer. J. of Orthopsychiatry* (1964) 34, 1–20.

Kluger, J. M. "The Uninsulated Caseload in a Neighborhood Mental Health Center, *Am. J. of Psychiatry* (1970) 126, 1430–1435.

Luechsler, H. "Transitional Residences for Former Mental Patients," *Mental Hygiene* (1961) 45, 65–76.

Raush, H. C., and C. L. Raush. *The Halfway House Movement.* New York: Appleton-Century-Crofts, 1968.

Smith, M. B., and N. Hobbs. "The Community and the Community Mental Health Center." Washington: *The American Psychological Assn.*, 1966.

Srole, L., et al. *Mental Health in the Metropolis.* New York: McGraw-Hill, 1962.

Psychotherapies:

Existential Therapy:

Frankl, Viktor. *Man's Search for Meaning.* New York: Simon & Schuster, 1959.

————. *The Doctor and the Soul.* New York: A. A. Knopf, 1957.

————. *The Will to Meaning.* New York: New American Library.

Greening, Thomas, ed. *Existential-Humanistic Psychology.* Belmont, California: Brooks/Cole, 1971.

May, Rollo, ed. *Existence.* New York: Simon & Shuster, 1967.

Hypnotherapy:

Moss, C. S. *Hypnosis in Perspective.* New York: Macmillan, 1965.

Shor, R. E., and M. T. Orne. *The Nature of Hypnosis.* New York: Holt, Rinehart & Winston, 1965.

Jungian Therapy (Analytical Psychology):

Jung, Carl G. *Modern Man in Search of a Soul.* New York: Harcourt, Brace, 1960.

————. *The Collected Works.* "The Psychogenesis of Mental Disease" (in *Vol. 3);* "Two Essays on Analytical Psychology" (in *Vol. 7);* "The Practice of Psychotherapy" (in *Vol. 16);* "The Development of Personality" (in *Vol. 16).* London: Routledge & Kegan Paul.

Kunkel, Fritz. *How Character Develops.* New York: Scribner's, 1940.

————. *In Search of Maturity.* New York: Scribner's, 1943.

Progoff, Ira. *Death and Rebirth of Psychology.* New York: Julian, 1956.

————. *Jung's Psychology and Its Social Meaning.* New York: Julian, 1953.

Sharp, Ella. *Dream Analysis.* Hogarth Press, 1937.

Play Therapy:

Anderson, Walt. "Don't Just Sit There—Play!" *Human Behavior,* January 1974.

Axline, Virginia. *DIBS: In Search of Self.* New York: Ballantine Books, 1964.

Psychodrama and Role-Playing:

Moreno, Jacob L. *Psychodrama.* New York: Beacon, 1946.

————. "The Viennese Origins of the Encounter Movement: Paving the Way for Existentialism, Group Psychotherapy, and Psychodrama," *Group Psychotherapy* (1969) XXII, No. 1-2, 7-16.

Solomon, M. L., and C. K. Solomon. "Psychodrama as an Ancillary Therapy on a Psychiatric Ward," *Canadian Psychiatric Association Journal* (1970) 15, 365–373.

Psychosurgery:

Trotter, R. J. "Peter Breggin's Private War," *Human Behavior.* November 1973.

The Radical Therapies:

Agel, Jerome. *The Radical Therapist.* New York: Ballantine, 1971.
Anderson, Walt. "Breaking out of the Establishment Vise," *Human Behavior,* November 1973.
Assagioli, Roberto. *The Act of Will.* New York: Viking Books, 1973. (Assagioli's Psychosynthesis is also part of the body-awareness movement.)
Laing, Ronald D. *The Divided Self.* New York: Pantheon, 1969.
_____. *The Politics of Experience.* New York: Ballantine, 1967.
_____. *The Self and Others.* New York: Pantheon, 1969.
Szasz, Thomas. *The Myth of Mental Illness.* New York: Harper & Row, 1961.

The Re-Evaluation Therapies:

Branden, Nathaniel. *The Psychology of Self-Esteem.* New York: Bantam Books, 1971.
Ellis, Albert. *Humanistic Psychotherapy.*
_____. *Homosexuality: Its Causes and Cures.* New York: Lyle Stuart, 1965.
_____. *Reason and Emotion in Psychotherapy.* New York: Lyle Stuart, 1962.
Glasser, William. *Reality Therapy.* New York: Harper & Row, 1970.
Johnson, W., and D. Moeller. *Living With Change.* New York: Harper & Row, 1972.
Maltz, Maxwell. *Psychocybernetics.* Englewood Cliffs, New Jersey: Prentice-Hall, 1960.
_____, and C. Barker. *The Conquest of Frustration.* New York: Grosset and Dunlap, 1969.
Orgler, H. *Alfred Adler: The Man and His Work.* New York: New American Library, 1972.
Rimm, D., and S. Litvak. "Self-Verbalization and Emotional Arousal," *J. Abnormal Psychology* (1969) 74, 181–187.
Rubin, Theodore. *The Winner's Notebook.* New York: Collier Books, 1969.
Sax, S., and S. Hollander. *Reality Games.* New York: Macmillan, 1972.

Rogerian (Client-Centered, Nondirective) Therapy:

Geiwitz, P. J. *Non-Freudian Personality Theories.* Belmont, California: Brooks/Cole, 1969.
Rogers, Carl R. *Client Centered Therapy.* Boston: Houghton-Mifflin Co., 1951.

_____. *Freedom to Learn.* Columbus, Ohio: C. E. Merrill, 1969.

_____. *On Becoming a Person.* New York: Sentry Editions, 1973.

Rogers, Carl R., and Barry Stevens, et al. *Person to Person.* New York: Pocket Books, 1971.

Transactional Analysis:

Eric Berne. *Games People Play.* New York: Grove Press, 1964.

_____. *Principles of Group Treatment.* New York: Oxford University Press, 1966.

_____. *Sex in Human Loving.* New York: Simon & Schuster, 1970.

_____. *Structure and Dynamics of Organizations and Groups, The.* New York: Ballantine Books, 1973.

_____. *What Do You Say after You Say Hello?* New York: Bantam Books, 1973.

Harris, Thomas. *I'm OK–You're OK.* New York: Avon Books, 1973.

James, Muriel, and Dorothy Jongeward. *Born to Win.* Reading, Maryland: Addison-Wesley, 1971.

Schiffman, Muriel. *Self-Therapy: Techniques for Personal Growth.* Menlo Park, California: Self-Therapy Press, 1967.

Steiner, Claude. *Games Alcoholics Play:* The Analysis of Life Scripts. New York: Grove Press, 1972.

Where to Go and Where to Write:

If you are interested in any of the programs described in this chapter and feel you are less interested in reading about them, here are some addresses:

American Psychiatric Association
420 E. 76th Street
New York, New York 10021

American Psychological Association
1200 17th Street N.W.
Washington, D.C. 20036

Association for Humanistic Psychology
574 Page Street
San Francisco, California 94117

Jacob L. Moreno
Psychodrama Institute
Beacon, New York

or:
236 W. 78th Street
New York, New York 10024

Guild for Structural Integration (Rolfing)
1874 Fell Street
San Francisco, California 94117

Ilana Rubenfeld
c/o American Center for the Alexander Technique
115 Waverly Place
New York, New York 10011

Esalen Institute
Big Sur, California 93920

or:
Esalen Institute
1776 Union, San Francisco, California 94123

Psychosynthesis Research Foundation
527 Lexington Avenue, Rm. 314
New York, New York 10017

11

Love Is All You Really Need

To love Someone
is to bid him to live
and invite him to grow.

ANONYMOUS

Americans are firmly of two minds about it all, simultaneously hardheaded and idealistic, uncouth and tender, libidinous and puritanical; they believe implicitly in every tenet of romantic love, and yet they know perfectly well that things don't really work that way.[1]

MORTON HUNT

Eros *is described as the desire for self-fulfillment by the other being,* agape *as the will to self-surrender for the sake of the other being. . . . No love is real without a unity of* eros *and* agape.[2]

PAUL TILLICH

Love does not cling to an I, *as if the* Thou *were merely its "content" or object; it is* between I *and* Thou.[3]

MARTIN BUBER

1. Morton M. Hunt, *The Natural History of Love* (New York: A. A. Knopf, 1959).
2. Paul Tillich, *The Dynamics of Faith* (New York: Harper & Row, 1957).
3. Martin Buber, *I and Thou* (New York: Scribner's, 1970).

We've been discussing a variety of methods, orientations, teachings, and techniques of "getting straight," of uncovering the hidden dimension of Self and reclaiming feelings of significance. The list includes many ideas that have been around for a few decades and many that aren't yet fully defined.

But there is another experience that actualizing human beings have always found to be fulfilling and expressive of their fullest and best selfhood. That is the experience of love.

The title of this chapter is catchy and easy to remember, and we would agree with John, Paul, George, and Ringo that it would be just "loverly" if love was all we really needed. We live in a world that has too often and too easily forgotten love. How many times have you been involved in a discussion or lecture on the problems of life—ecological abuse, poverty, racism, war, sexism, marital discord, child rearing, unemployment, international and intranational tension, political entanglement—and said to yourself (in a very low tone, because it sounded strange or irrelevant): "It would be different if we could just love each other"? We all have.

But loving is not a simple panacea, or perhaps it's better to say that learning to love isn't so simple. Perhaps if we *could* all love fully and effectively, we'd find that, indeed, that would solve many of these problems and conflicts. But interfering with loving, as well as with many other aspects of significance, are the biological and psychological traumas, the negativistic Life Scripts, the hurt, the bitterness, the fear, and most of all, the ignorance of how and why.

What do we mean by love? Do any two people mean the same thing by it? Look at the confusion engendered by the simple expression "I love you":

> Sometimes it means: *I desire you* or *I want you sexually*. It may mean: *I hope you love me* or *I hope that I will be able to love you*. Often it means: *It may be that a love relationship can develop between us* or even *I hate you*. Often it is a wish for emotional exchange: *I want your admiration in exchange for mine* or *I give my love in exchange for some passion* or *I want to feel cozy and at home with you* or *I admire some of your qualities*. A declaration of love is mostly a request: *I desire you* or *I want you to gratify me* or *I want your protection* or *I want to be intimate with you* or *I want to exploit your loveliness*.
>
> Sometimes it is the need for security and tenderness, for parental treatment. It may mean: *My self-love goes out to you*. But it may also express submissiveness: *Please take me as I am* or *I feel guilty about you. I want through you to correct the mistakes I have made in human relations*. It may be self-sacrifice and a masochistic wish for dependency. However, it may also be a full affirmation of the other, taking the responsibility for mutual exchange of feelings. It may be a weak feeling of friendliness, it may be the scarcely even whispered expression of ecstasy.

"I love you," wish, desire, submission, conquest; it is never the word itself that tells the real meaning here.[1]

The Meaning of Love

To the people who spoke Sanskrit, the word *lubhyati* meant "he desires." This is the root of the word that gives us so much pain in defining.[2] Most people feel pretty sure that they know what the word means when they use it. Some overuse and abuse it, but sincere people, even though unable to define it, are generally certain that they know what they mean. They also hope that the person hearing it from them knows what they mean; they expect that the two of them share a common meaning. Unfortunately, this isn't always the case.

Many thoughtful people, rather than abuse a meaningful word, or rather than use what they think is now a meaningless word, refuse to employ the word *love* at all. They will use terms that convey exactly what it is they mean. They are not afraid of emotionally laden terms. They are interested in getting their message across very clearly. If they mean "I like you," that's what they will say. If they mean "I'm sexually attracted to you," then that's what they will say. If they mean "We get along very well and I feel really comfortable with you," again, that is what they will say.

We've said that love is the point we arrive at when we go full circle in human experiencing. *Love is a creative relationship* in its most minimal definition. It is creative in the sense that something new or novel or important comes out of the relating. When two people love each other, something alive and vital happens. The relationship, not how it's expressed or consummated, is the important thing. A friendship between two people, whether of the opposite sex or the same sex, is a love relationship when certain important qualities are present. Erich Fromm, himself a loving and concerned human being, feels that any love relationship involves four elements: knowledge, care, respect, responsibility.[3]

Love Means Knowledge

To love, to be in a true loving relationship, the involved people must *know* each other. True love at first sight is possible under the

1. J. A. M. Meerloo, *Conversation and Communication* (New York: International Universities Press, 1952), p. 83.
2. E. H. Mudd, ed., *Man and Wife* (New York: Norton, 1957), p. 53.
3. Erich Fromm, *The Art of Loving* (New York: Harper and Row Publishers, Inc., 1956), p. 26.

rarest of circumstances and occurs only in the same kinds of ultra-sensitive people who may also be called "mind readers" or "superb judges of character." The common feeling of falling in love at first sight is a product of one or more things: fascination, fantasy, sexual arousal, admiration, appreciation, attraction, identification, or just plain "good vibes." If one defines *love* in any of these terms, then for all intents and purposes he loves. But love, for most people (and we must say *in reality*) is much more. It is really knowing another individual.

To know someone you must experience him. Not just on dates, and certainly not just by seeing him on a two-dimensional movie screen. In the typical dating experience, even in this modern, enlightened, up-to-date, anti-establishment world, people do unreal, phony and inauthentic things in an attempt to put their "best foot forward," basically to impress another person. So many things are artificially hidden—complexion flaws, food preferences, less-than-acceptable traits—that one person may require a great deal of time to penetrate the masks of another or to become acquainted with the games he plays. Mature, deep, and satisfying love comes from real, intimate, intensive, and extensive knowledge. It comes from wide and profound experiencing of the fullest self possible.

To know is more than intellectual insight. You don't know a woman simply because you know her name is Mary Elizabeth Jones, and she lives at 417 Seventeenth Street, that her phone number is 817-4435, that her measurements are 35-26-36, that her age is 20, that she works at . . . , that her parents are . . . , that she has certain color eyes, hair, skin, etc. This isn't the kind of knowledge we mean. This is Bureau of the Census information, almanac data. Fromm tries to impress on us that intimate, personal knowledge is a fundamental and basic part of a close relationship. We must, he says, know each other—each of us must understand the other's special uniqueness—before we consider our relationship one of love.

Love Means Caring

In addition to knowing, there must be *caring*. You must care, be concerned, about the other person's well-being, his growth, his health, his ups and his downs. A deeply felt and often expressed statement, verbal or not, that we convey to each other when we love is, "I *care* about you, how you are, what happens to you, about protecting you, about seeing you grow and become everything you can be." And it goes a bit further: "I hurt when you hurt: I feel your joy, your sorrow, your ecstasy, your loss, your fear, and your confidence."

The caring aspect of love is seen most vividly in the love expressed by a mother for her child. The child is not yet a full partner in the love relationship; he is a recipient of the mother's affection, concern,

and tenderness. What satisfies the mother, though, is response. The child can smile when filled or comfortable. He can gurgle and goo and wave his arms when he sees her coming. These simple expressions are sufficient for most of us.

But in a mature and authentic love relationship, if one person is inadequate or poorly equipped in responding, the other person may find that he cannot continue giving. Mutuality, the giving-taking circle, replenishes and nourishes and aids the growth of each person in a relationship.

Love Means Respect

The third aspect of a love relationship is *respect*. Not fear or awesome deference, but appreciation of the uniqueness and selfhood of another. In true respect there is no need to do anything to diminish or hurt the other person, to ridicule or damage another's integrity. There is acceptance in the active, positive sense: "There you *are*. I see, take in, readily acknowledge you and what you are. I really dig you!"

Respect also implies active concern. It means that if I respect you, I want the best for you: I want you to grow and become all that you are, and I don't want you to become anything for *me!* If you became what I wanted you to, then you wouldn't be you; you'd be some kind of *me*-shaped or *me*-colored reflection. Then, I wouldn't be acknowledging you as you. I'd be saying I can only love the me I see *in* you. And this is narcissism, an exploitative form of conceit far removed from real other-love.

Love Means Responsibility

Finally, Fromm tells us that we must experience *responsibility* with each other, and he suggests we spell it "response-ability," the ability and the readiness to respond to the other person. It means to be ready, willing, and able to meet another's needs—not to lead his life for him, or to promise to take care of all wants and needs, but to meet most of the important emotional needs.

Obviously, love as so defined is not a simple or even simply a complex emotion. It's a qualitative relationship, involving stimuli and responses, giving and taking. It also involves mutuality and reciprocity: there has to be some sort of two-way street involved. The tales told of the lovesick young man who adores a girl from afar are sometimes very good literature. They are very poor self-actualizing experiencing! He must know her, respect her, be concerned for her, and respond to her. Then, she must go through the same things with him. If she doesn't know he exists, has never even seen him, how can she love him? How can he love her if whatever he's feeling is all going *nowhere?*

More properly, he should call it fantasy, admiration, or something else. Love must be shared and returned.

Love Is Growth

One of the important things about authentic love is that it feels good. It does something *for* you, not *to* you. When you love and are loved, you are added to, not taken away from; you are made better, you feel more whole, you are more complete. If love is real, deep and mature, both people in a relationship experience all these good things. So often people tell us that loving someone takes everything out of them. This may not be authentic loving, especially in the sexual expression of love. If a person sighs with relief after sexual intercourse, if he feels diminished or lessened, he isn't entering into it with the kind of anticipation and giving attitude that it really needs.

When you love, you give without giving up. You give without losing. You gain from the giving. It's a shared experience, and it doesn't take anything away from you. The physical exhaustion following inter- course is partly fatigue that follows vigorous exertion and partly the letdown after the build-up and reduction of any kind of tension. But, in our counseling experience, this is the kind of thing we too often hear:

> Aw, I really hate to make love to my old lady! I always feel so weak afterward. I feel like I'm robbed of some of my strength. I don't have any energy or desire left to do anything but turn over and go to sleep.

Or, the picture is clouded by attitudes about the rightness of sexuality:

> I suppose it sounds funny, but I feel guilty about sex. It's so animal- like! My husband is so loud and excited. It frightens me. I don't know what I'd do if he woke the children up with his loud breathing and groaning. It all seems so . . . *bad, so abnormal.* Nice people don't carry on like bulls in a pasture!

Too bad for the nice people! One of the most significant things found in healthy, happy, well-married, and satisfied people is that their sexual lovemaking is free and unrestrained, full of abandon and vigorous responsiveness.

People who feel guilt or disgust about sexual lovemaking are likely to feel bad about it, before, during, and afterward, and anxiety will drain off energy and feelings of well-being. Self-actualizing people report the opposite feelings regarding what love and sexual expression do for them. Their expressions of love, whether verbal, gestural, visual, or sexual, are not "taking away from" experiences that "cost" them anything. They are always rejuvenating, strengthening, replenishing, and beneficial experiences. A loving person enjoys loving. He likes it; it "pleasures" him; it makes him feel good; it enlarges and broadens him; it creates something, and he wants to repeat these good feelings.

Trust

Basic to the love relationship is *trust*. Fromm's fourfold test of love assumes it: you must trust someone to know him and let him know you, to care and be cared for, to respect and be respected. And trust determines the quality of the responses made to another person.

Yet trust is difficult to come by. We acquire it in varying degrees throughout our growth cycles. A reliance on some sort of order helps one learn to trust. The most important aspect is what is internalized. Those who experience reliability, dependability, constancy in the people and objects around them tend to perceive reality in those terms, and the perception generalizes to include personal behavior—they gradually come to trust themselves.

Trust is a basic prerequisite for healthy, satisfying interpersonal relations. The truster is one who continues to believe in other people in general, even when individual people let him down, do him dirt, or even try to do him harm. He maintains a generalized good feeling about people, though he often develops a cautious attitude toward particular persons. One of the key concepts in the trust necessary for love relationships is *openness.*

Vulnerability

To be open to life, to love, to love another human being, is to trust that whatever else may come to you, mostly you will encounter good. To be open is to remove or discard defenses so that another person can have an authentic access to your fullest self. And that means you allow yourself to be vulnerable: you may be hurt, but you also may be loved. You make yourself susceptible to whatever life might offer: joy and pain, love and hatred, acceptance and rejection, pleasure and agony. The reward comes not in finding a balance between the "agony" and the "ecstasy," but in knowing yourself to be a courageous, vital person. Being a significant human being means that there is the "plus" of being one who dares, one who risks, one who experiments, one who invites life in. One who not only passively says yes to life, but goes out—wide open and vulnerable—and challenges life to be interesting, to be worthwhile, to be stimulating. This is the excitement that significant selfhood can bring. This is the very active element that loving can mean. We think love and live have more in common than a few similar letters and sounds. Our experience has been that loving people are living people. People who live life in this way also love well, for out of the basic, comfortable trust in themselves and their

ability to handle life, they communicate a trusting of others. Their attitude says in effect, "I believe in myself and Myself says that you are a person as worthwhile as I am. Let's exchange the gift of friendship and see what we can add to each other."

The Types of Love

The overall description of love is the joyous, unpremeditated experience of giving and taking that means knowing, caring, respecting, and responding. It means the giving that actually replenishes. But love wears many faces, and for those who know of only one or two we would name the forms it can take.

Self-love

The concept of self-love seems at first to be a contradiction in terms. If love involves giving and getting, how can one person do both? And how can he do both within one person? The ability to love means to break down any divisions between the "subject" and the "object"; as in the concept of the Yang and Yin from Taoist philosophy, mutually complementary halves become one whole with no *real* or important line between them. This is done, paradoxically, without either half (or either partner) losing his identity. Yang doesn't become Yin, nor does Yin become Yang: they only complete each other. There is unity without sameness.

In the attitude a person has toward himself, the distinction between *I*, the subject, and *Me*, the object, is only an academic exercise. *I* describes the active, knowing part of self; *Me* describes the known part of self. Both terms are fictions created for purposes of discourse. I can love myself, and indeed, I *must* love myself if I'm to talk about any meaningful, complementary relationship with another person. If I don't know, care about, respect, and respond to my needs, then I don't love myself and certainly can't love someone whom I experience less intimately. Furthermore, an unloved package is more likely to be a burden than a gift.

So, in spite of the seeming paradox, the person who loves others loves himself. He loves others *because* he loves himself. To become familiar with the fullest meanings of loving, you must begin "at home." The child who knows the affection, the caring, the respecting, the involving of loving parents begins to gain emotional as well as rational understanding of the love process, even though he may never be able to articulate or explain it, either to himself or to others. But he "knows" in the intuitive sense that he is loved, and he comes to value what his parents value—in this case, himself.

Harlow's classic study, with which most psychology students are familiar, points up the importance of body contact to the development of healthy adult relationships in monkeys. When infant monkeys were reared in isolation, with no interaction with others of its species, they were unable to enter into sexual relations as adults. In addition to deriving comfort from contact with a mother or mother substitute, the monkeys needed touching, fondling, playing, wrestling and even fighting with other monkeys in order to become social enough for sexual activity to take place—in spite of the fact that sexuality is instinctive in most lower animals.[4]

Humans are also in need of the kind of "loving" as infants and children that makes them comfortable with, and used to, contact. This kind of experience builds in them the first pleasurable sensations and satisfactions that are part of an emerging concept of self. When this develops in the normal, ordinary way, the child comes to know and accept and love himself.

Brotherly Love

Brotherly love still carries with it the characteristics and prerequisites of love in general, but its participants and expressions are spe-

4. G. L. Hershey and J. O. Lugo. *Living Psychology: An Experiential Approach* (New York: Macmillan, 1970), p. 116.

cialized. Brotherly love occurs between equals, peers, or those who can give and take in somewhat the same way and in about equal shares.

The child learns much about living life as he interacts with his own siblings. From older brothers, both boys and girls learn much of what it means to be male, just as sisters indirectly teach younger children about femaleness. Because a child may be scaled down more to his size or level, he may learn more naturally from a brother or sister than from a parent or teacher. Certainly the skills of communication and play are learned in this kind of interchange. Although the only child isn't automatically doomed to a tragic life because he doesn't have such built-in playmate-teachers, he does seem to have more difficulty acquiring some of the social skills.

Many parents think what goes on between their children scarcely resembles loving behavior. They see mostly squabbling, bickering, teasing, jealousy, tattling, and some physical abuse. As in any human enterprise, interaction may mean running some risks, but the benefits far outweigh the hurts in most cases. The ordinary play of ordinary children involves the testing and trying out that will enable the self to grow and mature. This includes hostile or aggressive behavior. Childhood is a good laboratory in which the child can get some idea of what it's like to be an adult, especially a social adult. His fighting and quarreling can prepare him for some of the hostile or competitive interaction that our particular society seems to prize, or at least to need.

One of the fortunate by-products of family living and the love it shares is a sense of kinship, of fellow-feeling. This feeling is one of the important attributes of the self-actualizing person. Developed by experiencing it with the ones around us, kinship gradually becomes a broader, more inclusive experience of identification and empathy with others.

Erotic Love

One of the first places that the child experiences sensations, after the mouth, is the pelvic region, for here his eliminatory experiences are focused, and these occur from Moment One. He is aware of the tension of the sphincters, of urination and elimination, and of the chafing that comes from wearing wet or soiled diapers. Actually, it's surprising that a child doesn't discover the stimulation of the genitals even earlier than he typically does. Random exploration of the body may lead to intentional stimulation as the infant discovers that the genitals are "alive" and contain many receptors for pleasure. The child doesn't experience orgasm in infancy, but he does experience the same pleasure that any of us do in stimulating or "playing with" the genitals.

Later, masturbation is coupled with conscious or active sexual behavior. The fantasy life of the preadolescent and adolescent is rich

and vivid with sexual imaginations. Dreams are filled with sexual activities and longings that come about naturally through the combined pressures of glandular secretions and external stimulation and memories. And let us underscore our unqualified affirmation and approval of these experiences and fantasies: *because they are normal, natural, and human, they are good.*

The child who is forbidden, or who forbids himself, to explore, to think or wonder about sexuality is crippled in his capacity for sexual love. Again, we can't be deterministic; we can only cite hundreds of cases in our own clinical practice in which otherwise fine and happy adults had great difficulty in experiencing the sexual side of their lives.

Sexual exploration, masturbation, sexual dreams, "wet dreams" or nocturnal emissions, and other infantile and juvenile experiences are natural processes that give a child experience and familiarity with his sexual nature.

In the adult sexual life, beginning with the necking, petting, and early quasi-intercourse experiences of adolescence, and concluding with the fullest, most satisfying orgasms of mature, wholesome, and totally free sexual lovemaking, there is the fullest, most intimate expression of love that can be found.

Some will say that we are making too much of sexual activity, overlooking "platonic" love relationships—the profound loves man has expressed for ideals, country, race, mankind, God, and altruistic, self-sacrificing love. We are not intentionally overlooking any form of love except insofar as our emphasis is on the *total* expression of self. Many forms of love, beautiful as they may be, deny sexuality—or try to.

Between two people, an enormous amount of communication goes on. There are contacts, moments of closeness, gestures, glances, intimations; many of these are erotic. The reason we emphasize this is that there is so much denial, so much repression, in our society. Much that is honestly and beautifully sexual is cheapened and hidden. Sexual love can be so deeply fulfilling and so beautiful that we wonder why anyone would want or need to minimize it, cheapen it, deny it.

Ways of Loving Erotically

Homosexuality: Let us be very specific. There are no such "things" as *homosexuals*. To classify these people as such, to give them a name, is to dehumanize and "thingify" them. They are human beings. They are people, anatomically, physiologically, and emotionally the same as people who practice only heterosexual lovemaking. Medical experts have found only an infinitesimal number of people whose hormones or genital structures seem to predispose them to what is called homosexuality. The majority of homosexual human beings have acquired a preference, a need for, a liking for sexual activity with members of their own gender. Through some learning experience, through some emotional reaction, they have found it easier, more comfortable, more tolerable, to have sexual involvement with those of their own sex.

Each human being is born with the latent potential of loving anyone, of either sex. If you have studied physiology and anatomy in any detail, you know that each of us carries not only the hormones, but also the primitive or vestigial sex organs of the opposite sex. Through combinations of experiences, through associations or traumas or accidents, some people come to prefer sexual companions of their own gender. Some feel actual fear, disgust or deep-seated hostility toward those of the opposite sex. These reactions can occur without any strong feelings *for* their own sex, but because of loneliness, or sexual drive, through isolation in certain settings (like prison, the military, parochial schools, private schools, or camps) they are involved in close associations with members of the same gender. In a friendship, there is usually a strong need for expression of affection. Often the close nonerotic love of two same-sex people is mistaken by the participants or by observers as "homosexual." A case in point:

> At a recent American Psychological Association Convention, one of the authors saw Dr. Frederick Perls greet several of his longtime friends, male and female. Dr. Perls—who died during the writing of this book—was a big bear of a man, with long gray hair and bushy whiskers. Because of his own sentimentality and his enormous capacity for affection, and because his experiences in Gestalt therapy, sensitivity sessions, and the Esalen Institute have enabled him to openly show affection, Dr. Perls greeted these friends with a big bearhug and often a kiss on the cheek—an honest and authentic display of affection between old friends. But a bystander said, loud enough to be overheard, that the "old fool was cavorting around like a flaming queer!" Several other observers uttered similar comments. Some found this kind of greeting to be offensive. Some must have been embarrassed and some may have been envious at Perls' open affections. Quite likely, not a few may have been concerned about their *own* sexual identity. Certainly our experience and knowledge of Fritz Perls convinces us that he wasn't in much conflict over his!

There is much more *homosexual panic* prevailing today than actual overt homosexual activity. Many men, feeling strong ties or inclinations of affection toward their fathers, brothers, friends, and acquaintances, are quite certain that they are "queer." They are not convinced of this because of any overt action on their part, but because their upbringing has made it difficult for them to show affection to anyone, especially to a member of the same sex. Women in this country are a bit more comfortable with contact and displayed affection among women. Yet, there is this same panic among many women, too.

The panic may occur for two social reasons: many religions teach that homosexual involvement is a sin; and most countries in Western civilization make it an *illegal* behavior. Great Britain, however, has recently changed its attitude toward homosexuality, viewing it now as a medical or emotional "situation," and not a matter of legalistics. Among the underground press in this country, over the past ten years, there has been a growing pressure to get society to let up on those who choose sexual partners who are different from those we call normative. The *Los Angeles Free Press* has a regular column devoted to news about the "Gay World." The Gay Liberation Front has linked arms and forces with the Women's Liberation Movements and the radical liberation groups.

Are people who live homosexual lives happy? This is a difficult question to answer. Our clinical experience has included psychotherapy with both males and females with homosexual love lives. Obviously, the person coming to a mental health clinic is unhappy about something.

Usually the person who wants to discuss his sexual life with a therapist is dissatisfied or unhappy about some aspect of it, even if it's only the reaction he gets from the larger society. Treatment is difficult, but certainly not impossible. The person with either a homosexual love life or "homosexual panic," who is motivated to explore his feelings about it and about himself, can come to a point where he may choose whichever form of sex life he prefers. A growing body of homosexuals are learning to accept their "different" preferences, and with that acceptance comes the ability to lead a productive, happy life.

Man-Woman Love: Austin Porterfield's book *Marriage and Family Living: As Self-Other Fulfillment* is one of the best approaches to love as a testimony of self-actualization that we know. Porterfield develops the concept of *interpersonal resonance.* To find fulfillment in love, and especially the sexual expressions of love, two people must 1) recognize the other self as similar to one's own, and 2) live with the concept of resonance. When you strike a chord on a piano which is perfectly attuned to another in the same room, the second piano echoes the chord. "In interpersonal resonance, the mutual echoing of two natures depends upon the recognition of similarities, and takes place through sympathetic imagination—the process of 'taking the role of the other,'

and imagining not only how the other feels, but why he feels as he does."[5]

This is what we're after: a way of looking at the deepest, most total expression of love. If two people feel their kinship as human beings, as actualized selves, then in their expressions of relatedness they will "tune" themselves in. The lovemaking is not a contest: who can reach a climax first, or who can hold it back longest, or who can have the biggest and best climax, or even "was it better than the last time?" Competition has no place in the bed of loving, actualized people. It belongs to "sexual athletes" or exhibitionists or sexual failures who cover up the failure with boasting and bragging about their sexual exploits. College students often spend hours recounting their sexual encounters, talking about the "notches on their belts," comparing numbers of "scores," or length of time before orgasm, or size of genitals or breasts. This isn't actualized sexuality, though it may be part of the open and honest enjoyment attitude actualizers have about sex! For most of these students it represents the most important part of sex: the story-telling, the reputation-building. This isn't self-love or love for another person: it's what Fromm calls *narcissism*, the phony self-appreciation that consists in boasting and flaunting oneself.

A truly loving, healthy, and fulfilled person doesn't need to *talk* about sexual exploits; he has too good a time experiencing them and strengthening his love relationships to spend time and energy worrying about his reputation. He also knows that statistics have little or nothing to do with sexual satisfaction, fulfillment, or mutual giving of pleasure. If he is male he does not worry about the size and development of his genitals. If she is female, she does not worry about the size and development of her bustline! These are only unimportant cultural values, and a truly self-actualizing person can live above them. The important factor in any sexual relationship is the two people involved— not the time, the place, the lighting, the candles, wine, violin music, or any other external factor.

The real giving and taking, or better, the "sharing" of self, that goes on in healthy, actualizing sexual lovemaking is relatively rare. Most people *use* sex. It's not uncommon to hear of people describing their sexual experiences in ways that are designed to build up their reputations, not as lovers in the meaningful sense, but as "lovers" in the sense of being smooth, competent, swinging, and very, very casual.

The language of sex often gives us clues to the intent of the user: "a piece," "tail," "a lay," "screw," "make" are all terms completely devoid of any human representation. These are impersonal, mechanical,

5. Austin Porterfield, *Marriage and Family Living: As Self-Other Fulfillment* (Philadelphia: F. A. Davis Co., 1962), p. 208.

dehumanized descriptions of acts, not relationships, and certainly don't involve the quality of involvement of one human being with another. Sometimes the partners are only referred to by the slang terms for their genital organs, or the roles they perform. Sexual love is just what its name should imply: love (or affection) expressed by the physical, mental, emotional, and spiritual coming together of two healthy, happy, total, and confident human beings.

There's an aura of overseriousness in the above paragraphs that indicates our deep concern for the preservation and respect of really human sexuality. But there's the problem, too, that the words used and the tone may cause some people to lose sight of one of the central aspects of human lovemaking: it's a joyous and wild and completely abandoned experience of losing oneself—that is, if it's good. Sexuality should be taken seriously, but should not be a serious business. It's play! It's re-creative childlikeness! Its most beautiful moments come when neither partner is involved in the mundane, everyday workaday affairs of life, when they forget everything, including themselves, and are concerned only with the pleasure and greater joy of the other person. Wholesome lovemaking is a spontaneous, unrehearsed, and certainly unselfconscious celebration of one's own love.

The Sexual Revolution—Fact or Fantasy?

Much discussion goes on today about sexual freedom. We are supposed to be living in a time of sexual revolution. We know that many people will criticize our efforts in this book by calling them part of the big conspiracy to destroy the morality of our youth! We *are* interested in changing repressive and guilt-producing attitudes about sexuality. We do want people to discover their own sexual natures and to grow from this discovery and to enable others to grow as well. We do hope that some sort of evolution, if not revolution, takes place in the area of sexual attitudes. We know that human beings who experience their love in satisfying and growth-producing sexual encounters are happier, healthier, and more loving people generally. This should continue.

Many high school and college students have difficulty with their sexual feelings. Our society makes no provision for their sexual needs. We condemn them for premarital sex and make them feel guilty or fear for their sanity if they admit masturbation. The problem is there for the unmarried, the widowed, divorced, or separated, too. Wives of servicemen tell us of the hardship of a sexless existence while their husbands are away. The serviceman himself is put in the awkward position of trying out a life of celibacy—made more difficult if he has had a happy and healthy sex life prior to his military involvement—or resorting to the less satisfying solution of masturbation. Often he's inclined to turn to prostitutes, which often is neither as fulfilling nor as hygienic as the relationship he had with his wife back home. Sometimes the serviceman is coaxed or seduced into homosexual patterns which at the very least produce some kind of guilt or shame, and which at their worst can cause him to doubt his heterosexuality and thereby interfere with his readjustment to married life when he comes home.

The sexual needs of prisoners in jails and penitentiaries are common problems today. Some solutions to this have included the right of conjugal visitation, where a man's wife or girl friend can spend a few hours or a night with him in a private cell. To those who criticize this, not on moral grounds, but on the basis that it's pampering a man who should be punished, we ask if having him turn to homosexuality is a consequence more to these critics' liking? How does your sense of morality or justice deal with that one?

It's important that our society examine its own attitudes toward the important area of human sexuality. Are they reasonable in the light of modern scientific findings? Are they in keeping with what we understand about the sexual side of human selfhood? And the feared problems that we think might result if sexual attitudes are made more human, do they really happen? Does full, free, warm, respectful, humanistic sex education (we prefer the term "Life Education") really cause children to go out and experiment, spreading disease and unwanted pregnancies and neuroses? Of course not! *Much more common are the diseases, conflicts, and pregnancies that result from ignorance, fear, and furtiveness.* This isn't a challenge to open the bedroom doors so that children can watch their parents making love; lovemaking, like all intimate shared experiences, needs and deserves uninterrupted privacy. It *is* a challenge to consider the fact that enlightening our children produces adults who respect knowledge and truth; keeping them in the dark usually produces adults who fear the light and the truth.

Marriage

An overwhelming percentage of the adults in our society are, or have been, married. It's part of the normative behavior of our people to find someone with whom we believe we can share a happy and productive life and make this decision public. This is such a strong pressure that people who don't or can't marry often are treated as peculiar, odd, perverse; or even subversive. The single person who prefers to remain unattached is subject to much criticism and pressure to "shape up," to conform.

Not everyone should marry. Some are not emotionally ready; some never will be. Others feel their particular talents lie in directions other than the traditional patterns of love-marriage-parenthood. This, like other important decisions, must be up to the significant person's own discretion.

Why marry? This is a question asked by increasing numbers of our students. They see the national ratio of marriages to divorces getting smaller. It's currently close to 3:1 in the nation as a whole. In Los Angeles County, it recently became 1:1! One divorce for every marriage! Perceptive and searching students look at the disharmony, the dissonance, the bickering, the infidelity, the mate-swapping, the marriage-divorce-remarriage-divorce-remarriage cycle, and throw their hands up in the air. Why, indeed, marry? Why not just keep things simple? If two people can agree to it, many of them are finding a satisfactory solution in simply living together for as long as they are both happy.

A number of radical solutions have recently been proposed as alternative "marriage" patterns. One solution is the above, to simply cohabit. Another is group cohabitation, or a number of people (not necessarily paired-off) living together as one big family. In this situation, there may be agreed-upon pairings or there may be agreement that anybody can have intercourse with anybody else. Researchers have yet to find communal situations where long-term nonpaired sexual relations have worked out, but this may be due to research techniques or other problems we haven't discovered yet. Potentially, it is one solution to the problems of marriage.

Another solution is contract agreements: two people marry and agree that at the end of a stipulated time—five or ten years—they will review their relationship and, if mutually agreed, will renew their contract. If one or both don't agree to it, the validity of the contract is declared null and void. Another suggested pattern is to have two different formats: for those who plan to have no children, a particular agreement is made; for those who want children, a different, more involved agreement is made.

Some are suggesting that two males (or two females) who profess their devotion and desire may enter into a marriage relationship. Some who have already done so have even succeeded in adopting children!

A number of other ideas are being discussed by sociologists and psychologists studying marriage and family living, including some of the longer-practiced patterns like polygyny and polyandry. In a society where there are more women than men, polygyny is often suggested as a logical solution to the companionship and sexual needs of single women.

In whatever form a particular culture develops it, marriage has survived when other patterns of behavior have succumbed to a variety of pressures. A behavior pattern continues as long as it proves itself functional, succeeds in meeting certain needs effectively and efficiently. The typical marriage pattern is developed as a response to needs for regulation of sexual activity, companionship, provision for giving birth and legitimacy to children, for socialization of the children, and for economic, emotional, and physical security. Most marriage patterns are reinforced by the religious teachings of a society. They are given legal status as well. So, marriage patterns are firmly entrenched.

Many sincere and mature social scientists are wondering if our traditional marriage patterns aren't moving toward dysfunctionality. The churches and synagogues take over the religious teaching that originally was the job of the parent. The society is providing economic security and police take care of physical security. Society is beginning to accept the job of caring for the illegitimate child and the older adult, so those family functions aren't quite so important any more. Schools, peer groups, and some religious groups are taking over most of the socialization functions. What's left for the family to do? Possibly the most important function still remains: to provide a situation in which deep affection and physical desires can be legally and morally expressed.

There is really nothing wrong with our present marriage patterns. But the ways in which we have come to regard human relationships do not fit into the ways in which traditional marriage patterns insist that we view them. Traditionally, two people are supposed to have all their needs met by each other. But today's world is much larger, more crowded than yesterday's. Both husband and wife travel further from the family hearth than they did even twenty years ago. The social and companionship needs of each are often well met by other people;

yet the spouse who isn't involved often feels hurt or left out. Even when a married person doesn't try to find outside sexual partners, he or she knows that intellectual, avocational, occupational, hobby, recreational, and companionship needs can be met by a variety of people other than his or her spouse. No one should expect one person to meet all his needs, nor should any one person expect that he or she can or ought to meet all the needs of his spouse.

A healthy marriage, a happy, actualizing marriage, is one in which two whole persons come together because they have much to share. They desire each other as persons, as sexual partners, and as companions. They also know that each of them, being whole and significant, is capable of meeting many of his own needs. It's also a happy realization that neither partner expects the other to be "all things" to him or her. Limitations and strengths are accepted and the two people try to lead realistic lives. Because of their mutual respect and affection, this can bring them into an even closer union. Their love relationship can grow, and they can grow because of it. The other people in their lives—fellow workers, friends, children, relatives—enter into the relationship, but not into the deepest part of it: that's the private shared world of the two people.

Love as Therapy

A tremendous amount of human misery is caused by lack of love. Not only do some people not love others; they don't love themselves. Some, having no love for themselves, play love games with other people. Some martyrs want hurt or even death, so they hurt or kill themselves in the name of "love for my fellowman." This is a lot of rot! No human being is helped by someone's killing himself! Mankind needs more people with healthy self-love, who also love others, who can *live*—not die.

Millions of miserable human beings could become unmiserable, even happy and creative, actualizing people if real love could enter their lives. There's more than just clever rhetoric in the phrase "behind every successful man is a woman." We'd like to run the risk of not-very-scientific generalizing by saying that behind every effective human being is some loving person or experience.

Love, real and meaningful love, is a form of therapy. We've seen violent patients turned into contented and responsive persons by simple acts of lovingkindness. We've seen fearful creatures become courageous humans when they know they're loved and respected. We've seen hostile rage reactions turned into quiet, creative dialogue when a loving person intervened. These are not fictions; they are realities.

Love isn't by itself a therapy, not in the strictest clinical sense. But love is therapeutic: it is enabling, releasing, quieting, uncovering, growth-producing, insight-giving, stimulating, enlivening, inspiring. People who discover that they are loved, even by one person, even when they themselves don't love anyone, often find new reasons to live. More importantly, they often find new reasons to be, to grow, to struggle to be more significant human beings.

The therapeutic aspects of real love are that the *person* is loved, not the man, the object, the member of *Homo sapiens*. It takes interacting human beings for love to take place. Your feelings about chocolate ice cream, Mick Jagger, Raquel Welch, or your dog are feelings of affection or admiration or pleasure, not love. To love, the other person must be one whom you know, care for, respect and respond to. If you show a person your love feelings, that communicates to him that he must, after all, be worthwhile: something he may never have known or felt before.

Another therapeutic aspect of love is that it gets you out of yourself. Many people are "sick" because they are lost inside their own heads or skin. They haven't ever "come outside to see whether or not it's raining." As the quotation at the beginning of this chapter says: "To love someone is to bid him to live and invite him to grow." If I love you, I invite you to come out and experience me and the rest of what's happening. This ability to experience a larger situation is a vital part of self-actualization.

Still another therapeutic function love performs is to open up communications. You must communicate love; it can't be experienced and then hidden away like a jar of pickled radishes. If it's good, it will be demonstrated, shared, given away. The person who is loved sooner or later knows it. He is given clues and if he's still too blind (or troubled or frightened) to pick up on these, then the lover will try another tack. Eventually, "love will out." It's beautiful to see.

There's a lingering or sticking-with-it aspect of love that's very therapeutic. The loved person takes this warm glow with him wherever he goes, like a hot coal carried in his pocket to keep his hands warm. He knows, even when alone, that he's loved. This shores him up, tides him over, carries him through many cold and lonely, frightening and defeating times. No professional advice or counsel ever has quite this potent an ability to hang on.

Being in a love relationship gives you the knowledge that you are appreciated, respected. You are, at least to one other human being, a significant and unique person. We can't quantitatively describe that feeling. If you know it, then it doesn't need description. If you don't, we can't create it for you by words.

Also, there is therapy in the fact that the loving person knows you. You may have shut out the entire world, kept it in the dark about you. But somebody, one lone person, found his way inside the central portion of your being and knows you and . . . lo, and behold! it didn't destroy you. You suddenly discover that being known isn't quite the totally devastating thing you thought it was. This often gives you incentive to expand this circle of awareness, to let others in on the secret, to invite other people into intimate nexus with you. This can be tremendous.

Therapy as Love

A good therapist thinks of himself as worthwhile, as a human being, as a person with enough good feeling spilling over to pass it on and share it with those who need it most. Sidney Jourard has said that therapists were something like *professional lovers:* psychotherapy that is effective is very much a love relationship. It's *like* loving, but it's also, in many aspects of it, *real* loving. For instance:

THERAPIST: Now, what's wrong?

CLIENT: Oh, you look at me as if you don't believe what I'm saying.

THERAPIST: Does it matter to you whether I do or not?

CLIENT: Of course! Why do you ask a question like that?

THERAPIST: I just like to know why my opinion or my facial expressions are important to you at all.

CLIENT: (Getting angry) Well, you're my therapist! What you say and think should matter.

THERAPIST: Why, because you've heard it should or you read somewhere . . .?

CLIENT: No, damn it! Because you're a real person to me. One of the few I've known. And you think *I'm* real and important. And I need that feeling.

THERAPIST: Maybe for now you need it from me and a few others, but eventually you're going to have to get that feeling of being real and important inside *you.* When you can do that, then you'll *be* real and important. Then you can tell other people to take their opinions and go to hell, because you won't need them to validate what you already feel deep inside. Still angry?

CLIENT: Yeah, because you're so damned smart! Besides, I'm entitled!

THERAPIST: You're entitled to feel anything you want to feel. You always have been, chum, you just never knew it before.

What we hope to illustrate in the above exchange is the quality of attachment and reality being given by each of them. It's right on the line: no fantasy roles, no symbolisms. Just straight give-and-take of feelings and insight. This is much more like a love exchange or, at the very least, an exchange of respect. This therapist is telling his client that he actually likes and appreciates him. It may be the first time it's ever really been communicated. He's inviting the client to experience that feeling and to practice communicating it to others. He is bidding the client to live and inviting him to grow.

Love comes from growth, encourages and fosters growth, and *is* a growth experience. The person struggling to actualize his own significant self will know love. He should glory in it, whenever it's offered, and should participate in it. We truly believe that "what the world needs now *is* love!"

Summary

Love is not an emotion, as commonly defined. It is a deep and dynamic relationship including attitudes and emotions. The attitudes are acceptance, trust, positive approval, helpful criticism, and a wish for the growth and well-being of the loved one. The emotions cover the full range of human feeling, but certainly include affection, joy, sexual desire, sexual pleasure, release, relief, respect, awe, sympathy, and empathy.

Love means a creative relationship. Erich Fromm gives us the important qualities of such a relationship: they are *knowledge* of the other, *caring concern* for his growth and well-being, *respect* for his unique selfhood, and *responsibility*, the willingness to respond to his emotional needs. Love involves growth, from smallness and fear into fullness and courage to be what you are.

Important in the love relationship are *empathy*, the ability to feel into the other person's life; *trust*, the willingness to "put yourself into the hands" of another person; *openness* and *vulnerability*, the willingness to experience, even though riskily, the other person and life together.

The types of love most easily studied are *self-love*, which is basic to the ability to love others; *brotherly love*, which begins with family members and gradually comes to include mankind; and *erotic love*, a relationship of physical intimacy and affection. In discussing erotic or sexual love, we find consideration must be given to homosexual as well as heterosexual relations.

Marriage is an important part of our society. We evaluated traditional marriage patterns and compared them to some suggested alternatives. Finally, we considered the therapeutic aspects of love and the love aspects of therapy.

Suggested Readings:

Aronoff, Joel. *Psychological Needs and Cultural Systems.* Princeton, New Jersey: D. Van Nostrand Co., 1967.

Barron, Frank. *Creativity and Personal Freedom.* Princeton, New Jersey: D. Van Nostrand Co., 1968.

Bartell, G. D. *Group Sex.* New York: Peter H. Wyden, 1971.

Bennis, Warren, and Phillip E. Slater. *The Temporary Society.* New York: Harper & Row, 1968.

Bernard, J. "Women, Marriage, and the Future," *The Futurist.* April 1970.

Buber, Martin. *I and Thou.* New York: Charles Scribner's Sons, 1968.

Byrne, Donn. *The Attraction Paradigm.* New York: Academic Press, 1971.

Cavan, Ruth S., ed. *Marriage and Family in the Modern World.* New York: Thos. Y. Crowell, 1969.

Chiang, Humg-min, and A. H. Maslow, eds. *The Healthy Personality.* New York: Van Nostrand and Reinhold Co., 1969.

Coopersmith, Stanley. *The Antecedents of Self-Esteem.* San Francisco: W. H. Freeman Co., 1967.

DeLora, Joan S., and Jack R. DeLora, eds. *Intimate Life Styles.* Pacific Palisades, California: Goodyear Publishing Co., 1972.

Fromm, Erich. *The Art of Loving.* New York: Harper & Row, 1956.

Hershey, G. L., and J. O. Lugo. *Living Psychology.* New York: Macmillan, 1970.

Hodge, Marshall. *Your Fear of Love.* New York: Doubleday, 1967.

Jourard, Sidney. *Self-Disclosure.* New York: Wiley, 1971.

Jourard, Sidney, and D. C. Overlade, eds. *Reconciliation.* Princeton, New Jersey: D. Van Nostrand Co., 1966.

Kanter, R. M. *Commitment and Community: Communes and Utopias.* Cambridge, Massachusetts: Harvard University Press, 1972.

Katchadourian, H. A., and D. T. Lunde. *Fundamentals of Human Sexuality.* New York: Holt, Rinehart & Winston, 1972.

Kirkendall, L. A., and R. H. Whitehurst, eds. *The New Sexual Revolution.* New York: D. W. Brown Co., 1971.

Lask, Angela, and R. Roe, eds. *This Is a Sociology Reader.* San Francisco: Rinehart Press, 1973.

Masters, W. H., and V. E. Johnson. *Human Sexual Response.* Boston: Little, Brown and Co., 1966.

May, Rollo. *Love and Will.* New York: Norton, 1969.

_____. *Psychology and the Human Dilemma.* Princeton, New Jersey: D. Van Nostrand Co., 1967.

Morihisa, J. "An Examination of Interpersonal Interaction in the Swinging Singles' Bar." Department of Social Relations, Harvard University, 1971.

Mudd, Emily H., ed. *Man and Wife.* New York: W. W. Norton, 1957.

Murstein, B., ed. *Theories of Attraction and Love.* New York: Springer, 1971.

O'Neill, Nena, and George O'Neill. *Open Marriage.* New York: Avon Books, 1972.

Otto, Herbert, ed. *Love Today.* New York: Association Press, 1972.

Packard, Vance. *The Sexual Wilderness.* New York: David McKay Co., Inc., 1968.

Porterfield, Austin. *Marriage and Family Living: As Self-Other Fulfillment.* Philadelphia: F. A. Davis Co., 1962.

Reik, Theodore. *Listening with the Third Ear.* New York: Farrar, Straus, 1949.

Roleder, George. *Marriage Means Encounter.* Dubuque, Iowa: Wm. C. Brown Co., 1973.

Rosenblatt, P. C. "Marital Residence and the Functions of Romantic Love," *Ethnology* (1967) 6, 471–480.

Rubin, Zick. *Liking and Loving.* New York: Holt, Rinehart, and Winston, 1973.

_____. "Measurement of Romantic Love," *J. Personal and Social Psychology* (1970) 16, 265–273.

Stephan, W., et al. "Sexual Arousal and Heterosexual Perception," *J. Personal and Social Psychology* (1971) 20, 93–101.

Wolf, Leonard, ed. *Voices from the Love Generation.* Boston: Little, Brown and Co., 1968.

Zimbardo, P., and C. Maslach, eds. *Psychology for our Times.* Glenview, Illinois: Scott, Foresman Co., 1973.

12

Come Up Higher

If psychic life consisted only of overt happenings—which on the primitive level is still the case—we could content ourselves with a sturdy empiricism. . . . Our psychic processes are made up to a large extent of reflections, doubts, and experiments, all of which are almost completely foreign to the unconscious, instinctive mind of primitive man. It is the growth of consciousness which we must thank for the existence of problems; they are the dubious gift of civilization.[1]

CARL GUSTAV JUNG

Biofeedback training has created the first revolution in the study of human consciousness. . . . Through biofeedback training man is learning to choose his state of being. He can explore new experiences in a systematic, controlled way without relying on unstable and often dangerous drugs.[2]

MARVIN KARLINS AND L. M. ANDREWS

. . . Psychoanalysis . . . strives to bring to the conscious state only the repressed material in the preconscious . . . but fails to correlate the conscious mind with the deeper levels of the subconscious and thus fails to uncover the latent faculties—to say nothing of reaching the state of pure consciousness beyond the subconscious . . .[3]

MAHARISHI MAHESH YOGI

1. C. G. Jung, *Modern Man in Search of a Soul* (New York: Harcourt, Brace & Co., 1960), p. 95.
2. M. Karlins & L. M. Andrews, *Biofeedback* (New York: Warner, 1973), p. 60.
3. Maharishi Mahesh Yogi, *Transcendental Meditation* (New York: Signet Books, 1968), p. 216.

So, love is an answer. Love, operating in its selfless and undemanding way, can provide the means and the incentive to growth and wholeness and personal significance. We've come a long way in this process of searching and examining the struggle we all must undergo to find Selfhood. And love appears to be at the end of that journey.

And so it is; but there is an incompleteness about this study if we leave it at that. Granted, for most of us, "leaving it at that" would be a monumental accomplishment, for how few of us really love or know love? But, what of the larger dimensions to Selfhood, the aspects that take us from our solitary, individuated selfhood out into the larger collective experience, what Jung has called the suprapersonal, what others call the *transpersonal?* Having learned to love, and to be loved, what does this do for us and urge us to do besides?

Aha! Now you may be imagining that we are going to abandon our scientific stance to dabble in the supernatural. But we are not. We want to explore the transcendent functions of human consciousness, and to do that we will indeed talk about some of the so-called parapsychological or occult phenomena. For, whether they in themselves have a reality or not, they are part of human experience. We want to demonstrate that they are far from "super-natural," that these unfamiliar or even unexplainable phenomena are very much part of the natural order.

Into the Unknown

What is the unknown? What is mysterious? We may think we know, but do we? It is possible that what we call mysterious, occult, extrasensory perceptions (ESP) are mysterious not so much because of their own inherent nature, but because of our inability and inexperience. We must acknowledge that limitations exist in human capacities: some are built into the structures of our bio-psycho-social substance: our bodies. The human eye, for example, can only respond to electromagnetic energy that pulsates at the range of wavelengths between about 4000 and 7000 angstrom units. But this is a tiny slice out of the entire electromagnetic spectrum. For on either side of this visible slice of the spectrum are X rays, infrared, ultraviolet, radio, gamma, and other rays, none of which are "visible" to the eye. Are these forms of electromagnetic energy mysterious, magical, supernatural? We think not. We think the limitations of our senses is the problem.

Besides this, there are imposed or acquired limitations, or those that happen because of insufficient development of the varying parts of the human nervous system. We know there are individual differences in the structures of our sense modalities (some function not at all;

others function extremely well because of more "perfect" structures: some can see light with wavelengths of 3900 angstrom units or over 7600 angstrom units, though the average is between 4000 and 7000). There are also differences in functioning that are due to development, learning, acquisition, or practice.

During World War II, members of military units that had to work at night learned to condition their eyes for night-seeing by sitting for a brief period in a room illuminated by red light. Then, when they went outside they could see much better than men who had the same visual apparatus, but who had not been "red-conditioned." Similarly, individual differences in functioning may come about through practice and training of perceptual processes. Did American Indians really have better hearing, smell, or vision than the white Europeans who studied them? Probably their eyes, ears, and sense of smell were nearly identical; biologists have not identified any racial or ethnic differences in perception that are attributed solely to genetics. In other words, apart from eye color and shape of the eyelids, no "racial" differences have been found between "Indian eyes" and "white eyes." Yet, European settlers and frontiersmen insisted that Indians could see in the dark, could hear like a forest animal, could pick up scent and so on. But many of the European frontiersmen, hunters and trappers, scouts and guides also came to develop similarly sharpened sensory skills. Why? For the simplest reason in all of nature—the principle underlying organic evolutionary theory—the need was there. If one's survival depends on sharpening and developing the sensory acuities, then one does that or perhaps dies! Though there is no actual evolution going on, the simple example of polishing these skills for personal survival is instructive.

None of these things could have happened had latent potential for such development not been present in the first place. If it's physically, physiologically, anatomically, and humanly impossible to run 100 yards in three seconds flat, no amount of "need" or practice, conditioning, training, or development of running, breathing, dietary, musculoskeletal, or any other physical skills is going to help. (We almost hate to mention a figure like three seconds, because it just might be possible after all! There were experts fifty years ago who dogmatically and categorically declared that human beings would never run the 100-yard dash in ten seconds! Yet the nine-second mark is being pushed every day.)

So, the sensory world, involving the most frequently used sense, vision, plus all the rest, presents us with an example of how events we might term "mysterious" may only be "unknown" or "unexplored" to us.

ESP, Hypnosis, and Other Crazy Things!

Among the subjects being studied along the cutting edge of psychological research, few have captured the imagination of the layman as strongly as have subjects like ESP, hypnosis, the supernatural and occult, and the spiritual. Let's be very clear at the outset: we have no definitive findings for you, to either accept or reject these areas of study. Most physical scientists and a large number of behavioral scientists do not study these areas. While not all refuse to believe in their possibilities,[4] many of them ignore or avoid any kind of study in these fields.

The best explanation for this—apart from the fact that these subjects do not seem to be even remotely connected to their areas of interest or exploration—is that scientists do not as yet know how to go about such study.

> Why do we not accept ESP as a psychological fact? Rhine has offered enough evidence to have convinced us on almost any other issue where one could make some guess as to the mechanics of the disputed process. Some of his evidence has been explained away, but as far as I can find out, not all of it. Until a complete rebuttal is provided or until we accept ESP, let us not talk about enlarging our notions of neurology to meet the psychological "facts" with no external criterion of what those facts are. We are still trying to find our way out of the magic woods of animism, where psychology began historically, and we cannot give up the talisman of a knowledge of material processes. Personally, I do not accept ESP for a moment, because it does not make sense. My external criteria, both of physics and of physiology, say that ESP is not a fact despite the behavioral evidence that has been reported. I cannot see what other basis my colleagues have for rejecting it; and if they are using my basis, they and I are allowing psychological evidence to be passed on by physical and physiological censors. Rhine may still turn out to be right, improbable as I think that is, and my own rejection of his views is—in the literal sense—prejudice.[5]

This quotation comes from D. O. Hebb, long associated with the most rigorous kinds of psychophysiological research. He alludes to

---

4. As long ago as 1952, Warner found that only 10 percent of psychologists surveyed believed that ESP is impossible. Yet, only 3 percent felt it to be an established fact. For your own perusal, this survey is described in L. Warner, "A Second Survey of Psychological Opinion on ESP," *Journal of Parapsychology* (152) 16, 284–295.

   Dr. Stanley Krippner reports that *New Scientist* polled its British readers and found that only 3 percent felt that parapsychological phenomena were impossible. The rest either accepted parapsychic events as real or as distinctly possible. *New Scientist* readers are largely professionals with advanced degrees. (See *Psychology Today*, October 1973.)

5. D. O. Hebb, "The Role of Neurological Ideas of Psychology," *Journal of Personality* (1951) XX, 39–55.

J. B. Rhine, who for over forty years did parapsychological research at Duke University. Rhine's research methods and statistical procedures were doubted at first, but in 1937, the American Institute of Mathematical Statistics studied his methodologies, research environments, and all pertinent conditions, and pronounced them acceptable and proper for valid research to take place.[6]

The word *science* is derived from the root *scientia,* which means "knowing." How do we "know"? We know through a dozen different means and methods. Science is undergoing a revolution in theory and methodology. The empiricism—based on the philosophical structures of logical positivism—that has characterized most of scientific research and theory for the past one hundred years has a long and respectable history and an extremely useful future. However, it is only one means by which knowledge can be obtained, and scientists are willing to acknowledge this.

> When we pass beyond the range of our senses, we find evidence that both we and the world we live in have been given a specious appearance of self-completeness. This does not merely mean that the human senses are limited; it means that the practical mind has been formed in such a way that it reinforces the impression given by the senses and takes for granted things which are not true, but which make for implicity and efficiency in practical life. . . . The great value of physical research is that it has begun to put perspective into the universe and to show us that neither we nor our world come to an end where we thought they did.[7]

This means we are beginning to open up our "eyes"—not only our physical organs of vision, but also the instrumentation and measurement techniques that have been devised to extend and amplify the functioning of our eyes and the other senses.

Extrasensory perception (ESP) is but one area that is being considered a valid area for further study. Only a few scientists continue to toss it into the same grab bag with astrology, witchcraft, and stage magic. Hypnosis has weathered a long and bitter battle to become accepted as a valid area of scientific study, and a natural phenomenon, within the potential experience of any one of us. We will take a look at hypnosis later, but we use it as a single example of how we have had to remove the blinders from our perceptions in order to accept areas of human experiencing.

6. Stanley Krippner and Gardner Murphy, "Humanistic Psychology and Parapsychology," *Journal of Humanistic Psychology* (Fall 1973), Vol. 13, No. 4, p. 4.
7. G. N. M. Tyrell, *The Nature of Human Personality* (London: Allen and Unwin, Ltd., 1954), p. 94.

CHRISTIANSON

There are still many unknowns—astrology, witchcraft, demonology, spiritualism—that deserve further study, though such study may be more difficult than trying to isolate the elements in a drop of rain water. (It is worth remembering that at one time, analysis of the chemical makeup of water was also considered "impossible" and outside of the realm of natural science.)

Turn on, Tune in, and Drop In!

When we do open up our minds and our methodologies, what we are learning about human experience is as fascinating and astounding as the most esoteric and exotic "magic" we could imagine. We are increasingly becoming aware that the human body is a marvelous creation. The brain and central nervous system, the peripheral systems, the glandular systems, indeed, the entire organism is turning out to be among the most fascinating areas of study.

We have long known, for instance, that humans use only a minuscule fraction of their brain's potential, but we haven't known why that was so. Now, scientists are gathering information about brain potential, and it leads us into areas so exciting we wonder why research hasn't concentrated on this area before. Part of the answer lies in the fact that we've only just developed the technological "hardware" to make such research possible, but that's come about only because we've allowed the technological "software" to develop: the ideas, theories, personnel, and experiences. Another part of the answer is that some areas—like altered states of consciousness—have been considered to belong to spiritualism, ESP, or drug-related experiences. As such, they were often thought to be "out of bounds" for valid, objective scientific research.

Today, the explanations for many hitherto "supernatural" events seem perfectly "natural": part of the nature of the human organism. Many of us are now willing to push out the boundaries on our previous storehouses of knowledge, for we know that human consciousness is far more extensive and complex than we've given it credit for being. To some degree, this more generous attitude comes about because some validation has been given to experiences belonging to Indian yogis and fakirs, to Buddhist meditators, to users of LSD and other psychedelic drugs, and to psychotics.

Carl G. Jung reminds us that consciousness has four functions. That is, we experience reality in four ways, none of which is "better" than any other, but all of which can be developed for more comprehensive and total experiencing. These four functions are *sensation, cognition, feeling,* and *intuition.*

Jung's professional training was medical—empirically scientific—and he considered his research to be scientifically valid throughout his life. However, the topic of his doctoral dissertation in 1902 was "On the Psychology and Pathology of So-called Occult Phenomena." His split with Freud was not alone because he rejected Freud's libido theory: Freud called Jung "crazy" for his interest in religion and the varieties of consciousness.

What these four functions mean to us is not fully appreciated, though we are beginning to understand them. We know that the sensory experiences are important, and though we understand how illusions can "fool" our senses, we still tend to use sensation as our primary function: especially in the sciences. This is the basis for logical positivism and empiricism. It is most simply expressed in the Missouri dictum: "Show me!" or in the proverb, "Seeing's believing." We are highly tuned to sensory phenomena, demanding stimulation and variety in all the sensory stimuli around us. We like color, movement, complexity of pattern (though some prefer simplicity), symmetry (though others lean more toward asymmetry), and all the cues and qualities of the sensory world about us.

Cognition ranks very high with most Western people, as well, because we pride ourselves on being rational and logical people. We seek to classify, name, encode, and "understand" things, in terms of previous experiences which have become part of our cognitive structures. We value learning and schooling (not necessarily the same things!) and many of us enjoy games that make us think, entertainments that provoke thought or elaboration. The cognitive function is extremely important: it provides us with much readily digestible information, enabling us to "make it" in the world more easily, more safely. If we had to experience everything sensorily at first hand, as people have done previously, we might get lost in the welter of sensations around us. But we have learned how to encode others' experiences and pass them on to the next generation, thus saving the young some headaches and hardships.

Feeling is the function that gets us off the so-called "scientific" track. This is the more subjective experience. It involves emotions, judgments, and values. The sensory function permits us to experience a collection of light, shadow, and shape; the cognitive enables us to identify this as a cloud formation at sunset; the feeling function enables us to say "How beautiful!" "I love it!" or "I'm so angry I could throw things!" We are learning that feeling is just as important a function as the others, that it provides us with another dimension of experience, that our emotions enrich our experiences and permit greater interpersonal relating.

Intuition is the least understood and least studied of the four functions. This is the one—experienced by all of us—that gives rise to hunches, guessing, "vibrations," and "knowing" in the sense of: "I can't tell you why; I just *know* I can trust you." Like Jung, we don't believe intuition to be any more paranormal than the other three functions. We do agree it is underdeveloped in most of us, and as a result, many intuitive experiences are scoffed at, disregarded, or devalued. They add the fourth dimension to consciousness, and help us to round out our experiences.

If we were to adapt the TA language to this discussion, we could say that the Parent "tapes" are involved in some of the feeling and cognitive experiences, the Child in most of the feeling, sensory, and the intuitive, and the Adult utilizes mostly cognitive, with healthy doses of sensory. The fully functioning, Self-actualizing person is one who functions as Adult, with harmonious balancing of Child and Parent ego states. Yet, in the Jungian sense, the individuated person is one who has developed all four functions to their fullest capacity.

Recently, Dr. Roberto Assagioli, founder of *Psychosynthesis,* has added to Jung's fourfold typology, saying that consciousness also consists of impulse-desire, imagination, and *will*—areas minimally explored by Jung. A drawing, on page 344, shows how Jung's four functions and Assagioli's might be graphically portrayed.

The concept of will, long neglected (partly because the vocabulary and methods of study were embarrassing and "unscientific" to scientific scholars) and largely misunderstood, is once again the subject of enormous interest in psychology.

For far too long the notions of biological determinism ("anatomy is destiny") and psychic determinism, especially from the Freudians, has dominated our understandings of consciousness and human behaviors in general. Rollo May, in *Love and Will,* has brought it back into popular awareness, as have Abraham A. Low *(Mental Health through*

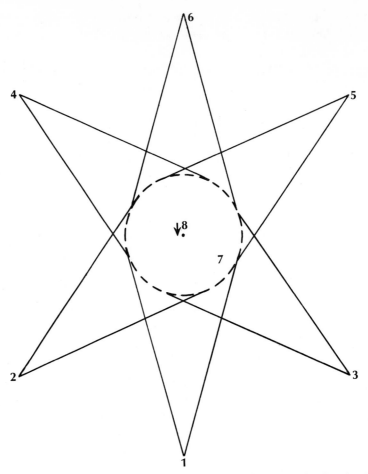

The Center of Consciousness and the Psychological Functions:

1. Sensation 2. Emotion-Feeling 3. Impulse-Desire 4. Imagination
5. Thought (cognition) 6. Intuition 7. Will 8. Central point: "I" or "ego"
(Adapted from Roberto Assagioli, *Psychosynthesis—A Manual of Principles and Techniques.* New York: Viking Press, 1971. See also Assagioli's *The Act of Will,* New York: Viking Press, 1973, and *Journal of Humanistic Psychology* (Winter 1974), Vol. 14, No. 1, "Jung and Psychosynthesis."

Will Training), Otto Rank *(Will Therapy and Truth and Reality),* and Leslie Farber *(The Ways of the Will).* We now accept and appreciate the possibilities that we are, after all, to a great extent aware of, and in charge of not only our consciousness but many other aspects of our behavior. Such notions have long been part of the theories and practices of humanistic psychologists, and the relative success of William Glasser's Reality Therapy and Schools without Failure programs attest to the very real possibilities for ordinary people—with help—to take responsibility and control of their own lives again.

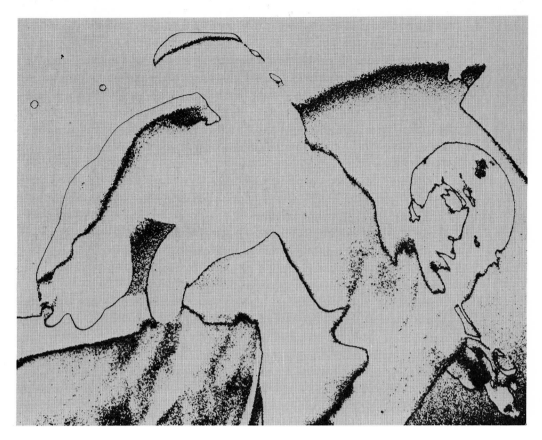

We are on the threshold of new insight into consciousness. The work of Robert Ornstein, Charles Tart, Jerome Bruner, Thomas Blackburn, Karl Pribram, R. W. Sperry, A. R. Luria, David Galin, Claudio Naranjo, Arthur Deikman, Stanley Krippner, Andrija Puharich, and Pierre Duval is ushering in a new age of understanding. (We don't like to name-drop, but this research is too exciting and needs so much support that we justify it on these grounds.)

Get This Through Your Thick Skull!

The research into consciousness begins where it properly should: with the organs of consciousness: the central and peripheral nervous systems. The brain isn't the mind, but it is where "mind" happens, in a strictly physiological sense. We aren't reducing all human experiences directly to neural and endocrine functions—not in the sense that if you add each neural, endocrinal, muscular, skeletal, gastrointestinal, and all other body functions together, they will add up to the sum total of human experience—but we are insisting that we have a lot to learn about biology before we jump off into too many other "unknowns."

The brain of the human being turns out to be far more complex and autonomous than we've ever known before. We have long known that the cerebral cortex is divided into two roughly equal hemispheres, connected by the fibers of the corpus callosum. We've long known that there are differences in the functions of both hemispheres, though we've tended to ignore these and concentrate on the similarities and duplications of function.

Roger W. Sperry's findings in the 1960s introduced us to the other possibilities. Dr. Sperry found that by severing the connecting nerves of the corpus callosum, sufferers of epileptic seizures could find remission. This led to other research into the two hemispheres. In most people, one hemisphere (usually the left) is "dominant." This dominance simply means that certain learning, memory, and speech functions are located in the left hemisphere.

Robert E. Ornstein is leading this exciting research in dual-hemisphere insights. He concludes that what we've called the "dominant" hemisphere is only dominant in a culture that places higher value on the functions of that hemisphere. He concludes that the left hemisphere (working through the right side of the body) controls in specific fashion the verbal, analytic, logical, and mathematical functions: all highly regarded functions in our "rational-analytic" cultures. The right hemisphere (operating mainly through the left side of the body) regulates in a more diffuse manner spatial awareness, musical ability, awareness of one's own body, and awareness of others. This is the "intuitive-holistic" function, not as highly valued in the West, but exceedingly prized in the Orient, Africa, and in outlying parts of our world.

The complementarity of these two modes of consciousness is manifest on several levels simultaneously—though we don't often realize it, stressing one side as we do. The two modes differ. Both hemispheres of the brain are responsible for the same functions in some cases (body sensing and body movement, for example), but each has its own specific functions. The table on page 347 may help us to understand these specific modes and how the insights of scientists and seers from all over can be fitted into this theory.

This is revolutionary information! It indicates that we have long-neglected areas of brain functioning to explore and that there is an imbalance in our appreciation of the whole of the brain. It also indicates that areas of experience that are not necessarily rational or empirically validated may be opened up for further study.

In a sense, we are going backward! The early psychologists were aware of many forms of input and experience, including intuition and

The Two Modes of Consciousness: A Tentative Dichotomy[8]

SOURCE:		
Many varied sources	Day	Night
Blackburn	Intellectual	Sensuous
Oppenheimer	Time, history	Eternity, timelessness
Deikman	Active	Receptive
Polanyi	Explicit	Implicit
Levy, Sperry	Analytic	Gestalt
Domhoff	Right side of body	Left side of body
Varied sources	Left brain hemisphere	Right brain hemisphere
Bogen	Propositional	Appositional
Lee	Lineal	Nonlineal
Luria	Sequential	Simultaneous
Semmes	Focal	Diffuse
I Ching	The creative: heaven, masculine, yang, light, time	The receptive: earth, feminine, yin, dark, space
Varied Sources	Verbal	Spatial
Varied Sources	Intellectual	Intuitive
Vedanta	Buddhi	Manas
Jung	Causal, Animus	Acausal, Anima
Bacon	Argument	Experience

introspection. The behaviorist movement halted this. William James was one of the few hard-nosed scientific psychologists to caution that we must not limit our knowledge to that received mechanically and from the senses alone:

> Our normal waking consciousness, rational consciousness as we call it, is but one special type of consciousness, whilst all about it, parted from it by the filmiest of screens, there lie potential forms of consciousness entirely different.[9]

Or, as Maslow has put it, "If the only tool you have is a hammer, you tend to treat everything as if it were a nail,"[10] referring to the reductionism of the behaviorists.

What are the "potential forms of consciousness" to which James alludes? Let's briefly explore the field of consciousness.

8. Modified from Robert E. Ornstein, *The Psychology of Consciousness* (San Francisco: W. H. Freeman, 1972).
9. William James, *The Varieties of Religious Experience* (New York: New American Library, 1958). Originally published in 1902.
10. Abraham Maslow, *The Psychology of Science* (Chicago: Henry Regnery, 1969).

Conscious Is as Conscious Does

The word *conscious* is an old one, but its most prevalent meaning is that given to it by Sigmund Freud. The German word Freud used was *bewusst*, a word that comes from *wissen* (to know), to which our expression *wit* is also related. *Bewusst* is more accurately translated "beknown," though that is an archaic expression (except in "unbeknownst to him"). We've typically defined *conscious* as *aware* so that *consciousness* meant *awareness*. Actually, then, *conscious* refers to that which is known, can be known, has been known.

Freud termed the unknown processes as *unconscious*. But, as we stressed at the beginning, our unknowing of something is less a comment on the qualities of that something than upon our own limitations. Freud felt that in the psychic process called the unconscious, there was no knowledge on the part of the person. In a "gray area" at the "lower" end of consciousness and at the "upper" end of unconsciousness, he postulated a "preconscious." In this transition zone, unconscious material could become conscious. In the preconscious lay the near-past events and experiences, now consciously forgotten or repressed, but able to come into consciousness through dreams, fantasies, slips of speech, and in some mental disorders, like schizophrenic hallucinations.[11]

Our present recognition of dual functioning in the two hemispheres may help us to understand some of the confusion that has long existed in the literature.

> This duality has been reflected in classical as well as modern literature as between reason and passion, or between mind and intuition. Perhaps the most famous of these dichotomies in psychology is that proposed by Sigmund Freud, of the split between the "conscious" mind and the "unconscious." The workings of the "conscious" mind are held to be accessible to language and to rational discourse and alteration; the "unconscious" is much less accessible to reason or to the verbal analysis. Some aspects of "unconscious" communications are gestures, facial and body movements, tone of voice.[12]

So, what we term consciousness refers to the processes of the brain and nervous system of which we are presently (naïvely?) aware. Is this all there is? We think the evidence mounting today is that it is not. However, let's look at what consciousness *does* involve to our best understanding.

11. Sigmund Freud, *A General Introduction to Psychoanalysis* (New York: Washington Square Press, 1952).
12. Robert E. Ornstein, op. cit., pp. 58–59.

Stanley Krippner has listed twenty states of consciousness[13] which we might use as a model for our searching. Briefly summarized, these twenty states are:

1. *The Dreaming State,* identified by EEG patterns and occurring periodically during the night, forming part of the sleep cycle.
2. *The Sleeping State,* identified also by EEG patterns; there is some evidence that some mental activity is present during nondream sleep, just as there is during dreaming.
3. *The Hypnagogic State,* that period known as "twilight sleep" just as we pass from wakefulness into the beginnings of the sleep-dream cycle.
4. *The Hypnopompic State,* occurring just as we begin the waking process, and containing mental and sensory activity different from any of the three previous states.
5. *The Hyperalert State,* in which we are intently vigilant. It may be induced through chemical means (such as caffeine, amphetamines, etc.) or through "duty" or obligation, as during cramming for exams, being on guard duty, or other periods of concentration.
6. *The Lethargic State,* involving sluggishness and dulled mental activity. Fatigue, sleep deprivation, malnutrition, dehydration, blood-sugar imbalance, depressant drugs, or despondent and depressive moods are often causative factors.
7. *States of Rapture,* often called ecstatic states, are characterized by overpowering emotions, usually positive in subjective evaluation. Examples are sexual stimulation or climax, frenzied dancing (as in the whirling of Sufi dervishes, voodoo dancing, and even modern-day dancing!), religious activities such as conversion, speaking in tongues (glossolalia), and certain drug-induced experiences.
8. *States of Hysteria,* involving negatively evaluated emotions of a strong and intense nature. These can be brought about by anger, rage, fear, terror, panic, jealousy, fear of being "bewitched" or "possessed," violent mob activity such as lynching parties, neurotic anxiety, and some drug-related experiences.
9. *States of Fragmentation* involve lack of integration among significant aspects or processes of the total psyche. These are parallel to (though not necessarily identical to) conditions

13. Stanley Krippner, "Altered States of Consciousness," in John White, ed., *The Highest State of Consciousness* (Garden City, New York: Doubleday & Co., Anchor Books edition, 1972), pp. 1–5.

referred to as psychosis, severe neurosis, dissociation, "multiple personality," amnesia, and fugue states. The causes are manifold and we have only touched briefly on them in chapter nine.

10. *Regressive States,* involving behavior that is clearly inappropriate to the person's physiological state and chronological age—though it is difficult to define "appropriate" behavior. This may involve physical deterioration (as in senility or "second childhood"), drug or hypnotic experiences, or neurotic needs.

11. *Meditative States* are characterized by minimal mental activity, lack of visual imagery, and recordings of continuous alpha waves on the EEG. These may or may not involve "esoteric" or Eastern rituals and practices, such as Zen, Yoga, Sufism.

12. *Trance States.* These record little or no continuity of alpha rhythms on the EEG, and involve extreme suggestibility, alertness, and concentration of attention on a single stimulus. Sources for this state have included hypnosis, chanting, prolonged observation of a whirling or revolving object, trance-induced rituals, brainwashing techniques, music, poetry, a charismatic speaker, watching a white line in the middle of the road while driving long distances, and even TV watching.

13. *Reverie,* characterized by rapid eye movements (as are found in dreaming), but occurring during a trance. It may also be part of the Daydreaming State.

14. *The Daydreaming State* is characterized by rapidly occurring thoughts that bear little relation to the external environment. Eyes may be open or closed. The causes are as many as there are people and environments.

15. *Internal Scanning* occurs when we become aware of bodily sensations in the organs, tissues, muscles, and so on. Consciousness is always present but exists on a non-reflective level unless the individual makes a concerted effort to become aware of these feelings, *or* unless the bodily feelings are intensified by pain, hunger, etc.

16. *Stupor* is characterized by reduced or suspended ability to perceive incoming stimuli. Language and motor activity may be impaired as well. The most frequent causes are opiates, alcohol, marijuana in some users, and certain types of psychotic reactions.

17. *Coma* is characterized by almost total inability to perceive incoming stimuli. Little motor activity and language is present, if at all. Illness, toxic agents, brain damage, epileptic seizures, or glandular dysfunction may cause comatose states.

18. *Stored Memory* involves past experience which isn't available immediately. The memory traces, or engrams, always exist on some level of the person's consciousness. These memories may be evoked by conscious effort, associations, electrical or chemical stimulation of the brain's cortex, free association or they may emerge spontaneously ("I haven't thought of him in ages!").

19. *"Expanded" Conscious States* involve a lowered threshold of sensory awareness and changed patterns of perception. They may occur spontaneously ("peak experiences") or by means of hypnosis, sensory bombardment, psychedelic ("mind-manifesting") drugs and plants. Krippner identifies four levels of progression in such experiences: *Sensory*, with subjective reports of alterations of space, time, and body image; *Recollective-Analytic*, with novel ideas and thoughts concerning the person's view of the world and his place in it; *Symbolic*, where the person identifies with historical or legendary people, with evolutionary processes, or with symbols; and the *Integral*, attained by very few, involving a "religious" or "spiritual" sense of confrontation with God (or the "Ground of Being," "Cosmos," "Eternal Mind"). This last level has been reported both by people involved with traditional religious beliefs and by others with little or no conventional religious background.

Synonyms for this level are found in every language: "satori," "samadhi," "oceanic unity," "cosmic consciousness," "peak experience," and many others.

20. *"Normal" everyday waking state* is characterized by logic, rationality, linear cause-and-effect thinking, awareness of emotions and ideas, goal-directedness, and the feeling that one is in control of one's mental activity, that Will is present.

Consciousness then encompasses a very extensive sweep of human experiences. It would appear, too, that Jung's idea that the "unconscious" is more an alteration of consciousness than an actual fact or situation is valid. Assagioli makes this point:

> Therefore, Jung maintains, the unconscious has no personal center. "Unconscious," as I have stressed elsewhere, should be considered an adjective, not a noun, and it indicates a temporary condition of the "psychic contents," many of which may have been conscious and may become so again.[14]

We want now to explore a state of consciousness that we feel is among the most important, among the most meaningful if we are to make real and lasting sense out of the concept of significance.

Unitive Consciousness

Alterations of consciousness have fascinated people for centuries. As we've noted before, Andrew Weil comments that nearly every culture ever studied has utilized some means of altering consciousness—through chemicals, plants, dance, trance, meditation, prayer, ritual, orgiastic experience, sensory bombardment and deprivation, or whatever.[15] This means that these altered states have had value for peoples in every part of the world for virtually all of man's history. It isn't enough to label alcohol and drug use as "escape behavior" from the routine, the ordinary, the dull, the fearsome, or the tragic experiences. It appears that a significant portion of all human populations has considered variations on ordinary consciousness as necessary in and of themselves.

Why should consciousness-alteration be such a universal? One reason that is mentioned frequently in a wide variety of literature is the motivation to explore other dimensions of selfhood. We know that a person may discover unknown or unacknowledged aspects of his

14. Roberto Assagioli, "Jung and Psychosynthesis," *Journal of Humanistic Psychology*, Vol. 14, No. 1, Winter 1974.
15. Andrew Weil, *The Natural Mind* (Boston: Houghton-Mifflin, 1973).

selfhood with the aid of alcohol, drugs, hypnosis, and meditative states. Here is Richard Alpert's account of his initial experiences with psilocybin:

> . . . I realized that although everything by which I knew myself, even my body and this life itself, was gone, still I was fully aware! Not only that, but this aware "I" was watching the entire drama, including the panic, with calm compassion. Instantly, with this recognition, I felt a new kind of calmness—one of a profundity never experienced before. I had just found that "I," that scanning device—that point—that essence—that place beyond. A place where "I" existed independent of social and physical identity.[16]

We could cite a hundred similar experiences from the literature and include a number of firsthand accounts from people around us. However, the interesting thing is that with only a few exceptions those who had such positive drug-induced experiences ultimately reached a stage wherein they found the drug experience to be only partial, only artificial, only fleeting.

The big excitement about psychedelia is behind us. Those who still insist that it's the Only Trip may be right, but it *is* only a "trip." As De Ropp, Watts, Alpert, Maharishi Mahesh Yogi, and countless others point out, the really significant and lasting search for Selfhood is a quiet, tedious, arduous, disciplined, and total search. The drug shortcut is often a detour and a deception, and frequently a cheat.

We do not disregard the insights found on drug-connected searches, and the so-called "drug culture" may have stimulated a larger and more responsible expedition into Selfhood:

> . . . These deductions from the nature of intense peak-experiences are given some support by general experience with LSD and psilocybin. Of course these preliminary reports also await confirmation.[17]

Our conviction is that no easily given answer by itself tells the whole story. We feel that these individual clues, these isolated and collective testimonies all serve to say to us: man is not nearly as simple and easily defined as he has been assumed to be; there is much more to the natural understanding of human behavior than we've known before; there are clues to a larger sense of Selfhood in all of these; there is a universality of human consciousness; and such clues only serve to firm up our basic belief that we are all integrally and interdependently linked up with each other, with other living forms, with the entire planet, and with the cosmos itself!

16. Baba Ram Dass (Richard Alpert), *BE HERE NOW* (New York: Crown Publishing, 1971).
17. Abraham H. Maslow, *Religions, Values, and Peak-Experiences* (New York: Viking Press, Compass Book, 1970).

The Mountaintop

One of the biggest problems we've had to do business with is the artificial and destructive split between "hard" science and the "softer" experiences, such as philosophy, religion, art, mythology, and literature. If behaviorism, with its strict emphasis on positivistic and reductionistic scientific methods, hadn't been turned from a means into an end, we might not have this problem today. And if psychoanalytic thinkers hadn't ruled out the long-standing and much needed areas of value and religion, the problem wouldn't have been compounded. These two isolated and stubborn orientations have virtually forced into existence the "third force" of humanistic psychology: to bring a wholism and unity to all human experiences. This isn't grandiose or arrogant. It is merely a restatement of the situation as it has existed for the past twenty years.

But because existential and humanistic scientists have kept their minds open and their methods flexible, with both behaviorism properly used as a tool and psychoanalysis properly used as a specialized study, we are now able to understand better what certain human beings have experienced for thousands of years: we've expanded our consciousnesses, our definitions, and our vocabulary.

If Abraham Maslow's samples of "self-actualizers" had been made up only of alcoholics, "acid-heads," and schizophrenics, the experience of "peaking" might have been kept in the closet with superstition and astrology and tarot cards. It was precisely the fact that the self-actualizers were men and women of extremely healthy physical, emotional, and mental systems that we are forced to see "peak experiences" as consequences of positive mental health, rather than of psychosis or brain trauma.

Suddenly, the writings of actualizers of every race, creed, sex, color, and ethnic group are being opened up for scientific study. The teachings of Buddha, Jesus, the Yogis, the Sufis, the mystics of the Jewish and Christian traditions are now found to be dealing with precisely the same kinds of experiences. Maslow, allowing for ethnocentric language and emphasis, has cut through them all and found at the heart of each of them what he calls the "core religious" experience.[18]

The laboratory studies of split-brain specialists, of biofeedback experts, of yogic trances have all yielded valid and reliable results. We know that self-actualizing people aren't "superhuman" people at all: they are merely ordinary people who have taken the time and

18. Ibid.

effort to actualize their fullest human potentials, to develop the most latent aspects of their being. William Blake said it:

> "If the doors of perception were cleansed, every thing would appear to man as it is, infinite."

The facts have been taught, preached, broadcast, hinted at, put into parables, riddles, koans, myths, legends, epic dramas[19] and revealed in dreams, trances, under hypnosis, and in drug trips. We are not surprised that the message has been so long and so easily ignored or missed; it doesn't fit in with our scientific pictures of ourselves, with the negative emphases of most of man's traditional religious dogmas or philosophical theories.

> Dissenting from the followers of those prophets who claimed direct revelation from God and from the nineteenth-century scientists who denied not only direct revelation, but God himself, the author [Maslow] declares that these revelations were, in his words, "peak-experiences" which are characteristic not only of specially ordained emissaries of God, but of mankind in general.[20]

19. See Nikos Kazantzakis, *Odysseus: A Modern Sequel* (New York: Simon & Schuster, 1958).
20. Maslow, op. cit.

This section sounds drastically philosophical, even religious, and it is! Religion in its root meaning (*religare:* to tie or bind together) is a perfectly good and useful concept. Organized religion, in the form of the institutions and dogmas most of us know, is too often a perversion or distortion of this deeper meaning. Yet, none of this section is pie in the sky or irrelevant: the peak experience, the consciousness of higher unity, "cosmic consciousness," is so important that it forms the bedrock foundation for our view that personal and social significance is built into human nature itself!

Each person finds this unitive consciousness for himself. It isn't a collective search, even though vast numbers of people are searching. It involves sincere and dedicated struggling with the other-directedness of our societies, with the transient and destructive values most of us have been taught. It often involves the experience of "going into the wilderness"[21] and coming to terms with your own weaknesses and strengths, goals and distractions.

Down in the Valley

Every actualizer who has climbed the mountaintops or gone into the inner desert wilderness has come to a further insight: that it is not necessary (indeed it is often irresponsible) to remain on the mountaintop or to live as a meditating hermit. Richard Alpert searched across India to find a guru to teach him to be enlightened, and was told to go home. Jesus, the Buddha, Albert Schweitzer, St. Francis, Gurdjieff, and the thousands of others like them all found that it was more important for them to come down from their "highs" and live in the valleys of everyday life.

> . . . The sacred is *in* the ordinary, that is, it is to be found in one's daily life, in one's neighbors, friends, and family, in one's back yard, and that travel may be a *flight* from confronting the sacred . . .[22]

The individuation process described by Jung is similar to the religious quest of these "high beings" (indeed, Jung speaks of people in analysis as being primarily in a "spiritual crisis"). Yet, individuation—the discovery of one's own personal uniqueness and value—is not the final goal of Jungian analysis. The final goal is to develop the transcendent function, to see, know, and appreciate our kinship with all others around us. This means to break down the false, cruel, and

21. Referring to Jesus' forty days in the desert.
22. Maslow, op. cit.

destructive barriers and boundaries we've created, and "join the human race"—and even beyond that to see ourselves as part of *all* that exists. This is religion in its root-meaning. This, for us, is the deepest and highest meaning of significance.

Most of us have been taught to define ourselves, our consciousness, our values, and our beliefs by basing them on some preexisting external source: something supernatural. Until recently—with the exception of actualizers down through the ages, and very few of them—most of us have denied our own inner experiences, our internal worlds. The Eastern writers have couched their insights in language often too esoteric for us, but Ornstein, Kamiya, and many others have brought such insights and such practices into the laboratory and we now see them to be extraordinary, but not extrahuman or superhuman! We are just beginning to appreciate what human beings are capable of.

We can individuate using any of the means described in chapters ten, eleven, and this one, and see in what ways we are unique from our parents, siblings, peers, and the society as a whole. And then, we can continue the growth of Self and recognize how individuated people make up the whole of life, the whole of cosmic reality. This cannot help but be important to us in trying to deal with the war, the racism, the deceit, the hostility, the violence we find all around us. For as we come to know and appreciate our Selves, we cannot help but know better and appreciate more the Selfhood of each and every other person. It's been said many times, but bears repetition here:

> I am life affirming itself in the midst of other lives affirming themselves.[23]

Summary

The recognition that love is therapeutic and a binding force in our lives is a valid and ultimate concern for most of us. But we find that further growth and development, into our own inner consciousness, is necessary. The scientific reductionism that has produced so much in the laboratory has also divided us from our integrated functioning and from each other, certainly from the nature of which we are so fundamentally a part (not *apart!*).

Scientific research into split-brain functioning, biofeedback, and other humanistic studies is beginning to "validate" (make scientifically respectable) many of the notions we have previously called parascientific or paranormal. While vast portions of human experience are still

23. *Albert Schweitzer: An Anthology*, edited by Charles R. Joy (Boston: The Beacon Press, 1956).

unknown to us, we are beginning to appreciate how complex and varied our consciousness actually is. Hypnosis, drug "trips," and other consciousness-expanding experiences are beginning to provide us with insights into varied and "higher" states of consciousness.

Maslow finds the "peak-experiences" of self-actualizers to be similar to, if not identical with, the Buddha-consciousness, Christ-consciousness, enlightenment, moksha, satori, and cosmic-consciousness described through the centuries. William James among the modern psychologists tried to help us to see the importance of incorporating these into our psychologies, but behaviorism and much of the Freudian tradition have taken us onto more conservative ground.

The insights of Jung, Adler, Assagioli, Naranjo, Ornstein, Tart, Krippner, and hundreds of others have given the humanistic orientation a stronger position. Self-actualization, finally, is seen fully as both development and growth toward individuated Selfhood and a recognition of the kinship we share with all others and that each of us occupies a vital and valid place in the cosmic order.

Suggested Readings:

Assagioli, Roberto. *The Act of Will.* New York: Viking, 1973.

————. "Jung and Psychosynthesis," *J. Humanistic Psychology* (Winter 1974) XIV, 1.

————. *Psychosynthesis.* New York: Viking, 1971.

Baba Ram Dass. *Be Here Now.* New York: Crown Publishing, 1971.

Bruner, Jerome. *On Knowing: Essays for the Left Hand.* Cambridge, Massachusetts: Belknap Press of Harvard University, 1962.

Bucke, Richard M. *Cosmic Consciousness.* New York: E. P. Dutton, Co., 1901, 1951.

Cohen, Allen Y. "The Journey Beyond Trips," *J. of Psychedelic Drugs* (Spring 1971), III, 2.

Cohen, J. *Psychological Time in Health and Disease.* Springfield, Illinois: Charles C. Thomas, 1967.

Cohen, Sidney. *The Beyond Within.* New York: Atheneum, 1965.

Deikman, A. J. "Experimental Meditation," *J. Nervous and Mental Diseases* (1963), Vol. 163.

De Ropp, Robert S. *The Master Game.* New York: Delacorte, 1968.

Eliade, M. *Cosmos and History.* New York: Harper Torchbooks, 1959.

Gooch, Stan. *Total Man.* New York: Ballantine Books, 1974.

Hall, Edward T. *The Hidden Dimension.* Garden City, New York: Doubleday, 1966.

Harold, P., and W. Babcock. *Cosmic Humanism and World Unity.* New York: Dodd, Mead, 1971.

Huxley, Aldous. *The Doors of Perception.* New York: Harper & Row, 1970.

Hyde, Margaret. O. *Mind Drugs.* New York: Pocket Books, 1969.

Jacobi, J. *The Psychology of Carl Gustav Jung.* New Haven, Connecticut: Yale University Press, 1962.

Jung, Carl G. *The Psychology of the Unconscious.* New York: Moffatt Yard, 1916.

_____. *The Structure and Dynamics of the Psyche.* New York: Pantheon, Bollingen Series, Vol. VIII.

_____. *Symbols of Transformation.* New York: Pantheon, Bollingen Series, Vol. V.

Kamiya, J. "Conscious Control of Brain Waves," *Psychology Today* (1968) 1, 56–60.

_____. "A Fourth Dimension of Consciousness," *J. of Experimental Medicine and Surgery* (1969) XXVII, 13–18.

Karlins, Marvin, and Lewis M. Andrews. *Biofeedback.* New York: Warner, 1973.

Kazantzakis, Nikos. *The Last Temptation of Christ.* New York: Bantam, 1968.

_____. *The Greek Passion.* New York: Ballantine Books, 1965.

_____. *The Odyssey: A Modern Sequel.* New York: Simon & Schuster, 1958.

_____. *Report to Greco.* New York: Simon & Schuster, 1965.

Kiefer, D. "Meditation and Biofeedback," in John White, ed., *The Highest State of Consciousness.* New York: Doubleday Anchor Books, 1972.

Kunkel, Fritz. *Creation Continues.* Waco, Texas: World Publishing, 1973.

Laski, M. *Ecstasy.* Bloomington, Indiana: Indiana University Press, 1962.

Luce, Gay G., and Erik Peper. "Mind over Body; Mind over Mind," *New York Times Magazine,* September 12, 1971.

Maharishi Mahesh Yogi. *Transcendental Meditation: Serenity without Drugs.* New York: Signet Books, New American Library, 1968.

Maslow, Abraham H. *Eupsychian Management.* Homewood, Illinois: Irwin-Dorsey, 1965.

_____. *The Farther Reaches of Human Nature.* New York: Viking, 1971.

_____. "Lessons from the Peak-Experiences," *J. Humanistic Psychology* (1962) II, 9–18.

_____. *Religions, Values, and Peak-Experiences.* Viking, 1970.

_____. *Toward a Psychology of Being.* Princeton, New Jersey: D. Van Nostrand Co., 1968, revised edition.

Maven, Alexander. "The Mystic Union," *J. Transpersonal Psychology* (Spring 1969) I, 1.

May, Rollo. *Love and Will.* New York: Dell Publishers, 1969.

Metzner, Ralph. *Maps of Consciousness.* New York: Collier Books, 1971.

Neumann, Erich. *The Origins and History of Consciousness,* Vol. II. New York: Harper Torchbooks, 1962.

Ornstein, Robert. *The Psychology of Consciousness.* San Francisco: W. H. Freeman, 1972.

Pauwels, L., and J. Bergier. *The Morning of the Magicians.* New York: Stein and Day, 1964.

Pearce, James. C. *The Crack in the Cosmic Egg.* New York: Pocket Books, 1973.

Peterson, Severin. *A Catalog of the Ways People Grow.* New York: Ballantine Books, 1971.

Phillips, Dorothy B., et al., eds. *The Choice Is Always Ours.* New York: Harper & Row, 1960.

Rudhyar, D. *The Planetization of Consciousness.* New York: Harper & Row, 1971.

Samples, B., and B. Wohlford. *Opening: A Primer for Self-Actualization.* Menlo Park, California: Addison-Wesley, 1973.

Tart, Charles T., ed. *Altered States of Consciousness.* New York: Viking, 1972.

————. "Transpersonal Potentialities and Deep Hypnosis," *J. of Transpersonal Psychology* (1970) II, 1.

Vasiliev, L. L. *Mysterious Phenomena of the Human Psyche.* New Hyde Park, New York: University Books, 1965.

Walker, Kenneth. "Mind Alive," *Image,* Hoffman-La Roche, 1964.

Watson, Lyall. *Super-Nature.* New York: Doubleday, 1973.

Weaver, W. *Science and Imagination.* New York: Basic Books, 1967.

White, John, ed. *The Highest State of Consciousness.* New York: Doubleday, 1972.

Wilhelm, R. "Death and Renewal," *Spring,* Analytic Psychology Club of New York, 1962.

Wooldridge, Dean E. *Mechanical Man.* New York: McGraw-Hill, 1968. (For the extreme in positivistic, behavioristic reductionism!)

Zaehner, R. C. *Mysticism: Sacred and Profane.* New York: Oxford University Press, 1961.

Zimbardo, P.; G. Marshall; and C. Maslach. "Liberating Behavior from Time-Bound Control," *J. Applied Social Psychology* (1971) I, 4, 305–323.

A Concluding Unscientific Postscript

With appreciation and apologies to Sören Kierkegaard

We named this book *The Struggle for Significance*, and struggle we all have: we to write it; you to wade through it. The very least you might expect after so many pages is a nice, cozy, *significant* answer to the questions raised. But if the answers were so easily available, so many busy and important people wouldn't have searched during the last 5,000 years for the answers.

As we intimated in chapter eleven, love is a possible answer to some of the questions. It is probably our best hope for anything like meaningful, significant living. So, part of the struggle and the search is done. But only part.

Out of the Orient comes a further wisdom, which might be paraphrased as follows to suit our limited, mechanical Occidental minds:

> The beginning of wisdom is this: the only Absolute is that there are no Absolutes; the only generalization is that one can't generalize.

We have been guilty of generalizing. It's easy; it's satisfying to be able to say: "There! *All* men need X." Yes, but, if X works *for* you, it may be just as likely to work *against* me. So, in all the preceding chapters, please remember that our generalized statements apply only to some people, though the wording might sound as though it applied to every one of us.

Each of us seems to need significance, a feeling of personal worth. We have tried to describe some of the traps, blocks, pitfalls, and hazards that accompany the search for this significance. We hope, though, that it hasn't been only a description of difficulties and struggles. We have found that, hard as it is, there are a multitude of benefits, enjoyment, wonderful people, and fun involved, as well.

We pass along one further bit of wisdom, despite the fact that just telling you won't do much, because you'll have to learn it for yourself: *Just as self-actualization is not to be grasped for, neither is personal significance.* We would say about personal significance what Viktor Frankl has said of self-actualization:

> Self-actualization, if made an end in itself, contradicts the self-transcending quality of human existence. . . . Self-actualization is, and must remain, an effect, namely the effect of meaning fulfillment. Only to the extent to which man fulfills a meaning out there in the world, does he fulfill himself. Conversely, if he sets out to actualize himself rather than fulfill a meaning, self-actualization would immediately lose its justification.[1]

Confusing? Of course! Like most truths, when we try to apply them to specific situations in our individual lives, we run the risk of failure. But let that bit of wisdom sink in: you cannot intentionally set out to create or capture your own personal significance—not as a goal in itself. As a result of immersing yourself in satisfying, creative work and love relations, spaced with peak-experiences of meditation, excursions into personal enjoyment, and experimental ventures into risky innovation, you *can*, as a by-product, discover your own significance.

In conclusion, you have just one life. Live it! Try to cram as much living into your existence as possible. You may not reach the "ultimate" height in every case, but we guarantee that you'll enjoy yourself a lot more than if you hadn't tried. We close with the words of a man who inspired us to write this book, a man who died during the writing of the first edition of this book, Abraham Maslow:

> It is true that human beings strive perpetually toward ultimate humanness, which itself may be anyway a different kind of Becoming and growing. It's as if we were doomed forever to try to arrive at a state to which we could never attain. Fortunately we now know this not to be true, or at least it is not the only truth. There is another truth which integrates with it. We are again and again rewarded for good Becoming by transient states of absolute Being, by peak-experiences. . . . This is like rejecting the notion that a Heaven lies someplace beyond the end of the path of life. Heaven, so to speak, lies waiting for us *through* life [italics ours], ready to step into for a time and to enjoy before we have to come back to our ordinary life of striving. And once we have been in it, we can remember it forever, and feed ourselves on this memory and be sustained in time of stress.[2]

1. Viktor E. Frankl, "Self-Transcendence as a Human Phenomenon," in Anthony J. Sutich and Miles A. Vich, editors, *Readings in Humanistic Psychology* (New York: The Free Press, 1969), p. 116.
2. Abraham H. Maslow, *Toward a Psychology of Being* (Princeton: D. Van Nostrand Co., Inc., 1968), pp. 145–146.

PEACE AND LOVE

John H. Brennecke
Robert G. Amick
Mt. San Antonio College
Walnut, California

Glossary

We have tried in this book to avoid clichés and the psychological jargon that is so often used to obscure a point or confuse the reader. The following terms, some fairly common, are part of the necessary vocabulary for this subject. Words having (TA) after them are from the working language of transactional analysis; (J) refers to the work of Carl G. Jung; (F) refers to Sigmund Freud.

acting-out. This is a term meaning that the observed behavior or speech is primarily a way of expressing (or covering) an internalized conflict situation. An example would be kissing everyone you meet because of inner fears of being unlovable.

adjustment. The traditional term for the study of ways and processes of coping, "making it," adapting to the pressures within us and around us. Adjustment psychology studies these problems.

Adult ego-state (TA). Refers to the data-processing, reality-oriented, rational part of the ego.

alienation. The feeling of being foreign or stranger to an aspect of one's self (self-alienation) or to others.

anima (J). The feminine component of personality, present in both sexes, but most manifest in women.

animism. The belief that every aspect of reality has a spirit or soul (Latin, *anima* = spirit, soul).

animus (J). The masculine component of personality, present in both sexes, but found most strongly developed in men.

anthropology. The scientific study of humankind, including fossil remains, social behaviors, and cultural traits.

Apollonian. Referring to cultural and personal patterns involving orderliness, sobriety, conservatism, rationality. Contrasted with *Dionysian.*

archaeology. The scientific study of artifacts of humankind, dealing with geological excavations, restoration, and measurement of tools, structures, and other "made" items of a culture.

archetype (J). A universal pattern or concept, modified by cultures, but independent of them. E.g., the archetype of the Great Mother, the Hero, Death, Birth, etc., is found in the history and mythology of most societies.

Jung felt they were genetically coded in and formed part of the *collective unconscious.*

autism. The disorder characterized by withdrawal, lack of communicativeness, an inner-oriented existence. Sometimes (not always) called childhood schizophrenia.

behaviorism. The scientific study of observable, measurable, objectively shared behaviors. Most highly developed in this country by John B. Watson, B. F. Skinner, and others. A valuable "tool" or approach to the study of human experience.

biofeedback. Any means whereby one receives information from his own body concerning its own processes, from the simple observation of perspiration in the palms to measured changes in brain-wave patterns on an *EEG.*

character disorder. A vague term describing behavior patterns whose origin cannot be clearly traced, with little or no anxiety, often involving the person in some difficulty with social, legal, or moral sanctions. Also called *personality disorders.* Examples: psychopathic personality, sexual deviation, passive-aggressive personality.

chauvinism. (From N. Chauvin, a Napoleonic soldier known for his loud and aggressive patriotism.) The term now refers to any exaggerated *ethnocentrism* or pattern of believing one's group or gender or race or religion is superior.

chemotherapy. The treatment of disease or illness by means of any chemical preparations. Specifically, the treatment of emotional or mental disorders through drugs or other medications, like tranquilizers, anti-depressants, mood elevators, or narcotics.

Child ego-state (TA). The patterns of emotionality, impulsivity, intuition, and dependency recorded into our *life scripts* during the first few years of life, remaining with us throughout life.

clinical psychology. That branch of psychology concerned with using psychological insights for the alleviation of emotional and mental distress, through hospitalization, psychoanalysis, and other psychotherapies.

cognition. The mental processes of the brain, including thinking, reasoning, fantasy, imagination, dreaming, and problem-solving. Others limit the word to intellectual functions.

collective unconscious (J). The core of human experiences, universal in nature, available to, and a part of, the individual and social and cultural experience of each of us. Dreams that transcend our personal, mundane experiences are said to come from this vast hidden process of consciousness.

conscious. The processes of our psyche of which we are aware, or, used as an adjective, being aware.

consciousness alteration. Modifying or changing the structure and functioning, even the "feel," of conscious awareness, as in stupor, sleep, dreaming, coma, ecstasy, "peak experiencing." (Sometimes referred to as "consciousness expansion.")

consciousness-raising. A term describing the various processes of increasing the awareness of a group's situation, both among members of the group and among the larger population as well. Examples: the beginning stages of the Black Power Movement involved raising the consciousness of blacks *and* whites to the facts of racism and oppression.

conversion (F). A term describing the transferring or expression of inner psychic conflicts into physical (somatic) symptoms, such as paralysis, blindness, aphasia. The term used to be called *hysteria*. It is generally included in traditional listings of neurotic patterns, and is also called conversion neurosis.

culture. The life-style of a given group of people (a society), including language, foods, dress, housing, religion, government, norms of behavior, and virtually all of the handed-down socialization patterns of the group. The layman usually means "artistic or aesthetic" when he speaks of someone having culture, but in fact, such matters as art, music, and going (or not going) to the opera are only specific traits of culture.

delusion. A distorted thought, idea, or belief, found in paranoid disturbances. Example: believing you are the target of an international conspiracy of authority figures.

DNA. Deoxyribonucleic acid. A protein, the molecules of which contain the genes responsible for transmission of inherited characteristics.

Dionysian. Behavior that is individualistic, unrestrained, impulsive, even reckless, often aided by the use of alcohol, drugs, or dance—though not always. It contrasts with *Apollonian.*

dualism. The belief or orientation that reality consists of divisions into two mutually opposed and exclusive principles, such as good and evil, mind and body, Democrat and Republican.

ecology. (Greek, *oikos* = household; *logos* = study.) The study of the various interwoven and interdependent relationships existing among the members of "the household of life." Examples: how humans and plants affect each other, as in agriculture, drought, pollution, housing developments.

ego. (Latin, *ego* = "I.") 1) (F) The process of personality involved with reality-testing and processing, the learned aspects of selfhood, having a mediating function between *id* and *superego* and external reality; 2) (J) the experiencing center of the psyche, the "I" that is aware of reality; 3) the lay use is simply that ego is a sense of self-awareness, which must be kept in balance; to have an "inflated ego" means to be conceited.

ego-state (TA). A process of the self, the three ego-states being the *Child*, the *Adult*, and the *Parent*. These ego-states are incorporated ("recorded" as "tapes" or "written down") and as they are replayed or remembered, they form the basis for the early *life scripts* by which we live our lives.

elitism. The belief that some individuals are superior to, or better than, others because of the social, racial, gender, economic, or religious groupings to which each belongs. The idea that there is a hierarchy of worth among people. Examples: believing that white-collar people are better than blue- or no-collar workers.

endemic. Contrasted with epidemic (an emergency or crisis situation), endemic means behaviors or traits that are consistent and ongoing. Examples: winter colds are endemic among many populations, though they may also reach epidemic proportions.

erogenous (F). Referring to sexual or *libidinous* energy. An erogenous zone is a part of the body especially sensitive to stimulation, which usually produces sexual arousal or receptivity. Examples: the genital organs, earlobes, breasts.

ethic. A word referring to a life-style of a particular group, similar in meaning, but stricter than the *culture.* It usually refers to the ethical or moral principles governing the culture of a group. Example: the Puritan ethic heavily influences most Western moral, economic, and political behavior.

ethnic. Referring to unique cultural traits (language, religion, dress, food, etc.) of a society, though often used to include skin color differences. Example: the ethnic dances of the Balkans; the ethnic attitudes of the Chinese.

ethnocentrism. Literally, the belief that one's own ethnic group is at the center of things, and that other groups revolve about it, or find their reference to that group. *Chauvinism, Jingoism, superpatriotism* are other terms having similar meaning.

etiology. The study or search for causes, origins, determining factors. Example: Freud's theory of the etiology of *neurosis* found it in reactions to repressed sexual or aggressive impulses.

existentialism. A philosophical position having many forms, but essentially finding its central focus in the fact of human existence, without reference to preceding or subsequent events. Other emphases are on choice, commitment, responsibility, and immediacy of experience. Sartre, Jaspers, Kierkegaard, Camus, and Rollo May are excellent sources of existentialist theory.

experimental psychology. The branch of psychological study emphasizing research, experimentation, and theory building. Laboratory studies, field studies, library research, and other methods are employed, basically following the scientific method.

feminism. A term covering a range of ideas and philosophies, but most often used to mean the theory of the economic, social, and political equality of the sexes, and actions to obtain or further that equality.

Freudian. Refers to Sigmund Freud, his ideas, and his disciples. It is also used to refer to what Freud called psychoanalytic theory.

Games (TA). Complex, complementary transactions between two or more persons having ulterior motives and a "payoff" or outcome, usually enabling the Gameplayer to avoid intimate and authentic encounter with others. Often the "payoff" involves hurting or rejecting another.

global consciousness. That form of consciousness wherein the experiencer is aware of the larger realities, the wholeness and integration of all separate forces. It is similar to Maslow's *peak experiences,* Bucke's cosmic consciousness, Freud's oceanic experiences, the illumination (*satori, moksha,* etc.) of various Eastern religions and philosophies, and unitive consciousness.

guru. A Sanskrit word referring to a "guide," though it is often used to mean *teacher.* It is always used in reference to the quest for spiritual enlightenment.

hallucination. A distortion of one or more sense perceptions, most frequently auditory and visual, experienced among many schizophrenics, but also among non*psychotics,* during times such as periods of fever, sleep deprivation, abstinence from food, sensory deprivation, alcoholic stupor, drug-related experiences, and other *consciousness alterations.* Basically, hallucinations are perceptions of events of a purely subjective nature, not observed or shared by others, though mass or group hallucinations are not unheard of.

holism. (See *wholism.*)

homeostasis. The optimum functioning of any physiological system or subsystem, such as bodily temperature at 98.6 degrees Fahrenheit. It is used to refer to balance, equilibrium within or among systems.

hypothalamus. That part of the midbrain involving a number of functions, but chiefly the hungers, drives, and emotional responses.

id (F). The primitive, inborn processes of personality which are formed in response to basic survival or physiological drive-states. The *id* operates on the pleasure principle, of deriving pleasure or satisfaction from basic tension reductions.

illusion. A disturbed or distorted perception due primarily to qualities within the perceived object itself, not entirely to subjective traits or needs in the perceiving person. Example: the illusion of water on the roadbed ahead is caused by heat, geography, distance, and perspective.

individualism. The belief that one is more important than others, that one is alone in the struggles of life, that collective endeavors or programs defeat one's solitary development.

individuation (J). The process of discovering, accepting, and developing one's own unique characteristics, those traits which set one off from his group, but do not put him in opposition to or at odds with any members of the group or the group's own goals. Individuation is the practical goal of Jungian analysis.

inferiority complex. Alfred Adler's view that inferiority feelings and experiences create an entire self-concept (a "complex") centered in inferiority, affecting virtually every thought, dream, activity, and expectation of the person.

insanity. A legal term, having an imprecise meaning, but being the society's legal definition of "mental incompetence" or "mental illness." Basically, it involves determining whether the subject is aware of the difference between right and wrong and is aware of his behavior in a given situation.

instinct. Species-specific behavior, inborn, unlearned, spontaneous, full-blown, and universal among that species. Example: the web-building of certain species of spiders; the homing tendencies of certain species of birds; often used to describe human behaviors such as drives and reflexes, and other behaviors, the instinctive nature of which is unproven—such as mothering, social grouping, warfare, etc.

instinctive aggression. A long-held and widely believed theory that aggressive, hostile, or pugnacious behaviors are instinctive and therefore unresponsive to learning processes. This idea is especially promoted by Robert Ardrey, Konrad Lorenz, and Desmond Morris. It is opposed by many, especially Ashley Montagu, Prince Pëtr Kropotkin, René Dubos, and the authors.

Our position is that while there are perhaps tendencies within human nature for these behaviors, humans also seem to have tendencies for mutual aid, cooperation, love, compassion, creativity, and peacemaking.

libido (F). The energy activating, and activated by, the *id* in human personality. It is generated by the *instinct* for life (Eros) and may be similar to the Hindu *pran,* the Chinese *K'i,* or *Ch'i,* and other bodily energy concepts.

"life script" (TA). The plan of living "composed" or "written" by a person in relation to the "tapes" he or she records in acquiring and developing the *ego-states.* It is considered by TA to be irrevocable, though new scripts can be written and added to the repertory of life possibilities.

lunacy. An older term for *insanity,* psychotic, or other unexplainable behavior. The word comes from *luna,* the Latin term for "moon"; it was commonly believed in medieval times that the full moon caused such behaviors ("moon madness").

marginality. Finding oneself on the edge or margin of social acceptability and membership. One may choose marginal existence ("loner," hermit, isolate, monastic, etc.), or one may be involuntarily made marginal ("reject," outcast, exile, etc.).

mask. In our conception, the presentation of oneself made to others, either from choice or involuntarily. It is similar to the Jungian *persona,* and corresponds to the social roles we play out. Its use refers to the limitation of oneself to that portrayal at the expense of disclosure of the rest of one's selfhood. *Stereotyping* is one way of forcing a person to wear a specific mask exclusive of other roles or aspects of selfhood that person may have.

masochism. The deriving of pleasure (or symbolic pleasure) from pain or punishment. Usually the cause is some deeply rooted sense of guilt.

moksha. A Sanskrit word used to describe the "liberation" achieved by a yogi or other searcher from the wheel of attachment and obligation (karma). It involves alterations of consciousness.

neural. Referring to the neurons or nervous system.

neurology. The study of the structure and function of the nervous system.

neuron. The nerve cell, the basic unit of the nervous system.

neurosis (plural, *neuroses*). Disorders of feeling, motivation, perception, thinking, and relationship. It has little or nothing to do directly with "nerves" or the nervous system. Anxiety is a basic characteristic of most neurotic behaviors. Neurotics seldom require hospitalization, though they usually profit from *psychotherapeutic* encounters. Example: an obsessive-compulsive neurosis involves ideas that take hold and force certain ritualized and/or fanatically repeated activities, such as hand washing or counting cracks in the sidewalk.

Not-OK (TA). The perception that oneself or another person is not functioning well, is not "good," is not "well," is not a fully functioning whole person. It may describe simple conflicts and *neuroses* or the extremes of *psychosis.*

OK (TA). The position that oneself or another is functioning well, is "in balance," is "healthy," is "good," is whole. In the TA conception, OK-ness is similar to, if not synonymous with, mental and emotional health, full functioning, individuation, significance, or self-actualization.

organism. Any whole system, be it a simple, separate subsystem of unicellular construction, such as a paramecium or amoeba, or a whole society. Organisms have identities and autonomies of their own.

Parent ego-state (TA). The *ego-state* involving judgments of right and wrong, evaluation, replaying of parental instructions, nurturing, examples, as contrasted with the ego-states of Child and Adult.

parochial. Of or pertaining to a single or narrow viewpoint; provincial; of or pertaining to a parish or parishes.

Persona (J). The social role or mask presented to others, often as an attempt to hide the rest of the psyche. It is real, but it is not the whole Self.

personal unconscious (J). The aspects of unconscious functioning that come from the individual's own personal experiences, needs, wishes or fears. These are considered to be as important as the correlative experiences coming from the *collective unconscious.*

philosophy. The study of knowledge and ideas, either as a separate and distinct discipline or the individual's own way of looking at, and conceptualizing, reality.

polarize. To draw apart into two opposing and exclusive "camps" or positions (coming from the two poles—north and south—on the earth's surface). If we dichotomize into good and evil, saved and unsaved, black and white, Democrats and Republicans, we are polarizing. Polarization has a long history.

prestige. The social evaluation or ranking of an individual's status or social position. Example: the status of teacher has more social prestige than the status of auto mechanic, though both may earn similar money.

primal. Refers to extremely early and primitive experiences, considered to be very important in psychic development. Here it has the meaning of "fundamental" or basic in psychic development.

psi. A term developed by J. B. Rhine to describe paranormal or parapsychological experiences, such as telepathy, clairvoyance, etc.

psyche. The totality of human personality. A synonym for personality, or the sense of being.

psychedelic. Refers to experiences (usually drug-induced) that alter or expand awareness, or the expanded awareness itself.

psychiatry. The medical specialty dealing with emotional or mental disorders. It basically utilizes the medical model of emotional disturbance, and may involve the use of medications, diet, hospitalization, shock treatments, or psychotherapy. A psychiatrist is a medical doctor with advanced training in psychological medicine.

psychic. A vague term. Among parapsychologists, it refers to experiences that fall outside the natural realm, such as ESP and other occult or spiritualistic experiences. We use it to refer simply (but inclusively) to all experiences of the psyche, or the personality in general.

psychoanalysis (F). The theory and technique developed by Sigmund Freud for the analysis and treatment of emotional conflicts, and subsequently for explaining the development of human personality. *Psychoanalytic* is the adjective referring either to this theory of personality or this technique of *psychotherapeutic* treatment. A *psychoanalyst* is usually an M.D. with six to eight years of advanced training in Freudian techniques, though in this country, Ph.D's in psychology may also obtain training and certification as psychoanalysts.

psychology. The study of human behavior and the functioning of the psyche, or personality.

psychosis (plural, *psychoses*). Severe disturbances of functioning, involving thinking, feeling, perception, and ideation. The major psychoses are schizophrenia, paranoia, and the manic-depressive psychoses. They involve separations from reality functioning and usually require hospitalization.

psychosomatic. Referring to the interplay between psysiological and neurological functioning, the so-called mind-over-matter problem, wherein an emotional conflict may find expression in a psysiological disorder, such as ulcers, sleeplessness, or a skin disorder. Also known as psychophysiological disorders.

psychotherapy. Any of the techniques or approaches to alleviate the inner and interpersonal distress of individuals, usually using talking over situations and feelings, but also getting into role-playing, acting out feelings, and other expressions of the inner conflicts. Psychotherapists are either psychiatrists, psychoanalysts, social workers, psychologists, or pastoral or educational counselors.

psychotic. Adjective, referring to the psychoses.

racism. The belief that inborn physical differences such as skin color, hair form, blood types, etc., create real differences among human beings and that these differences can be arrayed along a hierarchical ranking.

regression. The tendency to lapse into earlier modes of adaptation or reaction to stressful or threatening situations, such as throwing a tantrum under duress.

repression. The process of blocking out or hiding threatening or unpleasant experiences. Example: forgetting the name of someone you don't like or are afraid of.

RNA. Ribonucleic acid. A protein, molecules of which are apparently involved in a number of psychological processes of the nervous system, especially learning and memory.

samadhi. The Sanskrit term for cosmic or *global consciousness,* where a wholistic or "holy" view of reality is obtained, where subject and object distinctions are dissolved.

satori. The Japanese term describing the state of enlightenment or cosmic (*global*) *consciousness* arrived at through Zen Buddhist meditations and other techniques.

"Script." (See *life scripts.*)

self. A widely used term. It has a variety of meanings, such as the ego, identity, the "I," the awareness of being. In Jungian terms, it is similar to the ego, the experiencing center of being, but not the same as the *Self.*

Self (J). The center and integrating function of the psyche, involving perception and awareness of the totality of human experience. Jung himself identified the Self with "the God (or Christ) Within."

sensitivity group. A group of people trying to become aware of themselves as individual, experiencing persons.

sensory. Adjective referring to the senses such as seeing, hearing, feeling, tasting, and smelling, plus other bodily senses.

sexism. The belief that gender differences are aligned in hierarchical order, usually males' being supreme or superior to females, and the behavior that results from such beliefs.

social institutions. The collected activities, beliefs, and influences of a particular function of the society, such as family, economics, law, religion, and education, the media, and tradition.

socialization. The term used to describe the complex process by which a person (usually a child) learns and absorbs the norms and requirements of the culture in which he lives.

society. The people sharing a common or similar culture. Usually, such groupings are geographical or political, though they might be religious, economic, or familial as well.

sociology. The study of human social units and interactions.

stroke (TA). The acknowledgment of the existence of a person, either through a praising act or an act of punishment or rejection. Strokes are considered necessary for continued functioning and growth, whatever form they take.

superego (F). The conscience or valuing and judgmental processes of personality, constantly harassing and guiding the *id* and requiring the intervention of the *ego*.

symbiosis. The process of mutual, interdependent interaction and relationship. Example: mistletoe and the oak tree; the shark and the remora fish.

syndrome. A collection or pattern of symptoms, such as the cold syndrome, which involves sniffles, coughing, sore throat, congestion, and aches and pains; the paranoid syndrome, involving *delusions* of persecution or grandeur, mistrust, and a great gap between reality and perception.

TA. (See *transactional analysis.*)

Taoism. The religion-philosophy taught by Lao-tse.

tapes (TA). The unconscious and conscious remembrances of early experiences and teachings, comprising parts of *Child, Adult,* and *Parent ego-states.*

theology. The study of God, or the study of the religious forces or beliefs of humankind, regardless of the point of reference.

therapy. (See *psychotherapy.*)

transactional analysis (TA). The study of the ways in which human beings structure their time, their interactions; analysis of the pastimes, rituals, and *Games* we play with each other as ways of avoiding or denying intimate contact or encounter. Developed by Eric Berne, Thomas Harris, and others.

transpersonal psychology. The collective term describing the various ways in which we go beyond or transcend the animalistic or personal experiences of life, trying to reach a larger or more global experience of relatedness.

unconscious. The processes of personality and reality of which we are not, or cannot be, aware.

unitive consciousness. (See *global consciousness.*)

voyeurism. Deriving pleasure or gratification from observing others, especially nude people or those involved in sexual acts. (Synonyms: "peeping-tomism," scopophilia.)

wholism (holism). The practice or belief in the necessity for seeing and knowing the entirety of human experience, regardless of bias or orientation. A wholistic view encompasses, and accepts, all that the person is.

will. The function of personality involving decision-making, purpose, and intent. A long-neglected area, it has found explanation recently in the works of Assagioli and Rollo May.

work-sin ethic. The so-called Puritan or Protestant value-system, making hard work, temperance, moderation, thrift, and personal piety all-important, and finding its modern expression in the capitalist economic system.

Zen Buddhism. The Japanese tradition of Buddhist thought, emphasizing internal meditation and problem-solving, seeking, through the challenge of puzzle, riddle, and mental contest, the liberation and enlightenment (*satori*) that marks a Zen master.

Index

Jourard, Sidney, 258–259, 329
Jung, Carl Gustav:
  analytical psychology of, 204, 228,
    230, 281–282, 302
  and psychomotor therapy, 271
  therapy of, 103, 134, 266, 302
  on analysis, 356
  on collective unconscious, 230,
    281–282, 366
  on consciousness, 89, 228, 335,
    336, 342–343, 352

K

Kama Sutra, 28
Karlins, Marvin, 335
Kelly, George A., 284
Kierkegaard, Sören, 31–32, 361
Kinship feeling, 292, 317
Kluckhohn, Clyde, 119
Knowledge:
  love means, 309–310
  systems of, 101–102
Krippner, Stanley, 349–352
Kropotkin, Pëtr, 129

L

Laing, Ronald D., 227, 234, 283
Latency stage, 71
Leary, Timothy, 84
Leisure time. *See* Play; Recreation
Lethargic state, 349
Libido, 69–72, 370
Life roles, 1–18
Life scripts, 198–199, 261, 265, 370
Living: purpose in, 9–11
Lobotomy, 278
Long Day's Journey into Night (O'Neill),
  101
Lovaas, Ivor, 270
Love, 184–186, 307–330
  Fromm on, 123, 309, 310, 312, 314
  Gibran on, 139, 149
  meanings of, 308–315
  of self-actualizing persons, 292
  and therapy, 327–330
  types of, 315–323

Love needs, 58
Low, Abraham A., 343–344
LSD, 84, 87
  therapy, 272–273
Lunacy, 370
Luther, Martin, 30, 141

M

Maccoby, Eleanor, 238
Maharishi Mahesh Yogi, 335
Malthus, Thomas, 127–128
Man-woman love, 321–323
Manic reactions, 232
Marcuse, Herbert, 283
Marginality, 370
Marijuana, 85, 87–89
Marriage, 324–327
Marriage counseling, 273–274
Masks, 204, 242–243, 370
Maslow, Abraham:
  hierarchy of motives, 54–62, 289–296
  on behaviorists, 347
  on consciousness alteration, 89–90, 354
  on decision-making, 150–151
  on human beingness, 77, 104, 362
  on self-actualization, 16, 66
Masochism, 242, 243, 370
Masturbation, 317–318, 323, 324
May, Rollo, 13–14, 36–37, 228, 343
Mead, Margaret, 98, 238
Meaning: search for, 31–36
Medical model, 227–228, 264
Meditation, 278–279, 301
Meditative states, 350
Memory, 351
Mental health, 174–175, 196–197
  achieving, 263–289
  community centers, 268, 301–302
  dreams and, 172
  Freud's definition, 151
  humor and, 180–184
Mental hospitals, 268–269, 277–278
Mental illness, 231–234, 259
Meyer, Adolf, 284
Mistrust, 248–250
Moksha, 370
Montagu, Ashley, 98, 129
Mores, 119
Morris, Desmond, 97, 98, 118, 129

Significance: search for, 13–14,
   36–39, 361–362
Sleep, 171–172
Sleeping state, 349
Slums, 210
Social contract, 97
Social Darwinism, 125, 126–127, 144
Social environment, 112
Social institutions, 373
Social nature, 115–118
Social needs, 184–189
Social processes, 124–129
Social rules, 118–121
Socialization, 119, 201, 373
Society, 373
Sociodrama, 283
Sociology, 124, 373
Sociopath, 251
Solitude, 189–192, 291
Sorokin, Pitirim, 101
Specialism, vocational, 154
Spencer, Herbert, 124, 144
Sperry, Roger W., 346
Spinoza, 27
Statuses, 115–116
Steiner, Claude, 246–247, 283
Stereotyping, 205–206, 209–210, 370
Stroking, 188, 208, 242, 373
Stupor, 350
Subconscious, 355
Subjective awareness, 99–102
Suicide, 6–7
Sullivan, Harry Stack, 266
Superego, 74, 177, 228, 264–265,
   280, 373
Supernatural, 336, 342
Supportive environments, 151–153
Survival needs. See Physiological needs
Swift, Jonathan, 183
Symbiotic relationships, 132, 220, 373
Syndrome, 373
Synthesis: Western need for, 102–106
Szasz, Thomas, 6–7, 283

T

Taboos, 119
Tai Chi Chu'an, 271
Tapes, 373. See also Life scripts

Theology, 373
Therapy. See Psychotherapy
Thomas, Charles, 219
Thousand Clowns, A (Garner), 12–13
Tillich, Paul, 8, 25, 307
Trance states, 350
Tranquilizers, 272
Transactional analysis, 196–197, 206–209, 283,
   285–288, 304, 373. See also OK-ness
Transactions, 188, 197
Transcendent function, 282, 356–357
Transcending experiences, 291–292
Transpersonal experience, 336
Transpersonal psychology, 373
Trust, 117–118, 130, 248, 292, 314
Truth: systems of, 101–102
Twins, 110, 114

U

Unconscious, 228, 230, 281–282, 348,
   352, 373
Unitive consciousness, 352–356
Utilitarianism, 27

V

Value systems:
   developing personal, 145–146, 263
   of self-actualizing persons, 293–294
Values, 26–39
Vocations, 141, 142, 150, 151–153
Vonnegut, Kurt, Jr., 1, 2
Voyeurism, 374
Vulnerability, 314–315

W

Watson, John B., 39
Watts, Alan W., 84
Weil, Andrew, 352
Wholism, 266, 374
Will, 343, 374
Wisdom, search for, 30–31
Withdrawal, 245–246, 247